NATIONS OF THE MODERN WORLD

ARGENTINA | H. S. Ferns
Professor of Political Science,
University of Birmingham

AUSTRALIA | O. H. K. Spate
Director, Research School of Pacific Studies,
Australian National University, Canberra

CHINA | Victor Purcell, C.M.G.
Late Lecturer in Far Eastern History, Cambridge

CYPRUS | H. D. Purcell
Lecturer in English Literature, the Queen's
University, Belfast

ENGLAND | John Bowle
A Portrait
Professor of Political Theory, Collège d'Europe,
Bruges

MODERN EGYPT | Tom Little, M.B.E.
Regional News Services (Mid-East), London

FINLAND | W. R. Mead
Professor of Geography, University College, London

EAST | David Childs
GERMANY
Lecturer in Politics, University of Nottingham

WEST | Michael Balfour, C.B.E.
GERMANY
Reader in European History, University of
East Anglia

MODERN | John Campbell
GREECE
Fellow of St. Antony's College, Oxford
Philip Sherrard
Assistant Director, British School of Archaeology,
Athens, 1958–62

MODERN INDIA | Sir Percival Griffiths, K.B.E., C.I.E.,
I.C.S. (Ret.)
President India, Pakistan and Burma Association

MODERN IRAN	Peter Avery *Lecturer in Persian and Fellow of King's College,* *Cambridge*
ITALY	Muriel Grindrod *Formerly Editor of* International Affairs *and* The World Today *Assistant Editor of* The Annual Register
JAPAN	Sir Esler Dening *H.M. Ambassador to Japan, 1952–57*
KENYA	A. Marshall MacPhee *Formerly Managing Editor of* The East African Standard Group; *producer with British Broadcasting* *Corporation*
LIBYA	John Wright *Formerly of the* Sunday Ghibli, *Tripoli*
MALAYSIA	J. M. Gullick *Formerly of the Malayan Civil Service*
MOROCCO	Mark I. Cohen and Lorna Hahn
NEW ZEALAND	James W. Rowe *Director of New Zealand Institute of Economic* *Research, Inc.* Margaret A. Rowe *Tutor in English, Victoria University, Wellington*
NIGERIA	Sir Rex Niven *Colonial Service, Nigeria, 1921–59; Member of* *Northern House of Assembly, 1947–59*
PAKISTAN	Ian Stephens *Formerly Editor of* The Statesman *Calcutta and* *Delhi, 1942–51; Fellow of King's College,* *Cambridge, 1952–58*
SOUTH AFRICA	John Cope *Formerly Editor-in-Chief of* The Forum; *South* *African Correspondent of* The Guardian
SUDAN REPUBLIC	K. D. D. Henderson *Formerly of the Sudan Political Service; Governor of* *Darfur Province, 1949–53*
TURKEY	Geoffrey Lewis *Senior Lecturer on Islamic Studies, Oxford*

THE UNITED STATES OF AMERICA	H. C. Allen *Commonwealth Fund Professor of American History,* *University College, London*
WEST GERMANY	Michael Balfour *Reader in European History, University of* *East Anglia*
YUGOSLAVIA	Muriel Heppell and F. B. Singleton

NATIONS OF THE MODERN WORLD

MODERN GREECE

MODERN GREECE

By

JOHN CAMPBELL

and

PHILIP SHERRARD

FREDERICK A. PRAEGER, *Publishers*

New York · Washington

BOOKS THAT MATTER

Published in the United States of America in 1968
by Frederick A. Praeger, Inc., Publishers
111 Fourth Avenue, New York, N.Y. 10003

Second printing 1969

© 1968, in London, England, by John Campbell and Philip Sherrard

Library of Congress Catalog Card Number: 68–55984

Printed in Great Britain

FOR

J. T. C.

AND

R. J. H. J.

Preface

THE GREEKS have always believed since ancient times that they were an elect people, whether as in the world of city-states it was by virtue of the superiority of their language and culture or later as Byzantines in a Christian Empire which alone guarded the true faith. Yet in historical terms it is only recently that after three thousand years the Greek milieu has achieved an exclusive political identity through the establishment of the modern Greek state. Before its foundation the Greeks had lived since the fifteenth century as a subject people in the Ottoman Empire distinguished not by their ethnic singularity but as members of the Eastern Orthodox Church. The emergence of the new Greek state after the war of Greek Independence (1821–29) was preceded by the infiltration of secular and utilitarian notions of western culture into a still essentially eastern and traditional society. Since the eventual if grudging assistance of the European Powers was necessary to establish the Greek state it became inevitable that it would adopt western political and economic institutions. This surrender to the West implied a denial of the heritage that had in both the pre-Christian and the Christian past inspired the major spiritual and cultural achievements of the Greek milieu. Broadly speaking, its consequences, politically and culturally, are the subject of this volume.

There are many omissions in this survey whose content has been mainly determined by the interests of its authors. But for readers relatively unacquainted with Modern Greece we hope to make plain certain recurring themes in the country's modern history and the pattern of its principal institutions. However, an analytical approach carries certain disadvantages. It necessarily gives attention to many of the less admirable features of a society and may often suggest an author's prejudice which does not exist. And it dissolves away the richness, movement, and colour of life as it is immediately experienced. In the second respect, at least, we can make amends by directing readers to the books of such writers as Patrick Leigh Fermor and Kevin Andrews.

We wish to acknowledge gratefully assistance from the late Mrs

Marion Carr, Miss Susan Leys, R. E. Oakley and M. J. Llewellyn Smith. We owe thanks to Michael Kaser for his criticism of our treatment of Greece's economic problems. None of these ladies or gentlemen, of course, is responsible for the final form of anything we have written. Finally, the first named of the two authors gratefully acknowledges the assistance of a grant from the Leverhulme Foundation which materially aided the writing of this book.

St Antony's College, Oxford   J.K.C.
July 1968   P.O.A.S.

Contents

Preface   11
List of Illustrations   15
Acknowledgements   16

PART ONE

THE ORIGINS OF MODERN GREECE

1 The Idea of the Greek Nation   19
2 The Approach to Independence   50
3 The War of Independence   65

PART TWO

THE HISTORICAL DEVELOPMENT OF THE STATE

4 The New State and the Great Idea   83
5 Catastrophe and Reaction   127

PART THREE

TWO ASPECTS OF CULTURE

6 The Orthodox Church in Greece   189
7 Modern Greek Literature   214

PART FOUR

CONTEMPORARY GREECE

8   Political Events since the Civil War   247
9   Economic Dilemmas   299
10 The Greek Countryside   322
11 The City and the State   364

Bibliography   405
Index   413

Map

Greece, Physical and Political,   *facing page* 404
    with an inset showing the Greek Kingdom in 1832
    and neighbouring countries

List of Illustrations

[All are inserted between pages 224 and 225]

1 War of Independence. Fighting Priest and guerrillas, by Panayiotis Zographos (d. 1839)

2 Theodore Kolokotronis (1770–1843)

3 Charilaos Tricoupis (1832–96)

4 King Constantine I (1868–1922) during the Balkan wars. On his right Metaxas as a young staff officer

5 Eleutherios Venizelos (1864–1936)

6 Asia Minor refugees with their icons, 1922

7 Crown Prince Paul (later King; 1901–64), King George II (1890–1947), and General Metaxas (1871–1941)

8 The Italian war, 1940

9 Markos, the communist leader during the Civil War, and Zachariades

10 The victims who are not forgotten. Civil War, Athens, January 1945

11 Constantine Karamanlis, Prime Minister 1955–63. A new man for the new Greece

12 George Papandhreou

13 The poet George Seferis (Seferiades), Greek ambassador in London 1957–62

14 The village of Portaria in the Pelion range

15 Constitution Square, Athens. The Acropolis in the background

16   The Old Palace, Athens, since 1935 seat of the Greek parliament

17   The port of Piraeus

18   A wedding procession at Heracleion, Crete

19   The wife of a potter at Archangelos, Rhodes

20   An old man of Heracleion

21   The church of Moulki on Salamis

Acknowledgements

Plate 1, from the Royal Collection at Windsor, is reproduced by gracious permission of Her Majesty The Queen.

ACKNOWLEDGEMENT for kind permission to reproduce illustrations is also made to the following, to whom the copyright of the illustrations belongs.
Dimitri of Athens: 2, 3, 4, 5, 6, 7, 8, 10, 11, 14, 15, 16, 17, 18, 19, 20, 21.
Keystone Press Agency Ltd., London: 9, 12, 13.

PART ONE

The Origins of Modern Greece

Chapter 1

The Idea of the Greek Nation

I

THE NATIONAL and independent kingdom of Greece has been
in existence for less than a century and a half, and much of
its present territory has only been included within its frontiers
for a considerably shorter time. For some three and a half centuries
prior to this, the whole southerly area of the Balkan peninsula
formed part of the Ottoman Empire, and the peoples who occupied
it owed allegiance to the Sultan at Constantinople. Yet during the
comparatively short period that Greece has constituted one of the
nations of modern Europe, a very homogeneous state has grown
up. How did this nation come into being? How did the Greeks
themselves achieve their sense of national identity? What have been
the forces and ideas shaping their destiny and directing the pattern
of their historical life?

The answers to these questions can only be indicated by means of
a retrospective analysis of the growth and development of the
national Greek consciousness from the closing years of the Byzantine
Empire down to the outbreak of the Greek war of Independence
in 1821. It was as the result of this war that the Greeks achieved
partial liberation from their Turkish overlords and laid the foundations of the modern Greek state. As we noted, the Turks themselves
had been in occupation of the greater part of the lands that then
constituted the new Greek state for some three and a half centuries.
Constantinople, the capital of the Byzantine Empire, had fallen in
1453, and by 1460 the Greek mainland had been overrun. But the
Byzantines whose territories the Turks occupied in the fifteenth
century, and had been occupying in Asia Minor and further west
for several centuries prior to this, had no sense of nationhood in
the way that this was understood by the Greeks who fought for
their liberty in the opening years of the nineteenth century. The
Greeks who fought the war of Independence, in 1821 and after,
thought of themselves as, and called themselves, Hellenes, and the
state which was formed as a result of their struggle was given the
name Hellas. The Byzantines, on the contrary – with the exception

of a group of which we shall speak shortly –, did not either call themselves Hellenes, or think of themselves as Hellenes. They were members of the Roman Empire in that Eastern and Christian form which had been conferred on it by Constantine the Great. As such they were not only Roman citizens, but also God's chosen people, while their Empire was the area in which God's earthly kingdom was in the process of being fulfilled.

This notion of their status gave the Byzantines the sense that they possessed an elect and exclusive position in the universal scheme of things – a position so elect and exclusive that one Archbishop of Salonika found it necessary to remind his congregation that God had made the barbarians as well as the Byzantines, and heard their prayers no less. But the notion that they formed a nation or *ethnos* in the modern sense was something which they would have repudiated with distaste: the word *ethnos* (nation) served but to indicate lesser breeds without the law, tribes or races of barbarians or heretics (or both together) that had not the privilege of living within the bounds of Christ's terrestrial kingdom or of being ruled over by His divinely-appointed vicegerent, the Christian Emperor of Byzantium. Still more would they have repudiated the notion that they composed the nation of the Hellenes. Byzantium, as a Christian Empire, was an enemy of 'Hellenism', and throughout its history (again with few exceptions) regarded the philosophical, religious, and moral conceptions of antiquity with hostility – a hostility made manifest in the closing of the philosophical school of Athens in the sixth century by the Emperor Justinian. Particularly was this attitude towards everything Hellenic fostered by the main bearers of the Christian tradition of Byzantium, the monks; and seldom was their criticism of Hellenism more outspoken than towards the end of the Byzantine period, when the great theoreticians of the spiritual movement known as hesychasm were forced to defend their doctrine against attacks of those whose 'Hellenism' in one form or another was already directing their thought away from Orthodox Christianity. Hellenism was paganism and polytheism; and even the first Patriarch of Constantinople after the capture of that city by the Turks, George Scholarios, refused to allow himself to be called a Hellene.

Yet in spite of this official opposition to Hellenism as a philosophical or moral force, and in spite of the lack of attempts at 'ethnic' identification with the ancient Greeks, the Byzantines did maintain a tradition of Hellenic culture. This was chiefly reserved to what one might call the neutral zone of language and literature (de-mythologized), for ancient philosophy had more dangerous implications – the example of the Emperor Julian the Apostate was there to indicate what some of these could lead to – and hence its study as an end in itself was discouraged. But a classical education, and especially a knowledge of the ancient Greek language, tended to become a *sine qua non* of any advancement to the higher offices in the Byzantine state. Indeed, by the eleventh century this tendency had led to the formation of a kind of intellectual aristocracy, admission to whose ranks was open, or restricted, to those with a Hellenic education. It must be stressed however that initially this education was Hellenistic, or, rather, Romano–Hellenistic, in form, in the sense that it was directed above all to the study of grammar, syntax, and rhetoric – to the 'classics', that is, as understood and studied by the post-Renaissance classical scholar. It was not directly concerned with the life of the ancient Greek world itself, and nor did it imply any idealization of the social and religious forms of this life. Still less did it signify any romantic admiration for the present inhabitants of the lands of ancient Greece: these – 'Helladics' as they were called – were simply the occupiers of a not very important province in the Byzantine Empire, with no particular claim to deferential regard. In any case, after the conquest of Greece by Alexander the Great and the subsequent emigration of the native population to the new and prosperous centres of the Hellenistic world in Egypt and Asia; after the devastations of the Roman conquest, which included the destruction of Corinth and the bloodthirsty massacre of the Athenians; after the ravages of the Teutonic Herules in the third century A.D. and of the Goths of Alaric in the fourth; after the murderous mass invasions of the Slavs and their subsequent settlement chiefly in the sixth and seventh centuries; and after, finally, further mass invasions, this time by the Albanians, in the fourteenth century: after all this, and much more, these present inhabitants of the fifteenth-century Greek mainland were of a multi-racial stock to which the contribution of the ancient Hellenes can only have been modest.

In spite of this, towards the close of the Byzantine Empire a certain change did take place in the attitude of at least a section of the Byzantine cultural élite towards both the lands and the contemporary inhabitants of the ancient Greek world. As the territorial circumstances of the Empire became increasingly straitened as a result of the military activities of the Turks, and the claim to a cultural supremacy became more difficult to maintain in the face of the intellectual advances of the Latin West, a number of Byzantines felt challenged to reassess their position: in what after all did their particular excellence reside? They were still, and unquestionably, a chosen people; but the corollary which depended from this, that it was God's will that all peoples of the earth should be formed into a single body politic in universal subjection to His representative, the Byzantine Emperor, was now made to appear excessive: the Turks, whose military superiority was all too evident, were clear heretics; and the Christian West, now schismatic, made it a condition of any aid given in terms of arms and men to resist the Turkish inroads that the Emperor and his Church and people should acknowledge the universal authority of the Pope as God's vicegerent on earth. Threatened with this double loss – territorial and religious – of title, those members of the Byzantine cultural élite to whom reference has been made began, as a desperate rearguard endeavour to preserve an historical identity and continuity, to lay claim to a heritage that, extravagant as it was, neither the Turks nor the Latins could arrogate in quite the same way. They began to lay claim to a Hellenic inheritance distinct from the Romano–Hellenistic cultural tradition they shared with the Latin West; and they proclaimed – with, as we have seen, little or no historical justification – the contemporary inhabitants of the mainland of southern Greece, still unconquered by the advancing Turk, to be its true cultural and racial representatives.

Thus there developed among these Hellenizontes, or admirers of Hellas, a new attitude towards the Hellenic past with immediate religious and political implications for the present. Where the religious implications are concerned, it will be recalled that for the Christian Byzantines, Hellenism meant paganism and polytheism; it also meant, in the more dangerous matter of its philosophical principles, Platonism. Platonism, for reasons which need not be gone into here, had in the centuries preceding the fall of the Empire constituted an increasing temptation to some of the more philosophically-minded Byzantines; and this had produced a correspondingly strong reaction among the defenders of Orthodoxy: the eleventh-century neo-Platonist Psellus, for instance, who himself gave public offence by his 'Platonism', records that the monks in the monasteries of the Bithynian Olympus, where in 1055 he had taken refuge, crossed themselves at the mere mention of Plato's name and uttered anathemas against this 'hellenic' Satan; and in the fourteenth century an official anathema was declared by the Holy Synod against those believing in the 'Platonic ideas'. And in this Platonic tradition the new Hellenizontes now recognized, so they thought, the philosophical basis of their ancient Hellenic patrimony. As for the political implications of the new attitude, any 'ethnic' claim by the Hellenizontes that the inhabitants of the Peloponnese were the direct descendants of the ancient Greeks and should therefore re-establish a national state in the lands once occupied by the Hellenes of old was bound to involve a repudiation of the all-embracing and supranational universalism of Byzantine imperial and theocratic theory.

This 'hellenizing' movement came to a head in the first half of the fifteenth century – in the years, that is, which immediately preceded the fall of Constantinople in 1453; and it came to a head in the person of the remarkable George Gemistos Pletho. Pletho represents the crystallization of that change of attitude towards the ancient Greek world which we have been indicating, of that claim that the actual contemporary people of mainland Greece were the direct racial and spiritual descendants of the old Hellenes. 'We,' Pletho wrote in his memorandum to the Emperor Manuel II outlining features of his programme for the reconstitution of a national Hellenic state, 'We over whom you rule and hold sway are Hellenes by race, as is demonstrated by our language and ancestral education. And for Hellenes there is no more proper and peculiar land to be found than the Peloponnese, together with the neighbouring part of Europe and the islands that lie near to it. For it appears that this land has always been inhabited by the same Hellenes, as far as the memory of man reaches back: none lived here before them, nor have immigrants occupied it and expelled the others, later to be expelled themselves in the same way. No, on the contrary, the Hellenes themselves appear always to have been its possessors, and never to have left it.' The Peloponnese, once the ancient colony of the Dorians and now with its metropolis, Mistra (near ancient Sparta), the one place where it seemed possible to build a new Hellenic society to replace that of the rapidly disintegrating Byzantine Empire, was for Pletho the cradle *par excellence* of Hellenism. Combining the advantages of a large island with those of the continent, its inhabitants could not only defend it (to this end Pletho proposed the building of a wall across the isthmus of Corinth), but could extend their power over the surrounding districts. At the same time, its natural resources, correctly organized, would make it economically self-sufficient; and this correct organization meant for Pletho a virtual socialization of the land. What in fact Pletho envisaged was a kind of Platonic society; and in the formation of this society there is no doubt that Pletho wished to play a part in relation to the ruling Byzantine princes similar to that which Plato had sought to play in relation to the tyrants at the court of Syracuse.

But as in the Platonic inheritance (Pletho knew the Plato of the neo-Platonists, by way of Psellus), concrete theories of government in the sphere of political structure and economic obligation were for Pletho but translations of underlying philosophical principles into a more secular guise: the shape of the earthly society, if it is to have any stable existence, must be the reflection of the state of heaven. This meant that Pletho's proposals for the refounding of the ancient Hellenic state were accompanied by, indeed depended upon, proposals for a return to the religion of antiquity. 'I heard him say,' wrote George of Trebizond with reference to Pletho, 'when he was in Florence, that in the not distant future all men in the whole world would by common consent and in the same spirit embrace one and the same religion. And when I asked him whether this would be the religion of Jesus Christ or that of Mahomet, he replied: "neither the one nor the other, but a third, which would not be different from that of antiquity".' The political and social disintegration of the Byzantine Empire had convinced him that Orthodox Christianity was incapable of forming the religious basis of the new Hellenic state; for since the stability and vitality of the earthly state depends on metaphysical principles, it followed that this disintegration was indisputable evidence of the inadequacy of the metaphysical principles of which Byzantine society itself was a reflection; and these were those of Orthodox Christianity. At the same time the interminable discussions over the question of the union of the Orthodox and Roman Churches – in which Pletho himself, incidentally, took part – had likewise convinced him that it was not union with the 'Aristotelian' Latins that could save the Hellenes. The Hellenes could only save themselves, by purging away the accretions and errors which had obscured the lofty spiritual ideals of their ancestors, and in their light reforming their lives and the pattern of their human society. A myth had been born – the myth that the people now inhabiting the lands of ancient Greece were the direct descendants of the ancient Hellenes, and that only the thought and culture of their glorious ancestors could be relied upon to form the basis of the regeneration of the modern Hellenic nation.

In a way however the myth was still-born, for its growth in terms of practical implementation was cut short almost as soon as it was produced by the fall of Constantinople (1453) and the subsequent Turkish conquest of continental Greece. But quite apart from this it must be remembered that the movement and ideas of which Pletho was the chief spokesman were those of a small group of Byzantine intellectuals and had little influence among the great majority of the Byzantine educated classes, and still less among the mass of those actual inhabitants of Greek lands of whose pure Hellenic lineage Pletho had sought to be the sponsor. Both the majority of the educated Byzantines and the mass of the inhabitants of continental Greece remained loyal to the Orthodox Christian tradition – a tradition according to which Orthodox Christians were the chosen people of God's earthly kingdom whose consummation was, whatever the appearance of things, ultimately certain, and for which the names Hellene and Plato were still alien and abominable. For these Orthodox Christians therefore the Turkish conquest signified something quite different. It signified first of all a temporary punishment for the sins which His people had committed before God (similar to the punishment of the Babylonian captivity); and it also, though more obliquely perhaps, signified a divine intervention preventing the otherwise apparently inevitable subjugation of this people to the schismatic, not to say heretical, West and its Pope. 'Better the turban of the Muslim than the Latin mitre' was the classical formula in which the sense of the providential nature of this intervention was expressed. The Orthodox Christians then – and this is the only designation which the actual inhabitants of Greek lands at the time of the Turkish occupation had in common – accepted with the fall of Constantinople a mythological prospect quite other than that proposed by Pletho and his followers: they accepted as by right the prospect that one day, sooner or later (it mattered little when), God would lead His chosen people out of captivity, would restore to them all they had lost to the Turk and the Frank; and that, its sins and vices purged away, the Christian Empire – God's terrestrial kingdom – would be resurrected in all its pristine glory, not as the result of any particular effort, except that of repentance, made by Orthodox Christians themselves, but as part of a universal process directed by the divine will. Within a few years of the fall of Constantinople songs were already in circulation among these Christians announcing the future repossession of the city and of its great church, Santa Sophia:

Again with years, with time, again they will be ours.

Thus at the end of the Byzantine period the future of the Christian inhabitants of the late Empire was presented in the form of two incompatible myths, the first deriving from a faith in a classical past and the second from faith in the continuation of the imperial destiny of Christian Byzantium. It was the second, preserved and fostered above all by the Church, that made it possible for Orthodox Christians in Greek lands to maintain a sense of identity through the long centuries of Turkish occupation. But by curious irony it was the first that, though apparently cut off practically at birth in the way we have remarked, yet unpredictably reseeded itself in an alien soil where it grew with such vigour that when it was transplanted back into its native soil in the seventeenth and particularly in the eighteenth centuries it spread with an impetus that was astonishing.

The connection between the course of classical studies in western Europe from the time of the Renaissance down to the nineteenth century and beyond, and the destinies of the modern Greek nation, may not be obvious; and no doubt those pedagogues who initiated generations of students into the mysteries of Homeric participles and Attic metaphors would have been surprised had they been told that as an indirect result of their labours the peoples of a new Hellenic kingdom would one day erect, beneath the crippled Parthenon, their palace and state buildings with the firm conviction that they were at last resurrecting, in the land of its origin, the glorious heritage of their ancestors Pericles and Phidias. But between the time when the Greek-speaking Calabrian monk Barlaam began to teach the ageing Petrarch Greek and the day on which George Gordon, Lord Byron, lay dying amid the swamps of Mesolonghi, an extraordinary development took place in the mental outlook of the cultural European; and this development not only vitally affected the way he began to regard the contemporary inhabitants of the lands of the ancient Greeks; it also vitally affected the way these inhabitants began to regard themselves.

It used to be supposed that after the Crusades and particularly after the fall of Constantinople, the rediscovery of ancient Greek literature in the West provoked what has since been known as the Renaissance; and that this Renaissance signified the rebirth of the culture and thought of the ancient Greek world. It is now realized that this view is not altogether correct. The Renaissance reflects in the main a fusion of belated mediaeval French influences with a narrow and different native Italian tradition. This native tradition went back to Roman times, and found expression not so much in poetry and art as in lay education, legal custom, and a study of grammar and rhetoric. Where the literature of ancient Greece is concerned, in spite of strong political and commercial relationships between Italy and Constantinople in the Middle Ages, few Italians before the fifteenth century knew Greek, and fewer still read the ancient authors in the original. The Greek manuscripts translated into Latin in the twelfth and thirteenth centuries, mostly from Arabic translations, were almost entirely confined to mathematics, astrology, astronomy, medicine, and Aristotelian philosophy. It is true that after the middle of the fourteenth century other works of ancient Greek literature began to spread to the West in ever increasing volumes, both through the arrival of Byzantine scholars and through the exertions of Italian scholars who went to Constantinople in search of Greek learning; and that in this way Italian humanists, like Petrarch himself, began to read the 'classics'. But this interest in ancient Greek authors on the part of the humanists did not arise out of any concern for ancient Greece as such or for its inhabitants. It arose out of their grammatical and rhetorical studies. They were the heirs to the Latin tradition of *ars dictaminis* and *ars arengendi*, the art of epistolography and the art of eloquence; and they studied Greek authors because they found in them the best models for the cultivation of these arts. The Italian humanists introduced little new into the Roman tradition of rhetoric except a new 'classical' style. In fact, to think that humanism itself originally meant a new way of life is misleading. The humanism of the Renaissance was originally a technical term applied to a certain field of study, humanists being those whose studies centred in grammar and rhetoric as opposed to the logic and natural philosophy of the scholastics.

What this meant in terms that concern us here is that in spite of the increased respect for the literature of ancient Greece during the Renaissance, this did not at first imply any particular admiration for the actual physical monuments of ancient Greece, still less for the ancient Greeks as a whole or for their character or way of living; for this literature was approached by way of the Roman tradition and not directly. Hence the attitude of the Italian humanists to the ancient Greeks themselves was mainly derived from a reading of their favourite Latin authors of the Republic and the Empire; and the views they acquired from this reading were on the whole far from flattering. According to Plutarch, for instance, Grecian and scholar were the two terms of contempt which the artificers and other such 'base mechanical people' of Rome had ever ready at their lips; and, in agreement with the populace, the writings of Virgil, Plautus, Juvenal, the elder Pliny, Cicero, Livy, Seneca, and many others, all denigrated the Greeks in one way or another, and declared, often in highly vituperative terms, their dislike of or derision at their impudence, double-dealing, mendacity, lechery, vanity, and scurrilous servility. All this made a deep impression on the men of the Renaissance; and in fact the derogatory sense of the word Greek deriving from Latin literature has found an echo in modern European literature down at least to the nineteenth century. Moreover, these attitudes towards the Greek character were automatically and immediately transferred by the men of the Renaissance and by their classically-minded successors in Italy, France, England, and elsewhere to the contemporary peoples still inhabiting the southern part of the Balkan peninsula, the Aegean islands, and the Anatolian seaboard of Asia Minor; for these peoples were still quite naturally regarded, in the absence of those ethnological skills that have preoccupied later minds, as the descendants of the ancient Hellenes.

The reaffirmation therefore of the classical tradition at the time of the Renaissance in its Roman, or, more accurately perhaps, its Romano–Hellenistic form, had two consequences of considerable importance for the future Greek state. The first lay in the values of this tradition itself. And here it must be recalled that this 'classicizing' tradition was the fabrication first of all of the cities of the Hellenistic world. When, following the conquests of Alexander the Great, this world emerged, its chief centres were those commercial agglomerations like Alexandria, Antioch, Ephesus, which studded the whole middle-eastern area. These cities were laid out on the lines of the cities of ancient Greece, but laid out as it were *in vacuo*. They were culturally rootless, with no local traditions of their own. But they were the outcome of the Greek diaspora, and their main language was Greek. So that when it became a question of trying to fill the vacuum, of trying to find something to make up for their lack of native cultural roots, it was only natural that they should look back to ancient Greece. In the literature of ancient Greece the citizens of these new Hellenistic cities sought the cultural basis for their own civilization. They sought to imitate the models provided by ancient Greece, and to mould their world according to the patterns of fifth-century Athens. They adopted the language of the past, they tried to think in the categories of the past, to fit their lives into the framework of a bygone outmoded age. They wanted their epics and hymns to be like those of Homer, their prose to be like that of their Attic models. They produced glossaries of difficult poetic words, glossaries of Homer, systematic grammars, vast tomes on Attic syntax and on comic and tragic diction. What in fact they were trying to do was to fashion a perfect instrument for the imitation of those classical models which they regarded as the ideal forms of culture, of civilization itself. These models provided the norms according to which the value and beauty of everything was to be judged. The great process of the idealization of the classical golden age of ancient Greece which has so befuddled the subsequent intellectual history of Europe had begun. That this process of idealization involved an act of abstraction which effectively divorced the image of this golden past from any concrete historical reality and that what this image really represents is a mythological sanctioning of certain values which for quite local psychological reasons had become important, is no doubt typical of all such processes. As for these values themselves, they are above all those that envisage a purely human and secular excellence to be realized in and through a man-made civil and social order which reflects as far as is possible the norms of a rationalistic interpretation of life.

It was this cult of the classical golden age of Greece in which, it was supposed, the supreme ideals of human life and culture had been embodied, that Rome inherited from the Hellenistic age. Indeed, the whole imperial pattern of education for citizenship became increasingly devoted to inculcating and diffusing the classical ideals, and to erecting them into 'universal' standards of judgement and taste. But now the discipline of education itself became even more purely a matter of literary convention and scholarship, a system of *bonae* or *liberales artes* based on the study of grammar and rhetoric and the reading of classical philosophy. The consequence of this was to give classicism precisely that literary and aesthetic bias so strongly deprecated in fact by Plato himself; and it was this departure from the spirit and purpose of the Academic discipline that was to confer on the whole later development of western culture that rhetorical character, that concern with external form and aesthetic effect, from which it has scarcely even now been able to free itself.

For in reverting to Roman models of education, the men of the Renaissance were in fact ensuring the triumph of a new attitude to human life and relations. Humanism may have begun by being a technical term applied to a certain field of study; but implicit in this educational reorientation was an intellectual revolt against the papal–hierocratic doctrine of a universal *societas christiana* and all that it implied, and a growth in the belief in the natural, innate capacity of the human individual to regulate his own affairs and achieve his proper perfection through the activity of his unsanctified reason operating on the purely terrestrial and naturalistic level of the *societas humana*. For its philosophical basis this belief, systematized as it was above all in the Averro–Aristotelian schools of northern Italy, especially at the universities of Bologna and Padua, looked to the categories of Aristotle; while for its cultural counterpart it looked to those models, dominantly literary, enshrined in that Romano–Hellenistic classical tradition whose genesis and subsequent elaboration we have been indicating. Hence the Renaissance cry of 'back to the classics'. In the classics were to be found the values for the new civilization which was emerging, for the new humanist world. It is in this spirit that Petrarch, for instance, maintained that only Greek and Latin authors should be studied for guidance on how to live, how to enjoy nature, how to cultivate friendship, and so on. The great task of providing modern European civilization with its intellectual and cultural basis had begun—this in terms that involved an extraordinary respect for the philosophy of Aristotle, and an idealization of the culture of ancient Greece. That this respect and idealization went, as we have seen, with a

particularly cynical and disparaging view of the actual character
of the Greeks derived chiefly from Latin authors, was the second
consequence of considerable importance for the future Greek state
resulting from the reaffirmation of the classical tradition in its
Romano–Hellenistic form at the time of the Renaissance.

These consequences had already begun to acquire this importance
by the seventeenth century. For although the classical scholars had
fulfilled their role of giving a cultural basis to the middle-class
revolution of the Renaissance by the end of the sixteenth century,
the fact that their education was grounded in, and devoted to
promoting, an uncritical imitation of the models of the ancient world
meant not only that the more information that could be gathered
about this world the better, but also that a distinguishing mark of
proper and sophisticated cultivation was a taste for its artistic
masterpieces. This in its turn resulted in similar excursions for slightly different purposes. The first were those undertaken chiefly by the
scholars themselves. The number of works of ancient Greek literature available in the West had been enormously increased by those
brought by Greek exiles from Constantinople, Mistra, and other
centres of learning. But there might still be many more, especially
of course in Constantinople itself, where, it was felt, the accumulated
bibliographical wealth of several centuries could not all have been
destroyed or dispersed at the time of the conquest. Moreover,
other deposits of vital information were available in Greek lands
for those bent on supplementing their knowledge of antiquity,
deposits which would not only amplify the literary material but
would also serve to check it; and these were the constructions of
ancient Greek architects and engineers, sculptors and potters.

It is in connection with these latter in particular that the cultivated product of the classical discipline of Europe's schools and
universities was stirred into activity. The effect of propagating the
ideals of classicism among the new mercantile classes had led to a
new type of humanism. This was the humanism of those who had
made good in the new bourgeois world, had grown rich and
possibly picked up a title in the process, had imbibed through their
education the classical taste, and who were now consequently in a
financial and cultural condition to indulge this taste in a way which
flattered their own vanity and was in harmony with the finest ideals
of civilization. These dilettante gentlemen were concerned less with
the gathering of academic information about antiquity than with
the amassing of its solid stock: they wanted the objects of antiquity.
The nearest and, it was believed, most fertile source of such objects
was Italy; but here, naturally, the Italians had the advantage,
competition was intense, and prices high. Greek lands however

were still relatively unexplored and unexploited and might yield considerable booty. And for the actual transport of the goods they were to carry off as a result of the excursions they in fact made, these humanists were able to call upon the services of yet another class of foreigner in the east Mediterranean, the traders. In this respect the Venetians and Genoese had been prominent for several centuries before the fall of Constantinople, and had the advantages of actually being in possession of certain Greek territories: the Venetians, for instance, held Crete and the Ionian islands, the Genoese Chios. But by the sixteenth century the French and English were keen rivals. Through a commercial treaty concluded between France and Turkey in 1535 French traders acquired special privileges in the dominions of the Sultan; and in 1580 the Sultan Amurath III issued a charter of privileges to English traders, granting them the same rights as other European traders in the Ottoman Empire; while the following year saw the founding of the Levant Company.

All this meant that during the sixteenth, seventeenth, and eighteenth centuries the number of cultivated gentlemen from western Europe present in Greek lands, whether engaged in pilfering manuscripts from monastic libraries, copying inscriptions, measuring and drawing temples, dismantling pediments, acting as chaplains to merchants preoccupied with Malmsey wines or Corinthian currants, or simply as pilgrims of culture viewing the sites where those of old had wrought their heroic deeds and uttered their noble thoughts – the number of such gentlemen increased enormously. And wherever they travelled they carried with them their dream of the great golden age of Greece, their opinion of the Greek character derived from their reading of Latin authors, and the conviction, virtually unquestioned till after the end of the eighteenth century, that the native peoples they encountered on their journeys were the racial descendants of the ancients. Thus there begins to sound through the voluminous literature in which these travellers recorded their experiences or reported their findings that endless and inevitable refrain pointing the contrast between the ancient glory and the present degradation of the Greeks. From the beginning of the seventeenth century, when George Sandys published his *Relation of a Journey begun An Dom. 1610*—a journey to countries which 'once so glorious, and famous for their happy estate, are now through vice and ingratitude, become the most deplored spectacles of extreme misery'; through the eighteenth century, when a Gibbon, catching the note second hand from his reading of this travel literature, writes of the present-day Athenians that they 'walk with supine indifference among the glorious ruins of antiquity;

and such is the debasement of their character that they are incapable of admiring the genius of their predecessors'; down to the
clarion calls of Lord Byron, the refrain sounds. To us it may now
seem banal and invidious; but to those who uttered it, it was the
by-product of a passionate faith; and the least that can be said is
that it is hardly in worse taste than the cynicism about Greeks
which seems so often to be its alternative.

What was the effect of these visitations upon the actual living
inhabitants of these once glorious lands? To account for this it is
necessary to remember first that the conditions under which
Orthodox Christians in Greek lands lived during the centuries
succeeding the Turkish occupation had not produced among them
any radical change of mental or moral climate: they still remained
in this respect much as they had been in Byzantine times. The fact
that the Turkish Sultan in accordance with Islamic tradition
regarded his Orthodox Christian subjects as a 'nation' (*millet*) of
which the Oecumenical Patriarch of Constantinople was not simply
the spiritual but also the temporal ruler, led him to confer upon the
Patriarch privileges which gave the latter, within limits, responsibility for the whole civil and ecclesiastical administration of this
Christian 'nation'. In effect the Patriarch, combining the offices of
both Emperor and Patriarch, came to preside over a state within
a state; while Orthodox Christians themselves, protected from
forcible conversion on the part of the Turks by the principle of
Islamic sacred law that once non-Muslims who were 'People of the
Book' (both Old and New Testaments) had submitted to Muslim
rule and had agreed to pay tribute, then they could pursue their
traditional religion in freedom, were in practice left very much in
charge of their own affairs, both religious and civil. No doubt there
were hardships and grievances – the most bitter of these being
perhaps the system of child-tribute according to which the children
of Christians were selected and trained for positions in the Sultan's
army and slave household. But in general it may be said not only
that the territories over which the Patriarch came to preside formed
in a limited sense a reconstitution of Byzantium; but also that the
Orthodox Christians in Greek lands remained over this period of
Turkish occupation essentially a non-western people, not merely
because of their experiences under the Turks, but through the
continuity of the cultural and religious tradition of Byzantium,
whose Empire like that of the Ottomans did not have either its
centre in western Europe or even in European Greece.

In addition to this, it must also be remembered that the attitude
of Orthodox Christians to the peoples of western Europe was not
altogether favourable, either on an ecclesiastical or popular level.

First, western Europe as a whole represented a gigantic apostasy from Christ and the true faith, and its peoples were either schismatics or heretics, a matter of extreme importance and one that placed them on a lower level than the Islamic Turks. Then the Crusades, and particularly the sack of Constantinople by the 'Crusaders' in 1204, had left a legacy of extreme suspicion of, not to say hostility towards, the presence of western Europeans in the eastern Mediterranean and the adjacent lands; and this suspicion and hostility were nourished by the trading activities of, particularly, the Venetians and Genoese, for these in many cases led to the actual occupation of Orthodox Christian lands by the commercial communities in question. All this had given Orthodox Christians the opportunity of comparing western behaviour with that of the Turks, and again the result was seldom to the advantage of the westerners, whose general and particular rapacity came to be deeply resented – it is to be noted in this connection that when in the second half of the seventeenth century the Venetians, under the famous Morosini, were recapturing the Morea from the Turks, the enthusiasm and support of the local inhabitants for the Venetians were sadly lacking. Moreover, in the wake of the traders came the proselytizing religious orders of their schismatic or heretical brethren: the Jesuits were in Athens by 1645, and the French Capuchins by 1658; and the Jesuits also established themselves at Constantinople, Corfu, Zante, and other key positions in the Archipelago and elsewhere that came under Venetian domination or influence. This increased the already well-nourished animosity which the presence and pretensions of the western Franks provoked.

Thus the low esteem in which Orthodox Christians were held by western humanists might be said to be reciprocated, not to say exceeded, by the low opinion with which these Christians regarded the Franks. Unfortunately written testimony as to the Christian attitude is scarce; and in fact perhaps the most eloquent such testimony is to be found not in anything written by an Orthodox Christian but in a book written by one of the western Europeans in question. This book, *Athènes ancienne et nouvelle*, appeared in French in 1675, and in 1676 appeared in English with the title: *An Account of a Late Voyage to Athens, containing the Estate both Ancient and Modern of that Famous City*. Compiled by a Frenchman, de Guillet, it was based on several records, both literary and personal, about Athens, its monuments, and its people; and among the other items of interest reported is the speech of an Athenian ecclesiastic provoked by listening to the usual obtuse commonplaces about the present state of Greece and its inhabitants made by a group of travelling western gentlemen upon whom he was attending. The

C

speech is worth citing, for though it cannot claim to be a literal transcription, it does reflect what must have been the attitude of the more educated of the Sultan's Christian subjects in relation to the theme that we are examining.

'There is not a stranger comes to Athens, but observing the present condition of the Country, he deplores our misfortunes, with great expressions of sorrow, to see so Famous a City in the clutches of *Barbarians*, and in Pious Zeal cryes out against that ambition which animates your Princes, and prompts them rather to tear one another to pieces, than to confederate as well for their own interest, as ours against the tyranny of the Turks. This is the common sentiment and discourse of all Travellers that come hither. But what does it signifie? tis but impertinent talk, and I do not question but five or six hundred years hence they will complain to as little purpose of the ill management of the Liberty and Power among you, and the remedy will be as near. The half-witted people in your Country laugh at our ignorance, but I beseech you with what Justice? were we not ready in Old Times to communicate with you, and impart our Notions in all the excellent Sciences. When you had forgot what you had received from Plato, and Aristotle, and Epicurus, we were so kind in the middle of the fourteenth Century to supply you again with the Learning of Argyropoulos, Theodore Gaza, George Gemisto, and Antonicus: You look as you were surprized, but for whom do you take us Athenians? To silence you quite, I reserve for the last the poor but incomparable Caloyer Bessarion, who by one of your Popes was made a Cardinal, and sent Legate into France in 1472, to accomodate the difference betwixt Lewis XI and Charles the last Duke of Burgandy . . . I will not swear, that with your skill in the Latin Gibberish you ever heard this story that I shall tell you; George Gemisto was a Platonist, George of Trebezund a Peripatetik: these two Sects were formerly in great emulation, and perhaps are none of the best friends at this day; George of Trebezund writ against the Doctrine of Plato, and I question not but some of his works falling into your hands has been the occasion that Aristotle has been of late received into your Schools. Come to Constantinople, come to Sinope a Famous Port in the Black Sea, and you will find Professors in Philosophy that will discourse with you seven years together. My modesty will not suffer me to speak of those in Athens; In those three there are public Schools for the teaching of those Notions; but in the rest of the Towns of Greece, we have no Science but what teaches us contempt for this world, and preparation for the next. Our Philosophy teaches us to detest Sin, and our Theology to Pray. The great Apostle, to whom this Town is indebted for its Conversion, insinuates nothing else, and that is the main drift and scope of his Epistles to us. For you, I beseech you, what fruit is there of your Artificial Eloquence? of the confused tumult in your Schools? of the vain and obstinate contests of your Doctors, your chimerical dissertations upon what you call Criticisms, and we nothing but fooleries? Your great questions in Philosophy are rather subtilties and curiosities, than matter of use; in a word, mere Metaphysical reflections beyond, if not contrary to natural experience, serving rather to perplex, than to illustrate the Truth, while the niceties of your Great College are either the cause or support of New Heresies, extravagant Sects, monstrous Opinions, Confederacies, Civil Wars, and corruption in matters of Justice. Since Plato was rejected, and Aristotle received into your Schools, how many of your learned Doctors have there been, who make the Peripatetical Doctrine the foundation of their Christianity, declining the Authority of the Scripture, and not only doubting, but questioning and disputing Pro and Con with great ardency whether there be a God or not? . . . '

This speech is of interest from several points of view; for while it expresses a considerable awareness of the late Byzantine philosophical world, it yet makes it clear that the great body of Orthodox Christians remain entirely loyal to the Christian interpretation of life which they have inherited from Byzantium, and that it is in the light of this that they view the abnormalities and excesses of the West, attributing these precisely to the increasing prestige of the pagan philosophers and particularly of Aristotle. At the same time it indicates also that the Orthodox Christians – or at least those among them who are at all concerned with the matter – have completely accepted the western European version of their own genealogy: that the present inhabitants of the Helladic homeland are the legitimate and true-born heirs of the ancient Hellenes; that their language is the same; and that it is their forefathers who have written the great works and reared the magnificent monuments. Part of that myth, of which Pletho at the end of the Byzantine period had been the chief exponent, has returned in the way and form we have been examining, and from now on is firmly embedded in the consciousness of the modern Greek: he is the true descendant of the ancient Greek, and his sense of his historical identity is increasingly affected by this assumption.

This however does not explain how the other aspect of this myth – that only the values of the classical tradition are capable of forming the basis of the regeneration of the modern Hellenic nation – could so lead to the displacing of the traditional Christian values that by the time of the outbreak of the war of Independence in 1821 the ideals for which the Greeks were to fight were no longer those of a theocratic Christian Oecumene, but those of a nation state on a purely secular and western model. Partly this radical change in consciousness among Orthodox Christians – or at least among large and influential sections of them – can be accounted for by the change in attitude of western Europeans towards them in the latter half of the eighteenth century and particularly in the early nineteenth century. The victory of the western armies over the Turks at the siege of Vienna in September 1683 made it clear that the Ottoman Empire was no longer in a position to impose a military solution in its differences with Europe, and indeed encouraged the belief that Turkish domination in eastern Europe might soon be brought to an end. This meant that the question of who would succeed the Turks in these lands became one of immediate concern among the major European powers, including Russia; and this in its turn meant that the matter of the international sympathies of the Sultan's Christian subjects in Greek lands was no longer of comparative indifference.

Moreover, with this new sense of the possibilities of a restored Hellenic nation as an ally in the game of international power politics went a growing romanticization of the inherent properties and potentialities of the contemporary Greek character. The western idealization of everything Greek was bound sooner or later to affect the traditional Latin evaluation of this character; for whatever else they may have been the inhabitants of the lands of ancient Greece were by common confession genuine products of the ancient Hellenes, and so in this way were for the classical humanist objects of as direct a concern as he had for other such products; indeed they tended to become perhaps the most interesting of the relics littering the Greek scene, capable of throwing more light upon the customs and qualities of the ancients than columns, inscriptions, or vases. In addition to this it became increasingly difficult to admit that anything so genuinely Greek could be wholly without virtue; rather might it not be more true to say that the apparent failures of the Greek character were due to the intolerable conditions to which it had been reduced by the Turkish yoke? – the corollary that depended from this being that once this yoke was removed the pristine nature of this character would once more shine forth in all its glory. The fashionable theories of Rousseau about the natural goodness of man and that it is but the chains in which he is bound by crafty and powerful men that prevents this from being evident, lent support to these new philhellene sentiments. Man is virtuous in so far as he preserves or realizes his liberties and natural rights; in so far as he is deprived of these he becomes vicious and degenerate. Moreover, did not western Europeans, whose new civilization was built on the basis of values provided by the ancient Greeks, have a positive duty to make it possible for the descendants of these ancients to enter once more into the inheritance of which they had so unjustly been dispossessed? Hence sentiment could be reinforced by responsibility; and the great tidal wave of romantic philhellenism that was eventually to bear Byron to the shores of Mesolonghi began to gather strength.

Political expediency, then, and a new romantic philhellenism worked together to encourage the Greeks to shake off the Turkish yoke and to reconstitute themselves as a nation; and what both western politicians and philhellenes regarded as a nation was of course something on the lines of their own secular states and not at all anything that resembled a theocratic society either on the Byzantine or the Islamic model. (In any case very few western politicians or philhellenes had any knowledge of or interest in either Byzantium, the Orthodox Church, or the theocratic structure of Islamic society; and if they had had, it is most unlikely they would have been in the least enthusiastic about any of the three.) But neither philhellenism nor international politics alone can account for how, when in 1821 the Greeks eventually rose against the Turks, the decision as to whether the form of the society that was to issue from their struggles would be more in accordance with the Orthodox than with the 'hellenizing' myth had already been made in their national consciousness, and made in favour of the latter.

Reference has been made to the Averro–Aristotelian schools of northern Italy in the fourteenth century and to the schools of Constantinople, Sinope, and Athens of which the Orthodox ecclesiastic is said to have boasted in the middle of the seventeenth century. What has not been remarked upon however is the intimate connection between these schools, and the fact that it was by way of this connection that one of the most important influences shaping the formation of the national Greek consciousness in the century or more preceding the war of Independence was transmitted.

We noted that the great intellectual change which took place in western Europe as a consequence of the increasing importance attributed to the philosophy of Aristotle in the thirteenth and fourteenth centuries, was systematized particularly at the universities of Bologna and Padua. In effect the discovery of many of the lost works of Aristotle in the thirteenth century led in the West to a displacing of the hierocratic conception of a Christian society in favour of a laicalized and ultimately non-Christian conception of society, of a purely natural and secular state. No doubt the way in which great Arab scholars like Averroes himself interpreted

Aristotle made the opposition between Christian and Aristotelian thought appear more radical than it was; but even so the acceptance of the new Aristotelian standards was bound to result in the challenge to the established Christian outlook of an alternative system of thought. For these standards – finite, empirical, anthropocentric, concerned only with the mortal happiness of the individual and the welfare of the terrestrial political society conceived as an end in itself – could not finally be reconciled with those of the theocratic way of life that characterized the Christian Middle Ages and continued to assert its influence among the Orthodox Christians of the Ottoman Empire. Indeed the neo-Aristotelianism that in the fifteenth and sixteenth centuries supplanted at the university of Padua the Averro–Aristotelian tradition was frankly materialistic, everything being conceived in terms of a purely natural and organic causality; and it was this 'new' philosophy that provided the basis for those theories, political and other, which in the eighteenth century were to be propagated throughout Europe with such success by the various champions of Enlightenment.

All this might have been of no particular consequence where the formation of modern Greece is concerned had it not been for various coincidental circumstances. In 1405 Padua was occupied by the Venetians; the Venetian senate confirmed the autonomy and privileges of its University, and in fact this University became virtually that of the Venetian Republic. It was because of this that the Averro–Aristotelian teaching and the new spirit of scientific materialism which grew from it could develop there in a way that was impossible in any other European university; for the Court of Rome and the Inquisition were powerless to intervene in the internal affairs of the Venetian Republic. And it was precisely to the university of Padua that, after the fall of Constantinople and their consequent loss of facilities for higher education in their own lands, the Orthodox Christians of Greece came; for not only were many of their lands now in the hands of the same Venetian Republic that secured the independence of this University from Roman control; but, by virtue of that same independence, Padua was able to admit among its students those of the Orthodox faith. This not only meant that Padua was able to benefit from the services of the most outstanding Greek scholars of the time – scholars who in many cases had at their disposal sources until then unknown at the University and in western Europe generally; it also meant that what amounted to the whole higher education of Greeks from the fall of Constantinople down to the outbreak of the war of Independence in 1821, and hence some of the most powerful formative influences of the Greek intellectual and cultural mentality during this period, were dominated, directly or indirectly, by that same rationalizing and materialistic spirit which increasingly prevailed in the university of Padua itself.

In this way, then, those 'Aristotelian' trends of thought, with their corresponding notions of a purely natural and secular state, began to penetrate through Venice into Greek lands. Indeed, a leading Greek historian has asserted that modern Greece owes her renaissance to the Greek community of Venice. For not only were Greek commercial houses and printing works established at Venice during the fifteenth and sixteenth centuries, but also in 1550 the Republic of Venice authorized what she had previously forbidden in Greek lands under her control, the opening of schools; and these schools were largely staffed by teachers who had completed their education at Padua. Moreover, in the sixteenth century the Academy of the Patriarchate at Constantinople was revived and furnished with 'scholarchs' (directors), nearly all graduates from Padua. Of these directors, unquestionably the most important was Theophyllos Corydaleus, appointed in 1624 by the Patriarch Cyril Loukaris, and holding the position until 1641. Himself a student of philosophy and medicine at Padua, Corydaleus became the leading agent of western thought and culture in the Greek East, and perhaps more than any other individual was instrumental in reforging the intellectual links between the two halves of Europe. A fanatical devotee of neo-Aristotelianism, he reorganized the Academy of the Patriarchate along the lines of Padua University, and imposed the new philosophy as the basis of higher education, completely secularizing the latter and emancipating it from its connection with theology. In this way Corydaleus displaced the centre of Greek education from Italy to Constantinople – hence the boast of the Greek ecclesiastic in the speech cited –, and established the pattern of philosophical and scientific instruction which was to dominate Greek schools for the next century and a half. Other centres of education were founded in the seventeenth and eighteenth centuries in Greek lands, at Chios, on Athos, in Epirus and Macedonia, on Patmos – in fact in practically every town in Greek lands within and without the Ottoman Empire. All followed the lead and pattern Corydaleus had given, and all served as mediums for the transmission into Greek lands of the new humanist and secular ways of thought and culture.

Thus the slow process of undermining from within the Christian values and conceptions of the Greek-speaking Orthodox people, and of displacing these in favour of ideals of a 'hellenism' thought to stem from ancient Greece, was set in motion. Most receptive to start with to the disruptive influence of these ideals were, first, the

Phanariots, those Greek Constantinopolitans who filled the high offices of the Patriarch's civil administration and who came to believe that their task was to revive the thought and culture of their classical ancestors; and, second, and perhaps more important, the new merchant-bourgeoisie class which had indeed, both outside and inside Greek lands, increasing influence. Venice was by no means the only, even if she was the most important, Greek commercial colony. By the eighteenth century there were similar colonies in practically every large commercial centre in Europe: in London, Paris, Amsterdam, Manchester, Leghorn, Vienna, Marseilles, Trieste, to mention but a few. At the same time, from the opening of the seventeenth century Greeks began to acquire in the internal and external commerce and navigation of the Ottoman Empire an increasing ascendancy. This Greek merchant-bourgeoisie class, itself a reflection of its western prototype with its rational and materialistic values, saw in these same values and their political counterparts an ideological weapon with which to oppose inside Greek lands the vested interests, intellectual and economic, of the landed notables and the ecclesiastical administration. In this way both education and the economic interest of the rising class combined in preparing the ground for the intense propagation, during the closing years of the eighteenth and opening years of the nineteenth centuries, of the ideals of secular liberalism and classical enlightenment on the part of the man who, after Corydaleus, was perhaps the most important individual educator of the Greek people during the Turkish occupation: Adamantios Korais.

In a certain sense, it is with Korais (b. 1748) that the myth, of which Pletho had been the exponent and according to which not only are the inhabitants of Greek lands the direct racial descendants of the ancient Hellenes, but also that it is only upon the basis of Hellenic thought and culture that a new Greece may be born, comes full circle; though it must be added that it comes full circle, after its transmutations through the schools and learned societies of western Europe, in a form that Pletho himself would have been the first to repudiate. For Pletho was a religious Platonist for whom the shape of the human society had significance only in so far as it reflected principles of a metaphysical order; while the currents of thought of which Korais was a representative could be traced back directly to the rediscovery of Aristotelian standards in the thirteenth and fourteenth centuries – standards that envisaged no more than a purely terrestrial human welfare, to be achieved through a secular and ultimately non-religious political society. For Korais however, as for his counterparts in the West, these were genuine Hellenic standards. In effect, Korais, a devoted reader of Gibbon, saw civilization in terms of a 'classicism' which had been born in the Greece of Pericles, preserved through the Hellenistic and Roman periods, eclipsed in the 'dark' Christian Middle Ages, whether Latin or Byzantine, reborn in Italy with the Renaissance, and whose present bearers were the enlightened and liberal spirits of the eighteenth century. Greece, the birthplace of this civilization itself, was cut off from the western Europe where it was now flourishing by the abominable and barbaric Turk, and, worse still, the inhabitants of Greece, descendants of the glorious Hellenes, had fallen in their captivity into a state of ignorance and depression contrasting sadly with their past eminence. What therefore was demanded was the re-education of Greeks through the study of the classics which, just as they had brought enlightenment to western Europe at the time of the Renaissance, would revive in Greece itself a consciousness of her ancient heritage (thus providing the incentive to throw off the 'barbarian yoke'), restore her cultural dignity, and allow her to resume her rightful place among the nations of the civilized world. In short, what Korais envisaged was the 'emancipation' of Greece in terms of the secular liberalism and humanist enlightenment of the contemporary West; and it was with a view to this that he set about his intense campaign of propaganda in Greek lands.

The main direction of this propaganda was twofold: to revive the Greek language and to promote the education of modern Greeks through the study of the works of their ancestors. Pletho had already singled out the possession of a common language as evidence of the racial continuity of the Greeks, and indeed the similarities between the ancient and modern Greek language had become charged with an almost mystical significance in this respect. Moreover, by the late eighteenth century such notions had acquired a political extension through the labours of romantic philologists like the Germans Herder, Fichte, and Schlegel, for whom what distinguished a 'nation' is not its religion, or geographical factors, but the possession of a common language inherited through the centuries. This making a common language the criterion of nationality was later to have consequences of a violent nature where the future history of the Greek state is concerned; but for Korais it meant that a prerequisite of the development of a sense of nationality among the Greeks, as well as the subsequent unity of the nation, was a linguistic homogeneity; and to achieve this Korais advocated a language reform. The language he proposed was a mixture of the classical Greek language and the language of the modern educated middle class of which he was a spokesman (his anti-clericalism prevented him from considering the liturgical language of the

Orthodox Church, while the 'vulgar' language of the people was a little too remote from its classical prototype to be worthy of emulation); and the success of his reform can be measured by the incredible confusion of language that has been the bane of Greek life and letters ever since. As for education, it was the lack of this that was the root of all ills, and it would only be through the overcoming of this lack that the Greeks would again attain political and economic freedom: only when the Greeks became aware of the values of their ancient thought and culture would they set about freeing themselves. Hence education for Korais meant familiarization with the classics; and it was to this end that he embarked on a programme of the translation and publication of the main works of ancient Greek literature, and of their distribution in Greek lands.

The values that Korais desired to propagate through this programme and through the numberless pamphlets that poured from his pen – values which he regarded as *par excellence* those of Hellenism – were, we have noted, typical of the eighteenth-century West. Korais has no status as a thinker in his own right. His role was that of a popularizer of the dynamic western philosophy of secular liberalism and classical enlightenment which he himself accepted without question. His views on social morality were those of the School of Natural Rights, a simplified and doctrinaire mixture of Hobbes, Locke, and Rousseau, while on government they were those of such as Bentham and Blackstone. Theatre, press, universal elementary education, a subsidized religion, he regarded as indispensable instruments for the civilizing of society and for maintaining and strengthening its laws. His liberalism, his republican sentiments, and his middle-class concept of government, coloured with the notions of the Physiocrats and the reforming humanitarianism of the French *philosophes*, represented in an extreme form those systems of thought whose gradual pervasion of the Greek *milieu* in the preceding centuries we have noted; and it was because of these centuries of preparation that they found the ground so receptive and so favourable to their growth.

Their acceptance marks the crystallization of a long process. In that process those two ultimately incompatible mythological perspectives in which, at the time of the fall of Byzantium, Greek-speaking Orthodox Christians might, according to their various predilections, have seen their historical identity and future destinies defined – the one, looking back to the theocratic and imperial Christian society of Byzantium and forward to its resurrection, in which they were presented as God's chosen people, instruments in the inevitable consummation of His terrestrial kingdom; and the other, looking back to the ancient Greek world and forward to its rebirth in terms of a national state, in which they were presented as racial descendants of the glorious Hellenes: these two perspectives in that process merged and interacted in the way we have attempted to show. It would be rash to say that the result was a foregone conclusion, and that just as in the West the theocratic Christian vision and the way of life based upon it would not be able to resist the inroads of non-Christian materialistic thought and its corresponding social and political theories: the history of Orthodox imperial Russia is there to suggest other possibilities. But in the event, by the time of the outbreak of the Greek war of Independence in 1821 the Greeks' sense of who they were, and thus of the terms in which they were to seek to realize the shape of the modern Greek nation, reflected the ascendancy in their consciousness of the standards of the second of these two perspectives. Moreover, in gaining this ascendancy it had captured and harnessed to its own secular purposes many of the elements – the idea of a chosen people, the idea of an *imperium* – which had once belonged to the sacred system of its rival. The repercussions of this on the historical plane were to become all too evident in the formation and subsequent fortunes and misfortunes of the modern Greek state.

II

Ideas about nationality were not, of course, the constructs of the simple peasants and shepherds who peopled Greek lands at the beginning of the nineteenth century. Yet partly for these ideas they were about to fight a long war of intermittent savagery and suffering. And if we are to understand the form of this struggle and the subsequent efforts to establish a modern Greek state, some comments at least must be made about the institutions and attitudes of the countrymen.

Greek villagers at this time lived either on large estates generally in the more fertile plains which they worked as *métayers* sharing the produce with the landowner (who might be an individual proprietor or a religious institution): or in the broken upland country they cultivated smallholdings which were feudal land or private property. The countryside, it must be stressed, was largely untenanted, wide areas of the plains were left to grass where shepherd communities grazed transhumant flocks of sheep and goats each winter. Malaria oppressed low-lying lands and brigandage dominated whole districts in the mountains.

In these uncertain conditions the family and the village community were the social groups in which men placed their trust. Whether for security, water, or as a result of Ottoman fiscal and administrative arrangements, villages and hamlets, although often small in size, were nearly always compact settlements. Sheep and goats provided the wool, goatshair, and hide, from which shoes and clothes were made. Crops were grown mainly for subsistence, most taxes were in kind, and grain could be exchanged for the few necessities from outside, oil where olives were not grown, salt and simple utensils and tools of iron. There were variations in wealth but villagers shared a common style of life in a regime which was essentially autarkic. The group which in most contexts was responsible for an individual was his family, and to it, in turn, his obligations were absolute and categorical.

This was not only a domestic association of individuals with affections based on blood relationship, but a corporate group working together to provide the means for life and owning in common all significant property. It was, as it still is, a religious community with its own 'sacra', icons and other objects. The family is a divine institution and the figures of God the Father, the Mother of Christ, and Christ are in some sense a holy archetype family of which earthly families are an imperfect reflection. In the daily struggle to support a family a man was doing God's work and in preserving his relation with God through offerings to intercessory saints, through fasting and continence before important religious festivals, and especially in the Communion wine which normally he received only once or twice each year, a man might hope to draw down the Grace of God to assist him in the unequal battle.

The battle was unequal not only at the practical level of winning a living but also in the moral struggle to preserve the honour of the family in which the individual honour of each member was also implicated. The notion of *timē* is perhaps inadequately expressed by the English word honour. Subjectively it is a sense of integrity, of not being touched, or humiliated before others, or oneself, through particular kinds of failure. Outwardly *timē* is the recognition of social worth which is conceded grudgingly by the community. Two sentiments are closely related to it: that of *philotimo* which is the 'love of honour' that encourages a man to act rightly, and therefore is particularly sensitive to any suggestion that he has not done so; and *dropē*, shame, which is the fear of failure that prevents wrong actions, or a sense of acute discomfort which follows after them.

The intrinsic principles of personal honour refer to two sex-linked qualities that mark the ideal moral characters of Greek men and women: these are manliness (*andrismos*) in men, and sexual shame (*dropē*) in women. Manliness is, in part, a self-assertive courage and to have it a man must be *varvatos*, that is well endowed with testicles and the strength that is drawn from them. This power is not morally distinguished, for it may, if ill-employed, lead a man to rape or casual killing. The manliness which is related to honour requires this physical basis, yet it must discipline animal strength and passions to its own ideal ends.

In woman there are contradictory powers. The physical and moral capacities which enable her to bear children, especially sons, and to care for them, are valued. Yet ambiguity and awe surround the mysterious power of a woman's fertility, and the processes of menstruation and birth itself are peculiarly polluting and dangerous to others. The sensuality of woman, which even without her will must attract a man, is a threat to her life and honour, and to the honour and lives of those protecting her who after the discovery of a liaison may be obliged to kill both the woman and her seducer. Only in a legitimate marriage, which is the foundation of the family and the symbol of its honour, is sexual activity possible, and even then it holds an ambivalent quality. If it were possible to combine virginity and motherhood these would be the ideal qualities of a woman. There is no more direct, but also dishonouring, attack on a family than to sully or question the sexual honour of one of its women. Hence a woman must be governed by a sense of sexual shame, *dropē*, which is an instinctive revulsion from sexual activity, an attempt in dress, movement, and attitude to disguise the fact that she possesses the physical attributes of her sex.

One aspect of honour, then, was a struggle of self-discipline over brutality, cowardice, and sensuality, flaws of animal nature that continually threatened to limit the nobility of man. In this struggle men and women were helped by figures who are exemplars of certain patterns of ideal behaviour. Female values were referred to the qualities of the Mother of God: modesty, virginal attitudes, and selfless love. For men such horsed and warlike saints as George and Demetrius presented the pattern of assertive courage, physical, spiritual, and invulnerable. Or closer to the possibilities of this world the legendary image of the klephtic brigand hero was a man who had so refined his powers of courage and continence that he partly overcame the limitations of this life: neither could bullets strike him, nor a hundred foot chasm check his horse. Men and women struggled to attain these ideal modes of being and conduct. Where they fell too far short in the effort of identification, honour was lost. Thus in each family the courage and strength of the men had not to be seen to be diminished nor the purity of the women questioned. Where manliness and shame were complementary qualities in relation to honour it is not difficult to deduce the situations in which it was typically threatened: homicide, verbal insult or physical attack, seduction, rape, or a broken betrothal.

For any association between families unrelated by kinship or marriage these values had important implications. So exclusive were the obligations of members of the family to one another, so comprehensive were the consequences of the loss of honour, which was potentially at risk in dealings with outsiders, that distrust between unrelated families was virtually obligatory. Beyond the essentially negative prescriptions of neighbourly duty there was little sense of moral obligation. And since the preservation of social reputation depended on recognition unwillingly conceded by others, the denigration of other families, which might lead to their loss of prestige and even of honour itself, in a sense protected one's own position. The importance of name and reputation encouraged a man to much expressive boasting and self-assertion, for the need to equate the community's evaluation of himself with his own ideal image often encouraged a form of unconscious cheating, or self-deception. (Certainly, today, knives are pulled with greater bravado when it is certain that others are present to prevent their use.) It follows, too, that cleverness, skill, and cunning were prized because these were the capacities on which strength and success partly depended. Moreover, reputation was more easily preserved by families which had wealth and numbers of kinsmen and other clients to support them. In the court of honour strength was admired, weakness and poverty despised.

In the life of small mountain communities the sense of competitive opposition, struggle, and envy was intense. The values of honour, it is clear, were concerned with self-regard, not regard for others. In each case it was a question of a man attempting to realize, or at least to lay claim to, a particular ideal pattern of conduct. What interested him was the success of this quest, not the effect of his actions on the affairs of others. Self-regard forbade any action which might be interpreted as weakness. Cooperation and tolerance had generally to give way to the interests of the family group narrowly defined, and to arrogance and distrust. Even where a man moderated his actions because they might disastrously affect the fortunes of another family, this was the result of an acute concern about the purity of his own motives rather than concern for others.

In part these are the considerations and attitudes which underlie the often discussed individuality of the Greeks. Here some qualification is needed. In village society an individual seldom stood alone. He was judged and evaluated in relation to his membership in a family which he represented in his public actions and for which he was responsible. And since a family's reputation depended upon the judgement of other families the community was, in this respect, a field of common values. One of these values was that where a family's own interests were not prejudiced neighbours should be assisted, a category which could be extended to include most of those who lived in the same community. Despite the reality of competition and distrust men and women had to show each other sociability in the exchange of greetings when they met by chance, and in the acceptance of each other's company at the well or in the coffee-shop. Moreover, although a subsistence economy demanded a minimum of cooperation in a village each family in its need for the moral support which enhanced its influence and reputation had developed a net of friendships and alliances with certain other families which shared kinship or a common interest. But these relationships tended to be shifting and unstable. Favours were precisely accounted and accusations of ingratitude were not unusual. For whatever the altruistic ideal of friendship or patronage, in reality the relationship was limited by the exigence of family loyalties and the distrust of outsiders which accompanied it.

In terms of its internal structure the village community was divided and fragmented and it might seem unlikely that it could have acted in unison on any matter. Yet in certain circumstances the solidarity of purpose was considerable. The Ottoman form of government and tax collection in its unconcern with local administration preferred to deal with communities as entities represented by elected village notables and in this way created from without a sense of solidarity derived from the common problems which they imposed. But from within there also worked the complex notion of *patridha*, native place or country. This patriotism of peasants and shepherds was an organic growth, both emotional and pragmatic, a relationship with a place which supported life and with which the life of the family was intimately connected. There was a moral identification with a place where, symbolically, air was cooler and water purer than in other places. Any attack, or even administrative intrusion, upon the village and its land, was an attack upon the personal relationship between a man and his 'country', and consequently upon his honour. Men drew together to defend their own community and, by an extension of these sentiments, although at first with less certainty or enthusiasm, to defend other Greek communities.

This patriotism had a religious character. The village community, gathered about its church, was a space blessed and protected by God in opposition to the potentially destructive spiritual powers of the wilderness outside. And at the great religious festivals of the year, particularly at Easter, after a period of continence and fasting, men were drawn together in another way, if only briefly, in the general expression of enjoined goodwill.

In giving this admittedly schematic and incomplete account of values and attitudes in the small communities which mainly constituted the Greek population on the eve of the war of Independence we have wavered uncertainly between the use of the present and past tenses. For many of the values we have discussed were still valid a decade ago in traditional and remote mountain communities in Greece. Even today in the complex processes of social change which increasingly affect the countryside these values are not without effect. The writings of those, like General Makriyannis, who fought in the war of Independence are adequate sources for the attitudes which prevailed in the earlier period, and our account is not merely a projection into the past of conditions observed at the present.

The memoirs of Makriyannis show us his acute concern to justify his actions throughout his life in terms of the values of honour. A public whipping for a misdemeanour with a relative's gun was a searing and traumatic humiliation; yet a small fortune made through money-lending to hard-pressed farmers, and commercial deals in grain during a bread shortage which followed an outbreak of plague, is the object of self-congratulation because it saved him from an undignified dependence on others. For the intensity of responsibility and obligation to a restricted circle, and the extreme importance of honour and reputation which accompanied it, tended always to limit the range of moral obligation that a man could allow himself to feel. The extraordinary mosaic of heroism and self-seeking greed in the conduct of individual Greek leaders during the war of Independence is partly explicable in these terms. Reputation and power depended on followers, and the ability to hold followers on the means to support and pay them. Thus a man might too easily justify the methods he used to find these means. The temptation of personal and family advantage, and the priority that almost always was given to the settlement of personal slights and jealousies which in terms of honour were so consequential, continually threatened the unity of Greek military commands and the embryonic structures of civil administration; sometimes to the point of arrangements with the enemy. Where values were intrinsically self-regarding the margin which separated conduct that satisfied the reputation and interest of the individual, his family, and the community, from actions that were selfish in the dishonourable sense, was narrow and debatable.

In the society of Greek peasants and shepherds the typical relations of commitment were those within the family: they were few, unambiguous yet emotional, expressed through notions of honour and shame which were concerned with the assertive strivings of the total personality to realize a certain pattern of behaviour. They were not founded on limited or specific obligations. In such a community there was in men a stream of energy that might be channelled one way or another giving extreme and sometimes violent expression to opposite behaviour according to the situation and the social personalities involved. To a western European used to more universally applicable canons of conduct it was bewildering to find in the same individuals extraordinary proofs of heroism and self-sacrifice, spontaneous sincerity, and at other times evidence of treachery, brutality, and even cowardice. For the Greeks, too, who had to live by these values, there were problems of interpretation and judgement. The honour of Makriyannis was affronted when his brave soldiers looted a Greek village and after forcing four men to carry them on their shoulders across an icy river had, for this service, stripped them of their clothes and weapons and left them naked on the bank. Makriyannis in emotion and indignation left his men and refused to lead them until they restored what had been stolen, bound their ringleaders, and he had beaten them 'till the blood flowed from their buttocks'. 'I was worse off than they,' he added, 'my hands were bleeding and I was sick for many days after.'

The categorical quality of obligations to the family which normally take precedence over other loyalties, and its counterpart of distrust and relative moral unconcern outside that circle, go some way to explain these seeming anomalies. The local community, an army of irregulars, or the nation itself could stand united only when external threats were brutally evident or when such wider groupings could be seen as in some sense an enlargement of the family or a projection of its values.

D

Chapter 2

The Approach to Independence

ALTHOUGH AT THE BEGINNING of the nineteenth century the great majority of Greeks were illiterate peasants or shepherds, there were also small but important communities or classes of churchmen, administrators, and merchants, who by virtue of their occupation and influence profoundly affected the fortunes of their less prosperous compatriots. Not only were there considerable differences in wealth and education between these privileged groups and the rest of the Greeks, but the main theatres of their operations were generally removed from those areas of relatively homogeneous Greek-speaking population in the Peloponnese and southern continental Greece.

By the end of the seventeenth century economic expansion in central Europe had created a demand for Ottoman products, such as grain, leather, wool, and cotton, at a time when a general disorganization in the ports and markets of Syria and Egypt, due in part to Turkish wars with Persia, had removed the centre of Ottoman commercial life northwards to the cities of Salonika and Smyrna with their considerable Greek populations. With this advantage of locality Greek merchants with commendable opportunism and energy had captured the greater part of the Empire's internal trade by the middle of the eighteenth century; and whether as agents for European merchant houses, or on their own account, they were steadily extending their influence in external trade. In 1776 the French Consul in Salonika was reporting that Austrian houses could no longer face their competition in the market for cotton and woollen thread. By about the same date Greek merchants were a considerable force even in the domestic markets of Vienna. Other events in the eighteenth century assisted the impetus of Greek commercial advance. As a consequence of the treaties of Kutchuk Kainardji (1774) and Jassy (1792) which opened the Dardanelles to Russian and Austrian commerce and permitted Ottoman Greeks to fly the Russian flag, Greek colonies flourished at Odessa, the Chersonese, and Taganrog; and Black Sea commerce was controlled by Greek middlemen.

The result of the continental blockade during the Napoleonic wars was conclusive. French commerce in the Levant was destroyed. In 1771 French merchants controlled half the external trade of Salonika. After the Anglo–French wars three-quarters of the eastern Mediterranean trade had fallen into Greek hands, a great amount of it carried in Greek ships whose numbers had increased dramatically.

By the end of the eighteenth century a crescent of Greek merchant colonies might be traced from the south of France through central Europe to the Black Sea ports of southern Russia. As we have already observed in the previous chapter it was particularly through the channels opened by this merchant diaspora that novel western conceptions of 'progress', 'popular sovereignty', and the 'nation state' made their effect upon the Ottoman Greek world. Nor could these merchants fail to appreciate the advantage and profit that their businesses would enjoy if their own country were transformed to an efficiently ordered state on the European model. But here two things must be said. The commerce in which these merchants were engaged was an imperial trade in which the products of their compatriots were only one element. They operated from centres whether in Europe or the great market ports of Salonika and Smyrna that were distant or relatively unconcerned with the Peloponnese and Greece south of Macedonia.

At the political centre of the Empire in Constantinople, and therefore also removed from European Greece, was the Orthodox Patriarch, whose position under Ottoman rule we mentioned in the previous chapter. He held a detailed civil jurisdiction over the Christian community in the Empire, locally exercised through Metropolitans, bishops and the subordinate clergy, a jurisdiction which included the regulation of marriage, divorce, dowry, and inheritance. These, indeed, were the institutions that most intimately concerned the daily lives of men living in a society where the simple or extended family was the enduring unit of economic and social enterprise. But it was not only through these external sanctions that the Church held its members. It conserved and transmitted those liturgical and sacramental forms of worship that guided and sanctified a particular relation between men and God, a relation that appeared to Orthodox believers to be as practically necessary in their daily affairs as they were undoubtedly unquestioned values in an accepted way of living. It must be remembered that under unusual pressures apostasy was not common. This is perhaps surprising. The Greek Christians were impressed by Turkish morale and prestige. Their leaders often attempted to copy the external particulars of Turkish dress and manners as closely as they dared; and Greek pride suffered with difficulty the social humiliation of an inferior status. Yet each century of Turkish rule produced its martyrs to the faith.

The patriotism of the Ottoman Christian was in the first instance to his local community, a village or a ward in a small town grouped about its church where after the Sunday liturgy its congregated members discussed and argued over their parochial affairs, including at intervals the election of representatives to meet the demands of officials, tax-farmers, or feudal superiors. In itself the community was a microcosm, not simply a part, of the wider Orthodox Christian Oecumene: a Byzantine conception prolonged in the Ottoman recognition of Orthodox Christian subjects as a *millet* which had an ecclesiastical consciousness and unity.

But although this ecclesiastical consciousness was the predominant point of reference for Orthodox Christians of the Empire in the sixteenth and seventeenth centuries the Greek language prevented the total confusion of the Greek-speaking population with their Slav brothers. Moreover, since Greek was the official language of the Church, those who spoke a dialect version of it felt a certain superiority of status; while the hierarchy of the Church came to believe that they had a duty to preserve not only the Christian faith but Hellenism itself.

Yet by its very position in the structure of Ottoman government the Church was unfitted to lead a national rebellion. Appointment to, and deposition from, the Patriarchal throne were manipulated by the Turks through their encouragement of factions among the Metropolitans of the Synod. And the Patriarch and the members of the Synod were at all times hostages for their own proper behaviour. Although the people were no less devoted to their churches than before, criticism of the hierarchy became more general in the second half of the eighteenth century, stimulated no doubt by the anti-clerical views of the merchant diaspora. For these Greeks, already accustomed to question the value of traditional institutions, wrote bitterly on the simoniacal system of church appointments which demanded large sums from a successful candidate, who was then forced to recoup his debt by levies on subordinate clergy and the laiety. Nor with their utilitarian values could they consent to the 'un-productive' regime of monastic life and the great resources of land and wealth invested in it.

In a tract entitled 'Paternal Exhortation' (published in 1798) that was perhaps written by the Patriarch Gregory V, we have a most explicit defence of the Church's position. To preserve the holy Orthodox faith, the author tells us, the Lord had created from nothing the powerful Ottoman state to take the place of the Byzantine Empire which had begun to deviate from the true faith. (That is, it had compromised over theological principle with the West, just as many Greeks were now adopting western political values.) The new regime of Liberty, he continues, is a trick of the Devil, superficially attractive, but in fact contrary to the Holy Scriptures and designed to deprive men of every heavenly and earthly wealth. If the Patriarch was the author of this tract the irony that he was immediately strangled by the Turks after the first acts of violence which announced the revolution is indicative of his hopelessly vulnerable situation.

To assist the Patriarch and the Synod in their administrative work a class of lay officials, later known as Phanariots, had grown up at the Patriarchate. About the middle of the seventeenth century when the Turks could no longer attract European renegades to fill the specialist and diplomatic positions which required a knowledge of European languages and peoples, many of these officials found employment in the Ottoman government. In some instances the offices which became the regular perquisites of the Phanariots were positions of immense authority, such as that of Dragoman of the Porte who implemented the Empire's foreign policy, or the Dragoman of the Fleet who acted as a Secretary of State to the Ottoman Admiral, and, in effect, administered relations with the islands and their inhabitants. Later in 1709 the even more exalted appointments of Hospodar, or prince, to the tributary principalities of Moldavia and Wallachia were conferred on Phanariots. Indeed, between the middle of the eighteenth century and the outbreak of the revolution this Greek executive aristocracy might claim to have established a form of administrative diarchy. One consequence of this growth of Phanariot power was a diminution of the Patriarch's effective authority in the civil administration of the Orthodox Christians and even in his ability to reject a candidate for appointment to a see if he happened to be backed by Phanariot patronage.

In some respects the Phanariots were an aristocracy of merit; for they had to possess a wide range of linguistic and cultural abilities to claim and hold the monopoly of government entrusted to non-Muslims. Panayiotis Nikousios who became the first Phanariot Dragoman of the Porte in 1661 had studied mathematics and astronomy at Padua. Alexander Mavrocordatos, his successor, was also educated in Italy, was a doctor of medicine and philosophy, and wrote a thesis on the circulation of the blood. At Bucharest and Jassy in the Principalities the Phanariots encouraged and patronized the foundation of Greek schools in which the ideas of western philosophy, science, and political thought were current. But their mutually incompatible loyalties to ideals of Hellenism, to the Ottoman state as the institution through which they ruled, and to their families endemically intriguing for advancement, did not recommend them to Greeks who had begun to think of a more revolutionary solution for their grievances. Phanariots might effectively protect Greek commercial interests but they also acted as agents for the Ottoman government in the affairs of the Greek communities they administered. The more authority they acquired, the more serious their personal responsibility for internal order and, naturally, the greater their personal loss when they were driven from power. Phanariots perhaps hoped for a gradual development of Greek commerce and administrative function to a point where in all but name the Greeks would have usurped the Empire. And to this end it was not inconsistent that they, too, encouraged the growth of an Hellenic consciousness among their Greek-speaking compatriots. Unfortunately in encouraging this form of education it was impossible to censor the introduction of ideas which provoked developments the Phanariots could neither exploit nor sympathize with. As in the case of the church hierarchy, and for similar reasons, Phanariot power was always, at best, conditional and vulnerable.

The great majority of the Greek-speaking population at this time were, as they had always been, peasants living in small village communities. In Anatolia, Thrace, Macedonia, and Epirus they represented one element in a confused pattern of communities speaking different languages or professing different religious beliefs. But in the Peloponnese and southern continental Greece the peasant population was in most areas more homogeneously Greek.

Originally, after the conquest, the Sultan had distributed the more productive lands in fiefs. Some of these were associated with particular offices in the provincial administration, but the majority provided the physical means to support the permanent body of the Muslim feudal army. Considerable areas were also reserved for the endowment of religious and educational institutions and there were a restricted number of private estates. But in the precipitous mountains of the Peloponnese and continental Greece with difficult communications and an unproductive subsistence economy the Christian villagers were sometimes left in possession of their stony fields if taxes were paid without dispute. The most important of these were the head tax and the tithe of about one-seventh of their grain crops. During the first two centuries of Ottoman rule the regime for peasants living on feudal lands was by no means oppressive. According to law if a peasant cultivated his fields at least once in three years he could not be evicted from them. In taxes he paid the head tax to the Sultan's treasury, while the tithe of one-seventh of his produce and a number of inconsiderable dues were payable to the *Spahi*, his feudal lord. His obligations and his rights were generally in a predictable if not always equitable balance. The *Spahi* had an obvious interest in his peasant's prosperity, and the peasant could consider his land, at least in a contingent sense, as his own, since he could either bequeath the *tapu* (the right to cultivate it) to his son, or even sell it.

Towards the end of the seventeenth century conditions changed. The previously efficient provincial administration became capricious and corrupt. Defensive wars and local administrative anomalies led to increases in the amounts of extraordinary taxation levied and demanded from the peasantry on the one hand and, on the other, to the extension of oppressive methods of tax-farming in the collection of regular taxes. At the same time the general revival of trade brought a greater circulation of wealth in certain classes of society. Muslim officials and landowners, non-Muslim merchants including Greeks, wished to own or to invest in land. In this fashion many fiefs were illegally converted into private estates (*chiftliks*) or were gradually eroded to the same end by forcing, or persuading, the peasant to sell his rights because he needed protection or because he was in debt. However, the position of a peasant living on *chiftlik* lands was infinitely less favourable. His relation with the landowner was contractual, the latter generally providing the seed and taking half the produce of the land on which the peasant cultivator had no security of tenure whatsoever. Thus there came into being a considerable class of local Muslim and non-Muslim landowners in which, especially in the Peloponnese, the Greeks were well represented. It follows that the number of peasants without a title to land of any kind also increased, a development which was accentuated by the steady growth in population during the eighteenth century.

For the Christian peasantry who had to adapt themselves as best they could to whatever variation of taxation and land tenure was from time to time imposed on them, the village community was the refuge in which they found consolation and a collective moral strength produced by an autonomous social and religious life. This the static Ottoman state had conceded to them, as we have seen, through the *millet* system. There was no programme of agricultural or social innovation and therefore rarely need for any administrative interference. Provincial government was mainly concerned with elementary considerations of internal order and fiscal supply. And the fact that it often found the village community a convenient unit for collective responsibility in the first case and collective assessment in the second, greatly enhanced the political value of that institution. But the development of communal institutions was not uniform in all areas. The Turks tended to confirm existing institutions at the time of conquest or to tolerate their growth where they were locally convenient. Previous experience of communal self-government before conquest, a trading economy, and geographic position, mainly account for the developed forms of self-government which existed in many of the islands. After 1615 on the island of Mykonos, for instance, an assembly of the people elected annually two councillors who in consultation with the clergy regulated the internal life of the community, public order and worship, health and schools. They promulgated local market by-laws and arbitrated in internal disputes. Aggregate amounts of taxation demanded were divided among the citizen body and the sum was collected. In many districts of continental Greece, on the other hand, no explicit organization of this kind existed, the priest and local notables providing *ad hoc* representation when it was required. But everywhere the village was, at least, the means of keeping intact a culture and, as we have seen, a Christian ecclesiastical conscience of which the church was a physically present symbol. Collective opinion in a small, often insecure, community where one person was bound to the other members in a complex of personal obligations and animosities could never easily permit individual acts of apostasy.

But it was in the Peloponnese after its reconquest by the Turks from the Venetians in 1715 that these communal institutions reached their most elaborate development, at a time when the efficiency of provincial government was in decline and when self-government seemed to be one way of appeasing and directing the new economic power and ambition of the Greeks. The elected elders of the villages of each province, or *vilayet*, met to discuss their affairs and to choose from their number delegates to represent the *vilayet* to its Ottoman ruler, the Bey. Similarly delegates from all *vilayets* were convened in an assembly known as the Peloponnesian Senate which discussed administration and taxation. It also elected two delegates who with two Muslim representatives constituted the permanent council of the Vizier of the Peloponnesian *Pashalik*.

The Greeks in the Peloponnese had a further privilege of great practical value, the right to appoint two representatives, or *Vekyls*, to the Porte itself. At times these agents could exercise considerable influence by the distribution of bribes and presents to officials or by confidential reports on the conduct of the Vizier whom they intrigued to remove if his policies were displeasing. If we add to this influence the power of veto held by the Greek members of the Vizier's Council over all measures of extraordinary taxation, and the right to raise through their own institutions the amounts agreed upon, we see that in the Peloponnese there was a system that might reasonably be referred to as dual government.

In fact, a political life of some complexity had grown up in the Peloponnese. The leading personalities in the *vilayet* assemblies and in the Peloponnesian Senate were the Greek landowners whose emergence we have noted. There was no considerable class of merchants or artisans to rival their predominance. Internal trade was in any case largely in the hands of the landed families of which some owned or controlled entire districts in the plains: upon them very large numbers of peasants depended for land, employment, or protection. Opposed factions of these landed notables vied for ascendancy in the Senate and over the Vizier. A party temporarily in 'opposition' intrigued with Ottoman officials manoeuvring for appointment to the viziership, and despatched agents to Constantinople to oppose the official *Vekyls* of the party in power.

There were, then, two parallel hierarchies of government at village, province, and central administration levels. The first Ottoman, where power passed downwards from the highest authority; the second Greek where, through a form of popular election generally by acclamation, and in fact controlled through local patronage, authority passed in an upward direction. At any particular level individuals in either hierarchy were linked to one another, not only by the formal institutions we have described, but also through reciprocal favours received and returned, through presents, bribes, and even personal friendships; and these relationships were complicated by other considerations, the consciousness of religious difference between the two groups, and the existence of faction and personal rivalry within their own groups.

Finally, in the mountains, particularly in the Pindus mountains of continental Greece, there were institutions of resistance. Formally non-Muslims were forbidden to carry arms, but in the mountain areas many villagers and most shepherds were armed. Since the Turks seldom attempted to administer these districts in detail they licensed bodies of Christian irregulars, generally known as *armatoles*, to care for order and security particularly where important lines of communication led through vulnerable passes. The threat to peace was brigandage. Mountains, weak provincial administration, a simple fragmented social structure in which the family was the unit of ultimate loyalty, its social and economic interests apparently always in opposition to those of others, and a life led in accordance with those traditional notions of honour and prestige we have already described, are among factors that explain its existence. Men fearing vengeance for an 'honour' killing, men in debt or without land, might take to the hills to become *klephts*, as Greek brigands were known. As a body of *armatoles* were responsible for a district so a band of *klephts* would attempt to control a certain area in which for a fee they would claim to protect notables and villagers from the depredations of other *klephts*. Between *armatoles* and *klephts* hostilities alternated with collusion. Moreover, the roles were easily exchanged, a captain of *armatoles* dismissed by the authorities became at once a klephtic leader. *Klephts* preyed on Greeks as well as Turks, but as disturbers of the peace their opposition to the Ottoman administration was a permanent feature and in this sense their way of life became identified with a form of armed ethnic resistance against the Muslim rulers. Also the ideals of klephtic life were related closely to the traditional values of Greek mountain communities. *Klephts* were brave, brutal, anarchic, and cunning; but men of honour in the technical Greek sense, respecting women and requiring of themselves great physical strength and courage, and Odyssean cunning. The stereotype was certainly admired, if the excesses of particular *klephts* sometimes persuaded Greek communities to cooperate in delivering them to Turkish justice. But the importance of the *klephts* and *armatoles* was that they were a class of Greek hardened and practised in guerrilla war, an essential cadre for the promotion of a successful rising. It so happened that by the end of the eighteenth century Ali Pasha at Jannina had replaced many of the Greek *armatoles* in his *pashalik* with Albanian Muslims. And in 1806 his son Veli had conducted a successful campaign against the Peloponnesian *klephts* driving them out in various directions, to continental Greece and to the Ionian islands. In these places *klephts* were numerous and discontented.

Although most Greeks were peasants we have revealed a number of other important groups or occupations, both in Greek lands and beyond, with divergent interests and values. The instrument which drew together these different elements was the secret society and political conspiracy known as the *Philiki Hetairia* or Society of Friends. Faced with the problem of provoking to revolution men long accustomed to habits of compromise and often profitable co-operation in their relations with the Turks, its methods and organization were to some extent borrowed from freemasonry and the secret political societies in Europe. Ceremonies of initiation to different grades, solemn oaths of commitment, invested the duties of members with a sacred and categorical quality setting them apart from and above ordinary social life, even the obligations of family life. As far as was possible members knew only the individual who had initiated them. Through him, also, orders were transmitted or money was passed.

The Society had been founded at Odessa in 1814 by three Greek merchants of no particular repute who therefore found it necessary to hide their identity. Orders and exhortations issued from a

Supreme but unknown Authority situated in Russia gathered an almost numinous influence. Although the disastrous consequences of the Russian intervention which had encouraged the Peloponnesians to rebel unsuccessfully in 1770 had not been forgotten, it was natural for Greeks to look to Russia for their deliverance. Russia was the Orthodox Christian power entitled by treaty, after 1774, to 'protect' the Sultan's Orthodox subjects. And in Russia the Greek diaspora was an established influence in commerce, administration, the army and navy. It was difficult for Ottoman Greeks to believe that the orders received from Russia did not come with the blessing of her government. Some, indeed, believed the Authority of the *Hetairia* was the Tsar Alexander himself; others, more plausibly, that it was his Greek Foreign Minister Capodistrias. In 1816 Capodistrias, in fact, rejected an invitation to become leader of the conspiracy. A movement to win autonomy for Greece at that time would be, he realized, entirely unacceptable to any of the powers. On his own admission the incident vexed him so considerably that he fell ill.

The early years of the Society while its activities were confined almost exclusively to the Greek world outside the Ottoman Empire were not productive. But in 1818 the headquarters were moved to Constantinople and efforts to initiate Greek notables, churchmen, *klephts*, merchants, and sea-captains in the Peloponnese and continental Greece began to meet with some success. In August 1818 the Hetairists won the adherence of Petrobey Mavromichalis, ruler of Mani, the forbidding southern peninsula of the Peloponnese which enjoyed particular privileges of autonomy. This was an important accession of strength. The district although poor in resources was peopled by communities of practised guerrilla fighters and it lay at the furthest extremity of Turkish land communications. It was in 1818, also, that the Society initiated Theodore Kolokotronis, the klephtic leader, and Germanos, the Metropolitan Bishop of Patras. Yet many cautious men of influence declined to commit themselves while the leadership remained anonymous; now it was more than ever essential to reveal a leader whose name would give confidence to the waverers. Xanthos, an original founder of the *Hetairia*, travelled to St Petersburg to explain to Capodistrias the critical position of the society. Capodistrias once more rejected the invitation to lead the conspiracy but it is clear both that he sympathized with the struggle for independence, and that he advised the Hetairists to avoid direct revolutionary action for the time being. Xanthos turned then to Alexander Hypsilantis, a Greek Phanariot officer in the Russian army, who accepted the hazardous mission after only brief hesitation. Yet the balance of advantage was uncertain. The Greeks in the Empire were now caught up in a mood of incendiary expectation and their Ottoman rulers were distracted by the indiscipline of provincial Pashas. But there was little hope of support, or even tolerance from the powers, and no certainty of reliable cooperation from the other Balkan peoples.

The initial strategy of the Hetairists was the notion of simultaneous uprisings in Serbia and the Peloponnese. The military purpose of such a plan is obvious; but the political problems of implementing it were considerable. For another century the Greek popular imagination would continue to be obsessed by the idea of a political conversion of the original Byzantine Orthodox Christian Oecumene into a new Greek Empire. We have mentioned earlier that there were Phanariots who hoped to achieve this, almost incidentally, by progressive extension of their own administrative sphere. We referred also to the merchants and intellectuals of the Greek diaspora in Europe seeking the equation of a rediscovered ancient Hellas with a democratic nation state on the western model. These, one might say, were respectively the eastern and western solutions of the Greek problem. An earlier Greek propagandist and conspirator, Rhigas Pheraios (extradited by the Austrians and executed by the Turks in 1798), had attempted to reconcile these different conceptions in his projected constitution for a unitary Balkan nation for which a free adaptation of the French constitutions of 1793 and 1795 provided a framework. There would be religious and political equality, for Muslims as well as Christians would be citizens of it. But in the new state, titled 'The Hellenic Republic', Greek would be the official language, and clearly from its hellenized citizens a governing class would be recruited. It may be doubted whether Rhigas' revolutionary Balkan republic ruled by Greeks could have been established at the time its author was attempting to give it life. In the years following the birth of the *Hetairia* such a policy had ceased to be realistic. The Serbians, who had enjoyed a *de facto* autonomy since 1815, were already conscious of a political identity separate from the Greeks, and in the Principalities the Romanian discontent was directed in particular against the Phanariot Greeks who misgoverned them in the name of the Sultan. The dilemma of the Greek Hetairists was that while they needed the cooperation of their Balkan co-religionists if their revolution was to succeed, they simultaneously hoped to limit their participation to territories that would interfere as little as possible with the development of a Greater Hellenic state.

The first attempt of the Hetairists to convert the Serbs to their cause had been singularly inept. They initiated Karageorge, an exile in Bessarabia and the leader of the first Serbian revolt in 1804, and they encouraged him to return to his own country to negotiate with Prince Milosh Obrenovitch possible terms for concerted rebellion against the Turks, although they must have known that Milosh, who had recently achieved a precarious autonomy for his country, suspected Karageorge of poisoning his half-brother and was in any case prejudiced against him for his status as the alternative national leader. Predictably Karageorge was murdered soon after his arrival.

In Hypsilantis' first paper plans for a double rebellion in Serbia and the Peloponnese that would divide the enemy forces between two theatres distant from one another and with difficult lines of land communication, the role of the Principalities was altogether secondary. Recruits and money were to pass into Serbia but no aggressive operations were planned in these territories, an assessment that was to be proved very correct. But in the event the negotiations which the Hetairists attempted with Milosh Obrenovitch did not prosper. They were remarkable only for the courteous evasiveness of Milosh and for the form of a treaty proposed by Hypsilantis which used the designation 'confederate and allied provinces'. This was surely a far cry from a New Byzantium. The envoy bearing these proposals was captured by the Turks and in fact Hypsilantis went into his revolution with only vague expressions of goodwill to encourage his hope for Serbian participation. But Milosh had decided not to march.

Hypsilantis' later plan, to proceed with a rebellion based mainly on the Principalities with only the hope of Serbian support, seems extraordinarily rash in retrospect. That he did take this risk reflects very largely his judgement of the position of Ali Pasha and his probable fortunes.

Ali, the Lion of Jannina, an Albanian by origin, was one of a number of provincial rulers in the Ottoman Empire who in the late eighteenth century profited from the increasing inefficiency and incapacity of the imperial government. He established an almost autonomous despotate in the western Balkans which in 1818 at the period of its widest extent included the whole of Epirus, the heartland of his dominion, Thessaly, western Macedonia, the greater part of central Greece, and the Peloponnese. The Porte tolerated the growth of Ali's power partly because it believed it did not have the means to suppress him, partly because although personally rapacious he re-established order in districts where, as in Christian Souli, endemic brigandage had reduced both population and production, and might develop into political rebellion. But inevitably, in time, the extent of Ali's power and his exercise of an almost independent and frequently disloyal foreign policy, decided Sultan Mahmoud II to destroy him. In 1820, Ali's agents in Constantinople attempted to assassinate a personal enemy in a house close to the imperial palace. To make amends for this arrogance Ali tried to ingratiate himself with the Sultan by revealing the conspiracy of the *Hetairia*, but then, discovering that he was finally discredited and that even his revelations were disbelieved, he moved into open revolt, despatched envoys to the Serbs and Montenegrins, and summoned the Greek and Albanian leaders in his own dominions to a council. Here Ali, a tyrant renowned for his avarice, distributed gifts and promised a constitution. And for various motives his subjects decided to support him. What surprised contemporary observers was the rapidity with which Ali was driven back to Jannina by the imperial forces. It was the fear that this source of distraction would soon vanish that largely impelled Hypsilantis to launch his rebellion in the Principalities.

In some respects conditions in the Principalities may have appeared to Hypsilantis more propitious than they were. It was true that many Greeks in the Phanariot administration, including Michael Soutzos, Hospodar of Moldavia, had been initiated into the Society and that the Hetairists had formed an alliance with Tudor Vladimirescu, a Romanian who was opposed to the land-owning boyars. The economic disruption that was a consequence of the Russo-Turkish war and the exactions of the Romanian boyars and the Greek Phanariot rulers had caused sufficient distress to persuade some peasants to follow a rebel leader such as Vladi-mirescu. But the inappropriate character of the alliance between Romanian peasants and Greek Phanariots, and the remaining force of traditional social forms, made it, at least, doubtful whether an effective and universal uprising of Romanian peasants would occur. Hypsilantis publicly disavowed the Phanariot regime and declared that he would pass as soon as possible with his Greek volunteers through Serbia [*sic*] to join his own countrymen. In all this the reaction of Russia would be decisive. With little justification Hypsilantis hoped that Russia would refuse the Turks permission to enter the Principalities – a permission which the latter were bound by treaty to request. On 18 January 1821 Vladimirescu set out from Bucharest with moneys supplied by the Society to raise his rebellion in western Wallachia. And on 22 February 1821 Hypsilantis, although he knew the Powers of the Holy Alliance were at Laibach considering how they could contain revolutions in Spain, Naples, and South America, decided to cross the river Pruth into Moldavia. He believed that whatever international problems he might have to face he could not afford to miss the opportunity of a Balkan alliance with Vladimirescu's Romanians and Ali Pasha's Albanian Muslims.

Hypsilantis had been a competent officer in a regular army. However, the leadership of forces of guerrillas and civilian volunteers was beyond his abilities and the military progress of the rebellion was dilatory and ineffective. When Tsar Alexander condemned the rebellion and later permitted the Turkish forces to cross the Danube his situation became hopeless. The Serbians under Milosh Obrenovitch held carefully aloof. As soon as it was clear that Russia would not support the rebellion, Vladimirescu attempted to treat with the Turks; but not meeting with success he then came to an understanding with the boyars against whom in the first place his movement had been largely directed. Not surprisingly his men began to desert to their homes. Vladimirescu himself was captured by the Greeks and executed. Hypsilantis with his small forces, now without friends or resources, was locked in a territory from which he could not escape, and at the time it may even have been for him a certain relief when his force was overwhelmed at Dragatsani on 19 June 1821, and he was able to escape to internment in Austria.

Although in itself the insurrection in the Principalities failed completely it had important consequences. Many of the prosperous Peloponnesian notables, whatever their declarations in principle, were disinclined to commit themselves to the uncertainties of revolution when it came to the moment of decision. From the distant Principality the news of a Greek and Romanian uprising led by a Greek who was a Russian officer setting forth from Russian soil seemed to the volatile enthusiasm of a Greek population which for a number of years had been fed with the expectation of Russian aid to permit only the one interpretation. Papaphlessas, the Hetairist agitator in the Peloponnese, used this argument with effect to cajole or threaten reluctant leaders to action and in this he was fortunate that the first rumours of defeat arrived only after the rebellion in the Peloponnese had opened. Without this impetus it may be doubted if a movement without properly organized forces or an undisputed central authority could have overcome the self-interested caution of local notables. It is also certain that Turkish concern with events in Epirus and Wallachia allowed the precarious rebellion in Greece time to accustom men to their commitment before they had to experience the full weight of Turkish reprisal. Hypsilantis' failure to induce the Serbians and Romanians to form a Balkan Orthodox Christian front meant that the Greek struggle even if successful could hardly lead to the birth of a political unit that resembled the Balkan democracy of Rhigas, let alone any form of resurrected Byzantine *imperium*. Instead, almost at once, the revolution was to be driven back into the Peloponnese and southern continental Greece, areas of relatively homogeneous Greek population. This fact, too, had its fated consequences which we shall later be describing. Not the least of these was the fact that it was now clear the revolution could not succeed without foreign support.

Chapter 3

The War of Independence

I N T H E accepted popular history of the Greek war of Independence Bishop Germanos supported by other notables, lay and secular, raised the standard of national rebellion at the monastery of Aghia Lavra in the northern Peloponnese on 25 March 1821. It seems unlikely that this was their intention. They hoped at least to delay their commitment until they were assured of Russian support. The halt at the monastery was a despairing attempt at prevarication after they had been summoned by the Turkish authorities to Tripolitza, ostensibly for consultation, in fact as hostages.

The rising was precipitated in a manner quite contrary to the wishes of the Greek landowning notables by a number of local actions of small scale violence and looting directed or encouraged by such Hetairist leaders as Dikaios Papaphlessas, a patriot priest, and the Maniote chieftain Petrobey Mavromichalis. The bands of Greek irregulars were at first small, autonomous, and generally operated in the area from which they were recruited, while the Turkish forces they attacked were also dispersed in small groups to garrison towns and forts.

By the end of the year the Greeks had been generally victorious. Many of the earlier skirmishes were politically designed to compromise local Greek *Kodjabashis* (notables) to abandon their policy of inaction. As the insurrection gathered impetus it became, in the Peloponnese at least, increasingly difficult for individuals to withhold their support. We have already referred to the considerable complexity of the political and social relations which existed between Greeks and Turks particularly in the Peloponnese. The need, which was both psychological and political, to protect the novel revolutionary commitment from attempts to renew or maintain older political affiliations, was partly satisfied by savage acts of massacre such as the slaughter of Muslims at Tripolitza in October 1821. The religious difference which in the Ottoman state had been so intimately connected with questions of social status and rights over land, now prescribed a policy of extermination which would unite the Greek Christian population and might prevent any merely

E

political revision of the existing Ottoman government in a settlement imposed by the powers. Equally, for the Muslims, the struggle
now became a Holy War; and very soon Albanian Muslims, who
in the early days had agreed to cooperate with the Greeks, learned
the logic of the contest and resumed their proper alignment.

At first, as the Hetairists had foreseen, the Turks were prevented
by more serious distractions from dealing effectively with the
Peloponnesian rebellion: by a war with Persia, the Hetairist rising
in Wallachia, the Russian frontier, Ali Pasha in Epirus, and other
internal problems. At the close of the first year of war, although the
Turks had reduced most of the centres of rebellion north of Corinth,
the Peloponnese and a number of Aegean islands remained in
Greek hands, the political existence of the movement could not be
denied, and its primitive military organization had developed
sufficiently to present the Turks with a problem they did not solve,
in the military sense, until 1825.

The geography of Greece with its mountainous interior and
coastal plains gave the insurgents a critical advantage. The majority
of positions of military importance were accessible from the sea,
but the incapacity of the Ottoman fleet to meet the effective and
unconventional attacks of armed Greek merchantmen prevented
the regular supply of the Turkish army and its garrisons by ship.
Each year, before operations could be attempted in the Peloponnese, a preliminary campaign was required to clear the extended
lines of land communication running south from Jannina and
Larissa on either side of the central massif of the Pindus mountains.
By the time a Turkish force was prepared to cross into the Peloponnese the campaign season was too far advanced to accomplish the
work of pacification, which in any case was effective only where
the Turkish forces stood. Faced with insecurity of communications
and supply, and the onset of hard winter weather, the Ottoman
commanders retired to more secure bases at Lamia and Arta, the
military position essentially unchanged.

The defeat of Ali Pasha at Jannina in February 1822 released
the forces of Khurshid Pasha for other employment and changed
the military balance. The Phanariot Mavrocordatos, who had
assumed the political leadership of western Greece, ordered a force
including an international corps of philhellenes to move north from
Mesolonghi to support the Christian Souliotes. It was strategically
justifiable to attempt to prevent resistance from withering away in
Epirus, an area which politically and militarily it was not easy for
the Turks to control. Greek occupation of it would threaten the
route into western Greece and make it more likely that a Greater
Hellas would emerge from the struggle. But tactical misdirection

and treachery contributed to the destruction of the Greek force at the battle of Peta in July, and western Greece, except for Mesolonghi, was restored to Ottoman control.

In July, also, the Turkish general Dramali crossed the isthmus of Corinth into the Peloponnese with 20,000 men, but the threat to their security of irregular bands, and in particular the force which had recently captured Athens, on the flank of their supply route, was enough to force an early retreat which was considerably disordered and accelerated by the harassing attacks of Kolokotronis. In 1823 and 1824 the Turks contented themselves with operations north of the isthmus to clear their lines of communication, and with the investment of Mesolonghi; for with its capture they would control the whole of western Greece and a second approach route to the Peloponnese.

By now however the Sultan had determined on a more effective strategy. At length convinced that he could not overrun central Greece and the Peloponnese in a single campaign by advancing from the north, he overcame, for the moment at least, his apprehensions of the growing power of his Egyptian dependencies ruled by Mohammed Ali, and agreed to appoint Mohammed's adopted son Ibrahimas Pasha of the Peloponnese. The Egyptian undertaking was to secure the sea passages between Africa, Crete, and the Peloponnese, and to land an army on the peninsula, while Turkish forces continued to hold their ground in central Greece and completed the sieges of Mesolonghi and Athens. Attacked and ravaged from north and south it was believed that the rebellion must collapse. Although this was a sensible military judgement as such, the intricate development of the political situation both domestically and externally made the outcome less certain.

By the end of 1821 the very success of the Greeks in still being in the field at all brought with it the problem of how they were to govern themselves, at least for the time being. It was also evident that with the collapse of any form of Balkan cooperation the future of the Greek rebellion would largely turn on the possibility of obtaining foreign support; and this, again, would depend partly on the form of government adopted to represent the insurrection.

The first National Assembly was convened at Epidaurus in December 1821. Its members were delegates from Aegean islands and the three sectional assemblies already in existence in the principal revolutionary theatres of war in the Peloponnese and eastern and western continental Greece. Of these the Peloponnesian Senate was an experienced political assembly which had recently been part of the structure of the Ottoman government. The Senate of western Greece and the Areopagus of eastern Greece were *ad hoc* bodies respectively created by Mavrocordatos and a fellow Phanariot, Negris, not only to organize resistance and face the Turks in their localities but also to act as a political counterpoise against the Greeks in the Peloponnese. The membership of these bodies had been determined not by direct popular vote but through the indigenous system of communal representation which had developed under Ottoman rule. Thus the delegates of the Assembly were drawn from the landowning notables and church leaders, or men controlled by them, assisted by a number of Phanariots, merchants, and intellectuals mainly of the diaspora. Since it was constituted in this way it is not remarkable that the spirit of unity and common sacrifice which had flowered briefly after the first acts of rebellion was soon replaced by considerations of factional interest. For although the forms adopted by the first Assembly were borrowed from the constitutions of the French Revolution, their purpose in this context was to check the growth of executive power through a dominant legislature elected annually, and a collegiate executive of five members outside the membership of the legislature who in fact represented the different regional interests. The initiative of the executive in important measures of budgetary control and military appointment was limited. The consequence of this diffusion of power was that the political direction of affairs remained where it had been, with those who already controlled the regional assemblies.

The first Assembly although ineffective was not irrelevant. At this stage in the revolution it was perhaps the only political instrument that could give an impression of unity. The existence of a provisional Greek government was bound to impress the outside world. And its constitutional form appealed to western liberals. Local landed oligarchs and, in time, even European statesmen opposed to liberal constitutions, came to recognize that they could support a form of representative government in Greece where political conditions and attitudes made it possible to corrupt the system sufficiently for their own purposes.

Mavrocordatos, quickly appreciating the political reality, withdrew to western Greece to build an alliance of continental Greeks, islanders, and foreign philhellenes. In the Peloponnese itself, during 1822, the central government was powerless to give political or military direction. Ignored by the Peloponnesian notables who managed their own affairs as before, and disobeyed by the guerrilla captains who had no respect for an authority that did not provide them with supplies, it was forced ignominiously to evacuate its supposed seat of government at Corinth when Dramali in 1822 led the Turks into the Peloponnese.

Dramali's retreat left Kolokotronis in a position of considerable military and moral power. This was a development displeasing not only to the elements outside the Peloponnese but also to the landed notables of that province, such as Zaimis, whose local political position and patronage were threatened by the arbitrary exactions and terrorism of irregular bands living off their lands and oppressing the peasants they claimed to protect. This, as much as any concern for the proper prosecution of the war, determined the second National Assembly in December 1822 to decree the abolition of the three sectional governments and insist upon civil control of the military forces. But this was achieved only at the price of further concessions to regional interests. The Ministers of War and Naval Affairs were replaced by two committees of three, representing the Peloponnese, continental Greece and Mani, and the islands which mainly supported naval operations, Hydra, Spezzia, and Psara. In addition the powers of the executive were further diminished by limiting its initiative to legislate, while the legislature gained concurrent powers in the appointment of provincial Prefects, a concession extended in practice to every rank of government official. What in effect was demanded of the structure of government was that nobody should be able to gain a personal ascendancy in manipulating it, while each important sectional interest should have open access for its followers to appointments to a wonderfully proliferating array of posts and privileges.

After Dramali retreated in disorder Kolokotronis had captured Nauplion. But when the second Assembly wished to meet there he refused his permission and later followed it to Astros to watch its proceedings. The Assembly's decision to appoint a military committee of three was taken by him as a personal affront and he responded to it by simply carrying away the four members of the government executive to Nauplion under guard. As C. M. Woodhouse says, 'Never has the constitutional principle of dividing the legislative from the executive power been more drastically and literally enforced'. Zaimis, one member of the detained executive, managed to escape, but another, Petrobey Mavromichalis, openly joined forces with his captor and dispersed the legislature when it attempted to remain in Argos.

From late in the year 1823 until the summer of 1824 Kolokotronis and the central government were virtually at war. That the two parties could thus dissipate their strength certainly proclaimed the existence of a Greek jurisdiction over which it was possible to dispute; but it was a most dangerous indulgence. Kolokotronis, himself, did not have the power to resolve the deadlock. He could not continue the national struggle alone without the essential support of the Greek fleet. The legislature had now been joined by a reconstituted executive, the presidency of which had diplomatically been conferred on Kondouriotis, a leading notable from Hydra who would attract the loyalty of the islanders. Moreover, a foreign loan was now of the greatest urgency. All the factions within the Greek revolutionary camp needed money to buy supplies and to pay their followers. And ultimately the intricate negotiation of this matter had to be entrusted to Mavrocordatos, who held the confidence of western philhellenes.

His need to share in the first instalment of the foreign loan under the agreement signed by the Greeks and the London bankers in February at length persuaded Kolokotronis to a temporary reconciliation in the summer of 1824. For a brief period the Greeks lived in fictitious affluence, Phanariots and the professional men exchanged their rags for new suits and the soldiers suddenly appeared with gilded *yataghans* and silver mounted pistols. Very soon the greater part of the money was expended to satisfy private claims and to pay for the services of followers on whom the power of the factions depended.

In the autumn civil war broke out once more. The alignment was now more geographically precise since the Peloponnesian landowners led by Zaimis and Londos were supported by Kolokotronis in challenging the central government representing mainly non-Peloponnesian interests. This dangerous alliance was defeated by the government with the help of Roumeliote troops from continental Greece. But the victory was gained at an immense military and physical cost. Kolokotronis who combined an intuitive genius for guerrilla warfare with a capacity for popular leadership was imprisoned. The Roumeliote levies lived off the country as an army of occupation. At this moment of moral and political division Ibrahim deceived the Greek Admiral Miaoulis and his captains by making a sudden winter crossing from Crete. He landed at Modon in February 1825. Within a few months his disciplined regular forces, trained by French officers, reduced Greek resistance to its lowest ebb since the outbreak of hostilities. In the first campaign in the Peloponnese (1825) only Nauplion escaped his control. During the winter he crossed from Patras to join the Ottoman commander Kiutahi in front of Mesolonghi and ended the siege of that legendary town in April 1826. He then returned to the Peloponnese killing, burning, and destroying wherever resistance was rumoured. At the cost of admittedly dangerous concessions to his Egyptian vassal the Sultan had reasonable grounds for believing that he had won the Greek war.

Yet the success of this policy was partial. Although no military force now existed that could face Ibrahim in the open field, his communications were never secure, he controlled only the area where his forces stood, and his repressive terrorism drove desperate peasants to the hills to become guerrillas, who, under a firm but more flexible policy, might have prudently accepted his dominion. It also had some effect in checking the excesses of the factions. Kolokotronis was released and reinstated. Karaiskakis revived Greek resistance north of the isthmus. But the Egyptian operations had a more important consequence. They moved the British and the Russians, in reciprocal suspicion of the other's motives and intentions, to consider joint intervention. The advent of Ibrahim was the catalyst of the war.

*   *   *

When the news of revolution in Greece first became known the peace of Europe was already threatened by liberal revolution in Italy, Spain, and Portugal. The Holy Alliance of Russia, Austria, and Prussia guided by Tsar Alexander and Metternich was not alone in its opposition to liberal movements. The governments of Britain and France shared this attitude. And had the Turks been able to reduce their rebellious subjects to order within the first or second year of the war the powers would have accepted such a conclusion with general relief. It was the ability of the Greeks to prolong the insurrection into 1823 and 1824, and apparently indefinitely until the arrival of Ibrahim and the Egyptians, that disclosed differences of interest amongst the powers and prevented an agreed settlement. The longer this was delayed the more probable it became that the Greeks would have to be recognized as a party to any negotiation.

For some time Russian policy had been directed to a cautious expansion of influence. By a series of treaties (Kutchuk Kainardji, 1774, Jassy, 1792, Bucharest, 1812) Russia had obtained specific privileges for the Christians in Serbia and the Principalities, and general promises of fair treatment for those in other parts of the Empire. For her own purposes it was convenient to claim the privilege of protecting Orthodox Christians although this implied right of interference in Turkish domestic affairs was disputed by the Porte. She wanted, also, to dominate the Black Sea trade and extend her commercial interests in the Mediterranean. But although the recapture of Constantinople was as much a Russian as a Greek myth there was no consistent appetite for outright conquest. Her ability to wage an aggressive war over long lines of communication was limited, and was certainly often exaggerated by the western powers. The geographical extension of the Russian state already presented formidable problems of organization and there were Russians who feared that possession of Constantinople would divide Russia into two states looking respectively to St Petersburg and Constantinople. Moreover, apart from problems of control it would be exceedingly difficult to reach agreement with the other powers over the form of any partition of the Ottoman Empire. And unilateral action might lead to war. By the time of the Peace of Adrianople in 1829 the policy of maintaining the Ottoman Empire as a weak and dependent neighbour was preferred to the alternative of conquest.

Even at the outset of the Greek war in 1821 the position of Alexander was curiously ambiguous. He professed to be the protector of the Orthodox Christians yet, having by now outgrown the liberal sentiments of his youth, he disapproved of the Greeks as rebellious subjects. He was angered by Hypsilantis' claim to have acted in Wallachia with his consent and even more so by the appalling Turkish reprisal of hanging the Oecumenical Patriarch. This ambivalence was reflected in Russian actions. Hypsilantis was disavowed; but the Russian ambassador at Constantinople was recalled in July 1821.

The common element in the policies of England and Austria was opposition to the growth of Russian influence in the Balkans; and a concern to prevent a Russo–Turkish war which might have that as one of its consequences. But Austria wished to follow this policy within the Congress system; England outside it. Thus in the early years of the war Austria and Russia shared a devotion to the Congress system although with quite different ends in view. The Russians naturally wished for a settlement of the insurrection which served their policy. What this might be appeared in a *mémoire* circulated by Alexander in January 1824 which suggested the creation of three autonomous Greek provinces, a solution which had the double merit of preserving Turkish sovereignty while at the same time creating three political units which would be dependent on Russian protection and goodwill. A European Congress was required to confirm and guarantee such an arrangement. Austria on the other hand wished to invoke through a similar Congress the legitimist ideology of the Holy Alliance that would insist upon the entire reassertion of Turkish sovereignty. Indeed, for Metternich, the logical alternative to this solution was its opposite, sovereign independence for a new Greek state. It was the compromise policy of vassal status under the Sultan (and consequent dependence on Russian protection) that was most to be feared. This opposition of view between Austria and Russia was to lead in August 1825 to the dissolution of the Holy Alliance.

The practical consequences of the Greek war affected England at least as closely as Austria. The currant trade was interrupted, the commercial interests and political sympathies of the Ionian islanders living under a British protectorate were an embarrassment, and, more importantly, piracy in the Archipelago, which the Turkish fleet was unable to control, threatened the considerable British trade to Russia and Turkey.

There were, then, practical reasons why the British government would be driven at some stage to attempt to negotiate a settlement between the belligerents. But despite the policy and propaganda of Mavrocordatos to persuade England that Greek and English interests were identical, there was little reason in the early stages to suppose that such a settlement would favour the rebels. England was suspicious of Russian political and commercial ambitions in the eastern Mediterranean where her own trade was considerable and growing, and consequently she was unwilling to abandon her support of Turkey. Any concessions to the insurgents would have to be reasonably consistent with this general policy.

Nevertheless the disarray of the European powers worked to the advantage of the Greeks. Moreover, liberal groups in Europe and England, represented by men like Byron and Shelley, encouraged an astonishing growth of romantic philhellenism which was acceptable to men educated in a classical tradition, at least when no contrary arguments supervened. The Greeks, recently the acknowledged descendants of the ancients but decadent beyond redemption, were now presented as a race whose undoubted virtue the experience of freedom would soon restore. Such sentiments were cultivated also through the prejudiced reporting of a succession of dramatic and impressive events: the hanging of the Oecumenical Patriarch by the Sultan; the devotion to constitutional democratic government apparently evidenced by the Constitution of Epidaurus; the destruction almost to a man of the corps of philhellene volunteers at the battle of Peta in western Greece in 1822; the massacre by the Turks of the Christians on Chios in February 1822; the commitment implied in the raising of a foreign loan in London by the rebel Greeks; the siege of Mesolonghi; and the death there of Byron himself, the flower of romantic liberalism. As the months and years passed and a *de facto* government of free Greeks continued to exist on Greek soil, it became increasingly difficult for any power to demand a simple return to the original position.

Canning, who became Foreign Secretary in September 1822, was unaffected by philhellene sentiment; but he wished to separate England from the restrictive decisions of European Congresses which limited the political prestige and commercial advantage that

England might gain from developments in the international situation. His initial attitude to the Greek affair was one of strict neutrality. Yet since the Greeks were rebels even this was a policy which appeared to favour the Greeks. This impression was confirmed when Canning formally recognized the Greek blockade in March 1823. The measure was required by the genuine and practical interests of a trading nation; but it was not interpreted in this light by other powers or even by the ultra-Tories at home. And although in December 1824 a Greek appeal to Britain for help was answered by a formal reiteration of neutrality this again implied that at least England would not intervene against them.

In July 1825 the Greek provisional government, overwhelmed by the first impetus of Ibrahim's assault, passed an Act of submission to Great Britain. This was not accepted. But the pressure of liberal opinion at home, piracy in the eastern Mediterranean, and his concern that the Tsar who was no longer listening to Metternich would go to war, were turning Canning towards intervention. The rumour passed to him by the Russian ambassador that Ibrahim intended to repopulate the Peloponnese with Muslims may have been decisive. Canning decided to join with Russia in an attempt to establish an autonomous but tributary Greek state.

The terms of the protocol of St Petersburg signed on 4 April 1826 therefore indicated only a tributary vassal status for Greece; nor was this solution to be forced upon the Sultan. But Greek fortunes were now so low that they had already offered to accept mediation on approximately the terms of the protocol before they in fact knew of them. The Sultan, on the other hand, rejected the whole negotiation. With some justification he believed the military pacification of Greece was almost complete. And he settled Russia's more insistent demands through a separate negotiation in the convention of Ackerman in October 1826 which confirmed Serbian autonomy and demanded the evacuation of Turkish troops from the Principalities. Indeed knowledge of the Anglo–Russian agreement, as well as internal problems, had helped to persuade him to accept this settlement. For a while, at least, he felt safe.

Canning's next step was to draw in France to broaden the basis of the agreement and isolate Austria. This was personally acceptable to the French King, Charles X, who was much affected by philhellenic sentiments. And it suited French policy to join the new alliance to keep the principal partners in check and more generally to re-establish French influence in the Levant.

The Treaty of London was signed on 6 July 1827. It was based upon the terms of the protocol. Boundaries were to be negotiated by the contracting powers with the two belligerents. The Greeks, it was presumed, would acquiesce in accepting these terms since the intervention was partly based on their own invitations to the British and French governments as well as on the grounds of general commercial interest and the need to suppress piracy. On the other hand, if the Porte rejected the terms, the treaty powers agreed that consuls should be exchanged with the Greeks and that an armistice should be enforced; but without resort to hostilities.

The allied fleets received instructions that if necessary they were to achieve this simply by cutting off Ibrahim's supplies. These ambiguous orders precipitated a collision that was always probable. Sir Edward Codrington, the philhellene English admiral, was anxious to put an end to Ibrahim's renewed campaign of local devastations and he had been encouraged implicitly by the British ambassador at Constantinople, Stratford Canning, to use force if he saw the opportunity. His Russian colleague held a similar view. It would in any case be difficult to maintain an effective blockade in winter off the treacherous shores of the Peloponnese. He decided, therefore, on 20 October 1827, to lead his squadrons into Navarino Bay where the combined Ottoman and Turkish fleets lay at anchor. He hoped for, but did not expect to receive, provocation enough to justify a battle. But he was wrong and by dusk of the same day Ibrahim's navy had been annihilated.

The diplomatic and naval events of the months between April 1826 and October 1827, although they produced no agreed settlement, made it virtually certain that some form of Greek state could not be avoided. It is paradoxical that they should have occurred in the same period of time that saw the lowest point of Greek military fortunes. When Athens fell in June 1827 there was no organized Greek resistance north of Corinth and little enough in the Peloponnese itself. Yet in continuing the struggle for more than five years the Greeks had drawn the powers, through distrust of one another's motives, to move step by step towards recognizing their political existence and to insist upon a sovereign rather than a vassal status for the new state.

Much of this had been expressed in Canning's policy. He hoped to avoid a war between Russia and Turkey by urging the Sultan to make prudent concessions over a Greek settlement before he was forced to concede more. He realized he might not be able to prevent a war, but in that event, as an ally, he expected at least to be able to check the course of the Russian attack. To control his adversary it was necessary to act with him. Equally, of course, from the Russian point of view, anything achieved within an Anglo–Russian alliance that served the Russian interest could scarcely be challenged by any other power.

But Canning died two months before the battle of Navarino. The coherence of British policy passed with him, and the three powers of the London Treaty began openly to follow independent and often conflicting policies. International confusion was compounded by the growth of domestic faction among the Greeks, who, after the experience of Ibrahim's devastation of the Peloponnese, realized how completely they now relied on the European powers to save them. If after the signing of the St Petersburg protocol there were grounds for believing that some form of Greek state would be established, it was equally clear that neither economically nor politically would it be viable. Since the financial resources and the political constitution of any new state would depend in the first place upon the decisions of the powers, domestic factional politics were now ominously linked with the antagonisms and alliances of those powers. The Greeks abandoned themselves to a mood of calculating resignation. Political manoeuvre seemed more necessary than national unity or resolute military operations. And each party by acquiring an international patron hoped to become the exclusive agent of that power in its dealings with Greece, and to win appropriate benefits when the power it supported was in the ascendancy.

The disruptive effects of these factional disputes were to some extent checked by the arrival early in 1827 of two foreigners, Sir Richard Church and Lord Cochrane, to command the Greek military and naval forces. Their presence contributed relatively little to the conduct of operations except to precipitate a signal defeat at the battle of Phalerum and the consequent evacuation of the Acropolis by the Greeks. But at least it appeared to imply an English commitment to the Greek cause which lent some moral force to their demands for elementary order and discipline. Later the appointment of Capodistrias by the National Assembly at Troezene and his arrival in Greece in February 1828 were followed by a serious, although only partly successful, attempt to impose the will of the central government on the many local hegemonies of notables and captains.

The appointment of Capodistrias was partly a reaction of the Russian party to the apparent increase of Anglophile influence: partly it reflected the hope that the Greek cause would benefit if its affairs were guided by an established European diplomatic personality. But at this time the least concern of any power was the welfare of Greece. In the absence of any formulated British policy after Navarino, both Russia and France had recovered prestige and influence in the Levant. In January 1828 Wellington became Prime Minister. Policy was now less ambiguous but also less flexible. Wellington would not agree to terms of settlement satisfactory to

Russia and that power was consequently tempted to arrange matters for herself by a war declared on Turkey at the end of April 1828. Wellington did not have the military power to deflect Russia from this course. His own policies, indeed, resulted in the war which they were supposedly intended to prevent, and he had entirely abandoned Canning's subtle methods of indirect restraint. Stubbornly he fought to concede as little as possible over the question of boundaries. He wished neither to weaken Turkey nor to include in the new state any portion of the western coastline of continental Greece facing the Ionian islands of the British protectorate whose security he believed was essential for maintaining British influence in the eastern Mediterranean. He believed also that any Greek state would be patronized and protected by Russia. Initially, therefore, he advocated dependent status for a midget state restricted to only the Peloponnese and the Cyclades; but later under the pressure of events he attempted to make these narrow geographical limits more palatable by suggesting that they should be accompanied by full independence.

Wellington was equally distrustful of the French who had the wit and opportunism to see that a viable Greek state might replace Ottoman rule in the southern Balkans and that support of it might serve French interests. In the spirit of the terms of the Treaty of London they were anxious to send a force to the Peloponnese to superintend the repatriation of Ibrahim's troops. Wellington, typically, at first refused to agree to this proposal and then as suddenly consented, in the belief that the evacuation of the Egyptians would make it difficult for the Russians to justify continuing the war. The report of the three allied ambassadors in the Aegean on the boundary problem completed the discomfiture of the Duke, for it recommended a line drawn between the gulf of Arta and Zeitoun. This would include Athens and concede to the Sultan only the right of investing a hereditary ruler, but not of nominating him.

Greek freedom was not the concern of the Russians in going to war with Turkey. This was a general ambition to expand their political and commercial interest in the area, checked only by the fear that they might not be able to manage events if they precipitated the collapse of the Ottoman Empire. The thought that this familiar if unloved landmark on the eastern landscape might at last be removed had a singular power to reverse policies. When in August 1829 it seemed that the Russian army might take Constantinople, Wellington was so alarmed at this vision that for a brief period he contemplated creating a new Greek Empire on both shores of the Aegean as a counterpoise to the Russians. The Russians themselves drew back for reasons we have already considered. The Peace of

Adrianople, therefore, was relatively lenient. The Russian aim was now to retain Turkey as a weak and dependent neighbour, a policy which clearly might conflict with the interests of the Greeks in certain circumstances.

After their military victory it remained for the Russians to negotiate a settlement of the Greek affair with the other powers. Wellington and Metternich, by this time, were set upon a fully independent Greece within moderate limits. They now realized that vassal status would afford Russia too many opportunities for intervention. And Wellington also insisted on the exclusion of Acarnania. By protocols signed on 3 February 1830 the crown of an independent kingdom was offered to Prince Leopold of Saxe-Coburg. The boundary of the new state would be from only the river Aspropotamos in the west to Zeitoun. Crete and Samos were excluded. Russia had won immense prestige from the military success which had brought her army almost within sight of Constantinople. She could afford to be compliant to the requests of the other powers in return for their tolerance of her latest advances. The details of the settlement might offend the Greeks but this was a trifling price to pay.

In response to the military and diplomatic manoeuvres of the powers after Navarino there was little that Capodistrias could do to alter their views. But presiding over the affairs of the *de facto* state with an authoritarian resolution he purposefully followed a policy of concentrating in western Greece, north and west of the Aspropotamos, such irregular forces as his limited monetary resources would support. These resources were from time to time either Russian or French, whenever these governments thought it was in their interest to support the Greeks. The frontier question was a main concern for Capodistrias. Apart from any other consideration if he agreed to the Aspropotamos frontier it would arm domestic opposition. It may also be true that he was pleased to use the proposed Aspropotamos line as a means of persuading Leopold to revoke his acceptance of the throne on the grounds that the Greek people would not willingly receive him with so limiting a frontier. Capodistrias had initially supported Leopold's candidature but the implications of full independent status for Greece, and of Leopold's English connections, may have caused him to change his mind. Leopold withdrew his acceptance on 21 May 1830.

Although the treaty powers, under pressure from Wellington, now formally directed Capodistrias to evacuate Acarnania and Aetolia in western Greece, he stubbornly delayed. And the French and Russians did not particularly press him. Finally his shrewd procrastination was rewarded in November 1830 when the Whigs came to power and Palmerston at the Foreign Office abruptly altered the objectives of British policy in Greece. The evacuation of Acarnania and Aetolia was postponed. Meanwhile the search for a prince continued and at last settled upon Otho, a younger son of King Ludwig of Bavaria, a choice much influenced by the absence of other candidates acceptable to each of the powers. A long negotiation preceded the Convention of 7 May 1832 which settled the conditions of acceptance. Otho, a Catholic, was not to be forced to become Orthodox, nor was he obliged to grant a constitution. But his sovereignty, assumed entirely by favour of the powers and accepted for the present with relief by his new subjects, brought with it a renegotiated continental frontier following a line between the gulfs of Arta and Volos.

In the meantime, on 9 October 1831, Capodistrias had been assassinated by two of his opponents, the Maniotes Constantine and George Mavromichalis, at that time under ineffective detention at Nauplion. With the removal of the man who had attempted to suppress factionalism, the triumvirate of Agostino Capodistrias, the dead man's brother, Kolokotronis, and Kolettis, appointed by the Senate to succeed him, almost immediately fell apart into two factions, Peloponnesian and Roumeliote, which with characteristic ruthlessness disputed control of the country. Indeed the condition of anarchy to which Greece was now reduced was a factor in hastening the powers to a settlement.

This settlement was not unfavourable to the Greeks in the circumstances of their weak bargaining position and the balance of mutual suspicion between England and Russia. Also the limits of the new Greece, although narrow, happened to reflect what philhellene Europeans then considered to be homogeneously 'Greek' and what, moreover, their classical education had taught them ought to be Greek. This area was undoubtedly Greek, since most of the Turks had fled or been massacred and the communities of Albanian Christians had little difficulty in assimilating Hellenic ideals. However, the new state included only a minority of the Greeks in the Ottoman Empire: and its military and economic weakness made it dependent on the goodwill of the protecting powers. Since in every probability its policy would be directed to extending its territory and liberating the unredeemed Greeks, and the generosity of different powers would vary according to the warmth of their attitudes to Turkey, the role of Greece in the development of the Eastern Question was already foreshadowed. After the establishment in 1843 of a form of parliamentary government the political parties and followings which grew out of the same warring factions that dominated the country when Otho first arrived in 1833, and whose relation to the traditional institutions and values of Greek society we have mentioned, partly expressed their mutual opposition through becoming the clients of particular powers – attachments which at moments of national crisis undermined the country's solidarity. Disunity at home, dependence abroad, and a stubborn devotion to an irredentist ideal which Greece could not hope to realize unaided, were continually evidenced during the course of the war. The conditions of the settlement only confirmed that they would continue to be leading motifs in the future history of the new state.

PART TWO

The Historical Development of the
State

F

Chapter 4

The New State and the Great Idea

I

Greece under King Otho, 1833-1862

THE TRANSITION of part of the Greek world from a peripheral province of the Ottoman Empire, subject to its particular forms of decentralized administration and communal self-government, to a small nation state on the European model affected fundamentally certain aspects of the social structure. Where previously local oligarchies of landowners and clergy, sometimes with the support or tolerance of *armatoles* and *klephts*, had played a complementary role in government and could claim to represent their districts, if not on rigorously democratic criteria, at least by the force of their influence and ability to negotiate effectively with Ottoman officials, the introduction of centralized government and bureaucracy now submitted both landowners and peasants to a common dependence on the local representatives of a distant and unsympathetic authority. While it is true that powerful landowners exploited the families which worked their estates they did not constitute an exclusive or culturally distinguishable class of gentry. Politically they had been vulnerable to Ottoman hostility, socially they were the centre of complex networks of customary obligations and relationships. Despite their wealth and the support of dependants who had no other choice, they were subject to moral and practical checks which under Ottoman rule both limited their power and sometimes made them acceptable representatives of their communities. The situation of the local representative of the new Greek state was different in two respects. He was not dependent . on the local community of which he might have no previous knowledge or experience; he came as the representative of an alien and 'Frankish' form of government whose tyrannies were the more insupportable since it claimed to act in the name of the nation.

Already the processes of centralized administration had been given an institutional form by Capodistrias in the municipal organization established in 1828. Although the election of local councillors appeared to continue the tradition of local self-government the extraordinary Commissioner (appointed by Capodistrias to administer each province), or his agent, presided over the electoral committee, invalidating the candidature of persons uncongenial to the government and in some instances suggesting candidates and enforcing their election. By such methods Capodistrias removed from official positions notables and klephtic captains whom he held responsible for reducing the country during the war of Independence to the local rule of tyrannous chieftains taxing village communities and dispensing their own justice to a helpless population. The councillors elected in their place owed their office to the government and acted as its agents receiving through the provincial Commissioners the President's instructions for the welfare of his people.

After a further instructive period of anarchy and civil war which followed the assassination of Capodistrias in October 1831 (itself a sympton of the frustration of disregarded notables), the foundation of the new kingdom and arrival of the seventeen-years-old King Otho returned the country to the ordered paternalistic rule of government without parliamentary representation. Under the Bavarian regents until 1835 while Otho was yet a minor, and afterwards during the period of the King's personal government, a centralized and inflexible administration consolidated the changes already attempted by Capodistrias. The state was divided into ten Nomarchies (prefectures), fifty-nine Eparchies (sub-prefectures), and 468 Demes (communes). Nomarchs and Eparchs were directly nominated by the King. The Demarch, too, was appointed by the King from a list of three candidates elected by a restricted number of the more highly taxed members of the Deme. The right of the Eparch to supervise the elections in practice resulted in the nomination of persons suggested by, or agreeable to, the government. Nor did the election of a consultative council by each Deme offer any defence against the administration of local affairs by the agents of central government which in such matters as taxation or village disputes could disastrously affect the fortunes of peasant families living at the margin of subsistence. Unlike the Ottoman Empire in its unconcern with the detailed administration of local Christian communities or the improvement of their economies, the new state under the influence of the western concept of progress intervened in the affairs of villages in a manner which brought few improvements but disproportionate frustration. But also the conscious insecurity of the central government in forestalling and disarming local opposition to its monopoly of power led to the same end. The closer the administrative supervision of the countryside, as far as the very difficult communications allowed, the more secure the government's control of the country. The reaction of individuals and factions in protecting their interests against the interference of government officials resulted in a search for protecting patrons with political influence which inevitably weakened the traditional solidarity of the community. And the constitution of the Demes added to this weakening of local institutions since they were arbitrary administrative areas generally including a number of villages,[1] often with a history of long-standing hostilities.

In the severe conditions of disorganization and poverty existing in the early years of Otho's reign taxation was the greatest burden and raised the greatest resentment in the countryside. Whether taxes were farmed out to individuals (in theory by public auction, in practice by royal patronage), or were collected by government agents, the consequences for the peasants were broadly similar. One-tenth of the gross agricultural produce was paid over, generally in kind, and a further one-fifteenth as ground tax if the crops were grown on National Lands, that is lands which had belonged to the Ottoman government before the war of Independence. While these fractions were not in themselves unreasonable the methods of collection were exceedingly oppressive. In the first place there was no land register. The agent, by inspecting the crops while they were still growing, assessed the amounts to be surrendered. Appeal was almost futile because even where argument was possible, too many of the highest functionaries were interested parties in the agent's extortion. Further, the peasant was not allowed to harvest his crops until the agent gave his permission. Particularly in the case of perishable crops, he could be ruined so easily that he was willing to hand over quantities greatly in excess of his true obligations. The agent directed to what threshing ground and within what dates crops had to be carried. After a journey sometimes of many miles the peasant lived in the open protecting his grain from the attacks of birds and rats until the agent decided to appear and claim his portion. Corruption did not stop at the threshing floor. The grain was taken into the public magazines with one set of false measures and was sold from them to the public with another set, also false. The villager was aware that the greater part of the reduced revenue which finally reached the King's treasury was paid out to maintain the administration, the army, and police, which in the next year would again take perhaps half his crop. Such forms of extortion were seen as a direct assault on a man's family and a threat to its survival.

Although this current of general discontent existed the principal factor in the movement which in 1843 challenged the personal rule of Otho was the disaffection of politicians and unemployed

[1] The 468 Demes included 2,783 village communities.

klephtic captains who had formed the controlling oligarchy during the war of Independence. The government of the country by Bavarian officials, in whose administration only subordinate positions with few prospects for individual initiative were open to Greeks, barred their ambition and wounded their pride. Except for a force of 2,000 men the Greek irregular forces were disbanded and replaced by Bavarian troops whose excessive rates of pay consumed the greater part of the loan made to Greece by the Protecting Powers. This amounted to little less than the humiliation of colonial status. Even when in 1837 Otho recognized the need for a purely Greek Ministry only those men who were believed to be obedient to his wishes and European in outlook received appointments. In their religious life, also, Otho's subjects had been early offended under the regency by the declaration of an autocephalous Church of Greece administratively independent of the Patriarch in Constantinople. This separation and Otho's continuing loyalty to his Roman Catholic faith disturbed a still devoutly Orthodox people. Thus there was no popular resistance to the almost bloodless *coup d'état* on 15 September 1843 by the Athens garrison under the command of Colonel Kallergis.

Under duress Otho agreed to grant a constitution. Its form, however, which he negotiated with the National Assembly summoned in November 1843, was anything but liberal in spirit. For although it provided for a parliament with a lower chamber elected on a wide franchise, the King shared with parliament the legislative power and retained the right to veto measures of which he disapproved; and while executive powers were to be exercised only through his responsible Ministers he had the right both to appoint and dismiss them without consulting the elected chamber. In addition he was empowered to summon parliament to an extraordinary session or dissolve it before new elections. With the counter-signature of a Minister he could issue executive decrees and with that of the Prime Minister make appointments for life to the upper chamber, the Senate. Thus even in terms of a rigorous interpretation of the constitution Otho's position in the state continued to be dominant.

In practice the King soon learned the ways of corrupting or controlling deputies. His mentor was Kolettis, whom as the leader of the largest party in the chamber he appointed as Prime Minister after the first elections in 1844. Kolettis, a politician of Koutsovlach[1] descent who had studied the arts of patronage and intrigue as a physician in Ali Pasha's retinue, had built by 1847,

---

[1] Koutsovlachs were an ethnic minority group speaking a dialect resembling Romanian.

the year of his death, a popular following by openly corrupt methods which he justified by the observation that parliamentary democracy was unsuited to the conditions of Greek society. His methods, therefore, are of some importance since they set unfortunate standards. Briefly political dependants could be recruited and disciplined in three ways: by bribes, promises, and violence. Small presents of money or political favours created an initial obligation of goodwill. No consideration of propriety deflected Kolettis from the use of public funds to hold his following; although, in fact, his disbursements were seldom lavish. Having once established a relationship Kolettis made subtle use of promises of government patronage to maintain it, in matters such as land grants or public appointments. Few of these undertakings were ever honoured. Kolettis himself shrewdly remarked that when an office was filled he made one friend and twenty enemies. By the exercise of his personal charm, by never refusing to receive a petitioner and never disagreeing with him, Kolettis held in hope an infinitely larger number of supporters than he could have done by attempting to satisfy their demands, which neither the monetary resources nor the limited number of official positions available during this early period of the Greek state could have supported. No doubt Kolettis could not have profited indefinitely from these tactics. After his death when Otho less skilfully employed the same manipulations the government had to distribute more patronage but sometimes had a less certain control over the kingdom. The King's resources of patronage were nevertheless impressive, including appointments to the public service and the positions of Demarch and aldermen in the communes; appointments to the Senate for life at £20 a month; the profitable operations of tax farming; commissions, decorations, and promotions in the army (there was one officer for every seven men and seventy generals in a force of 10,000); and the Phalanx, a body of the heroes of the revolution who received pensions for past services to the nation, to which political supporters who had never fired a shot might be admitted. To an impoverished deputy facing the importunate petitions of clients whom he was obliged to feed and lodge during their visits to Athens, access to privileges for their satisfaction, or for his own profit, seemed well worth his attachment to the royal interest.

When bribes and promises were not appropriate or effective Kolettis and other party leaders had already shown in the first elections of 1844 that the use of force could also secure the return of their candidates. Street riots in Athens were used by Kolettis to discredit the government of Mavrocordatos which held office between March 1844 and the first parliamentary elections. How-

ever, the principal method of intimidation widely used in the countryside was brigandage. In earlier chapters we have already discussed
the traditional origins of this institution, the general significance of
the klephtic ideals of continence and courage, and the ambivalence
of brigands' relations with the general population. After the
foundation of the kingdom the disbanded and disregarded irregulars
as well as men in danger of arrest by the authorities for such
causes as honour killings, theft, or debt, provided no lack of recruits.
In principle their role changed remarkably little. They continued
to exploit or defend the districts in which they operated, brutally
killing hostages who were not ransomed yet protecting their own
clients or friends against the exactions of tax collectors. By the
implication of its illegality their activity was in some sense associated
with popular opposition to the 'injustice' of centralized administration, and in the earlier years more specifically the 'tyranny' of
the 'Bavarian occupation'. Nevertheless, after the introduction of
parliamentary government in 1844, many brigand bands took
service under the King, or his agents, to terrorize electors to cast
their votes as they ought to, or at least to prevent opponents from
reaching the ballot-boxes, but also from time to time in the more
honourable work of creating disorder on the Turkish frontier when
Otho wished to convince the powers of the strength of irredentist
feelings. In return for these commissions brigands enjoyed the
protection of their political patrons if they were arrested for crimes
of theft or murder in the course of their normal business.

When these methods had given Otho's party a majority in the .
chamber, its consolidation of this position was arranged by allegations of irregularities in the elections of the deputies of defeated
parties which were debated and voted on as the first business of the
chamber. Thus in the first parliament only twelve of the fifty-three
deputies of the Mavrocordatos party originally elected survived to
take their seats. The structure and values of the western society
from which parliamentary institutions were imported differed so
extremely from those of Greece in the first half of the nineteenth
century that the divorce between ideals and practice in their functioning should have surprised no one. Indeed, Greeks became adept at
manipulating principles (as in the instance of alleged electoral
irregularities) in order to justify and facilitate further malpractices.

* * *

As the pioneer of parliamentary management in Greece Kolettis
did not rely only on the sordid methods of intimidation and corruption. As many of his successors were to do in years to come he

courted easy popularity by expressive exhortations for unity in the nation's crusade to redeem the Greeks of the Ottoman Empire. We have already discussed the origins of the Great Idea in the opening chapter. The principal characteristic of this national obsession in the present context was the disparity between the means at the disposal of a bankrupt nation of less than a million souls and its ambition to re-establish the Byzantine *imperium* in the form of a modern state. Yet for Kolettis' purposes the very fact that in relation to this ideal (as to other important values) Greeks lived on two levels of consciousness meant that when attention could be directed to the brilliant vision of the nation's destiny, with the powerful confusion of religious and ethnic beliefs which this involved, neither the primitive state of its army, lack of numbers, money, or preparation, nor the disorder of the country's adminis-tration or the corruption of its parliament, seemed to be of the least consequence, or indeed to exist at all.

While these demagogic temptations to distract popular criticism from domestic shortcomings were seldom resisted the government and political parties had to consider their relations with other powers concerned in the Eastern Question, in particular the Pro-tecting Powers, England, France, and Russia, which had established the kingdom; for these were the countries which from time to time according to their interests and circumstances might assist or hinder the Greek pretensions. The Greeks were quick to exploit these rivalries in which England was in principle opposed to Russia and France played a vacillating role. The political dependence of the country was clearly exposed by the development of three parties each attached to one of the country's three international patrons. In this way, until the Crimean war, the English, French, and Russian ambassadors unofficially presided over parties led domestic-ally by Mavrocordatos, Kolettis, and Metaxas respectively. The fact that they used these parties as instruments of their Greek policy made it curiously difficult for them to agree even when their governments instructed them to do so. When Guizot hoped in 1843 that Kolettis would form a joint Ministry with Mavro-cordatos the former declined to halve his resources of patronage by sharing power with another political party and proceeded to fight the election alone. Thus mutual hostilities of the parties and the belief of the Greeks in the mutual hostilities of the powers reacted on and intensified each other. Although the agreement of the Protecting Powers to the constitution of 1844 seemed to confirm the sovereignty of Greece, in fact this development increased the opportunities for foreign intervention.

The powers' choice of a monarch for the new Greek state, the regulation of his regency and succession, their guarantee of a loan to the King of Greece, and the powers given to their diplomatic representatives under the treaty of 7 May 1832 to ensure that interest and amortization payments were a first charge on the national receipts, had been from the foundation of the kingdom grounds for continuous interference in the country's internal affairs. After the revolution of 1843 the terms of the constitution were almost identical with the 'suggestions' of Lord Aberdeen. Britain welcomed the constitutional checks to Otho's personal rule but neither the British cabinet nor the Tsar intended to allow principles of popular democracy to be enshrined in constitutional forms. When between 1844 and 1847 the Kolettis governments supported by France began to advance the nation's irredentist claims both as a justification for the inadequacies of the domestic economy and administration and as their only cure, the British policy expressed through the party of Mavrocordatos was the opposite advice that Greece should build a well administered state within her original boundaries and await with patience the eventual collapse of the Ottoman Empire. Since this counsel had little appeal in a society where the notion of present investment or restraint for future advantages (whether in the economic or the political field), was little appreciated, and was correctly interpreted as simply an aspect of the policy of guaranteeing the integrity of the Ottoman Empire, Anglo-Greek relations were not cordial. Exhortations to restrict military expenditure were particularly resented.

Otho was alarmed by the revolutionary events of 1848 in Europe. He turned for support to the Tsar who was soon to abandon the uneasy agreement with England that the two powers should prevent further erosion of the Ottoman domain, an understanding which since 1829 had prevented open conflict between these countries despite the suspicions of Palmerston and the growth of an irrational Russophobia in England. In 1850 Palmerston's dislike of Otho's person as well as his policies overcame his better judgement. Using as pretexts the exorbitant claim for damages to personal property by Don Pacifico (a Gibraltar Jew and a British subject), a land dispute between King Otho and the historian George Finlay, and the question of the status of two unimportant islands, Cervi and Sapienza, which Great Britain claimed as part of her protectorate over the Ionian islands, Palmerston ordered the Royal Navy to blockade Greece in January 1850. He achieved little for his country by this display of force but much for Otho, reviving his popularity at home and justifying his new policy of reliance on Russia. The dispute between France and Russia over the rights of the Roman Catholic and Orthodox Churches at the Holy Sepulchre in Jerusalem was a further excitement of religious and national enthusiasm from which the King benefited. With the outbreak of hostilities between Turkey and Russia in October 1853 and the withdrawal of Ottoman forces from the Greek frontier the temptation to promote popular insurrections in Macedonia, Thessaly, and Epirus, became too great. King Otho and his pro-Russian consort Amalia were briefly and intensely popular while ill-disciplined bands of brigands, convicts, demobilized soldiers, and patriotic volunteers, crossed the frontier. Yet before the Anglo-French naval forces could intervene to check the Greeks, the Turks had already stifled the revolt. By May 1854 the majority of the irregular bands had withdrawn behind the Greek frontier and in the same month an Anglo-French force was landed at Piraeus. Otho was compelled to abandon the Russian alliance, to accept an imposed government led by the English party leader Mavrocordatos, and to endure an allied occupation and surveillance which continued after the ending of the Crimean war until February 1857.

This chronicle of events indicates the enduring pattern of Greek foreign relations. Three European powers manipulated their rights of 'protection' in the course of their mutual hostilities and com-binations with little sincere concern for the country they had guaranteed. Greece, endowed with frontiers which condemned her to military and economic weakness, but inheriting ideals which forced her into irredentist ventures and were the only source of internal unity in a politically fragmented society, was compelled to become the client of the power, or powers, which favoured her claims. The same choice earned her the hostility of others, and the humiliation of cynical interventions by their armies and navies.

Although at first this humiliation of their King was seen by his subjects as the martyrdom of a patriot, changing political attitudes and the gradual expansion of certain aspects of the economy under-mined the King's position.

After the Crimean war communications in Otho's kingdom remained primitive. Few roads existed which were fit for wheeled traffic; goods were carried almost exclusively by pack animals, and for them many of the Turkish bridges were unrepaired from the days of the Independence war. Local taxation added a fiscal barrier to the circulation of goods. Except in well developed areas such as the coastal plain of the northern Peloponnese the agricultural economy of peasants aimed at little more than subsistence. We have noted the hostility provoked by Otho's centralized administration. Relations between local communities and the centre were charac-terized by a relative absence of trade or the movement of goods except in the context of taxation. The government and the towns where it was principally established were morally and geographically isolated from the peasantry and the countryside to which they returned few services for the revenues exacted. Although by 1860 the number of landless families had been much reduced and the majority owned smallholdings of between 10 and 15 acres, the grants of national land through channels of patronage, or its simple occupation by squatters without legal titles, were expressions of local habits of fraud and violence in dealings with authorities which from time to time were also exploited by discontented notables in the organization of local rebellions against the King. Often the notables and their agents lived in symbiotic alliance with brigand chiefs who protected their estates and intimidated their enemies in exchange for food, information, and promises of political rewards. The employment of brigands by the King's agents has been mentioned; yet as many worked for patrons in the opposition. At moments of national crisis, or exceptional local grievance, the bolder spirits of the mountain villages rallied to klephtic leaders who might raise large but ill-disciplined forces which local notables and their parties used to embarrass the government.

After the Crimean war, however, Otho had to face new forms of opposition in Athens and other small towns where since the foundation of his kingdom a small but increasingly influential bourgeoisie of merchants and public servants had become established. Athens itself in 1855 was a town of only 20,000 people living in 2,000 houses. Its size and constitution was almost entirely explained by the presence of the court and the government. The population was anything but homogeneous. There were certain leading elements such as Phanariot families who had settled there in the hope of winning positions at court, men of cosmopolitan culture and learning; rich merchant families from the islands, especially Syra and Hydra; and some of the military chieftains who had distinguished themselves in the Independence war, men like Kolokotronis and Makriyannis. But a large fraction of the population represented the families of the place-holders and the place-hunters at more humble levels in the government administration. There was, too, a growing class of shopkeepers and artisans serving this rather incongruous society. Productive industry beyond the scale of simple workshops, however, was absent. In the lower reaches of society several thousand people literally lived in the streets and off their wits trying to pick up something in the performance of personal services and from the changes and agitations of the political situation in which as street rioters they were themselves sometimes actors.

We have mentioned the divorce between this urban world and the countryside. To a considerable degree its political and economic interests were directed outside the national frontiers. At its foundation the Greek kingdom had a population of about 800,000 while two and a half million Greeks remained in the unredeemed provinces. Not only were the political ambitions of the incomplete state naturally attracted by the principal centres of their ethnic influence in the Ottoman Empire at Constantinople, Salonika, and Smyrna, but these were cities of Greek commercial enterprise still dominant in Balkan trade and incomparably more important than ports within the kingdom. Thus it was to their share in this carrying trade, and in that of the Middle East which after the Crimean war was developed by French and British enterprise, that the Greek merchants of Syra, Piraeus, and Patras principally looked. Despite the steady growth of Athens in commercial importance Constantinople remained until the end of the nineteenth century the centre of the Greek mercantile world. Nevertheless the attraction was reciprocal. The unredeemed Greeks looked to the Athens government for political support in the improvement of their status; Athens and its University became the cultural centre of Hellenism; Greek merchants in the Empire established agencies in the kingdom where they expected to develop a market in which they would have a natural advantage over foreign competitors. In their own commercial interests they began to demand that the government should provide the minimum services of safe communication and local order in the interior of its territory.

By 1860 the mutual awareness of the divided communities of the Hellenic world was united in renewed fervour for the Great Idea, now linked with notions of liberal constitutional democracy which Otho found it impossible to approve. Students at Athens University, mainly the sons of the Greek middle classes but including many youths from outside the kingdom, followed with enthusiasm the struggles of the Italians for their liberty, and were indignant at King Otho's preference for the Austrians. They read uncritically about the French Revolution and wrote romantically violent pieces in the newspapers. 'A Revolution without blood is like a battlefield without dead men, music without harmony. The Revolution must be baptised in blood.' The dissemination of such inflammatory texts was assisted by the freedom of the press written into the 1844 constitution and only partly frustrated by Otho's censure. In this tiny capital, in 1860, there were no less than twenty-two newspapers and four periodicals. Most of these sheets poured out a ceaseless stream of criticism against the regime, full of scandalous details of oppression, without doubt greatly exaggerated, but well suited to the general feeling of stifled frustration in the country. They reached also to the provincial towns and even to many villages giving large sections of the population highly coloured and superficial versions of the principles of the French Revolution and the struggle for freedom in Italy and other parts of Europe.

A new generation of politicians represented by such men as Deligeorgis gave political expression to this dissatisfaction with Otho's government. They asserted that once the country was administered by a genuine parliamentary government, freely elected by the people and uninfluenced by monarchical intervention and powers of appointment, the nation's problems would be quickly resolved. Under a rational administration new roads and more secure communications would make it possible to distribute local surpluses of grain and other produce. Less taxation, lower interest rates, and protected rights of communal grazing, would reduce indebtedness in the countryside and increase production. Thus villagers would become more prosperous and the smaller amounts of imported grain would assist the balance of trade. But the significant benefit from genuinely constitutional government would be to regain for Greece the favour of the western powers. The inability of Russia to help the Greeks during the Crimean war, the country's vulnerability to naval power, and new apprehensions about the growing nationalism of Slav populations in the north, indicated the need to end the personal foreign policy of King Otho who was disliked by Napoleon III because of his support of Austria, and wholly distrusted by the British since he would not guarantee the integrity of the Ottoman Empire. Thus, paradoxically, King Otho, the devoted supporter of the Great Idea, was increasingly regarded by many of his subjects as the principal impediment to its realization.

An attempt by students to assassinate the Queen in May 1861 and an unsuccessful military revolt in Nauplion in February 1862 were preliminary warnings little heeded by Otho. The army had become undisciplined and unreliable. Junior officers, and even N.C.O.'s, affected partly by fashionable ideas of constitutionalism and partly by hopes of rapid promotion, conspired with opposition deputies. Although the army's inefficiency had doomed the isolated and unsupported revolt of the Nauplion garrison in February, it was for the same reason a useless instrument of repression for Otho's government when a general civil rebellion broke out in October 1862. The insurrection was declared in Acarnania by the local chieftain Theodore Grivas and supported almost immediately by the landed notable Rouphos at Patras. A few days later when the effectiveness of the movement in the provinces had been established beyond doubt the Athens garrison broke into disorderly revolt and a provisional government led by the Hydriote politician Voulgaris declared an end to the reign of King Otho, and called for a National Assembly to find a new King and to frame a new constitution. The departure of Otho was little regretted. Slow, pedantic, and childless, gossips had at different times claimed that he was impotent and mentally backward. Even on a more charitable interpretation neither his character, childlessness, nor political philosophy, any longer recommended him to the Greeks.

II

1863-1897; Tricoupis' Attempt to build a State

Although mutual suspicion between the Protecting Powers resulted in the strict application of the protocol of February 1830 which barred members of the reigning families of the Protecting Powers from the Greek throne, the National Assembly was caught by the general enthusiasm for a close connection with Great Britain inspired partly by that country's role as a patron of constitutional governments, partly by speculative hopes that the Ionian islands might be ceded to Greece. It persisted, therefore, in promoting the candidature of Prince Alfred, Queen Victoria's second son, who in a plebiscite held in December received 230,016 votes in a total of 241,202. Although his election was inevitably set aside, this expression of the popular will justified the Assembly, after its request to the Protecting Powers to take up the search for a monarch, in paying particular attention to the opinions of the British. For the latter the initiative in suggesting a candidate for the throne was a difficult but valuable mission which eventually resulted in October 1863 in the declaration of the eighteen-years-old Prince William George, younger son of the King of Denmark, as George the First, King of the Hellenes; a title reflecting both the popular origin of his sovereignty and the nation's irredentist hopes.

Greek political parties as well as Protecting Powers were competing for a predominant position in the country's affairs which, each hoped, would compel the King's goodwill for their faction on his arrival. Although the Assembly included representatives from Hellenism outside the kingdom, and although the majority of its members were drawn from the new political generation and had not been deputies in King Otho's managed parliaments, the disputes between the two principal parties led by Voulgaris and Admiral Kanaris showed too clearly that the political practice of those who claimed that only the end of royal interference was necessary to allow representative institutions to work their inevitable therapy, was an exchange of corrupt paternalism for anarchy and irresponsibility. Not for the first or last time in Greek experience it seemed difficult to find a middle way between these alternatives. Where no moral restraints limited the means which might be used to win power, its pursuit became an end which prevented any honest consideration of the country's problems. Soon factional quarrels descended into civil war between different units of the army which was barely resolved in time for the young King's introduction to his realm.

It was not uncharacteristic of Greek political life that the same Assembly involved in these hostilities should also be considering the principles and provisions of the new constitution. The constitutional nature of the monarchy was the important premise. The King held only those powers which were expressly vested in him. Unlike King Otho, he could not claim in any sense to share the constituent power with the representatives of his people. In practical terms, however, the provisions of the constitution left the King with powers similar to his predecessor's. Although the Senate was abolished he retained considerable powers of appointment, the right to dissolve parliament and to appoint and dismiss his Ministers, to declare war and contract treaties. The crisis in the dynasty's fortunes in the reign of King George's son would be precisely the conflict between the King's apparent right to intervene in the conduct of foreign policy and the popular will expressed through the elected parliamentary majority, a conflict not adequately provided for in this constitution or its revision in 1911. But in 1864, with the constitution passed by the Assembly, with a young and inexperienced King, but a ruler nevertheless more flexible by temperament and more prepared by upbringing to accept constitutional forms than Otho, it seemed possible to optimistic spirits that, as a 'crowned democracy', the country would at last find order and prosperity. As a settlement of the new King's accession England ceded to Greece the Ionian islands which had been held by her since 1814 and whose government for a professedly liberal nation had become an increasing embarrassment. The cultural maturity and political experience of their leading families might be expected to make a contribution to Greece out of all proportion to the islands' physical area and wealth. On these arrangements the powers set their seal by recognizing the wish of the Greek people to live in a constitutional state.

Despite serious financial crises and the uneven fortunes of her pursuit of irredentist dreams, the two being sometimes intimately related, Greece experienced a considerable expansion of her economy during the last four decades of the nineteenth century.

Fundamentally this was a concomitant of the general advance of trade in Europe, the availability of foreign capital for public investment in Greece, and the growth of population. The change in 1864 to a more open although still corrupt political system assisted this movement indirectly in the sense that the bourgeois interests dominant in the parties did not consciously introduce measures likely to restrict their trading interests, while the need to win the allegiance of voters resulted in some distribution of national resources particularly in a more rapid disbursement of national lands to small peasant farmers. Subsistence farming continued to be the occupation of the great majority of Greeks. But with the very gradual improvement of communications, particularly in the 1880's with the construction of a modest network of paved roads and of railways, larger quantities of export crops were marketed; particularly of currants, which increased from 42,800 tons in 1861 to 100,700 tons in 1878, an improvement principally due to the ravages of the Phylloxera epidemic in French vineyards. The improvement in communications also made possible a wider internal distribution of local surpluses of grain, olives, and cheese. The abolition of the tithe in 1880, and with it the extortions of its collection which we have described, encouraged farmers to increase their production. But Greece continued to depend heavily on the importation of grain partly paid for with the earnings of exported currants. The dangers of this reliance on one predominant export crop were distressingly exposed in 1892 when France introduced a high tariff against Greek currants, the price of which on the London market fell overnight by 70 per cent. Even before this disaster the extension of the national frontier in 1881 to include the fertile plains of Thessaly had not cured the chronically adverse balance of trade. The province was dominated by large estates (*chiftliks*) whose owners preferred to lease large areas of grassland to families of Koutsovlach and Sarakatsan[1] shepherds for winter grazing. This limited the production of grain on these plains where in any case under the traditional system of fallow only one-third of the arable land was cropped each year; and where, on *chiftliks*, peasants obliged to surrender between one-third and one-half of their produce to the owner of the estate had little incentive to increase production or make improvements. The currant disaster had repercussions throughout the economy which were compounded by the costs of mobilization and military defeat in the Greco-Turkish war of 1897. Thus the 1890s saw a recession that helped to begin the migratory movement to the United States, which between 1906 and 1914 attracted more than a quarter of a million

[1] Communities of transhumant shepherds of Greek ethnic origin.

migrants. But in time their remittances and the development of tobacco as an export crop contributed to a new phase of modest economic growth in the years before the First World war.

Industry beyond the modest scale of artisans' workshops was established only after 1880 when a policy of tariff protection and the attempts to provide public services and better communications provided a more encouraging environment. Native entrepreneurs and Greek merchants from Turkey were now more willing to invest capital in productive as opposed to commercial enterprises, banking and credit facilities were developed, and the growth of Athens and other towns provided the necessary domestic market. The urban population which in 1853 was only 8 per cent of the total, by 1878 had risen to 28 per cent. One must not, however, exaggerate the extent of industrial development which in 1877 employed 7,000 workers and in 1917, despite the territorial expansion of the state, only 36,000. The range of industrial production was restricted to small shipbuilding, the processing of olives, and simpler consumer goods such as Textiles and pottery.

On the other hand the extent of Greek foreign commerce and the size of the Merchant Marine had become considerable. The latter, which in 1875 had a fleet of sailing ships and small craft of a quarter of a million tons in aggregate had to survive the crisis posed by the foreign competition of steamships of which one effect was a fall in the population and influence of the island communities. By investing in older ships Greeks had already acquired a fleet of 107 steamships in 1895 and by 1915 this had been increased to 475 with a total tonnage of 893,650 tons. Among other consequences of this entry into international commerce outside the confines of the Mediterranean were the development of port facilities at Piraeus and the establishment of shipping firms and agencies. We have already mentioned the importance of banking and credit facilities for these commercial activities. Besides the National and Ionian Banks already in existence, five others were founded between 1882 and 1907. To establish the elementary public services which these changes in the economy required, and to tax and regulate the affairs of new enterprises the number of civil servants and the frequency of their interventions increased; and this in turn was accompanied by a greater demand for the services of lawyers whether in litigation or as mediators. Therefore the last forty years of the century saw a very considerable expansion of the world of professional men and salaried clerks working in financial, commercial, and government institutions. These with the great number of small wholesale and retail traders formed the nucleus of a growing urban middle class wearing European clothes, priding themselves on having an education and attitudes similar to their western counterparts, and while they were no less devoted to the Great Idea than other Greeks (being indeed more open to literary theories of nationalism) many of them appreciated the need for an ordered and efficient state if Greece was to be successful in her commercial or irredentist pursuits. The growth of this middle-class urban electorate had its effect in the development of political life.

Already before the dethronement of Otho the factions exclusively dependent on the ambassadors of the Protecting Powers, which had their origin in the internal dissensions of the Greek insurgents during the war of Independence, had lost their definition; partly because of the allied interventions in Greece during the Crimean war and King Otho's corrupt support of monarchical candidates during the later elections of his reign; partly because of the independent spirit of many younger men in the anti-dynastic opposition. In the early years of the new reign the alignment of deputies in parliament was essentially undifferentiated by their policies or principles. The personal position of each deputy depended on his local influence determined by the size of the clientele which he could hold by various forms of intimidation or promise. Although this situation was inherent in more general institutions and attitudes in the Greek countryside it was also confirmed by the introduction in 1864 of peculiar electoral procedures borrowed from the Ionian islands. The voting papers used in elections under the first dynasty, which had obvious disadvantages in a largely illiterate electorate and were open to various forms of falsification, were replaced by the use of lead ballots. At each voting station separate boxes were displayed for each candidate. Into each box, which was divided into two sections by a partition, the right hand painted white and entitled 'Yes', the left hand painted black and entitled 'No', the voter placed in the appropriate section the ballot provided for him. Since by law a voter had to cast a ballot in each box he was compelled to express his judgement negatively or positively on each candidate. Although this fairly represented the character of relationships in small communities where not to be 'for' was indeed to be 'against', as well as the ambition of the ordinary man to have as many patrons as possible, it resulted in some voters approving or disapproving of all the candidates. But whatever combination of negatives and positives a voter might decide upon, such a system inhibited the growth of corporate parties and loyalties which are encouraged by the need to make a clear choice for one candidate only and the party he represents.

Under the new dynasty until 1881 personal parties in parliament were numerous and their membership unstable, each faction operating in temporary coalition with, or opposition to, the government which was appointed by the King without particular reference to its voting strength in the chamber. It became customary for a minority government to dissolve the chamber and use the apparatus of state, including the armed forces and brigand bands, to press the electorate to increase its strength at new elections; either simply by their presence or by physically preventing known opponents from reaching the voting stations. Parliamentary elections began to resemble civil war. Nor did these methods encourage political stability; in the first seventeen years of the new reign there were nine elections and thirty-one governments. By 1875 public agitation against these arbitrary practices was so evident that King George, with that sense of political realism which distinguished him from his predecessor, invited Charilaos Tricoupis, a leading critic of the prevailing system, to form a government. Although from the elections which he conducted without the assistance of the customary pressures his 'Constitutional' or 'Liberal' Party did not emerge as the strongest group of deputies in the new parliament, his policies began to gain acceptance. In the same year the King in his speech from the throne recognized the principle that a government should command the confidence of parliament by a majority of votes. Tricoupis himself had to wait until the election of December 1881 before his party could claim a parliamentary majority which he then gained principally through the support of thirty of the thirty-five representatives of the new territories in Thessaly and Epirus which were ceded to Greece in that year.

For fifteen years after 1882 something resembling a two-party system was developed in Greece with government alternately shared by the parties of Tricoupis and Deligiannis. Tricoupis' purposeful leadership was derived from the indignation of the urban middle class at the corrupt confusion of public administration and from his conviction that Greece must acquire the values as well as the formal institutions of western democracy. The King's recognition of the principle of government by majority parties enabled Tricoupis to discipline his deputies and insist upon unpopular measures. Deputies now had to keep their place in the ranks of the party if they wished to share the perquisites and favours of government on which their own local influences partly depended. Since majority governments might remain in power for a period of years desertion became a costly gesture.

Tricoupis' policy was one of economic expansion and administrative reorganization. Between 1879 and 1893 the aggregate of foreign loans was almost 640 million francs but since they were issued below par only about three-quarters of the nominal amount

was available to Greece. After this had been drawn on to buy
armaments, to support the National Bank, and to repay internal
loans, eventually little more than six per cent of the original sum
was invested in productive works. Meanwhile one-third of the
state's revenues, increased under Tricoupis by unpopular taxes on
such items as tobacco and matches, was used to service the Public
Debt. Nevertheless, whatever may have been the cost, it was
mainly due to Tricoupis that there were improvements in the
defective communications which had limited economic development.
Tricoupis also established tariffs to protect infant industries. In the
administrative sphere he attempted to reorganize the army and
the police, set educational qualifications for civil service appointments, establish the neutrality of the judiciary by protecting judges
from dismissal, and improve the methods and honesty of tax
collection. And in a revision of the electoral system he introduced
a law to increase the size of constituencies, arguing that political
life must move towards problems and principles and away from
obligations to personalities.

The more traditional party of Deligiannis which opposed
Tricoupis was strongest in the country areas of Old Greece, the
original kingdom, but it also had supporters among the less prosperous urban workers who resented Tricoupis' measures of high
indirect taxation. Its policies tended to be those simply of opposition
and expediency. Tricoupis' attachment to the interests of those
with capital and a willingness to risk it in the national development,
and his relative unconcern with the individual hardships which
his reforms might cause, gave his opponent sufficient issues for a
basis of popular support. He repealed Tricoupis' tax measures. He
reversed the legislation for wider constituencies, claiming that if
the personal bonds between a deputy and his constituents were
weakened the electorate would become unhealthily apathetic
about political problems. In other words, the efficacy of patronage
might be diminished. For similar reasons he removed the qualifications for employment in the civil service. More seriously his party
was less able than Tricoupis to resist irresponsible irredentist
responses to any crisis in the country's external affairs. After
periods of Tricoupis' rule his party was the natural beneficiary of
the former's cautious and mainly pro-British foreign policy. Yet
while it lasted, and despite King George's continued interventions,
there existed for the first time in Greek experience a certain consensus about the conventions of an essentially two-party parliament
which provided the country with majority governments. It is true
that both parties remained alliances of personalities rather than
corporate entities, more evidently so in the case of Deligiannis'

group. Despite better party discipline it was still possible to lose an election but later acquire a majority in the same parliament. In the countryside which included the great majority of the population men still voted for protectors rather than principles. But the readiness of the political world to accept these conventions at the time and thereby contribute to a measure of political stability, was not unconnected with the flexibility of membership and the fact that neither party remained continuously in power for any considerable period of years beyond the life of a single parliament. Consequently no large body of deputies, and their more considerable following of clients, were excluded for too long from necessary access to political benefits.

Throughout the period which stretches from the Crimean war to the end of the century, the development of the domestic economy and political life was never unaffected by the continuing concern with the problem of the unredeemed Greeks.

It was now increasingly clear that other Balkan peoples in Serbia, Montenegro, Bulgaria, and the Danubian Principalities were intent on claiming their share of the Ottoman Empire. Russian policy, from time to time affected by Panslavist sympathies for the Bulgars and the Serbs, was a less reliable support for the Greeks than in the past. Little more was to be expected from the British who still pursued, if less certainly, their traditional policy of maintaining the integrity of the Ottoman Empire. The Greeks were asked, for the present, to be content with the reforms which periodically the European powers pressed on the Sultan; for instance the 'Law of Vilayets' in 1864 which entitled non-Muslims to membership of provincial and communal councils. Measures of this kind merely increased the appetite for a full national independence; yet Great Britain's naval power and financial influence left Greece little freedom of independent action.

The situation in the island of Crete illustrated these problems. With an ethnic and religious tradition of rebellious independence in the mountain villages and the discontent of peasants in the plain who worked on the estates of a renegade Muslim minority, the island experienced periodic outbreaks of insurrection in 1841, 1858, and again in 1866. When the Cretans proclaimed their union with Greece on this occasion the government of Koumoundouros in Athens made a serious attempt to form a common front against Turkey. Talks with leaders in Romania, Montenegro, and Egypt were held. More significantly a treaty was signed with Serbia in 1867 which recognized the right to national independence of the different ethnic communities in the Christian East. But although this agreement was consolidated by a military convention in February 1868, already in January King George, who listened attentively to British advice, had dismissed the Koumoundouros government and enforced his own policy through a more compliant cabinet. The Cretan question was referred to the Protecting Powers. In 1868 the Turks had been pressed by the powers to announce reforms, known as the Organic Statute. In 1869 at a conference in Paris when the rebellion had already been suppressed Greece was sternly instructed to cease the recruitment and despatch of volunteers for Crete. The only serious attempt at combination in the Balkans before 1912 had ended in inaction.

In 1870 the isolation of the Greeks and the beginning of a grim struggle to protect the interests of Hellenism on its northern frontier in Macedonia were foreshadowed by the Turkish concession to the Bulgarians of an autonomous Church, or Exarchate, in which their own clergy would celebrate the liturgy in the Slavonic language, not always more intelligible to peasants than the Greek but at least indicative of a growing national consciousness. The reaction of the Greek Patriarchate of Constantinople, which now held only a tenuous spiritual jurisdiction over the Exarchate, in declaring it to be schismatic recognized the grave setback to the work of the Greek clergy and schools in their hellenizing mission in areas where Greek and Slav communities were intermixed.

It is therefore no surprise that Serbian suggestions to Greece in 1875 and 1876 for a common struggle went unheard. By that time Greece needed little prompting from the British to appreciate the Slav threat to their ambitions, or even to consider some *rapprochement* with the Turks as temporarily the lesser evil. In 1875 the Slav population in Bosnia and Herzegovina had broken into armed revolt. Serbia and Montenegro unofficially encouraged by the Russian consul in Belgrade moved to their aid in May 1876. In the same month a rising of Bulgarian peasants was savagely repressed and Turkey again showed by summarily defeating the Serbs how unwise it was for weak Balkan states to attack her unaided. For the Greeks there was even a certain satisfaction to be drawn from these events. Nevertheless after the efforts of the powers had failed to make a peace and war had broken out in April 1877 between Russia and Turkey, the arrival of the Tsar's army within striking distance of Constantinople so excited popular hopes for the liberation of unredeemed Greeks and fears that they might pass to a worse subjection, if Greeks everywhere remained inactive, that local uprisings in Epirus, Thessaly, and Crete, broke out. But before the Greek army could march to their support the Treaty of San Stefano signed by Russia and Turkey on 3 March

1878 ended the war, released Turkish forces, and made any venture by the Greeks unrealistic.

The concessions demanded by the Russians and accepted by the Turks included the creation of a Greater Bulgaria reaching to the Aegean and excluding only Salonika and Adrianople. Although these arrangements were wholly unacceptable both to the Austrians who would not agree to the establishment of any large Balkan state which could oppose her interests, or to the British in the person of Disraeli who believed that Bulgaria would be used as an instrument of Russian commercial and strategic penetration in the eastern Mediterranean, even the subsequent partition of territory decided on at the Congress of Berlin in July 1878 was a most severe shock for Greek hopes. An autonomous principality of Bulgaria, still tributary to Turkey, was established north of the Balkan mountains; to the south a further region, eastern Rumelia, was created under the rule of a Christian governor appointed by the Turks and approved by the powers. Greece's claims to Epirus, Thessaly, and Crete were disregarded. Only the customary promises of reformed administration were made by the Turks, and in the case of Crete the negotiation of specific concessions in October 1878 (known as the Halepa Pact). While it was true that the Berlin Treaty barred, for the time being, any direct access for Bulgarians to the Aegean they had reached a line which coincided with a liberal interpretation of Greece's ethnic frontier just as it also threatened areas claimed by the Serbs. Turkey in Europe had now been reduced to its ethnically most disputable regions, Epirus, Macedonia, and Thrace. Although it was some compensation that at a conference of the powers in Constantinople in 1881 Turkey under pressure from Great Britain eventually ceded to Greece the greater part of Thessaly and the district of Arta in Epirus, in another sense it brought the Greek state physically closer to the problem of these sensitive areas. The situation became even more acute in 1885 when an insurrection in eastern Rumelia in September declared for union with Bulgaria. This provoked an attack by Serbia on Bulgaria in November (which was repulsed) and persuaded the government of Deligiannis, whose party in April had defeated Tricoupis, to bend to the storm of popular excitement by restating Greece's claim to Epirus. When Deligiannis refused to reverse his order for the mobilization of the Greek army, the powers used their now established sanction of a naval blockade to force an acceptance of their demands.

Deligiannis' resignation followed. When Tricoupis returned to office in May 1886 not only had a great part of his earlier constructive legislation been repealed but the expenditure on military preparations had created a serious budgetary deficit. From these difficulties he never wholly recovered. The necessary increases in taxation, his cautious and undemonstrative response to renewed disturbances in Crete in 1889, brought about the defeat of his party in the elections of 1890. Under the Deligiannis government which succeeded him the economic position worsened, and once more his reformist legislation was repealed. Again in office with a parliamentary majority after the elections in May 1892, Tricoupis was never to be on terms with the deteriorating position. The service of foreign debts was now consuming 33 per cent of the budgetary receipts and in 1893 the effects of the disastrous fall in the price of currants, Greece's principal export, compelled Tricoupis to admit that the state was bankrupt. The inevitable reduction of the interest paid to foreign bondholders earned him the hostility of their governments. When he failed to win the election of 1895 Tricoupis withdrew from politics. In the following year he died, defeated by political and economic forces which he could not control, but spared the humiliation of the military defeat which ultimately compelled the country to adopt some of the policies he had advocated.

The control of Macedonia had become the central issue in Balkan politics. The lines of communication passing through it from the Vardar valley, its fertile plain, and important commercial centre at Salonika had long marked the importance of this area imprecisely bounded by Lake Ochrida in the west, the river Nestos in the east, with the Shar and Rhodope mountains indicating the northern limits, Salonika and the Aegean Sea the southern. Its importance and geographic position during centuries of rule under the theocratic Byzantine and Ottoman empires had resulted, as in parts of Asia Minor, in a complex intermingling of local communities of different ethnic origin and religious attachment. And when the area was claimed by the conflicting nationalisms of the new Balkan states the census categories of the Ottoman administration based on the formal jurisdictions of different Orthodox Churches were objectively useless for any prospect of rational division. Added to the conflict between those who were claimed as Greeks, Serbs, or Bulgars by the three predominant national communities, were the disputed existence and numbers of a separate Macedonian community speaking its own Slavonic dialect, and a further confusion of other minorities, Jews, Koutsovlachs, Albanians, and Turks.

We have mentioned the establishment of the Bulgarian Exarchate Church as a symptom of the developing national consciousness of the Bulgars and their wish to resist hellenizing influences. Until

1894 the Exarchate extended its influence southwards adding a number of bishoprics by peaceful infiltration, propaganda, and calculated Turkish partiality. After this date policies changed. The Internal Macedonian Revolutionary Organization (IMRO) was founded in Macedonia to prepare and arm the Slav population in the struggle for an autonomous Macedonian state. Originally influenced by socialist thinking and the ideal of equal treatment for all nationalities, IMRO's policy was soon affected by a 'Supreme Committee' in Sofia bent on the simple annexation of Macedonia by Bulgaria. In support of these intentions bands of *komitadji* irregulars began a tradition of destructive raids initially against the Turks but soon more generally against any villages which still owed religious loyalties to the Greek Patriarchate in Constantinople.

Both Serbs and Greeks responded to these Bulgarian advances by founding secret organizations, at first to support schools and nationalist propaganda, later to resist with guerrilla forces the depredations of *komitadjis*. By 1895 the Serbian society of Saint Sava had established a hundred schools in the vilayet of Kosovo. The Greek 'National Society' formed in November 1894 could soon claim to assist schools instructing 80,000 pupils. Although events in Macedonia had not yet impressed the Greek public with the force they were to hold after 1897, the pressure put on the government of Deligiannis by the 'National Society' (to which perhaps three-quarters of the army's officers belonged) had already embarrassed its position when an outbreak of rebellion in Crete in 1896, and a declaration of the island's union with Greece in the following year, precipitated a new crisis. The inability of the powers to act effectively in concert encouraged Greek reluctance to accept an offer of autonomy and influenced their refusal to withdraw troops from the island. Although the powers wished to avoid a war which might grow into a wider conflict, the British government under pressure at home from liberal opinion would not co-operate with other powers to establish a naval blockade. Russia and Germany would not permit the union of Crete with Greece. Unwillingly forced on by the frenzy of popular indignation Deligiannis declared a general mobilization in March and in April after a series of incidents on the Thessaly frontier Greece and Turkey were at war.

Financially bankrupt and militarily unprepared the Greeks suffered humiliating defeat in a war which lasted only thirty days. The Turkish army which had been recently reorganized and equipped by German officers was superior in every respect to a force more used to its role in domestic politics than modern war. The Serbs and Bulgars, who had been warned by Russia and

Austria not to intervene and were more concerned about possible Greek gains than Turkish tyranny, offered no aid. On 19 May an armistice was signed. The peace terms agreed by the Powers and forced upon the Sultan were extraordinarily lenient to Greece. The British argued that territory once received from Turks could not be retroceded by a Christian state. There were small rectifications of the frontier in Thessaly and an indemnity to Turkey. Since it was difficult to see how this could be paid by an insolvent state with profligate habits the Germans insisted that Greece's public finances should be controlled by an international financial commission. But in the matter which began the war the defeated country won unexpected advantages. Crete was granted complete autonomy under Ottoman sovereignty and in 1898 the King's second son Prince George was appointed as governor. The war and the negotiations for a peace settlement after the brief hostilities underlined yet again the lesson that the Ottoman army was a formidable foe for weak Balkan states which could not compose their differences. This defeat damped their eagerness for open war; but it did not diminish their appetite for irregular warfare in Macedonia to maintain their claims and interests while they awaited the chances of new circumstances and combinations among the powers. Turkey was finding a new patron in Germany. Great Britain, isolated and distrusted in the uncertain concert of Europe, was now less concerned about the area of the Straits or the integrity of the Ottoman Empire.

III
1897-1914: The Advent of Venizelos

The aftermath of their abject defeat in 1897 was a period of intense national frustration for the Greeks. The struggle in Macedonia continued unabated. The Bulgarians were not deflected by the repression of the rebellion of Macedonian Slavs in 1903. Despite the intervention of the powers and the establishment of an international gendarmerie the raids of *komitadjis* against villages with loyalties to the Greek Patriarchate became more frequent, and after 1904 the Greeks responded by committing to the struggle more bands of their own irregulars led by *klephts* or volunteer army officers. At home the generation which grew up in the decade after 1897 was no less nationalist than its predecessors. But its dissatisfaction with the past handling of the nation's affairs and its feeling for a new orientation found expression politically in anti-dynastic agitation, and intellectually in an attachment to the demotic school of writing led by Psycharis.

Yet the means for realizing Greek aspirations seemed extremely inadequate. A lesson of the military débâcle in 1897 was the quality of the Ottoman army in equipment and morale. The illusion that the Empire could be taken by the uprising of a few thousand klephtic irregulars was finally destroyed. But while the need for military organization and modern armaments was acknowledged, the tutelage of the International Financial Commission prevented the expenditure which these demanded. If in the long term this control safeguarded the state from chronic bankruptcy, the knowledge that the restraint was imposed in the interests of foreign bondholders and at the expense of the country's domestic development and military preparedness was a continuing humiliation.

Political life during these years reflected the national circumstances. Without resources, policies, or leaders, the two-party system broke down to unstable combinations of a number of larger and smaller factions whose aims were too evidently the pursuit of privilege and patronage. The quality of public administration suffered also. The King's manipulation of the parties in his concern to protect his dynasty and disarm irredentist conspiracies was a source of general discontent. Grievances and their cures were many and contradictory. Some like the political theorist Ion Dragoumis rejected western ideas and habits as destructive of the demotic tradition which alone could nourish a distinctively Greek culture. He believed particularly that European parliamentary institutions were not compatible with two ideal aspects of Greek society; the self-governing life of local communities, and the unity of the national community (*ethnos*) which the divisive forces of western political party organization and of European bureaucratic administration (*kratos*) threatened. Western values of profit and individual rights distracted Greeks from the sacrifices which the national struggle demanded of them. Agrarian unrest had more parochial concerns. A consequence of foreign investment in roads and railways was a conflict between the certainties of subsistence agriculture (other than the traditional hazards of weather and political disturbances) and the insecure advantages of the new market economy. Through improved communications peasants became vulnerable to the terms of international trade for the produce which they sold, and to some extent dependent on goods which were not manufactured locally, and were paid for in money and not in kind. Meanwhile the real wealth of peasant families did not increase. Growing population led to smaller and more fragmented farms, and in Thessaly, the main area of large estates, to increased numbers of landless and under-employed labourers. There were demands for the expropriation of large estates, a moratorium on peasants' debts, and lower taxation. In the towns dominated by government, commerce, and the professions, the practical interests of the urban bourgeoisie and their romantic identification with the national struggle called for a more efficient and impartial administration of the armed forces and the public services, for the bureaucratic integration of the state on the model of Bismarck's Germany. More radical solutions were proposed by socialist circles, but although associations and newspapers with these opinions had appeared in a number of towns in the 1880's, and from 1895 there had been efforts to promote trade unions, the total effect of these activities had been negligible. The 'Sociological Society', formed in 1908, supported the collective organization of workers and the political expression of their interests through a Socialist Party. Its intellectual propaganda made some impression on young and radical officers in the army. Nevertheless in a nation predominantly composed of peasant proprietors, small shopkeepers, and hawkers, socialism lacked any popular basis. Even in its own esoteric circles members held divided and incompatible loyalties to Marx and to the Great Idea. In the state of growing but imprecise public dissatisfaction the problem of the unredeemed populations remained the single issue on which the great majority of Greeks felt a common frustration and indignation. The greater their division, uncertainty, and sense of grievance about the imperfections of their own society, the more unquestioned was their unity of purpose, at least in an expressive sense, in relation to the Great Idea; and more specifically to the fate of Macedonia, Epirus, and Crete. These interests were now affected by the revolutionary movement of young Turkish officers at Salonika who with the aid of the Macedonian garrison overthrew the autocratic government of Sultan Abdul Hamid in July 1908. Although the Young Turks, as the ruling circle of officers were collectively known, claimed to recognize the rights of other nationalities in the Empire, they expected in return loyalty to the Ottoman state. In the Balkan countries there were mixed reactions: doubt about the true intentions of the Young Turks towards the other nationalities, a desire among younger officers to imitate their decisive action in reforming the state, and the temptation to pursue irredentist claims before the Turks had recovered from their political crisis. On 5 October 1908 Bulgaria dared to declare her full independence from the Ottoman Empire; on the following day Bosnia and Herzegovina were annexed by Austria. But two days later when the Cretans proclaimed their union with Greece, the government at Athens, conscious of the surveillance of the International

Financial Commission, the navies of the powers, and the memories of 1897, was too circumspect to support the move. The Young Turks needing a success to offset the concessions they had already made to Austria and Bulgaria became increasingly bellicose and demanding over the formal question of the island's status. When the powers took their troops from Crete on 27 July 1909 the islanders raised the Greek flag on official buildings in denial of the Sultan's sovereign rights. The Turks threatened, Rallis, the Greek Prime Minister, pleaded that he could not control Cretan passions, and on 18 August 250 marines of the powers landed at Chania to lower the Greek flag. Such symbolic exchanges, and the evidence of their government's impotence, enraged the Athenian press and populace. The situation was particularly unacceptable to the army's military self-respect, always sensitive since its humiliation in 1897. In May 1909 an organization of young officers, known as the Military League, had been formed. Its original concern had been a general grievance at the 'improper' promotion of officers in the favour of the Commander-in-Chief, Crown Prince Constantine. The anti-dynastic bias involved in this self-interested issue was then extended to a demand for wider national reforms in the manner of the Young Turk movement of which the League was in some sense an imitation. On 28 August 1909, 3,000 officers and men of the Athens garrison marched from the capital to Goudi on its outskirts. From this threatening encampment the League's demands were eventually accepted by a new Prime Minister, Mavromichalis. Among other reforms the royal princes would no longer hold responsible offices. The two Ministers for the army and navy would be serving officers. A general reorganization was demanded in the administration, the judiciary, and education. The armed forces were to be strengthened, taxation was to be lowered.

With Mavromichalis as a titular Prime Minister the leaders of the Military League became the effective rulers of the country. By the end of the year the government had passed a mass of ill-considered and often impractical legislation which included bills for the abolition of the office of Commander-in-Chief and of the General Staff, and others for the dismissal of officers and officials not in sympathy with the ruling clique. The anomalous character of this military influence, and the plain inability of the officers to realize their aims of reforming the political system and the army, had already cost the League some loss of respect when it was decided to enlist the services of the Cretan leader Eleutherios Venizelos. Venizelos had two important qualifications for this consultative role: he had apparently shown his disapproval of the dynasty by opposing Prince George and driving him from office in 1906 when the latter had been High Commissioner in Crete; and more importantly he was uncommitted to the traditional parties of the existing political system. His advice that a National Assembly should be elected to revise the constitution, but not to alter its fundamental articles, and that the dissolution of the League should be linked to the Assembly's convocation, was eventually accepted, by the King because he realized that his dynasty was in danger, by the League because it offered a realistic retreat from an untenable position.

The Assembly which met in September reflected the sectional grievances which have been mentioned. It included a considerable number of independent representatives, forty-five Agrarians, and ten Socialists. Its mood was strongly anti-dynastic. On 18 October 1910 King George, having failed to form a stable government from the resources of the traditional parties, called Venizelos to the premiership. He did this with reluctance and suspicion; yet it was essential to satisfy the officers and to appease the extraordinary popular fervour in favour of Venizelos which indicated popular disenchantment with the old political world. The absence of acceptable native leadership, Venizelos' revolutionary past, and the charismatic power of his personality contributed to his remarkable rise to power. The King's suspicions were partly disarmed by Venizelos' insistence on the merely revisionary powers of the Assembly, and by the fact that, as yet, he lacked a party.

The obstructive tactics of those attached to the traditional parties, however, soon offered Venizelos an opportunity to create a personal following. His threatened resignation when the opposition prevented a quorum by boycotting the Assembly's proceedings was refused by the King under the pressure of repeated public demonstrations. From this position of strength Venizelos persuaded the King to dissolve the Assembly and hold new elections. Without the support of an established party he was compelled to give his campaign a novel and plebiscitary form in which through the press and indefatigable travelling he offered himself personally to the electors as the architect of an honest and modern administration which would bring, eventually, domestic prosperity and compel attention at the negotiating table of the powers. The corruption and failure of previous governments had ended in intolerable humiliations against which the army had justifiably rebelled. Having created this opportunity for a national renaissance the army would now return to its proper concerns. By this declaration Venizelos freed himself from the criticism that he had been imposed on the country by the Military League and the suspicion that he would continue to be subject to the army's influence. Spirited homilies about the politician's moral duties to those he represented seemed convincingly sincere. The men with political ambitions who now linked their fortunes to his rising star were aware that despite the necessary basis of a personal following their success considerably depended on the voters' acceptance or rejection of Venizelos as a national leader. The political programme which he offered answered the aspirations of the overwhelming majority. In the Revisionist Assembly of January 1911 300 of the 364 representatives were Venizelists.

His position in the Assembly now unassailable Venizelos set about his legislative tasks with vigour. Among the revisions to the constitution of 1864 the inviolability of private property was qualified to permit the expropriation, with compensation, of large estates for the settlement of landless peasants. The quorum of the chamber was reduced to one-third to prevent irresponsible obstruction by opposition parties. Serving officers became ineligible as deputies. Established civil servants were entitled to security of tenure. Social legislation was introduced for employers' liability and for sickness and old age pensions. A bill was passed which prevented employers from interfering in the affairs of workers' organizations. A Ministry of Agriculture was established. Foreign advisers were introduced, particularly from Great Britain and France on whose influence and assistance Venizelos had already chosen to rely. With the appearance of political stability and this readiness to defer to foreign advice, and even control, capital flowed in from abroad to finance ambitious programmes of public works and road construction. Although a number of the laws passed in this period were not immediately implemented, for instance in the field of social legislation or in the provisions for the redistribution of large estates, the promise of these measures had already at the time of the elections for the second Revisionary Assembly in December 1910 destroyed the independent threat of the Agrarians and Socialists whose support in a country with little industry and a population mainly consisting of peasant proprietors was local and limited even under favourable circumstances. With most sections of the community and particularly the urban bourgeoisie of merchants, entrepreneurs, and public servants, in general approval of the intentions embodied in Venizelos' first period of legislative and administrative effort, his Liberal Party won a second overwhelming victory at the elections for a normal parliamentary chamber held on 25 March 1912 in which it won 150 of the 181 seats.

It is said sometimes that Venizelos' rise to power represented the victory of the urban middle class over a traditional political oligarchy of families some of which drew their influence from the ownership of land. It is true that part of Venizelos' political success was that he responded to the needs of the former class. But members of families which owned estates were themselves involved in commerce and professional life and were part of the world of the Athenian upper bourgeoisie. They did not constitute a socially separated class or caste. While popular discontent with the restricted circle of families which traditionally had dominated the represent- ation in parliament, whether as landowners or as patrons with other kinds of influence, gave a particular opportunity to new men, mainly merchants or lawyers with local clienteles, who entered the first Revisionary Assembly as independents, and the second as adherents of Venizelos, it would be too strong an emphasis to suggest that they represented a radically different political type from the men who had served in parliament before 1909, and a number of whom continued to do so afterwards. Although, as we have said, Venizelist deputies might not be politically independent of their dynamic leader, the system of local notabilities and patron- age persisted, particularly in the countryside where the majority of the electorate still lived. The achievement of Venizelos was to have persuaded his countrymen that by a flurry of apparently radical legislation the nation had been reborn. By this illusion he in fact preserved the dynasty and the existing structure of society of which he mainly approved. For at heart Venizelos was a national, not a social, revolutionary. A steady advance had already been made before 1909 in the stability of the state's finances and the expansion of small-scale industry. After 1909 Venizelos' legislation encouraged this economic growth and improved the country's institutional structures; but it is an exaggeration to suggest that by the eve of the Balkan wars in 1912 he had miraculously recreated the Greek state. The miracle consisted in the general belief that he had done so.

In one respect, however, Venizelos' intervention was decisive. In the armed forces, also, there had been improvements before 1909 in both training and equipment. A number of younger officers who had studied in France and Germany formed the nucleus of a professionally trained staff. Nevertheless the involve- ment of ambitious officers in the factional politics of the period undermined the discipline of the army and the country's confidence in its effectiveness. Venizelos took two significant measures. He reappointed to a military command Crown Prince Constantine after his dismissal by the Military League and thus disarmed the grievances of Constantine's following in the officer corps. He introduced military and naval missions, from France and Great

H

Britain respectively, to reform the technical organization of the two services. With the military reassurance which improvements in equipment and morale soon provided Venizelos was able to negotiate for his country's participation in the alliance of the Balkan League which had developed in reaction to the nationalist policies of the Young Turks and with the encouragement of Russia's concern to limit Austria's influence in the Balkan peninsula. The war between Italy and Turkey in 1911 which opened a tempting prospect of Turkish collapse was a further incentive to the temporary unity of the Balkan neighbours. Greece's adherence fitted logically with a change in Great Britain's previously inflexible policy in favour of the integrity of Ottoman territories, a change which had developed with Germany's increased military and economic influence in Turkey. A settlement of accounts seemed also to be forced on the Greeks by the Turkish policy of 'Ottomanizing' the Empire which might soon threaten the predominance of the Greeks in the Empire's commerce and rudely interrupted their dreams of political infiltration. For Greece the critical agreement which committed her to the alliance was a treaty with Bulgaria signed on 29 May 1912. Significantly, it did not define the line of any future frontier between the two nations.

Although none of the powers wished for hostilities in the Balkans their deadlocked opposition prevented any effective intervention when Montenegro declared war on Turkey on 8 October 1912, and ten days later was joined by her allies, Bulgaria, Serbia, and Greece. The moment was well chosen. Turkey had been weakened and distracted by war with Italy and revolt in Albania. The size of her forces in Europe, whose morale and organization had been gravely disrupted by Turkey's internal crises, was less than half the strength of the armies which advanced against her. A rapid reinforcement of her own army by sea was barred by the superiority of the Greek navy. For geographical reasons the Bulgarians faced the main strength of the Turks but within a month they had driven their enemy back to the Chatalja lines before Constantinople. Meanwhile the Serbs cleared Old Serbia, western Macedonia, and the Sanjak of Novi Bazar; and the Greeks, meeting only light resistance, had invested Jannina and, more importantly, had captured Salonika in November only a few hours before the arrival of the Bulgars, with whom they declined to share their authority. Apart from the towns of Adrianople, Jannina, and Scutari, whose garrisons were to resist for a few weeks longer, the Turks had been everywhere defeated. In December 1912 peace negotiations opened in London. Although these were interrupted by a resumption of hostilities in February 1913, the signature of the Treaty of London on 20 May finally confirmed that Turkey would abandon her sovereignty over all lands to the west of the Maritsa river, virtually the whole of her remaining European dominion; by the same treaty Crete was finally united with Greece, southern Epirus was secured, and the status of certain Aegean islands and Albania remained to be settled by the powers.

Almost immediately the victors quarrelled. During the war Bulgaria had been compelled to fight in the east while her political objectives in Macedonia and at Salonika were captured by her allies. Serbia was now claiming areas in Macedonia assigned by the terms of the alliance to Bulgaria. Between Greece and Bulgaria the whole question of a frontier had yet to be negotiated. On 1 June 1913 Serbia and Greece concluded an alliance directed against Bulgaria. The Bulgarian government driven on by an unreasoning public demand for the occupation of the whole of Macedonia ordered a foolish advance against the Serbian lines on 29 June. Although the attack was probably intended as a political demonstration the Greeks and Serbs chose to declare war. Montenegro, Romania, and Turkey also accepted the unusual opportunity. Surrounded and outnumbered the Bulgarians were swiftly defeated. By the Peace of Bucharest signed on 10 August Greece received Salonika, the town of Kavalla, and the province of southern Macedonia. Serbia was given northern and central Macedonia, while Romanian opportunism was rewarded with part of the Dobrudja, and Turkey, the lately defeated enemy, was permitted to reoccupy eastern Thrace. Bulgaria, in many ways the principal force in the first Balkan war, received, for her pains, only a small area in Macedonia and an outlet to the Aegean Sea at Dedeagatch. Predictably her humiliations and discontents would continue to threaten the peace of the area.

At the moment of these victories Venizelos had already built at the elections of 11 March 1912 a parliamentary party whose position seemed impregnable. Since the new parliament was a normal chamber with half the number of deputies summoned to the preceding National Revisionist Assembly for constitutional deliberations, Venizelos had been able to test and select only the most devoted members among his 300 followers in that body for inclusion in the list of adopted candidates for the elections of 1912. During his first two years in office, moreover, he had founded throughout the country local associations of his Liberal Party in the effort to form for the first time in Greece a mass party whose adherents would admit a permanent and corporate loyalty which depended on their approval of national policies rather than local personalities. Although the electoral system, and more fundamentally the social structure of Greek society, prevented the attainment of this ideal, and although Venizelos himself contradicted it by choosing candidates with preexisting social, commercial, or professional clienteles, the awareness of candidates that their hopes of election except as members of the Liberal Party were slight, created a parliamentary party discipline which if still flexible in many individual cases was sufficiently effective to ensure the obedience of most deputies. It is significant that many of those adopted and elected as Liberals in the 1912 parliament remained with the party until Venizelos' death. The point in political evolution had been reached where the party still required notables as candidates but where the development of communications and the press made it possible for the political personality and policies of a leader such as Venizelos to become the important issue in many voters' decision.

Yet this new political stability created problems which even today remain unsolved. The expansion of the state apparatus over which Venizelos presided during five years of uninterrupted office between 1910 and 1915, together with the legal safeguards for their employment which the revised constitution of 1911 provided for public servants, meant in practice the disbursement of valuable patronage and the establishment of an apparently permanent public service very largely Venizelist in its loyalties. Although the coherence of the Liberal Party encouraged the growth of an opposition party, the National Opinion Party (renamed in 1920 the Populist Party) under the leadership of Gounaris, which in the new parliament elected on 13 June 1915 held 90 seats against the 187 of the Liberals, its prospects of a parliamentary majority seemed distant and the future resources of patronage pre-empted. Patronage remained, it must be emphasized, an important means to political power; and an important end in itself because of the prestige its distribution conferred. The working of a two-party system in Greece without the dangerous accumulation of discontent depends considerably on a frequent exchange of office. In conditions where the numerical strength and discipline of one party were incomparably greater than that of the other, even the flexibility given by the individual defections of deputies (which had been a characteristic of the parties before 1909) were now pointless in the one direction, and without profit in the other. Thus by 1915 the Greek political world was already seriously divided between those who had held office and patronage in their hands since 1910 and those who had been excluded from the privileges which in Greece affect material interests and personal prestige so intimately.

There existed an incompatibility between the values and institutions of traditional Greece, in particular categorical obligations to families and communities, the absence of wider corporate loyalties either in the countryside or the town, and the growth of patronage which protected or promoted these interests in relations with the state, and on the other hand the effort to govern the country through the western institutions of corporate parliamentary parties, and a centralized bureaucracy, elaborate and overstaffed, in theory impartial, in practice too closely allied to the party which had appointed its members. It was this incompatibility which Ion Dragoumis understood and Venizelos' policies accentuated.

IV

1914-1922: Schism and Defeat

The force and bitterness of this existing division were given an additional and disastrous emphasis by the different foreign policies favoured by Venizelos and King Constantine[1] after the outbreak of the First World war, a conflict of opinion which implicitly concerned the future of the unredeemed communities in Turkey. The Great Idea, which with weak political parties and acceptance of the King's right to intervene in decisions of foreign policy, had invariably in the past served as the single issue on which unity could be assured, now fatally divided the Greek nation.

Although the threat of a Bulgarian attack prevented Venizelos from offering Serbia more than a benevolent neutrality in her struggle with Austria, as early as 18 August 1914 he indicated his wish to place Greece at the side of the Entente Powers, Russia, France, and Great Britain. In his judgement both Bulgaria and Turkey, countries where German influence was already strong, would ultimately declare their support for the Central Powers. Bulgaria in particular had claims on Serbia and Greece, consequences of her defeat in the second Balkan war which naturally led her to the side of the Central Powers. At first the Entente allies noted Venizelos' offer with satisfaction but declined to take the matter further in their anxiety not to compromise negotiations with Turkey and Bulgaria. By January 1915 with Serbia hard pressed, Turkey in the enemy camp, and their own consideration of an operation against the Dardanelles, Greece had become a more desirable ally. On 24 January the British Foreign Secretary Sir Edward Grey offered Greece 'important territorial concessions on the coast of Asia Minor' if she entered the war; although to

---

[1] On 18 March 1913 King George had been murdered by a deranged Greek in Salonika.

attract the support or neutrality of the still uncommitted Bulgarians Greece was asked to cede to that power unspecified territory which Venizelos suggested should be provided by the districts which include the towns of Drama and Kavalla with a Greek population of 30,000. In exchange for this concession Venizelos supported a Greek claim on Smyrna and its hinterland with an area of 125,000 square kilometres and a Greek population of 800,000.

There is evidence that until December 1914 Venizelos did not favour territorial claims in Asia Minor where Greek communities were generally dispersed and outnumbered. But information which he received from his minister in Rome in the middle of that month about projected divisions of the Ottoman domain between the allies, and rewards in Asia Minor for Italy if she entered the war, apparently convinced him that Greece must claim the Smyrna region even at the cost of ceding territory to Bulgaria. The obligations of the Great Idea were a moral imperative in circumstances where Hellenism in Asia Minor might suffer a new subjection to Italian or other foreign control if the Greek state did not intervene. With this justification the vision of a Greater Greece on both sides of the Aegean Sea became difficult to resist. Nevertheless Venizelos' conditional acceptance given on 26 January prudently depended on the assurance that at least Romania, and preferably Bulgaria also, would declare their support for the Entente. Since these conditions could not be fulfilled the matter temporarily rested. But by the end of February the allies with renewed insistence were again pressing Greece to join their ranks. On this occasion, discounting the advice of his acting Chief of the General Staff, Colonel Metaxas, who had warned him not only of the immediate consequences of a Bulgarian attack if Greek forces were committed to operations at the Dardanelles or in Serbia, but of the strategic impracticability of holding indefinitely territory in the physically inhospitable and politically hostile interior of Asia Minor, Venizelos recommended on 3 March Greece's participation in the attack on the Dardanelles. Convinced of the magnitude of this error Metaxas resigned. King Constantine, reversing his earlier reluctant approval of the venture, supported his military adviser, and in his turn Venizelos resigned on 6 March. Both sides had now taken up their positions on the issue that would divide the nation. Constantine, an admirer of German military efficiency, the husband of the Kaiser's sister, did not disguise his preference for the Central Powers whose arms he expected to prevail. If the geographical vulnerability of Greece to naval power prevented its expression more forcibly than in a formal neutrality, the opposition of the two policies in terms of the Great Idea was unequivocal. Venizelos now unreservedly offered the prospect of the partial fulfilment of the age old dream of a New Byzantium. His political opponents, exploiting the opposition of the King, a vacillating and not particularly intelligent man too easily affected by the overshadowing stature and condescension of his Premier, argued against the irresponsible acceptance of uncertain promises and in particular the inadmissible undertaking to cede to Bulgaria territory which had been redeemed; for whatever the advantages in area and population of the suggested exchange, sacred national territory was inalienable.

Venizelos did not question the King's constitutional right to dismiss him, particularly over a profound issue of foreign policy. At the general election of 13 June 1915, to which the minority government of Gounaris led the country, the Liberal Party again emerged victorious with 184 seats in a chamber of 310, despite the allegations of many administrative irregularities. After this consultation of the popular will on the specific issue of the country's position in the war Venizelos believed that any further obstruction of his policy by the King was a contravention of the constitution. Yet his opponents by exploiting the illness of the King kept him out of office until 23 August. The next crisis in his relations with Constantine was not long delayed. On 22 September the Bulgarian army was mobilized. With the defeat of Serbia imminent the opportunity to occupy territory in Macedonia lost to Serbia after the second Balkan war seemed to King Ferdinand too favourable to postpone, particularly as the Austrian interest in Salonika was well known. After some resistance Constantine agreed to a Greek mobilization. It was clear, however, that while Venizelos was intent on fulfilling Greek treaty obligations to Serbia if that country was attacked by Bulgaria, the General Staff regarded mobilization purely as a defensive measure. In particular they objected that Serbia could not provide the force of 150,000 men for operations on the Bulgarian front which the treaty stipulated. In response to this argument the ingenious suggestion of Venizelos that the two western allies should provide the men which Serbia could not, was immediately accepted by France and Great Britain. By the time the King had objected that, if Bulgaria did not attack, the neutrality of his country would have been compromised, it was too late. The two powers declared that the landing of troops was their responsibility, a curious justification; although it is true that under the 1864 treaty in which Great Britain, France, and Russia guaranteed the country's constitution they were entitled to land forces in Greece if the three Protecting Powers were in agreement. On 4 October, the day Bulgaria declared war, Venizelos reiterated in parliament the intention of his government to honour its obligations to Serbia. The policy was approved by 147 votes to 110. On the next day King Constantine told Venizelos he could not accept his policy. Consequently the Prime Minister resigned and on the same day allied troops landed at Salonika.

These events marked the final breakdown of relations between Venizelos and Constantine. The former believed that after the King had correctly exercised his right to refer an issue to the decision of the people by the dissolution of parliament, he must accept afterwards their verdict even on questions of peace and war. Constantine partly based his position on the traditional identification of the dynasty with the state in which the monarch's personal and kinship relations were used to advance the nation's interests. During the reigns of King Otho and King George I the constitutional correctness of the Crown's initiative in questions of foreign affairs had not been seriously questioned. King Constantine's claim that as the embodiment of the nation, responsible only to God, his opinion on the fundamental question of peace or war must be preferred to that of the accidental leader of a transient parliamentary majority attempted to attribute a metaphysical validity to a conventional arrangement. But the constitutional difference between Venizelos and Constantine should not obscure the fundamental issues which had precipitated it: in the first place the protracted dominance of the Venizelists over office and privilege, and secondly the differences of policy affecting the sacred matter of the Great Idea which convinced both political factions that each was the authentic author of the ethnic truth.

We cannot follow within the limits of this chapter the complex development of the 'National Schism' which now divided the nation. The experience of succeeding crises merely hardened the lines of opposition and eroded what little mutual understanding or communication had originally existed. The reverses of the allies in the war, the general resentment of the allied landing at Salonika, which the royalist press stigmatized as a brutal attempt to force Greece into the war, decided Constantine to test public opinion once more at elections on 19 December 1915. The abstention of the Liberal Party, on the ground that a second dissolution of parliament within six months was unconstitutional (and partly in fear of an electoral defeat), intensified the schism by placing the opposition in an extra-parliamentary and therefore potentially revolutionary position which encouraged the anti-Venizelist governments of a one-sided chamber to remove Venizelists from the civil service and the armed forces.

Greece had now become an arena in which German and allied

sympathizers and intelligence agents conspired with increasingly arbitrary methods. The royal government reacted to the presence of the allies at Salonika by refusing transit rights for the re-equipped Serbian units to move from Corfu to Salonika, and more seriously by surrendering to a force of Germans and Bulgarians on 23 May 1916 Fort Rupel, the key to eastern Macedonia. The overrunning of eastern Macedonia by Bulgarian forces during the summer of 1916 with only nominal resistance from the Greek army, and the royal government's hardly disguised benevolence towards the Central Powers, even after the Romanian entry into the war on the side of the Entente, ensured that the indignation of Venizelists never flagged. On 21 June 1916 the allies demanded the dissolution of the chamber, a new government, and demobilization of the army. The King yielded to these demands to the extent of replacing his Prime Minister but then avoided implementing the others; in the case of demobilization by organizing 'Leagues of Reservists' which were later used both for propaganda and intimidation.

On 9 October Venizelos followed the logic of his extra-parliamentary opposition by establishing a rival 'provisional government' at Salonika. Although Venizelos' 'National Movement' was not, at first, formally recognized by the allies for fear of provoking open civil war, in practical terms Greece was now physically divided between two states, one intriguing openly with the Central Powers from a position of enforced neutrality, the other pledged to support the allies with the men which it was soon recruiting to its separate army. This development lifted the struggle to a new intensity of emotion and indignation. On 1 December when French and British contingents landed near Athens to receive guns and war materials which the allies had demanded as a guarantee of the royal government's neutral intentions, and in compensation for artillery and supplies surrendered to the enemy at Fort Rupel and in Macedonia, the allied force was attacked and after suffering heavy casualties was forced to retire in some disorder to its ships. The exaltation of this much exaggerated victory and the orgy of murder and maltreatment of Venizelists which followed proved the strength of the festering resentment of royalists at the many humiliations they had suffered at allied hands.

These events inevitably brought their retribution. The Venizelist movement at Salonika acquired a clearly anti-dynastic colour and the allies recognized the provisional government by appointing diplomatic representatives at Salonika. On 7 December a blockade of royalist Greece was declared which caused suffering and further resentment in Old Greece. (For 104 days no cargo of wheat passed through to any port under King Constantine's jurisdiction.) And

on 29 January 1917 at a solemn ceremony in Athens the Greek
army saluted the colours of the allies in expiation of its sins. By
June 1917 with Venizelos now firmly established in Salonika the
allies decided to end the danger and discomfort of Constantine's
political disloyalty behind their Macedonian front. The King did
not resist the demand for his departure which was made more
palatable by a promise to raise the blockade. He agreed to the
succession of his second son Alexander without, however, giving a
formal admission of his abdication. For many Greeks the impression
of their King driven from his throne was painful and deeply
wounding. Simple people seeing Constantine as the hero of the
Balkan wars, the King by name and destiny chosen to free Constantinople, silently waited in the streets to mourn his going. At
Oropos where he embarked fishermen knelt and wept. Others had
more material reasons to resent his expulsion. Venizelos, soon
reinstated in power at Athens as Prime Minister, asked for the
recall of the chamber elected in June 1915 which in his view had
been unconstitutionally dissolved. Without delay the civil service,
army, and navy, were reorganized to become as exclusively
Venizelist as previously they had been Constantinian. As the
schism became more clear and more uncompromising each turn of
fortune temporarily destroyed the professional positions of an
increasing number of families, and the existence of duplicate
officer corps and civil services itself made difficult the prospect of
reconciliation.

   Greece, reprovisioned with foodstuffs and war materials by the
allies, was now able to make her contribution to their cause.
Ten divisions fought with valour on the Macedonian front in the
campaign of autumn 1918 which broke the German and Bulgarian
resistance. The general collapse of Germany and her allies followed.
And in the triumphant entry of the allies into Constantinople
Greek troops and ships took their place. For Greece this was merely
the preliminary to the real struggle. Venizelos' interventionist
argument and his bitter opposition to Constantine had been based
on the belief that by joining the ranks of the allies he would achieve
in victory the redemption of Hellenism in Turkey. He could not
now withdraw from this task whatever the risk. From December
1918 when Venizelos arrived in Paris for the Peace Conference he
was almost continuously abroad as principal advocate of Greece's
claims. Although the original offer of territory in Asia Minor made
by Grey in 1915 had not been taken up, the allies accepted the
plea that Greece's services on the Macedonian front in 1918 and
her part in France's unsuccessful expedition to the Ukraine merited
proper reward. By personal charm, persuasive rhetoric, and

doubtful statistics Venizelos fought with fluctuating success at the negotiating table for the ends he desired too much, international control of Constantinople and the cession to Greece of northern Epirus, the Dodecanese islands, eastern Thrace, and Smyrna with its hinterland.

Unhappily the problem of making peace with Germany and the complexities of the Armenian question, the Straits, and conditions in Anatolia, among other factors, delayed the peace treaty of Sèvres with Turkey. It was not signed until August 1920. Although Constantinople was to remain the Sultan's capital, Greece was given eastern Thrace as far as the Chatalja Lines, the islands of Tenedos and Imbros, and the administration of the Smyrna district under formal Turkish sovereignty for five years. By a plebiscite at the end of this period the population could ask for incorporation within the Greek state. The dream of the Great Idea, of Greece astride the Aegean, seemed within reach. Yet even on the day of the treaty's signature it was difficult to see how its conditions could be enforced in the face of the intransigent opposition of the Turkish National Movement led by Mustapha Kemal.

At the end of March 1919 the Italians had landed troops at Adalia in Asia Minor south of Smyrna to secure the territorial and commercial concessions promised to them under the Treaty of London in 1915. In their anxiety to check this Italian advance, in a period when widespread demands were being made on their shrinking reserves of military manpower, the allies were very willing to accept Venizelos' calculated offer to occupy and administer Smyrna and its hinterland on their behalf. Thus it was under cover of the guns of British, French, and American warships that the Greeks landed at Smyrna on 15 May 1919. Venizelos' telegrams and correspondence during these days betray his excitement. Whatever the formalities of his position as an agent of the allies a politically irreversible step had been taken. To protect more than one and a half million Christian Greeks from worsening persecution and to realize in some political form the Great Idea it was necessary now to claim to rule a population of Turkish Muslims two or three times as numerous. Such was the incompatibility between the distribution of populations in a theocratic empire ruling inter-mingled communities of different ethnic and religious complexion, and the western institution of the homogeneous nation state now to be established in its place. Venizelos' excitement was balanced by Turkish fear and humiliation. The arrival of the Greeks, the despised religious enemy of many centuries, gave a new and decisive impetus to the still uncertain movement of national resistance led by Kemal which other factors also encouraged, the growing disunity of the allies, their inability effectively to disarm Turkish forces in central Anatolia, and the support of Bolshevik Russia. As the months passed the guerrilla forces of Kemal, already receiving unofficial supplies of arms from the French, grew stronger and more bold, pushing British forces out of the Izmit peninsula. Once again Venizelos was conveniently at hand offering to assist the harassed allies with his army. In June 1920 with the reluctant assent of France the allies empowered him to clear Thrace and western Anatolia of Kemalist forces. In ten days Brussa was captured, the Greeks reached the sea of Marmora, and Thrace was occupied. The allies were impressed. On 10 August the treaty of Sèvres was signed.

With these diplomatic and military achievements to his credit, and in view of the many perils the country would have to face before its position in Asia Minor was secured, Venizelos judged that it was an appropriate moment to renew his mandate from the people. That two disaffected naval officers attempted to assassinate him in the Gare du Lyon as he set out on his journey home was a sign that the bitterness of the national division had not abated. During Venizelos' absence from the country the Liberal government had been neither lenient to its opponents nor incorrupt in its administration. The resentment of that section of the middle class which suffered from its hostility kept fresh their anger at the treatment of Constantine and the brutal interventions of the allies. Among the general population, and particularly in the countryside, the effects of the continued mobilization of an army of 300,000 men (necessary for Venizelos' policy of supplying the Allies with the force they needed to implement their policies) were causing growing discontent in a land which had been intermittently at war since 1912. The fortune, status, and indeed subsistence of a family were threatened by the absence of the bread-winner. The force of the Great Idea as an expressive ideal was not necessarily diminished by such discontent. Smyrna and Thrace were already Greek, by the decision and with the support of the powerful western allies. To simple men peace and demobilization were not incompatible with the defence of these just awards. The anti-Venizelist electoral campaign based on such implications was more successful than its authors could have imagined. It did not aid Venizelos' fortunes that on 25 October King Alexander died of blood poisoning from the bite of a pet monkey. When his younger brother Prince Paul refused the throne, arguing that neither his father nor elder brother had resigned their rights, the issue of the general election on 14 November 1920 became a choice between Venizelos and Constantine. The result was a disastrous defeat for the Liberal Party which held only 120 seats in a chamber of 370. On 17 November with many of his Ministers and officials Venizelos boarded a British yacht and left the country. Exile had become an institution.

The defeat of Venizelos allowed certain developments in the relations between Greece, Turkey, and the allied powers to take a more radical turn. The French hoped to prevent the return of Constantine, for them a symbol of political perfidy, and to modify the Treaty of Sèvres which created a Greater Greece too closely allied to British interests threatening their commercial position in the Levant. Conversely the British felt less strongly the opposition to Constantine but were more concerned to save the treaty. A strong and friendly ally in the eastern Mediterranean might be used to support British political and commercial policies in the area. This was now less certain under Constantine than under Venizelos and to that extent the British government was willing to support the French in a note delivered to the Greeks on 3 December in which they were warned that if Constantine was recalled the allies reserved to themselves every freedom of action. The royalists aware of growing dissension among the allies preferred to believe that the British would not abandon them. A plebiscite on Constantine's return provided an overwhelming affirmation on 5 December. Three days later the allies informed the Greeks that they could no longer continue their financial support. And on 19 December amid popular rejoicing the King returned to his people.

The royalists neither demobilized their army nor made an attempt to reduce their commitments in Asia Minor as they had promised in their election statements. The fateful seduction of the Byzantine myth, the implied abandonment of one and a half million Greek Christians made such an action almost as politically difficult for them as for Venizelos. Moreover they discerned, not incorrectly, that British policy in support of the Hellenic cause, now freed of its moral obligation to Venizelos which Lloyd George felt so personally, would depend on the success of the Greek army in standing its ground in Anatolia and upholding the treaty. But the growing strength of Kemal's forces was overturning every prediction. At a new conference in London on 21 February 1921 Kemal's representative was already negotiating privately with the French and Italians. The growing disarray in the allied front was evident. In June the Italians evacuated their forces from Adalia. In October France without informing her British ally signed the Franklin-Bouillon pact with Kemal in which, broadly, she gave up to the Turks Cilicia and large quantities of arms for peace on her Syrian border and promises of commercial concessions. At the official sessions of the conference in February and March a fruitless attempt was made to find an acceptable compromise between Greeks and Turks. The suggestion that the Smyrna district should be controlled by an international gendarmerie, while only a small garrison of Greek troops should remain in the city, was rejected by both sides.

Instead of concentrating the scattered elements of the Greek army inside the Smyrna zone, the Greek government, under the influence of Gounaris, a man with little practical understanding of military strategy or international relations, ordered a general offensive. By thus abruptly ending the efforts of the powers to find a peaceful solution the Greek government isolated itself diplomatically and freed the allies from any responsibility for the military catastrophe which would inevitably follow. The army ill-equipped, the morale of its officer corps impaired by the pressure of royalist officers to replace the Venizelists, which only the exigencies of active service partly prevented, had advanced to Sivri Hissar in June, a point sixty miles from Ankara, Kemal's capital. Misled by the motives of the Turkish withdrawal and overruling the advice of their own General Staff, the Prime Minister Gounaris and Theotokis, his Minister of War, ordered a final offensive to capture Ankara. On 7 August 1921 the Greek army at the end of long and vulnerable lines of communication attacked the Turkish army entrenched behind the formidable banks of the Sakarya river. After twenty-two days of bitter and bloody fighting the Turks still held their positions and the Greeks withdrew from the decisive engagement of a war in which the further they advanced the more certain was their ultimate defeat. Militarily they could do no more. In March 1922 at a conference in Paris an armistice was proposed; but the Turks insisted that evacuation should precede its signing. The final act in the tragedy was the carefully prepared offensive of the Turks in August 1922. In two weeks they split the Greek defence and drove the survivors to Smyrna which was given up to flames and massacre. Such was the brutal ending of the long history of Hellenism in Asia Minor.

Chapter 5

Catastrophe and Reaction

I

The Lausanne Treaty and the Greek Republic

THE SHOCK OF defeat was profound and paralysing. In the space of two weeks it became certain that the Greek culture and population which had developed in Asia Minor for three thousand years would be driven out. The dream of recapturing the 'City' which had given courage to Orthodox Christians under Ottoman rule, and in the form of an ambition to establish a state with territory on both sides of the Aegean Sea had for almost a century dominated the foreign and domestic policies of Greece, adding illusions of political greatness to religious sentiments, would not be realized. The arrival of ships packed with broken and destitute refugees appeared to confirm this.

At this moment of national crisis a 'revolutionary' committee of army officers led by Colonels Plastiras and Gonatas assumed the powers of government. None could immediately dispute their control of the country. Twenty thousand troops from Mytilene and Chios had landed at Lavrion in support of their cause. King Constantine accepting an ultimatum handed to him on 26 September 1922 had precipitately left the country and the throne, which now passed to his son Prince George. The arrest and arraignment of eight of the King's Ministers and military advisers followed. In the mood of unreasoning anger, which particularly affected the refugees and the army, Plastiras reluctantly agreed to respect the verdict of the court-martial. In the event five Ministers (including Gounaris), and the unfortunate Commander-in-Chief Hadjianestis, were executed by a firing squad on 28 November.

In Greece anger changed at once to horror. Athens became a city of mourning. The British minister was withdrawn as an expression of Lord Curzon's extreme displeasure. It is true that in the short term the executions had certain beneficial effects. The very severity of the act extinguished all sentiments of further revenge. By concentrating the responsibility for defeat on a number of luckless scapegoats it absolved the army from blame and made it possible to revive its morale and efficiency. And it shocked the general population into a sober realization of the country's immediate dangers. Yet if the executions were perhaps inevitable, and not without benefit, they were to provide in the future a compelling emotional justification for the social and political schism between monarchists and republicans which in the earlier form of a national division between the supporters of Constantine and Venizelos already had, as we have seen, a basis in the experiences of the Great war and the structure of Greek political life.

The non-parliamentary government of the Revolution, with Plastiras as its 'Leader' and Gonatas as his Prime Minister, faced the two formidable tasks of making peace and settling the refugees. An Armistice agreement had been signed at Mudanya on 11 October 1922. When the Peace Conference assembled at Lausanne on 21 November the position of the Greek delegation led by Venizelos was not enviable. It had been strengthened only by the rapid and effective reorganization of the army in Thrace under the impetuous leadership of General Pangalos. Yet if his unrealistic but seriously intended threats to renew the war perhaps moderated some demands of the Turkish delegate, Ismet Inonu, it is certain that they also embarrassed the work of Venizelos in his search for an acceptable settlement. The principal factor in the negotiations was simply the military victory of the Turks and the disarray which this had introduced into the ranks of the allies. France had already come to terms with Turkey over Cilicia and Alexandretta, Lloyd George had resigned, and although Curzon was determined to uphold the prestige and interests of Britain the situation of Greece was no longer particularly identified with these.

The difficult negotiations which were delayed by a lengthy adjournment of almost three months between February and April were finally concluded by the signing of the Treaty of Lausanne on 24 July 1923. Among the conditions which affected Greece, the islands of Imbros and Tenedos close to the Straits reverted to Turkey. Italy continued to control the Dodecanese islands, and Britain the island of Cyprus. Turkey recovered eastern Thrace. But for Greece the crucial decision of the Conference was contained in a separate convention signed on 30 January 1923 by Greece and Turkey for the return of prisoners of war and political hostages, and the compulsory exchange of the Greek and Turkish minorities in the two countries. From this arrangement only the Turkish population in western Thrace and the Greeks of Constantinople were excepted.

The first compulsory exchange of its kind in modern times it seemed, at first sight, a cruel and radical solution, uprooting entire communities from the environment in which their ancestors had lived for centuries. The Turkish representative had insisted that in no circumstances would the refugees who had already fled from Turkey be permitted to return. He said they could no longer tolerate in their midst a population foreign in blood and religion, living by the commercial exploitation of the faithful and conspiring ultimately to resume an ancient sovereignty over the land. Yet, in defeat, there were advantages for the Greeks. Already more than a million refugees had fled or been driven from Asia Minor. Excluding the 100,000 Greeks of Constantinople only 150,000 Greeks then remained to be exchanged against 388,000 Turks who were still living undisturbed in Greece. The departure of the Turks from Greece released land for the settlement of refugees already a charge on the county's limited resources. It improved, particularly in Macedonia – an area disputed by Balkan neighbours, the percentage of Greeks among the total population of northern Greece and therefore the political security of that region. Above all by removing the irredentist temptation which the dispersed communities of Greeks in Asia Minor had represented it removed at last the inconsistency between the modern ambitions of Greeks (which they had learned from the West) to live in a single nation state, and their geographical dispersion which had resulted from their historical existence within the 'Oecumene' of a theocratic empire.

Although the Treaty of Lausanne formally ended the war with Turkey domestic debate to determine the responsibility for military defeat and the destruction of national ideals had inaugurated a new cycle of political hostilities at home which only the dictatorship of Metaxas in 1936 temporarily suppressed. With the destruction of the Great Idea through which the state had hitherto found its national mission, political life was largely reduced to the sterile attribution of blame and the cynical manoeuvres of personal followings for office and patronage. The principal threat to Plastiras' position was neither the making of peace nor the settling of refugees but the undermining of his regime by dissident factions of ambitious or discontented officers who considered that justice and honour were not satisfied by Constantine's abdication and the executions. The monarchy as an institution had also to be removed.

In July 1923 the anti-monarchist Military League was formed to organize senior and junior officers with republican opinions. The more extreme and republican the solution of the constitutional issue which they had insisted on raising, the greater would be the number of even moderate officers who might be retired on grounds of a doubtful allegiance, and the more rapid the promotion of

I

mose whose loyalty could be relied on. The organization of the
League is worth remarking on. A representative was elected by the
thembers of the League in each battalion. In each division an
officer was chosen by the representatives elected by the battalions,
and similarly in each army corps another was appointed by the
representatives from divisions. The effects upon military discipline
of such alternative loyalties and chains of command may be
imagined. Since the League's leaders were senior officers such as
Generals Pangalos, Othonaios, and Kondylis, and Admiral
Chatzikyriakos, their juniors felt little remorse in preferring to
obey the League's instructions rather than those of their unit
commanders. The situation was further confused by the ambitions
and mutual distrust of the men whose names we have mentioned.
They were extreme in their republican sympathies, and in the
methods they were prepared to use, rather than in their respect for
democratic processes, for which Pangalos and Kondylis, indeed,
were soon to show a complete disregard.

Officers of all political persuasions had now assimilated the
simple lesson of the years between the revolution of Goudi in
1909 and the movement of Plastiras and Gonatas in 1922 that
government was at the mercy of the armed forces. Thus the
extremism of the Military League soon produced an opposite conspiracy. Monarchist officers still serving in the army, Venizelists who
were not republicans, and other officers who for personal reasons of
jealousy or their exclusion from controlling cliques were discontented
with Plastiras (and a fortiori apprehensive of the convinced republicans who wished to replace him), shared a general grievance that
the Revolution had ceased to be a national and patriotic movement
and had increasingly identified itself politically with republican
forms of Venizelism. It has to be remembered that some who
originally supported the Revolution had been anti-Venizelists,
including Gonatas. Although the leaders of the Revolution had
announced elections for a National Assembly to be held on 16
December 1923, it was now clear that the constitutional issue
would be involved and almost certainly prejudged, and that under
the electoral conditions imposed by the regime the non-Venizelist
parties would have little hope of success. Indeed, the Populists
were so convinced of failure that they decided to boycott the contest,
avoiding in this way the recognition of any constitutional change
and the humiliation of defeat.

In these circumstances and before the elections had been held,
an attempt on 21 October 1923 to overthrow the Revolutionary
government by force was made by two disaffected Venizelist
generals, Leonardopoulos and Gargalides, supported by junior

officers, both monarchist and Venizelist. Many were moderate men disillusioned with political factions and anxious to end the National Schism. They recruited to their ranks the anti-Venizelist Metaxas who had consistently disapproved of the Asia Minor adventure and was proclaiming moderate policies of reconciliation. But his professional advice to concentrate on a rapid *coup* in Athens was disregarded and in the event the counter-revolution was energetically suppressed by Plastiras.

Until this mismanaged rebellion altered the political balance Plastiras and Gonatas, influenced by the wishes of Venizelos himself, had resisted the arguments and manoeuvres of the more extreme officers who wished to remove the dynasty. Although a motive of many who supported the *coup* was distaste or fear of extreme republicanism, its failure probably ended any hope of saving the monarchy. More than five hundred officers whose involvement in the rebellion was proved or suspected, were dismissed, and immediately following the December election petitions presented to the government by the Military League demanding the dethronement of the King now reflected an almost unanimous opinion among serving officers whatever their previous political affiliations might have been. It was a question, principally, of professional survival.

At the elections in December 1923 the abstention of the anti-Venizelist parties had returned a National Assembly almost exclusively composed of delegates from parties of Venizelist origin. Papanastasiou's radical 'Republican Union' in alliance with a group of republican Liberals controlled 120 of the 397 seats, while the Liberal Party itself held 250. Yet although the Assembly was dominated numerically by conservative Liberals, the majority of whom would have preferred to avoid constitutional changes, it was also overawed by the vociferous propaganda of republicans inside the Assembly and by the threats of the Military League outside. The latter had an almost immediate effect. Only a few days after the election King George accepted the advice of Gonatas that he should travel abroad until the future of the monarchy was decided.

With the transfer of power to an elected assembly Venizelos who had recently returned to Greece became Prime Minister in January 1924. If he could not prevent the change from kingdom to republic he hoped at least that it might be accomplished in a manner that would bring back stability and continuity to parliamentary life. In time a republic might become generally accepted in a way that possibly the monarchy could not. But in any constitutional changes the popular will must be seen to be genuine and unforced. Therefore

Venizelos favoured a plebiscite with only limited canvassing of support to be confirmed afterwards, if necessary, by legislative acts of the Assembly. The Republican Union and the Military League, on the other hand, required the immediate establishment of the republic by a decree of the Assembly to be approved or rejected later by the will of the people, an important difference in Greek plebiscitary procedure. These bodies had no interest in reconciliation; for reasons of professional advantage the soldiers wanted the schism in the officer corps to become permanent, while Papanastasiou's supporters in the Republican Union were pressing for social reforms unacceptable to the other parties. But even over those followers who supported him on the constitutional issue Venizelos discovered that his control was not complete. In a one-sided Assembly which lacked the unifying opposition of the monarchists he was at odds with a Venizelism fragmented into the personal followings of his principal lieutenants. Temperamentally he found it difficult to accept these limitations to his authority, nor did he want to bear the responsibility for the establishment of a republic in the way that it was likely to be effected. After only nineteen days in office he resigned on grounds of health and early in March withdrew to Paris to the relief of both his political enemies and more independent colleagues.

Between January 1924 and June in the following year the Assembly provided the country with six short-lived governments and a greater number of attempted military *coups*. With the resignation of Venizelos the Liberals were distributed among the followings of Kaphantaris, Michalocopoulos, Roussos, Sophoulis, and others. Since no party now commanded a majority, political life was filled with intricate manoeuvres to create coalitions whose brief lives indicated the mutual personal distrust of the sectional leaders and their consuming ambition for the premiership under the most unpromising conditions. The influence of Venizelos' advice, even after he had gone abroad, on the Liberal leaders, particularly Kaphantaris, further confused the scene. When he was not himself in power his restless nature seldom allowed any situation to develop unaided by his often impulsive interventions. But, above all, the Assembly's behaviour was dominated by sectional bargaining for military support, a process which in its turn introduced indiscipline and inefficiency into the armed forces to the point that the *coups* themselves were comically ineffective.

Following a brief period in office of Kaphantaris, Papanastasiou became Prime Minister on 12 March. With those forceful heroes Kondylis and Chatzikyriakos in his cabinet he judged correctly that although the Republican Union Party did not command a

majority, military pressure and a growing public opinion in favour
of a quick constitutional settlement would enable him to pass a
decree establishing a republic. On 25 March 1924 by 259 votes to 3,
with the party of Kaphantaris abstaining, the motion was carried.
On 13 April in the plebiscite, 69 per cent of the voters approved
the National Assembly's decision. In this measure of popular support
there was as little deep conviction or emotional commitment to
republicanism in an ideological sense as there was later in 1935
any convinced attachment to monarchy as an institution when
King George returned. In both instances a plebiscite on the constitution came after periods of political confusion. On both occasions,
with little justification, despairing voters hoped that constitutional
change might produce political stability. This does not contradict
the existence of the bitter political schism between Venizelist and
anti-Venizelist parties which fed on memories of the conflict
between Venizelos and Constantine and the betrayal of the Great
Idea. But this was most acute as an opposition between party
hierarchies, their agents, and more important clients. It is true
that at any time ordinary countrymen and townsmen were attached
to parties through channels of patronage which in particular
districts or families might remain unchanged for many years. But
generally political loyalties were not so inflexible that in the
matter of constitutional forms views could not change considerably
after long and distressing periods of political instability.

With the republic established Papanastasiou quickly lost the
support of the other groups outside his party. They had no wish to
support the radical economic and social reforms which were his
ultimate aim. A mass resignation of officers in the navy was obliquely
aimed at bringing down the government. Two weeks earlier the
resignation of Kondylis on the grounds that the Prime Minister
had been too lenient with the Communists and too ready to be
reconciled with the monarchists also had the same object in view,
with the intended consequence that he might himself be called on
to form a government. As it happened a weak compromise cabinet
led by Sophoulis succeeded Papanastasiou. Indeed Sophoulis'
position was so insecure that his only means of controlling an
obstructive faction of naval officers was the ingenious but humiliating
stratagem of demobilizing the crews of their ships. The government
of Michalocopoulos which succeeded him was hardly more effective,
continuously attacked by the radical Papanastasiou in the Assembly
and hampered by a succession of labour disputes. There was now
general popular discontent with the whole apparatus of state,
with the Assembly, with military irresponsibility, with the loss of
international respect for the country to which successive govern-

ments had contributed. Moreover, the growing unrest among urban workers, especially in the refugee quarters, showed clearly that in the towns and cities some were not satisfied with a merely constitutional revision of the old order. With such revolutionary possibilities in the air many middle-class citizens were relieved that on 25 June 1925 General Pangalos at last carried through successfully the *coup d'état* which he had so often threatened.

Having proclaimed his intention to introduce honest and effective administration Pangalos had little difficulty in obtaining a formal vote of confidence from the Assembly for a government established by military *coup*. The basis of this support was the support of Papanastasiou given in exchange for various undertakings which Panagalos had little intention of honouring. On 30 September, after the signing on the previous day of a republican constitution – itself, in the circumstances, a somewhat meaningless act, the Assembly was dissolved. The end of this disastrous National Assembly was little regretted but the announcement that elections for a new chamber would not be held until March or April 1926 provoked increasing opposition from the Venizelists; a number of Ministers resigned and were replaced by anti-Venizelist personalities to whom the General now began to look for support. The final break with the forms of legality came on 5 January when elections for the new Senate (the second chamber under the republican constitution) were set aside. And on 11 April the new dictator was elected by popular vote as President of the Republic, having earlier added to this office, by his own constituent act, important executive powers.

Pangalos ruled, even while he yet observed the outward forms of parliamentary government, with a fine arbitrary zeal. Immediately following the *coup* restrictions were imposed on press criticism of the government's acts and its personalities. Legislation was passed to make corrupt practices in public administration a capital offence and under this law, applied retrospectively, two hapless army officers were publicly hanged on 28 November. After the government became openly dictatorial there were precautionary arrests of officers and politicians. Attempts were even made to regulate conventional behaviour in such matters as the length of women's skirts or the removal of their hats in cinemas. Pangalos had no original political philosophy beyond the puritan and authoritarian outlook which is still, today, common among senior officers in Greece.

His policy in foreign affairs was an unrealistic ambition to revise the territorial consequences of the Treaty of Lausanne. In October 1925 he used a border incident to stage a foolish invasion

of Bulgarian territory for which Greece was condemned by a
League of Nations commission. And later in August 1926 he made
diplomatically unwise concessions to Yugoslavia, including the
recognition of the Slavophone minority in western Macedonia as
Serbian, in order to protect his flank in some projected stroke
against Turkish Thrace. Since these expansionist fantasies required
additional military expenditure at a time when the state was
bankrupt under the extraordinary burden of refugee settlement
Pangalos resorted to a forced national loan by removing a quarter
of the face value from banknotes. Yet the army with its discipline
destroyed by political entanglements was no longer reliable even
for the maintenance of the dictatorship's internal security. The
economic and diplomatic mishandling of national affairs had
reached such a point of scandal that when in August 1926 Pangalos
was at length overthrown in a *coup* organized by that more sagacious
political warrior General Kondylis relief was at least as general
at his passing as it had been on his arrival.

It was in character with the swift treachery of this time that
Kondylis achieved his purpose with the assistance of the battalions
of the Republican Guard, Pangalos' own selected security troops
whose attachment, however, he had increasingly strained by his
new alliance with personalities outside the republican camp.
Since the commanders of these troops had hardly more faith in
Kondylis than in Pangalos, they had obtained a written undertaking that elections would be held without undue delay. But
they had not foreseen the more immediate risk they ran. Two
battalions were unsuspectingly lured to positions where with some
loss of life they were surrounded, shelled and disbanded. Nevertheless when their leaders were put on trial the production of Kondylis'
undertaking played some part in forcing him to accede to the
general wish for a return at last to normal parliamentary government.

The elections held on 7 November 1926, for the first time under
a system of proportional representation, clearly indicated that the
country was still broadly divided between Venizelists and anti-
Venizelists; out of 286 seats the former held 143, the latter 127.
They also showed however that in each camp the moderate parties
had received increased support. Among the Venizelists the radical
Republican Union had won only 17 seats, while in the opposite
camp the moderate Free Opinion Party of Metaxas, which had
accepted the republican constitution as a basis for political life,
now held almost as many seats as the Populist Party which threatened to reopen the constitutional issue. A national coalition under
the neutral leadership of Zaimis gave expression to this general

feeling for conciliation. Even the Populists, unwilling to concede an advantage to Metaxas, were drawn into the government.

After a period of national bankruptcy, inflation, and political disorder, the principal achievements of the coalition were the re-establishment of parliamentary government and a more responsible economic administration. Kaphantaris courageously guided the country's economy by the current orthodox principles of increased taxation, balanced budget, resistance to the temptation to print money, and a stabilized exchange rate. From this policy of sound finance the country benefited by a £9 million sterling loan issued under the aegis of the League of Nations.

On 2 June 1927 the chamber passed the definitive version of the republican constitution in place of General Pangalos' invalid instrument. Politically however the policy of national reconciliation was a failure. Although its desirability was recognized, the structure of political relations made its success improbable. Apart from the bitterness of their past hostilities the parties and personalities in the coalition were inevitably in competition for the distribution of patronage to their followers. A point of fundamental dispute was the return of anti-Venizelist officers to active service as part of the bargain accepted for the support of the Populists. Inevitably the two sides had different views about the number of combatant officers who should be reinstated. Soon the more extreme parties began to undermine the coalition. The Populists by continually reaffirming their intention to reconsider the constitutional question hoped to draw support away from Metaxas and underlined their independence by withdrawing from the government over changes in the banking structure. On the other side, Papanastasiou led the Republican Union out of the government over a disagreement about public works contracts which reflected a more general frustration with an alliance which offered little advantage to a radical party.

The fate of the reduced coalition was settled by Venizelos. He returned to Chania in Crete from abroad in April 1927. Publicly he had repeated his decision not to return to active politics. But predictably he was soon surrounded by the republicans and Liberals, both officers and civilians, who were discontented with the government. By his presence and the advice which he was able to offer without the responsibilities of office he seriously embarrassed the position of Kaphantaris who led the Progressive Liberals. Unable to form a genuine party of his own the latter resigned from the leadership in May 1928. And after some weeks of uncertainty the government of Zaimis also resigned.

The elections which followed on 19 August 1928 were conducted by a government led by Venizelos. Having in effect driven out Kaphantaris he declared that he could not leave the Liberal Party leaderless and vulnerable while it remained the only political force capable of protecting the republic against its monarchist or dictatorial opponents. Tactically Venizelos had chosen his ground well. By 1928, the continual shifts and compromises of the coalition government had become unsatisfactory for most parties and for many of their followers. The mood of the country was now for a strong government and an undisputed leader. The general belief that Venizelos supported by the votes of the refugees would win the election induced many other voters to change their allegiance. Venizelos, haunted by the memory of his defeat in November 1920, was less certain of the result. He offered, once more, to leave party politics if Tsaldaris and the Populists would recognize the republican constitution. The ambition to refashion the national unity which he had helped to destroy still affected him almost as strongly as the older ambition for office. Tsaldaris, the Populist leader, probably discounted too easily the sincerity of this offer, but in any case he believed that his patient intransigence in emphasizing everything which divided Populists from republicans must eventually bring his party to office when discontented voters turned away from Venizelism. He was not wholly displeased when Venizelos persuaded the President of the Republic, by a decree the constitutional validity of which was doubtful, to return to an electoral system of simple majorities. The purpose of this change was clear. Uncertain of his electoral prospects Venizelos needed the assurance that the smaller republican parties, including Papanastasiou's, would enter the elections as a united force. In this he was successful; only Kaphantaris and his friends fought the campaign independently. The electoral result was an overwhelming triumph for Venizelos, the republican parties won 223 out of the 250 seats, and of these 178 were Liberals owing a personal allegiance to Venizelos. Despite the volatile structure of Greek parties he had become, as he admitted in a letter to his wife, 'a parliamentary dictator'.

Whatever the sincerity of Venizelos' desire to unite the nation, a consequence of the return, for tactical reasons, to the majority system was that it helped to polarize the political forces of the country between the irreconcilable opposition of the republicans and the Populists. The attempt to forget the past had failed. Among the anti-Venizelists the party of Metaxas, moderate at least in constitutional matters, had been almost obliterated. It must be stressed that what remained was not an opposition between two parties reasonably disputing office through the institutions of an accepted constitution, but a struggle between factions to determine the form of the constitution itself, and through it the partisan loyalties of the armed forces, with the intention of holding a permanent monopoly of political power. The principle of expediency in redetermining the electoral system at each general election and Tsaldaris' reluctance to recognize the republic were both indications of this situation and the attitudes which it encouraged. The memory of defeat in Anatolia, the execution of the Six, the unending debate about the responsibilities for these events and for the settlement of the refugees, and the very logic of the political patronage system which provided privileges for adherents but not for opponents, contributed to emphasize a schism that particularly in the urban middle classes was social as well as political, often preventing personal relationships of friendship or marriage across the political line.

Above all, the personality and presence of Venizelos represented the principal impediment to any kind of political consensus. Both in his effort to preserve a constitutional monarchy after the Asia Minor catastrophe, and later in his attempt to persuade the Populists to accept the republican constitution in the interests of national unity, he had failed. By 1928 the Republic stood for Venizelos and Venizelism, the Monarchy for his opponents.

II

The Refugees

An abbreviated account of political events in the years which immediately followed the defeat in Asia Minor cannot do justice to the consequences of this catastrophe for every aspect of Greek existence. Of these the settlement of 1,300,000 refugees who had come to Greece before and during the occupation of Anatolia, or as a result of the compulsory exchange of minorities between Greece and Turkey after the war, was a moral and practical problem whose solution was clearly beyond the unaided resources of the Greek state, bankrupt after ten years of intermittent war and political crisis and now called upon to accept a destitute population equal to about one-quarter of its own.

The very gravity however of the situation both in humanitarian terms and its possible political consequences brought assistance from the international community, initially through relief offered by voluntary organizations, particularly the American Red Cross, and later in November 1923 through the establishment by the Greek government, with the support of the League of Nations, of the Refugee Settlement Commission. The importance of this step was to remove the practical administration of refugee settlement from its dependence on the defective machinery of Greek government. The Commission was an independent corporation with full legal personality under Greek law. It had four members. Two were appointed by the Greek government, one by the Council of the League. The fourth member, and chairman, was a national of the United States representing the relief organizations. The Greek government initially undertook to transfer to the Commission 1,200,000 acres of cultivable land for the establishment of refugee families. Funds for the Commission's work were partly provided by loans raised on the international money market: £10 million in 1924 and a further £6,500,000 in 1927. That these financial operations were possible, despite the instability of Greek political life during these years, was due to the initiative of the League in sponsoring an independent organization with international affiliations in which foreign lenders had confidence and refugees and Greek officials could work with energy and purpose.

Although no accurate figures existed for the previous occupations of refugees the Commission discovered that considerable numbers were not farmers. Particularly in Anatolia many Greeks had been artisans, traders and labourers. Professional men, doctors, lawyers, and teachers also were numerous. Nevertheless it was inevitable that the Commission should place the emphasis of its programme on farming. Not only did a farm give means of subsistence for a family but the abandoned estates of Muslims, particularly in Macedonia and western Thrace, provided land and some of the necessary housing. The balance of the land required, about half the total area, was found from state lands and the expropriation of private estates, which under the pressure of the settlement crisis was administered with such radical zeal that by 1930 arable farms or estates of even a modest size had ceased to exist. In 1928 90 per cent of the country's 953,000 farms were of 12·5 acres or less. And by 1930 when the Commission was dissolved 145,758 families had been settled on the land.

Although the economic and social costs of the refugee problem were very considerable it is important to recognize that the settlement of Asia Minor Greeks in the countryside had a number of beneficial consequences. Intensively, and extensively, agricultural resources were more productively used. In the decade after the Asia Minor catastrophe the area under cultivation in Greece increased by 55 per cent. Due to the stimulus of the Commission's work in refugee settlements crop rotation was adopted in many others. Tractors and steel ploughs were introduced to cultivate the pasture lands of northern Greece. Refugees developed the cultivation of tobacco. Two-thirds of the production of this valuable export crop in 1926 could be attributed to their enterprise. And a decade after 1922 the value of agricultural production in the country had doubled. Against these advances we must weigh the effects of the fragmentation of farmland into smallholdings consisting generally of separated plots. We return to this problem in Chapter 10.

The settlement of the urban refugees was a more complex problem. Mainly they were congregated on the outskirts of Athens, Piraeus, and Salonika where the opportunities for employment were greatest. But their situation was difficult. Large-scale industry did not exist and even for the more humble forms of personal service they had to compete for work with native Greeks. In cities overcrowded before they arrived their housing conditions were deplorable. Although by 1930 the Commission had built 27,000 houses in 125 urban refugee settlements there were still 30,000 families living in barracks or shanties. When the Second World war broke out the problem still remained.

Nevertheless, as in agriculture, the arrival of the refugees added some impetus to industrial development. Their numbers widened the very limited domestic market. Even a family living at subsistence level had to make certain essential purchases. Moreover, the refugees who were officially exchanged after the war were able to bring with them money, jewellery, and moveable goods which in value, it is believed, amounted to 56 million gold pounds. With part of this wealth refugees opened workshops and small factories, in some cases introducing skills and manufactures new to Greece, for instance silkworm breeding and carpet-making. It was chiefly due to refugees that between 1923 and 1930 the capacity of the textile industry was doubled. And it is a remarkable fact that even today 20 per cent of Greece's entrepreneurs were born in Asia Minor.

Less fortunate refugees were a reservoir of cheap labour. Owing to the practice of high tariff protection which grew up in Europe after the First World war the Greeks in their efforts to become less dependent on imported goods resorted to the same restrictive trade policies and to programmes of public and private investment by which they hoped to produce domestically a range of essential goods. For this expansion the cheap labour of refugees was a fortunate advantage and it was not accidental that many factories were built close to urban refugee settlements. Inevitably the availability of labour and the pressure of personal needs led to a tacit disregard of regulations and agreements on hours of work, wage rates, and the employment of women and children.

Economic growth in such an environment protected by a tariff wall created too many small, inefficient, and labour intensive enterprises using a minimum of capital equipment. This is a problem to which we shall return in Chapter 11. In the short run it was a partial solution to the employment problem and between 1921 and 1929 the value of industrial production, admittedly starting from a very low base, was multiplied seven times. From a situation after the First World war where industry contributed only marginally to the economy, in 1940 it produced 18 per cent of the national income and employed 15 per cent of the working population. Although without the refugees industry and agriculture would not have remained stagnant after the war, the stimulus of the settlement problem and the energy and numbers of the refugees greatly accelerated the rhythm of Greek economic life. This must be remembered when we consider the cost of supporting and settling refugees, which consumed half the country's ordinary budget for many years and the external loans which have been mentioned. The total cost was claimed by Venizelos to be £83 million, an estimate probably close to the truth.

Politically the refugees had in their great majority supported republicanism. Not only did they believe that King Constantine and the Populists were responsible for their exile, but monarchy, and the party which supported it, represented for them the established structure of privileged society from which as destitute newcomers they were excluded. Since their voting strength was geographically dispersed they could not form a separate political force, but their 300,000 voters altered the balance between the Venizelist and anti-Venizelist parties in favour of the former. In the election of 1928 they had no hesitation in supporting Venizelos whom they revered as their irredentist champion. Nevertheless it was during Venizelos' period of office from 1928 to 1932 that many refugees became seriously discontented and although this was not immediately reflected in any dramatic change of political allegiance it was a warning which Venizelos did not fully appreciate. In 1930 the Refugee Settlement Commission was dissolved. With the majority of the refugees permanently if not contentedly established it was left to the government to complete the work. It was perhaps natural, after the more visible and acute aspects of the problem had been solved, that the sense of urgency would be lost. At the same time the commercial and financial effects of the world trade depression became serious in Greece. Refugees were among the first to suffer through unemployment and a further depression of wage rates, for instance in the tobacco industry at Salonika and Kavalla. These were additional misfortunes to add to the primitive housing conditions which many urban refugees still had to face. It was therefore unfortunate that Venizelos, secure behind his formidable majority, should have signed in 1930 the Ankara Convention. Under the original terms of the agreement on the exchange of populations it had been arranged that the properties of both minorities would be valued and liquidated for the compensation of their former owners. Almost no headway had been made in this intractable task. In search of a realistic relationship between the two countries Venizelos agreed under the Ankara Convention to consider the property of the two minorities as being equivalent in value. The Turks insisted on a small additional monetary payment in settlement. To satisfy Turkish pride and establish friendly relations this seemed to Venizelos a reasonable price to pay. To the refugees, whose property was certainly more valuable than that of the Muslim minority which had left Greece, the Convention was both a national humiliation and an abandonment of their rights.

Such disappointments were a factor in the steady recruitment of refugees into the Greek Communist Party (K.K.E.). This had grown out of the Socialist Party, which in 1918 had been formed from small groups of socialist intellectuals and Marxists who had little support in the country outside their own esoteric circles. By 1920 it had changed its name to the Communist Party of Greece and was already using in its literature the familiar terminology. Not surprisingly the party made particular efforts to win adherents among the discontented urban refugees. They had some success, particularly among tobacco workers in Macedonia where wages were low and workers were easily organized. In 1926 when elections were held under a proportional system of representation the country was surprised to find ten communist deputies in parliament, eight of whom were from Macedonia. After the disillusionment of the Ankara Convention in 1930 leftist tendencies among refugees became more pronounced. They were assisted, naturally, by rising prices and the general economic distress which became worse after Britain left the gold standard in September 1931. The majority of refugees, it must be said, remained faithful to the bourgeois parties. But for the less fortunate or more radical among them the propaganda of communism had an appeal. Since their own world had been erased some refugees were prepared without compunction to overturn the inadequate society of the Greek state to which they had no traditional attachment. As a subject category of Christian Greeks in Turkey they had been despised. In Greece, too, they soon discovered that their presence was resented and their social status inferior. In the circumstances it was not difficult for some to stand their Orthodox belief on its head and embrace communism.

Yet even among discontented urban refugees the number of Greeks who could accept the anti-Hellenic policy of an autonomous Macedonian republic, which the Comintern under the influence of the Bulgarian Party insistently demanded, were a small and uneasy minority. This policy which after the exchanges of population had no ethnic basis did much to discredit the party in the eyes of many who might otherwise have supported it. For this reason the consolidation of Macedonia and western Thrace through intense settlement by refugee farmers was a consequence of the agreement on the exchange of populations which was to prove critically important. In 1912 Greece had been a nationally homogeneous state with the exception of 6,000 Muslims living on their properties in Thessaly. With the annexations in northern Greece after the Balkan wars minorities suddenly represented 13 per cent of the total population, including in 1913 370,000 Turks and 104,000 Bulgars. The effect of the agreement with Turkey, and of an earlier arrangement under the Treaty of Neuilly with Bulgaria which provided for a voluntary exchange of minorities, was that in Greek Macedonia the Greek element which in 1912 was merely 42 per cent of the population had by 1926 mounted to 88·8 per cent; in western Thrace at the time of the Paris Peace Conference the proportion was as low as 17 per cent but by 1924 had become a respectable majority of 62·1 per cent. By the mid-twenties the possibility of the Communists successfully inciting a popular movement for an autonomous Macedonia had passed. Nor could the governments of Yugoslavia and Bulgaria advance any serious territorial claims on the basis of the small Slav minority of 80,000 which still remained in Greece. Due mainly to refugee settlement the security of Greek Macedonia, at least in a cultural sense, was assured. And the only effect of the continued insistence of the Greek Communists that Macedonia should form an autonomous state[1] was to divide and weaken their party during a period when many conditions favoured its advance.

The symptoms of malaise in Greek society between the two World wars, of which the appearance and growth of the Communist Party was merely one, must not be attributed only to the physical disruption of war, refugees, and a world slump. In the new state of modern Greece the notion of the Great Idea had offered a supra-local loyalty which transcended the opposed parochial interests of village communities, and the deracinated individualism of those who in increasing numbers moved to the cities. In that

[1] In 1935, in the interests of the anti-fascist struggle, this principle was exchanged for the recognition of the 'equality of all minorities'.

particular respect the ideals of this national conception partly replaced, partly were confused with, those of the Orthodox Church which had united Christians under Ottoman rule. When after the military defeat in Asia Minor the ideal was destroyed Hellenism seemed to have been emptied of its meaning and purpose. As George Theotokas, one of Greece's most significant novelists and thinkers, has written: 'The moral influence of defeat has been and continues to be profound in our country. The first post-war decade has everywhere been a period of resurgence and great efforts. For us it has been a period of despair. Our elders lost in the harbour of Smyrna not only their power but also their ideals and self-conviction. In 1922 they ceased to have confidence in Greece. The disaster choked every breath of idealism . . . No one expects anything of value from Greece.'[1] It is partly in the light of this reaction that we must attempt to understand the confused chronicle of prejudice and self-interest in Greek political life between the wars.

III

The Return of Venizelos

When Venizelos returned to office in 1928 there is no reason to question that he believed sincerely in his new mission, to forget the wrongs of the past, rediscover national unity through the institutions of the republic, and fashion a prosperous and well administered bourgeois democracy. The new ideal seemed more practical if less ennobling than the dream which had preceded. Yet without considering more fundamental difficulties the vulnerable condition of the economy shortly to be assaulted by the international financial crisis, and the tactical shifts in his own political behaviour more often directed by the wishes of self-interested advisers such as Maris and Skoulas than by his own statesmanship, were soon to make it appear equally unrealistic.

Nevertheless until these difficulties had largely restricted his freedom of action Venizelos made a courageous attempt to solve intractable problems. In particular the serious deficit in the balance of payments made more acute by the need to service the foreign debt, which had been greatly increased by the refugee loans, threatened the stability of the currency. Inheriting from the previous government plans for the extensive drainage of potentially rich agricultural lands in northern Greece, Venizelos exploited the confidence that his name encouraged in the international money market and with a £10 million loan energetically initiated a

[1] George Theotokas, *Free Spirit*, Athens, 1929, pp. 103-4.

programme of public works which eventually provided, as well as 2,750,000 additional *stremmata*[1] of farmland, an improvement and extension of the existing road and rail networks. The loan offered the immediate advantage of a capital inflow to assist the balance of payments; its service and amortization would be offset, it was hoped, by the savings in imported grain resulting from the production of the reclaimed lands. And although Greece was soon to be swept along in the tide of general financial disaster the employment, which public contracts offered, cushioned for a time the effects of the depression for many families of peasants and labourers.

The interrelated benefits of increased agricultural production, reductions in grain imports, and the political credit for a modest improvement in farmers' income, also led Venizelos to introduce more general reforms in the countryside. The establishment in 1929 of the Agricultural Bank offered an alternative source of credit to the loans of merchants and private money-lenders to whom the great majority of peasant farmers had been permanently indebted. Since this form of economic subjection was frequently accompanied by political obligations to creditors, the wisdom of this reform for a party whose electoral strength was less evident in the traditional countryside is obvious. But undoubtedly the most effective technical action in the government's policy was the introduction of new strains of seed which by 1932 had in many cases increased wheat yields by as much as 75 per cent.

In so far as Venizelos' programme was not simply a matter of party advantage its purposes were conservative. The expropriation of large estates, for which legislation during his earlier period of office in 1917 was originally responsible, had produced an agricultural population of small peasant proprietors. These changes had limited the political influence both of landowning families and agrarian agitators which in different ways had threatened the position of the Liberal Party in the countryside. But after 1928 agricultural and social policy in the villages was principally concerned with greater production and the alleviation of more conscious grievances.

In the towns legislation was passed for somewhat similar purposes to create an environment which favoured the operations of the bourgeoisie of merchants and small manufacturers who in their majority supported the Liberals. The protective tariffs behind which this often inefficient and small-scale industry and commerce grew up were justified on the grounds of the undeniable need for import substitutes and the general international trend towards policies of self-sufficiency. For the settlement of the urban refugees

[1] One *stremma* is approximately ·247 of an acre.

K

who disturbed this scene the minimum rate of rehousing calculated as compatible with internal security and the retention of their political support proved to be a gravely mistaken estimate; and in 1931 even this rate of advance could not be maintained as the effects of the financial crisis brought public programmes to a standstill. But already at an earlier date, in 1929, a sense of insecurity and unease in the cities, where visible differences in living standards which ranged from wealth to destitution were clearly visible, persuaded the government to pass the so-called 'idionym' law. This legislation directed against the Communist Party made agitation for the overthrow of 'the existing social order' a criminal offence. It implied a subtle distinction between the traditional military *coup* which presumably did not threaten the bourgeois order of urban society and any violence which Communists might intend through exploitation of popular discontent – a discontent which the government could only think to check by a combination of repressive measures and the minimum of social relief.

Yet perhaps Venizelos' attempted reform of the education system shows most clearly the premises of his social policy. A loan of £1 million was contracted from which grants in aid were made to local communities to build primary schools. During the first years after Venizelos' return in 1928 these were constructed at a rate unprecedented in the country's history. At the same time there was an effort to make the syllabuses less classical and more practical; and the demotic language was established as the teaching medium for both primary and secondary schools. On the other hand while Venizelos ensured that in the future all Greeks would be literate he reduced the number of classical gymnasia which in practice represented the only available form of secondary education. The number of students in secondary schools fell from 96,000 in 1928 to 57,000 in 1932. Similarly entrance examinations and quotas for admissions to different faculties were introduced for the universities. Consciously he wished to reserve the benefits and limitations of classical secondary and university education for those who would enter the professions and provide the ruling class; and to check the unhealthy growth of the legal profession and the pressure of too numerous and half-educated holders of diplomas for employment in the public service and similar unproductive positions. Ambitious villagers were encouraged to send their sons to agricultural schools instead of the classical gymnasium; urban workers and artisans to send children to technical schools to learn a practical trade. While this attempted revision of the education system, the full development of which was prevented by the financial crisis, was concerned with a genuine problem, its form tended to differentiate between the education that was supposed to be appropriate for the sons of peasants, workers, or the bourgeoisie, prescribing practical training for the complementary tasks of different social categories. Although nothing approaching this was achieved, or indeed was possible, the policy indicated Venizelos' conservative and static ideal of Greek society in the later period of his career.

The incessant movement of personal manoeuvre which so generally characterizes political life in Greece, and under all governments takes precedence over the practical implementation of policies, soon compromised its efficiency. Both intrigue and Venizelos' mainly fruitless search for effective Ministers caused frequent disruptive changes in the cabinet. In the four years of his government he appointed six Ministers of Justice and five for external affairs. The final Venizelos cabinet included no survivor from his first except himself. It is true that for the first year of office Venizelos lost nothing of his popular appeal. Indeed at the elections in April 1929 for the Senate the Liberals' success was even greater than in 1928. But already during these Senate elections errors of judgement were apparent. Although Venizelos was sincere in his ambition to build a bridge between the two factions and find a political consensus in which parliamentary government could function normally, he wrongly supposed that this had already been achieved within the limits of the republican camp. The very scale of his electoral success led him to think that the Populists were a spent force whose sensitivities he need no longer consider. Therefore in response to the growing independence and opposition of the other republican parties and of personal followings within the Liberal Party itself, which in 1928 had only accepted the discipline of a united front to survive the electoral hazards of a simple majority system, Venizelos believed he was free to consolidate his control over the Liberal Party by provocatively bringing back to active political life as candidates for the Senate in 1929 the controversial figures of Gonatas and Plastiras. As it happened Plastiras refused to stand, but Gonatas who had been his Prime Minister in the regime of the Revolution was elected; and shortly afterwards became a Minister in company with Karapanayiotis who had served as a member of the court which condemned the Six. Secure behind republican numbers Venizelos also reinstated the president of that court, General Othonaios, as head of the Greek army. The anti-Venizelist world felt, as the paper *Kathimerini* put it, that it had been spat upon. Certainly no acts could have more effectively offended moderate anti-Venizelists who otherwise might have been less attracted by the arguments of those who wished to restore the monarchy.

The choice of a successor to the aged Admiral Koundouriotis who resigned as President of the Republic in December 1929 weakened the position of the republic in a different sense. Although at first Venizelos was prepared to accept Kaphantaris, a candidature which pleased the majority of Liberals and was acceptable to other party leaders as opposed as Tsaldaris and Papanastasiou, further reflection and the advice of his wife and close associates reminded him of past difficulties and disagreements between himself and his former lieutenant. The need to believe that he could impose his will on those with whom he had to deal was a facet of Venizelos' temperament which became more compulsive as he grew older and less confident. It was also a weakness which advisers such as Maris and Skoulas used with skill for their own tactical advantage. By contrast with Kaphantaris, Zaimis, the eventual choice as Head of State, was politically neutral, compliant, and aged. As we have said, the republic had no emotional roots in the minds of those born in Old Greece, just as the monarchy had little appeal for the refugees or the Greeks of the new territories in the north. The former might tolerate a republic if it guaranteed political stability. Yet with Venizelos' promises that he had returned to bridge the chasm of national division still fresh in their memories, they could not fail to reflect that the Populist Party, though reduced in strength, were as adamant as ever on the constitutional question. In this situation Venizelos chose to appoint to the office which symbolized the republic an undistinguished personality whose main interventions in the political life of the past three decades had been to lead governments of short duration at moments of national disorientation when none of the greater political figures was appropriate or willing to accept office. Although the assumption may have been incorrect such a choice suggested that Venizelos himself had no great hopes for the republic. During these negotiations, moreover, he had offered Tsaldaris a plebiscite on the constitutional question. And if there was little prospect that Tsaldaris would accept a contest which at this time would have certainly been lost, it was an error of judgement to suggest that the issue was even open to debate.

The growing disarray in the republican ranks which had made the candidature of Kaphantaris for the Presidency too great a risk in Venizelos' mind now began to be reflected in direct attacks on Venizelos by the leaders of the smaller republican parties, attacks which were also, to a degree, the outcome of the appointment of Zaimis. By June 1930 Kondylis, Papanastasiou, Kaphantaris, and Zavitsianos had accused the government of a variety of sins;

Kondylis because its policies had created a general condition of political anarchy; Papanastasiou and Kaphantaris because Venizelos concentrated all executive power in his own hands, and because he had intentionally kept alive the constitutional issue to use the threat of 'troubles' as a stratagem for preserving his influence over the electorate; and Zavitsianos because the government had taken no steps to protect the economy against the impending financial crisis.

Disclosures of alleged corruption added to the government's discomfiture. In the middle of October 1930 it was discovered that quinine tablets produced in government laboratories contained only flour. The government's Chief Chemist, whose 'exemplary honesty' in a quite separate matter the Prime Minister had only recently guaranteed, was arrested. The fact that a verdict on the charge against the accused man was not arrived at until June 1931, or that he was acquitted, hardly restrained public judgements. During these months, and afterwards, Venizelos was freely accused of deliberately attempting to alter the course of justice.

Before the quinine scandal had run its course, Karapanayiotis, the Minister of the Interior who had earlier held the Ministry of Communications, was advised by Venizelos to resign from office after it became known that a company, in which a brother-in-law of the Minister had been a partner for twenty-seven days in 1929, had received a road-making contract in Mytilene. Possibly Venizelos hoped by this display of moral sensitivity to protect the government's reputation from the taint of Karapanayiotis' alleged 'corruption'. But it was hardly consistent virtually to remove a Minister from office because his brother-in-law had been twenty-seven days in a company which had obtained a government contract, when it was an accepted practice that most Ministers and many deputies saw to it that road-works in their own constituencies were given to contractors who were politically 'friendly' to them. A more serious error was that he refused to permit an inquiry, for this allowed the opposition press to accuse him of concealing his colleague's guilt. Yet although the Populists felt an emotional satisfaction in harrying Karapanayiotis who had been a member of the infamous court-martial of 1922, their true quarry was Venizelos himself. Venizelos might be personally incorrupt but if by proof or imputation they could show him to be surrounded by unworthy men, they might yet drag him down.

By the middle of 1931 the prolonged attacks both of Populists and the republican parties, now estranged from the Liberals, had begun to erode the strength of Venizelos' position. This was ultimately undermined by events beyond his control. It had been possible to withstand the early effects of the depression in 1930 and during the first six months of 1931, but after 20 September 1931 when Britain left the gold standard, to which the drachma was linked through holdings of sterling, Greece could not maintain convertibility. As the crisis deepened the effects on Greece's foreign commerce were increasingly serious. The prices of her agricultural exports and the amounts she was able to sell abroad fell disastrously; and emigrants' remittances and the earnings of shipping were greatly reduced. Venizelos' attempt to offset the adverse balance of payments and save the failing reserves of foreign exchange by soliciting loans from foreign governments was a failure. At home urban unemployment brought hardship, especially to the refugees; and the unavoidable decision taken on 15 April 1932 to suspend interest and amortization payments on foreign loans was received abroad with unsympathetic hostility. The economic strategy of the government had depended on preserving the country's credit-worthiness to attract foreign loans for a programme of public works which would increase exports and modernize the economy. After the suspension of loan payments there was little hope of receiving substantial foreign aid. For the scale, if not the causes, of these misfortunes Venizelos was held responsible. Greeks, particularly, expect their rulers to have luck as well as merit.

An appeal from Venizelos to Tsaldaris to form an emergency coalition was rejected. It was characteristic of political life between the two wars that the recriminations now exchanged between Liberals and Populists on the question of the nation's finances should be referred to events which preceded the catastrophe in Asia Minor. Venizelos reminded the chamber that by recalling King Constantine in 1920 the Populists had lost the country promised allied credits of 40 million gold pounds. Tsaldaris criticized Venizelos for his irresponsible contribution to the Treaty of Sèvres and while disclaiming any crude intention of revenge he rehearsed the qualities and experience of the executed Six which the nation could have used so well in its present crisis. These retrospective considerations, set out at length, were wholly irrelevant to the country's financial problems; but for both parties they served once more to remind their followers of past bitterness and present loyalties. Venizelos, who in 1928 had hoped to build a bridge across the political chasm, now believed that he must destroy whatever inadequate communication still existed between the factions if he was to remain in power or at least prevent Tsaldaris from forming an effective government.

In an effort to distract criticism during the weeks before the election Venizelos resigned on 21 May 1932. But he was in office again on 8 June when he brought down the Papanastasiou minority government which had succeeded him. The Liberals feared the popular character of Papanastasiou's programme and the practical handicap of an election conducted by a government of the Republican Union. Venizelos' programme for the election in September was simply to reduce the issues to the single question of the constitution. He made much of a joint declaration by Tsaldaris and the republicans in which they claimed that the assertion that the republic was in danger was an electoral fabrication. He stressed, as indeed was the case, that Tsaldaris had been careful to avoid giving any categorical assurance that the Populists if returned to power would in no circumstances consider restoring the monarchy. They merely guaranteed that they would do nothing by *coup d'état*. Tsaldaris was in some difficulty. If he recognized the republic as the nation's permanent constitutional form he would destroy the unity of the Populist Party to the advantage of other anti-Venizelist groups, in particular Metaxas'. If he did not recognize it, he might remain dominant in the anti-Venizelist faction, but he gave his principal opponent a similar advantage in his own camp and the opportunity to use a potent election slogan 'that the Constitution was in danger'. Moreover, danger to the constitution was a convenient cover for military action by republican officers anxious to guard their professional careers against the re-introduction of anti-Venizelist officers. In fact on 11 June Papanastasiou revealed the existence of a republican Military League in the officer corps sworn to prevent a Populist government assuming office. Unabashed Venizelos declared that he would sternly repress any attempt at military pressure during the election, but after the result he would not stand in the way of officers defending the constitution. In other words he would not allow Tsaldaris to form a government if he did not first make a clear declaration that he accepted the republic finally and without reservation – a declaration which, it was supposed, would sooner or later divide the Populist Party between monarchists and republicans.

In these circumstances the country approached the elections on 25 September 1932. Again there was a change in the electoral system, an expedient reversion to proportional representation to minimize the effects of popular discontent with the Liberals. The result was an even balance of forces. Neither the Liberals (98 seats) nor the Populists (95 seats) with their allies could form a majority in the new chamber. There had been a marked increase in the strength of the Left, Communists and Agrarians who between them won 11 per cent of the votes and 21 seats out of 250. Venizelos for reasons similar to those which had prompted his resignation in

May was not immediately anxious for office. If Tsaldaris could be persuaded to recognize the republic and form a government under unfavourable conditions where without a majority in parliament it would be permanently vulnerable to Liberal attack, neither the popularity of the Populist Party nor its internal cohesion would be likely to survive. At the time it seemed a folly only attributable to a period of years without office and its privileges which induced Tsaldaris to accept the President's invitation to form a government. Earlier on 3 October 1932 Tsaldaris had given the form of recognition of the republic which Venizelos had required, and on 4 November his first cabinet was sworn in, including Metaxas but also those opportunist republican warriors Kondylis and Chatzikyriakos.

It did not last for long. Whatever tactical reasons Venizelos might have had for allowing Tsaldaris to take office, neither he nor his immediate circle could tolerate emotionally the reality of a Populist government, however weak. There were also more practical fears as the Populists began to make modest changes in the military hierarchy and the civil service. On the night of 12/13 January 1933 the government fell. Venizelos formed his last government on 16 January. With the smaller republican parties once more in alliance and another change of electoral rules to a simple majority system his advisers believed the Liberals would win a sweeping victory. In these hopes the chamber was dissolved and elections declared for 5 March. Although the 'United Opposition' in which the Populists were the leading party won 46·19 per cent of the votes against 46·32 per cent claimed by the Venizelist coalition, the effects of the distribution of seats in this election gave the anti-Venizelists a clear majority in the chamber with 136 against 110.

News of the defeat on the night of the elections brought General Plastiras to Venizelos' home at midnight. The atmosphere was one of desperation and panic. After ten years of almost uninterrupted control of the state the republicans were about to lose immense resources of power and patronage. Reminding his audience of the persecution suffered by Venizelists after their electoral defeat in November 1920 Plastiras announced that he would go to the refugee quarters and raise a popular revolution. Venizelos appears not to have wanted to assume responsibility for any kind of *coup d'état*. At the same time he did not use his personal influence over Plastiras expressly to prevent him. Indeed by arguing that the complexity of the country's problems would soon destroy Plastiras if he established a dictatorship he seemed not to be opposing the plan in principle.

During the night Plastiras with the support of the 1st Infantry

Brigade seized the Ministry of War where he announced to General Manettas and other senior officers of the Athens garrison that he was already in communication with the corps commanders in the provinces and that it was his intention to establish a dictatorship 'by the will of God, to save the nation'. It was soon apparent that Plastiras had little support. Generals Othonaios and Manettas were aware that Venizelos was unconvinced that a Plastiras dictatorship would help the republican case. Despite their reputations as dedicated republicans they decided not to back the *coup*. In the short time that Tsaldaris had held office before the elections attitudes had changed. Admittedly in a position of political weakness he had acted with moderation and no doubt had come to an understanding with members of the military hierarchy. The generals understood that Populist rule within a republican constitution was acceptable to the general population whereas government by *coup* was not. Moreover, the context of a lost election without any other substantial justification was the worst possible basis on which to establish an authoritarian regime. The movement collapsed. The President appointed General Othonaios as an interim Premier to restore order and within a few days he had handed over to Tsaldaris who formed his second Populist government on 10 March.

The attempted *coup* of 6 March 1933 was an act of tragic folly. After Tsaldaris had accepted without qualification the legality of the republican constitution it seemed that at last the country might be governed in a reasonably orderly fashion through the processes of parliamentary government. The bitterness which the events of 6 March added to attitudes and emotions already long established rekindled factional passions. Metaxas disillusioned by the failure of his conciliatory policies in earlier years took the opportunity in the new parliament to make a detailed and devastating attack on Venizelos to whom the moral responsibility for the *coup* was wholly attributed. While the country was still debating the question of his complicity in the plot Venizelos on 6 June had a miraculous escape from assassination in which his car was pursued three miles along the road between Athens and Kifissia and shattered by bullets. Evidence which could not be suppressed implicated the police. The car used by the assassins belonged to the brother of the Athens chief of police who had been personally appointed to his position by Tsaldaris. The inquiry which followed was conducted with a lack of zeal well calculated to keep political tension at almost insupportable levels. Nor did the government's legislative programme do anything to calm the apprehensions of their opponents. In August 1933 Kondylis, the Minister of War, who as a lapsed republican was particularly disliked and suspected by his former colleagues, announced the introduction of a bill to empower the government to retire officers from the three services. Although through its continued control of the Senate the opposition's ability to obstruct the bill resulted in a compromise by which the number of officers to be retired was limited to the modest number of forty-five, the future intentions of the Minister not only as to the retirement of officers but in the use of his powers of appointment, and a proposal to revise the methods by which officers' seniority on the army list had been calculated in the past, again convinced many republican officers that they must defend their careers by force.

Their political friends felt hardly less insecure or outraged when in March 1934 the government introduced a bill revising the electoral law with a return to the majority system and alterations to the boundaries of constituencies in Athens, Piraeus, and Salonika which were intended to favour the Populists. The attempt to pass such bills despite the veto of the Senate and the anti-Venizelist campaign for the abolition of the obstructive Upper House were adequate proofs for many republicans that the constitution was in danger. And when, after it had required the intervention of Venizelos' 'private' police to arrest a known brigand for his part in the attempted assassination, the first two attempts to hold the trial of the accused men on 24 November 1934 and again on 22 December were prevented by technical objections of the defence lawyers, and then the open intimidation of jurors, the frustration of Venizelists had passed its breaking point. Before the third attempt to hold the trial could be completed the republicans had made their final bid to recover power.

The republican *coup d'état* of 1 March 1935 like its predecessor in 1933 was a failure. In the army it was supported by those who believed the government was about to purge the armed forces of officers who would resist a restoration of the monarchy. Simultaneously they were defending the republic and personal careers. But the *coup* was ineptly directed and except in the navy and some army units in Macedonia (but not in Salonika), it failed to win any widespread support because few believed it could succeed. In this belief even convinced republican officers were affected by their knowledge that outside the circle of those immediately involved in the political game people in all classes were weary of military *coups* and political instability. But the initial prostration of the Tsaldaris government at the news of a *coup*, of which they had received many warnings, suggests that with better planning and leadership it might have succeeded.

For the future its principal political significance was the admitted participation of Venizelos. He had known of the preparations since December when anger and impatience over the delay of the assassination trial may have played their part in his giving the plan his conditional approval if the conspirators would wait until the Populists attempted to restore the monarchy. Although they had not taken his advice on this point it was difficult then to disown his connection with them. He therefore put himself at the head of the movement in Crete where the naval units had concentrated. With the collapse of the revolt on the mainland the futility of local resistance was obvious and by 13 March Venizelos and the rebel naval officers had fled to Rhodes. Now finally compromised by his revolutionary spirit, which was compatible with parliamentary life only when his party was in power, his political career had come to its end.

IV

Monarchy and Dictatorship

The principal effect of the attempted *coup* by the republicans was to precipitate the events they most feared. Kondylis at once removed Othonaios and other senior Venizelist officers from active service. By a number of arbitrary constituent acts submitted to the Lower House of parliament the chamber was dissolved, the Senate abolished, and the permanency of the judiciary and civil servants was suspended. Elections were to be held for a National Assembly which would revise the constitution. Even to moderate anti-Venizelists it seemed clear that on this occasion the entire Venizelist apparatus must be finally dismantled. The trials followed. More than a thousand soldiers and civilians were convicted. One serving officer was executed. Two retired generals, the heads of a republican officers' organization who had taken no active part in the rebellion, met the same fate. Their deaths appeased the extremists and offered a formal revenge for the Six. The political leaders of the revolt, Venizelos and Plastiras, were condemned to death *in absentia*.

During the electoral campaign Tsaldaris disclaimed any intention of ending the republic. This was not simply a tactical policy to avoid losing the votes of dissatisfied Venizelists. By temperament intensely conservative and fearful of violence he preferred to work within the existing system. He recognized correctly that after two unsuccessful Venizelist *coups* the Populists no longer needed the insurance of the monarchical institution to enable them to rule. Such a restoration could now only benefit the declared monarchists in the anti-Venizelist camp, in particular Metaxas whom he feared and distrusted. And it was the articulate propaganda of the latter that forced him to concede that after the elections a plebiscite on the constitution would be held.

Other factors however made it increasingly difficult to hold moderate views. Since the Venizelists decided not to fight the elections on the grounds that the lifting of censorship and the release of their leaders from detention were permitted too late to allow proper preparation, their consequent absence from the Assembly allowed them to view its proceedings as invalid and unconstitutional, an attitude which provoked their opponents to more extreme solutions.[1] When they did not have to debate in parliament with a republican opposition, however weak, the Populists had no reason to consider any concession to their viewpoint. On the contrary the only opposition they then faced was that of Metaxas' Monarchist Party and the right wing of the Populist Party itself which also was in favour of a restoration, and it was in this direction that the government had to make its accommodations. As in the republican Assembly of 1924 the one-sided character of the representation assisted the policies of the constitutional extremists and undermined the unity of the principal party whose customary function was to oppose an enemy who for the time being had disappeared from the parliamentary scene.

After the election Kondylis publicly declared his support for the King on 21 June. His opportune appearance, during the March *coup*, among the troops in Macedonia had enabled him to claim the credit for suppressing the rebels. Now his influence over anti-Venizelist officers who adopted him as their political representative made it difficult for Tsaldaris and his cabinet to oppose his wishes in case his resignation was the signal for military action. Both Tsaldaris' agreement on 18 September to fix the date for a plebiscite (3 November), which he had wished to postpone, and his earlier statement on 9 September that he favoured the return of the King, were unwilling concessions made in the hope of restraining Kondylis and his allies. But his slow retreat brought him little benefit. With the Italian invasion of Abyssinia threatening to precipitate a European war, there was a respectable argument for settling the constitutional question without delay as well as the apparent personal advantages for those who could claim to have brought the King back to his throne. On the morning of 10 October three senior officers, one from each service, led by General Papagos, stopped Tsaldaris' car on the Kifissia road and returned with him to his home to inform him that the armed forces insisted that the

[1] The distribution of votes at the election gave 65 per cent to Tsaldaris, 14·8 per cent to Metaxas and 9·6 per cent to the Communists.

monarchy be restored by a decree of the Assembly. At the cabinet meeting which immediately followed this ultimatum Tsaldaris announced that his government had been overthrown by force.

Events moved swiftly. Supported by the armed forces Kondylis formed a government. In the absence of Tsaldaris and his followers a rump Assembly declared the restoration of the monarchy. Further measures were rushed through to sweep away the last vestiges of Venizelism in official positions. The confirmatory plebiscite which followed on 3 November was conducted with more enthusiasm than good judgement. Despite the official abstention of the republican parties 356,000 more voters apparently came to the polls than in the general election of 1932 and 97 per cent of those who voted were alleged to have done so in the King's favour. Yet although the figures were certainly false the result no doubt reflected the hope of a weary and disillusioned population that with the King political stability might also return. That Kondylis who as Minister of War in 1924 played his part in organizing the plebiscite which confirmed the exile of King George, also led the government which in 1935 restored him to his throne, only illustrated how little questions of political principle hampered the opportunism of a determined man.

The King returned to Greece on 25 November 1935. His honest intentions to reunite the conflicting political factions were an unexpected disappointment for Kondylis who was soon compelled to resign over the King's insistence that there should be a general amnesty for those involved in the recent rebellion. A non-political Prime Minister, Demertzis, was appointed to lead the country to elections to be conducted under a system of proportional represent-ation which offered a guarantee that the influence of each political party would be justly reflected in the first parliament under an impartial and constitutional sovereign.

The elections of 26 January 1936 could not have had a less satisfactory outcome. The royalist parties held 143 seats, the republicans 141. Between the two groups the Communists with fifteen seats held the balance. The King had no choice but to retain Demertzis while the parties negotiated throughout February. There was now a history of bitterness between the two political camps which stretched back in time beyond the execution of the Six and had only recently been refreshed by the three executions and the destruction of many careers after the abortive *coup* in 1935. No differences of social philosophy divided the essentially bourgeois interests of the majority of the men who had influence in the two factions. But they represented not only alternative governments but, as we have said before, two exclusive systems of patronage which offered employment and social status over a very wide conspectus of public and professional life. Fundamentally this was why the attempt in 1926 at a national coalition government failed and there were many in all parties who had no wish to repeat the experiment, whatever the cost. Even the moderate elements showed little will to impose a solution. Sophoulis and Tsaldaris were prepared to collaborate in principle but the former was held back by Kaphantaris and other Liberals who required a guarantee of reinstatement for republican officers, while the latter governed as always by his cautious and narrow calculation of party interest declined to enter a coalition without Theotokis' ultra-royalists whose electoral strength, he feared, might be improved in opposition. In any case the two leaders had found it impossible to agree upon the distribution of controversial Ministries.

Both factions were also negotiating with the Communists. Reports of these discussions considerably alarmed the armed forces. The Minister of War, Papagos, as their spokesman, informed the King on 5 March that they would not tolerate a coalition which included Communists. Threatened by the arbitrary intervention of soldiers which the return of the monarchy was supposed to have ended the King dismissed Papagos and invited Metaxas to take his place, a man who had supported his cause and shared his intolerance of military indiscipline. By a characteristically swift manoeuvre Metaxas occupied the Ministry and used the communications network to assume a control which senior officers immediately respected.

On the following day, 6 March, parliament assembled. With the aid of communist votes the Liberal leader Sophoulis was elected President of the Chamber, and following the customary procedure the King then requested him to form a government. The parties now faced their crucial test of responsibility in providing the country with government. Hitler's recent occupation of the Rhineland and general fears for a European war added a pressing reason for cooperation. Yet again agreement eluded the negatiators and Sophoulis advised the King to call again upon Demertzis on the condition that Metaxas should remain at the Ministry of War to guarantee that the army kept to its proper tasks, a curious compliment from a political opponent, repeated also in the relief expressed by Venizelos in a letter, possibly the last he ever wrote, in which he approved the King's appointment of Metaxas.

The coincidence of death soon altered every expectation. Kondylis had died suddenly on 31 January; in Paris the great Venizelos found his peace at last on 18 March. Now on 13 April 1936 the Prime Minister Demertzis died of a sudden heart attack. The King without hesitation or consultation immediately appointed Metaxas to succeed him. This development provoked one more attempt by Populists and Liberals to form a coalition. Although some judged that Metaxas had merit as a Minister they remembered that he had openly advocated dictatorial government and as Prime Minister might put an end to the party game. Tsaldaris, sick and uncertain, feared that Metaxas would use his position to capture the leadership of the anti-Venizelist camp which had eluded him for so many years. Once more however the fundamental question of the reinstatement of republican officers prevented the formation of a coalition government.

The case for strong extra-parliamentary government had been strengthened on 3 April when the Communists published the terms of the agreement between the party and Sophoulis. For the support of communist votes in the election to the presidency of the chamber, and subsequently in a vote of confidence which would establish a Liberal government, Sophoulis had given a variety of serious under-takings including the repeal of the 'Idionym' law which proscribed agitation against the social order, the disbandment of security organizations and a moratorium on peasants' debts. Since in the event Sophoulis thought better of forming a government which depended on communist votes, publication was a form of revenge for the Communists well calculated to disturb the political scene. Its effects were compounded ten days later when in the debate on a motion of censure against Sophoulis it was also revealed by the Communists that similar though unsuccessful negotiations had been held with the Populists. The two major political parties having failed to give the country the government which they owed it, and having been discovered in negotiations with a party whose intentions against the existing social order were well understood, were thus in no position to deny the community the services of Metaxas' administration. On 25 April on a formal vote of confidence 241 votes were in his favour, only sixteen against. Parliament, having provided the government with the necessary powers to pass legislative decrees subject to the approval of a parliamentary committee of forty members while it was not in session, then adjourned for the summer recess. It did not meet again until after the Second World war.

For the Communists Metaxas' appointment was both a danger and an opportunity. Taking advantage of political disillusionment and depressed living conditions among urban workers a campaign of industrial unrest was promoted to discredit his government. The events of 9 and 10 May in Salonika were the culmination of agitation which provoked 344 strikes of varying scale and severity during the

first six months of 1936. Five thousand tobacco workers striking
for higher wages, joined in sympathy by twenty thousand other
workers, were caught in a struggle with armed police in which
twelve demonstrators were killed. Blood spilled in police action is
in Greece a symbol of the state's tyranny. For a day the general
population made common cause with the strikers in a collective
protest of such intensity that police were withdrawn to barracks
and army units with local conscripts broke their ranks. For some
hours Salonika was without authorities until army units arrived
from Larissa.

This not inconsiderable success led the Communists to believe
that they were now in a position to manipulate the popular masses
in the cities. Their confidence was particularly flattered by the
progress they had made in infiltrating military units, proof of
which, they thought, had appeared in the indiscipline of certain
regiments at Salonika. The effect of these events on Metaxas was
equally marked. They offered him arguments for an emergency
dictatorial government in a situation where he could claim that
both the internal and external security of the nation was endangered.
His persuasion of the King was successful and, as it happened,
timely, for Sophoulis had made it plain that the Liberals would
withdraw their support from Metaxas when parliament reassembled
in October. Fortunately for Metaxas King George was more
impressed by the present dangers to the country than by Sophoulis'
plan to form a coalition in the autumn with the group of Populists
led by Theotokis, which the Liberal leader had confided to him on
22 July. Although King George disliked the political philosophy of
Metaxas he shared his intolerance of political disorder and agreed
that in the existing circumstances an extra-parliamentary government was a necessary but strictly temporary expedient. Unfortunately for his subsequent reputation international events never gave
him the opportunity to claim that the emergency had ended. On
the contrary he understood that only Metaxas could adequately
prepare the country for the probability of war. In this judgement
he was almost certainly correct.

The dictatorship was formally established by the signing of a
document at a cabinet meeting on the evening of 4 August 1936,
the date by which the regime was to be known in the future.
Various articles of the constitution were suspended, press censorship
was established, and parliament was dissolved without provision
for new elections. The announcement provoked little public
reaction. Apart from a few armoured cars in the main streets of
Athens no show of force was necessary. Without newspapers the
protests of the political world were scarcely heard and in the case

of the Liberal Party, which still hoped that Metaxas would keep his undertaking to restore republican officers to their positions in the army, none was made.

The motives of Metaxas were more complex than those of the King. He chose to declare the dictatorship on the eve of a 24-hour general strike organized by the Communists in protest against the introduction of compulsory arbitration in labour disputes. But although he used the threat to the existing social order, the inability of the existing parties and parliament to provide strong and decisive government, and external dangers, as principal reasons for the change to an authoritarian regime, these were the precipitating rather than the fundamental causes of his action. Like Venizelos his political career was coloured by the early history of the National Schism in which as an adviser of King Constantine in 1915 he had played an important part, the consequences of which he admitted had contributed to the disastrous national division in 1917. Like Venizelos he hoped to close the rift which he had helped to create. Since he had bravely disapproved of the Asia Minor policy of the anti-Venizelist government which came to power in 1920, he had been well placed after the catastrophe in 1922 to lead those moderate anti-Venizelists who looked for a rational programme of political and economic reconstruction freed from party bitterness and retrospective debate. Despite his half-hearted involvement in the unsuccessful counter-revolution of 1923 which had been provoked by the extremist tendencies of republican officers, he consistently pursued this moderate policy to a point of some success in the elections of 1926 when his party held almost as many seats as the Populists. By agreeing to serve in a national coalition government he set an example which the Populists could not afford to ignore. But the experience of internecine party warfare within this government, the personal humiliation of accusations about his handling of public contracts as Minister of Public Works, and the subsequent annihilation of his party when Venizelos returned to office in 1928, made him personally bitter against the Greek form of parliamentary government of which the excesses and inefficiency had certainly been remarkable since the First World war. The ruthless exploitation of party interest by the Venizelists between 1928 and 1932, followed by their two armed insurrections in 1933 and 1935 to remove the Populists from the power which they had legitimately won, convinced Metaxas not merely that it was necessary to bring back the monarchy if political stability was to be restored, but also that the only method by which the political schism could be repaired was by suppressing the historical parties which had created it. It is

L

significant that when Tsaldaris died in May 1936 Metaxas made
no attempt to claim the vacant leadership of the Populists. For by
that time he had been persuaded that only a strong extra-parliamentary government could save Greece from political ruin.
Nevertheless, although Metaxas enjoyed the respect of the officer
corps, which following the purge of many republican officers by
Kondylis in 1935 was predominantly monarchist, he had no
personal following in the army; and it is true, as Kaphantaris
bluntly told the King, that without his agreement and support no
Metaxas dictatorship could have been established.

The regime of the Fourth of August offered the advantages and
drawbacks often associated with relatively efficient dictatorships
in countries with predominantly agricultural economies and
political instability. Metaxas instituted a systematic programme of
public works, particularly drainage and irrigation schemes to
increase the supply of arable land. His most important contribution
to solving the human problems of the countryside was to declare a
moratorium on farmers' debts. Guaranteed prices for wheat were
assured. There were also new regulations for the central collection
of this crop, a measure which was to ensure an equitable distribution
of bread to the army and the civilian population when eventually
the country went to war. In industrial and urban employment an
attempt was made to protect workers from the worst abuses of
depressed wage rates. Although strikes became illegal and arbitration by representatives of the Ministry of Labour in disputes about
pay and conditions was compulsory, minimum rates of pay were
negotiated for different categories of workers. Many employers
undoubtedly evaded these regulations by threatening to dismiss
men who did not sign a receipt for wages which were greater than
the amount in fact received; but the right of direct appeal which
Metaxas encouraged had an effect on the degree of this exploitation.

In the civil service there was an assault on bureaucratic indifference and delay in attending to citizens' affairs which had some effect
in matters of simple routine. In more complex questions the greater
centralization of decision making which Metaxas' distrustful temperament encouraged partly offset the improvement in the efficiency
of the service. Yet in matters which he judged to be supremely
important such as the re-equipment of the armed forces, the
efficiency of the system of civilian and military mobilization, the
productivity of agriculture, and the establishment of a national
youth movement, Metaxas' remarkable powers of personal application and administrative insight inspired or drove his Ministers
and senior civil servants, often men of limited ability, to carry out

his policies with an urgency and conscientiousness unprecedented at that time.

Metaxas' regime only briefly and imperfectly resembled a national government of public men acting together to carry the country through an emergency. Always believing his position in the country to be less secure than in fact it was, by 1937 Metaxas had already converted it into a purely personal administration, appointment to which principally depended on hard work and personal loyalty. Opposition and obstruction were treasonable. Distrusting both the ambitions and abilities of most of his Ministers Metaxas exercised a remarkable control over their departmental work, reading and drafting memoranda on any important issue. The Greek economy and the structure of government were not then as complex as they have become in the period of expansion after 1950 so that with some strain this degree of detailed supervision by a determined and dominant Prime Minister was possible. Over the internal administration of the army, however, Metaxas did not attempt to keep the same close control. Its corporate organization, conventions of seniority, and the relationship between the King and the officer corps made this more difficult. But working through General Papagos, whom he appointed as the Chief of the General Staff, Metaxas insisted on standards of efficiency and discipline long forgotten or disregarded. Since discipline was partly a question of changing old habits of political conspiracy, Metaxas adamantly resisted every pressure to reinstate republican officers. At the cost of the services of some capable officers the army recovered a strictly professional morale and the individual interests of the majority of officers were identified with those of the regime.

Before the Italian attack in 1940 it could not be claimed that the Metaxas government had won the hearts of the Greeks. In popular understanding any Greek government is alienated from the ordinary people it governs, even those who have supported it with their votes, until it has provided them personally with material benefits or privileges. It was exactly this market in favours, *rousfetia*, and the philosophy underlying it, which Metaxas aimed to eradicate. Generally the government was opposed for obvious reasons by all those in the old political world which it had replaced, as well as by the many middle-class professional men such as lawyers and doctors, the extent of whose practices was not unconnected with their political influence. And like all Greeks with secondary education they had been brought up in the traditions of western liberal democracy and its version of the ideals of classical Athens. Similarly, intellectuals, writers, school-teachers were in their majority opposed to the regime on principle, and in reaction to the foolish logic of censors who in their surveillance of art, literature, and education, believed, for instance, that it was necessary to excise Pericles' funeral oration from school textbooks. Many entrepreneurs and businessmen also disapproved of the regime because of its labour regulations and high taxation. The reaction of the great majority of the population, on the other hand, was rather one of resigned acceptance, an appreciation of the advantages of stability and order, which had previously been so signally lacking, balanced by the frustrations which no Greek lightly accepts of weighing his words. As in all authoritarian states, fear of the security police was an important pressure for conformity.

During the four and a half years of the dictatorship there was only one open rebellion, a short-lived affair of only a few hours duration in the traditional Venizelist stronghold of Crete. There were a number of conspiracies involving Ministers and officers in the armed forces but these were discovered before they could develop. Most of the former political leaders either from conviction or the frustration of unemployment attempted to make declarations of their opposition to Metaxas, or more seriously, like Michalo-copoulos, tried to negotiate with foreign governments and the King for a change of regime. Discovery carried the penalty of exile to different Aegean islands, a reasonably humane solution except in the instance of Michalocopoulos whose exile to Paros when he was unwell contributed to death. In combating the Communist Party the security police under the shrewd direction of Maniadakis were no less successful. With the establishment of a dictatorship the party became illegal and vulnerable at a moment when it believed that its growing influence would soon lead to a revolutionary seizure of power. Overnight a number of its leaders, betrayed by police agents in the party, were arrested. The publication, later, of 'declarations of repentance' by many members caused confusion and paralysis in an organization where the integration of self-contained cell memberships, with rules of secrecy and anonymity in their outside contacts, depended on absolute loyalty and confidence. The party itself was later to admit that the regime of the Fourth of August had 'decapitated' its organization.

Metaxas was not satisfied with merely negative or repressive measures. He wished to create a new Greek society, to replace the selfish individualism and disillusionment which seemed to characterize especially the life of middle-class Greeks after the 1922 catastrophe, with new corporate and Christian loyalties. A third Greek civilization had been born on 4 August 1936 which would draw the best elements from classical Greece and Christian Byzantium, and add its own. It was to be built about the simple and categorical loyalties to King, country, religion, and family in which individual interests would be transcended by more spiritual values, drawn from genuinely Greek sources and not from corrupt imitations of a western liberalism unsuited to the Greek scene. These were themes which appeared frequently in his speeches and in other propaganda.

It is doubtful if these somewhat abstract notions had much effect. In the Youth Movement (E.O.N.), however, Metaxas found a practical instrument to help him mould a new generation that in time might have responded to his vision. E.O.N.'s activities were a mixture of para-military training and athletics for boys, domestic science and dress-making for girls, nationalist indoctrination, excursions, and camping for all. It must be remembered how limited were the recreational facilities open to the children of most Greek families at this time. All these were now offered at the state's expense. The uniform, parades, comradeship, and sense of national purpose, however naïvely expressed, made an undoubted appeal to the children of the towns. At first, in the countryside its purpose was less easily understood, and less appealing. Since E.O.N. disputed their guidance of the moral development of young people it was resisted by many school-teachers and middle-class parents. The latter objected to their children mixing with those whose fathers were labourers or factory workers. But Metaxas persisted. Despite his careful husbandry of the country's limited resources in other respects, he spared no expense to establish a classless organization which he believed would provide in ten years a new basis for national solidarity and a popular commitment to the ideals of his regime. E.O.N., in fact, was the only attempt Metaxas made to create anything resembling a party, in this case a party of the future. We cannot know how Greek political life would have developed if there had been no war. E.O.N. was an educational and political venture which Metaxas hoped would give him support in the future either for a continuation of the dictatorship or a cautious return to some limited form of representative government. He understood that it was relatively easy to become a dictator but a greater problem to provide either a method of legitimate succession, or any more liberal form of government after a dictatorship that would not be even more unstable than that which had preceded it. As it happened other events beyond the control of Metaxas or his country did not allow him even half the ten years he believed he needed. Only a few weeks after his death in January 1941 when Greece was occupied

by the Germans in April, it seemed as if, outwardly at least, his
government and its work had never existed.

V

The Italian War: the Nation United

The foreign policy of Greece in the years immediately after the
defeat in Asia Minor was weak and confused. In August 1923
Mussolini took advantage of the murder of an Italian member of
the Greek-Albanian frontier commission to bombard and occupy
Corfu, from which only the pressure of international opinion
persuaded him to withdraw a month later. In October 1925
during Pangalos' period of power there was the foolish invasion
of Bulgarian territory already mentioned earlier in this chapter.
With Yugoslavia continuous friction over the extent of the Free
Zone in the port of Salonika, and the privileges and regulations of
communications with it, embittered relations. With both Yugoslavia and Bulgaria there were the perennial problems of the recognition and definition of the Slavophone minority in Macedonia.
And in Constantinople the difficulty in deciding which Greeks
were exempted from the exchange of populations, and which
were not, provoked a crisis in which the Turks expelled the Patriarch
in January 1925 as an 'exchangeable person'.

During his period of office after 1928 Venizelos attempted a
radical alteration of Greece's traditional policy. Released from
the incubus of the 'Great Idea' Greece was no longer obliged to
court the favour of whichever great power seemed currently
willing to support her irredentist ambitions. Avoiding undue
attachment to any power Venizelos hoped to negotiate treaties of
friendship with as many neighbouring states as possible. The
point of danger was Italy which since 1927 held Albania virtually
as a protectorate and publicly proclaimed her interests as a Balkan
power. A treaty of friendship and arbitration was signed between
Greece and Italy on 23 September 1928 and, although it implied
a tacit acceptance of the Italian presence in the Dodecanese
islands held by Italy since 1912, it offered temporary security from
Italian designs as well as a bargaining counter in other negotiations
with Yugoslavia. Yugoslavia herself feared the same Italian
ambitions in the Balkans and realized that she might be isolated
from her Greek neighbour. With this advantage Venizelos successfully settled the problems of the Free Zone in Salonika and negotiated
a treaty of friendship. Similar overtures to Bulgaria were rebuffed.
In Turkey however Venizelos had a considerable success where,

by the force of his persuasive personality and the practical argument of the concessions made by Greece in the Ankara Convention, which finally determined the question of refugee property claims, he convinced the Turks that Greece had permanently given up her territorial ambitions in Asia Minor. As a result, on 30 October 1930, later in the same year, a treaty of friendship and commerce was signed between the two countries. In a reasonable and peaceful world such a network of friendship treaties with immediate neighbours might have served. In the coming years it would be proved both valueless and delusory. Greece's only ally in 1940 was again one of the traditional and not disinterested 'Protecting' Powers, Britain.

In October 1930 the first of four Balkan Conferences was held by unofficial delegations from the different countries of the region to consider how they might improve cooperation in political, economic, and cultural problems of common concern. It was a response both to the economic difficulties of the depression and to the political insecurity of the 'satisfied' Balkan countries (Greece, Yugoslavia, Romania) in resisting the efforts of Bulgaria to reverse or revise the conditions of the treaties of Bucharest and Neuilly, and the ambitions of non-Balkan powers, particularly at this time Italy, to exploit this Bulgarian discontent. The marriage of King Boris of Bulgaria to an Italian princess in 1930 marked a general *rapprochement* between Italy and Bulgaria which was particularly alarming.

The concern for collective security later resulted in the signing of the Balkan Entente in February 1934 between Greece, Romania, Yugoslavia, and Turkey. Its purpose was to guarantee the security of existing frontiers in the area. It represented, in effect, a defensive alliance against Bulgaria. But since this country could hardly attack its neighbours without the assistance of an outside aggressor that eventuality had also to be covered by the terms of the alliance. The weakness of this pact, inherent in the signatories' mutual distrust and their different relationships with the Great Powers which in the event of war might be enemies or allies (circumstances often affected by the simple facts of geographical position), was evident from the outset. Turkey qualified her acceptance by indicating that she could not assist Romania against Bulgaria if the latter was supported by Russia. And in Greece the Populist government of Tsaldaris, pressed by the personal opposition of both Venizelos and Metaxas, had to ask the treaty partners for an undertaking that Greece would not be automatically bound to enter a struggle involving her in war with a great power. In this instance the fear was that Greece might be obliged to fight Italy to protect the frontiers of Yugoslavia.

Such were the international obligations and policies which
Metaxas inherited. His own foreign policy was clear and cautious.
By a formal attitude of neutrality he hoped to limit his dependence
either on Germany or the western democracies. Of Italy he was
consistently suspicious. While he worked for what he believed to be
the regeneration of Greece he sought to isolate his country as far
as this was possible. Although he believed another European war
was inevitable he hoped by some miracle Greece would not be
drawn into it. He realized that a policy of isolation presented
obvious risks but he judged, correctly, that in a crisis Greece
would have to rely principally on her own resources. As early as
1936, however, he had decided that if Greece had to fight she
could only do so at the side of the western allies, France and
Britain. This was so not only because Greece was vulnerable to
naval powers which controlled the eastern Mediterranean but
because Metaxas understood that the ambitions of the democracies
were limited to the indirect imperialism of financial and strategic
influence while Italy and Germany were bent on territorial
aggrandisement. In the efficacy of the Balkan Entente he put
little faith. The German occupation of the Rhineland on 7 March
1936 set a physical barrier between France, the guarantor of the
status quo, and her smaller allies in the Little Entente (Romania,
Yugoslavia, Czechoslovakia) and the Balkan alliance. As the
German advance proceeded to the northern boundaries of the
Balkans through the annexation of Austria in March 1938, and as
Mussolini renewed his threat in the military occupation of Albania
on 7 April 1939, the Balkan countries alternated between desperate
attempts to organize their collective security among themselves
and individual negotiations with the powers which threatened them.
Already in 1937 Yugoslavia, assured that neither Greece nor
Turkey would assist her against Italy, had attempted to secure
the latter's sympathy by a treaty of non-aggression signed on 25
March 1937 which had been preceded on 24 January by a similar
engagement of 'perpetual friendship' between Yugoslavia and
Bulgaria. But almost all the arrangements between Balkan countries,
whether collective or bilateral, were soon to be proved equally
futile; none more so than the attempt of the Balkan Entente
powers to come to terms with Bulgaria by signing on 31 July 1938
a treaty of 'Friendship and Non-aggression' which allowed Bulgaria
to rearm and to disregard the clause in the Lausanne Treaty
concerning the demilitarization of her frontiers with Greece and
Turkey. Significantly, Bulgaria undertook not to attempt to alter
her frontiers by force, but to submit all disputes to arbitration.
Implicitly the *status quo* had been abandoned.

As war approached Metaxas found it increasingly difficult to balance his relations with the powers. After the occupation of Albania, France and Britain had given Greece and Romania unsolicited guarantees of their territorial integrity. This was a cause of frequent complaints made by the Italians to the Greeks during the summer of 1939. The disinclination of Metaxas to renew the 1928 treaty with Italy was another. Nevertheless when the World war broke out in September 1939 the Balkans were not immediately involved. Italy was unprepared, and the form of the Nazi-Soviet Pact implied for its signatories a policy of non-involvement in the area south of the Danube. Greece welcomed the negotiations between Turkey, France, and Britain formalized in a tripartite treaty signed in October 1939 which indirectly included Greece through the French and British guarantes. On the other hand Greece made repeated public protestations of her peaceful intentions towards Italy. And when it suited Mussolini in September 1939 temporarily to relax the tension between the two countries by suggesting that their respective forces should be withdrawn 20 kilometres on either side of the Greek-Albanian frontier, Metaxas was quick to respond. But if Greece's ultimate political alignment, however carefully Metaxas attempted to disguise it, was in fact with the western alliance, her commercial dependence on the German market for her exported produce, which was directly exchanged for German manufactured goods and armaments, inevitably continued. The British complained of this exclusive trading relationship but could not themselves guarantee to buy the quantities of Greek tobacco offered to them. In turn the Germans were to complain that Greek ships carried cargoes for the allies although in seas dominated by the British and French navies it was clear no profitable alternative existed. For a country militarily weak, strategically important, and highly dependent on trade, neutrality, let alone isolation, was hardly possible. Yet Metaxas persisted in his policy to which various considerations continued to bind him. From personal experience of war and religious conviction he was, despite his authoritarian temperament and political beliefs, a man of peace to the point that bellicose critics have said that he was timid. Politically, since it was clear that Bulgaria's revisionist ambitions would sooner or later draw her into the war on the side of the Axis, there was little safety for Greece in seeking a similar alliance. But the ultimate value against which any policy had to be measured in Metaxas' mind was the country's territorial integrity. For this even temporary defeat had to be endured, as well as the consequence which Metaxas most feared, the ruin of his uncompleted work in reshaping Greece.

After Germany had overrun western Europe in May 1940 and Mussolini had made his inglorious entry into the war, relations between Italy and Greece began to deteriorate despite the initial assurances that Greece had nothing to fear from Italy's new belligerent status. Metaxas suffered Italian provocations in dignified silence. Greece was accused of harbouring British warships while her own ships were bombed or machine-gunned by Italian planes which daily flew over Greek territory. As soon as it was clear that Italy's profit from the French adventure would be negligible Mussolini looked for compensation in the Balkans. Episodes multiplied, culminating in the sinking of the Greek cruiser *Helle* by a submarine attack as she rode at anchor off the island of Tinos on the morning of 15 August 1940, the feast day of the Virgin's assumption which the ship had come to honour. Recovered fragments of the torpedo casing bore Italian lettering. Still Metaxas refused to respond. Information that Greece had been saved from attack by the intervention of Hitler, who was unwilling at this time to see the war extended to the Balkans, seemed to justify his policy. But in October Mussolini decided to disregard German wishes; indeed, Hitler's own occupation of Romania earlier in the same month without consulting his ally hardened Mussolini's resolve to strike out for himself. Italian intelligence reported that the morale of the Greek army was low and its equipment obsolete. Occupation of the Greek mainland and islands would threaten the British position in Egypt. Greece appeared to be the appropriate target. The ultimatum dramatically delivered to Metaxas in his house at Kifissia by Grazzi, the Italian minister, at 3 a.m. on 28 October was firmly rejected. It stated that it was necessary for Italian forces to occupy certain strategic positions in Greek territory. After reading it Metaxas replied simply 'It is war.'

Greek strategy was determined by the two weeks required to mobilize the army's reserves. Although some reserves had been secretly called up as early as May Metaxas had for some time resisted the General Staff's pressure for a full mobilization, not only because this could be interpreted as provocation by Italy, but because the national economy would be seriously weakened by the costs of maintaining a fully mobilized army and by the dislocation it would cause in domestic production. Only Italy knew when she would attack. If Greece responded to a continuing series of provocative incidents by mobilizing her forces she could be seriously weakened, if not bankrupted, without a shot fired. In these circumstances it was necessary in the early days of the struggle for the Greek forces on the frontier to fight a containing action, giving ground where necessary, until the rapid concentration of reserves, the administration of which had been carefully prepared and rehearsed, was completed. But already during this defensive phase the Greeks had won a notable success on their right flank in the narrow difficult valleys of the Pindus mountains north of Metsovo where they trapped and defeated the 3rd Alpine Iulia Division. By 14 November they had concentrated their forces and passed to the offensive, driving for the high ground around the Albanian town of Koritsa which they captured on 22 November; then, transferring the weight of their attack to the coastal sector where supplies could be brought in by sea, they forced the enemy to withdraw into Albania along the entire front, capturing the important base at Argyrokastron on 8 December and the port of Santi Quaranta two days earlier. Although the advance continued, the extremely severe weather with deep snow drifts, the poor communications, lack of air cover, and the arrival of Italian reinforcements which the Greeks could not match in numbers, prevented them from reaching the more distant objective of Valona.

Nevertheless the Greek victories had a wider significance than their modest military results. At a time when England alone faced Germany and Europe was prostrate, the Albanian campaign was the first defeat suffered by the Axis. The sympathy and admiration of the free world was consequently unstinted. Moreover, the success had been achieved with only limited assistance from the British, partly because they had few resources to spare and were perhaps unwilling to send material aid to an ally whom at first they under-valued, and partly because Metaxas did not wish to provoke Germany by introducing British ground forces in numbers which would not be decisive. Thus British aid against the Italians was limited to modest amounts of financial credit and war supplies, air support provided as late as January 1941 by only four squadrons based in Greece, and naval cooperation.

On 29 January after a short illness Metaxas died. Already there were signs that Hitler was preparing to move into the Balkans, as we now know to secure his southern flank before he launched his attack on Russia. Metaxas had agreed with Wavell, the British Commander-in-Chief in the Middle East, that whatever ground forces he could spare would be sent to Greece when the German army crossed the Danube into Bulgaria. This movement of German troops from Romania commenced in January and on 8 February 1941 the Greeks appealed to Britain for troops which began to disembark at Piraeus during March. The prospects for this campaign were from the first forlorn. The British force, mainly troops from Australia and New Zealand, was too small for its task. The Turks impressed by its inadequacy, could not be tempted into a

war they still hoped to avoid. The Yugoslavs, far from offering any
hope of forming a united Balkan front with Turkey and Greece,
capitulated to German threats and signed the Tripartite Pact on
25 March, a step already taken by Bulgaria on the first day of the
same month. A military *coup* in Belgrade on 26 March supported
by anti-German public opinion came too late. Threatened by
German forces on long and vulnerable frontiers the government
of General Simovitch vainly hoped to appease Hitler by an attitude
of strict neutrality which included the rejection of British and Greek
proposals for military cooperation.

On 6 April the Germans invaded Yugoslavia and Greece. By the
swift and efficient manoeuvre of their forces against static defences
the battle was virtually decided in the first three days. There was
no contact between Greek and Yugoslav forces. In Greece itself no
attempt was made to draw back Greek divisions from eastern
Macedonia and Thrace, or from the main concentration of the
Greek army still facing the Italians in Albania, to form a coherent
front south of Salonika with the Anglo-Greek force, from which they
were, in fact, almost immediately separated. Lack of transport and
air cover would have made such moves hazardous in any case.
General Papagos, the Greek Commander-in-Chief, claimed that
the only effect of such withdrawals would have been to destroy
morale, if not the units themselves. 'Metaxas might have done it,'
he said, 'I cannot.' Since the death of Metaxas and the certainty
of an overwhelming German attack the resolve of a number of
senior officers and Ministers had begun to falter. Shortly before
his death, in discussing with a foreigner the will of the Greek
people to resist, Metaxas had said that after all for the Greek
Orthodox believers death was only an episode. But now lacking the
moral example of his leadership many in positions of responsibility
began to question whether further resistance was not futile and
self-destructive. On 20 April, despite specific orders to fight on,
General Tsolakoglou surrendered the forces on the Epirus front.
Already Koryzis who had succeeded Metaxas as Premier had committed suicide two days earlier, overcome by the implications of
the impending collapse and the discovery of defeatism in his
cabinet. On 21 April King George and General Wavell agreed to
the evacuation of the British forces, the greater part of which with
the help of the navy and a succession of moonless nights were taken
off before the end of the month. With them went the King and the
new Prime Minister Tsoudheros. By the end of May when Crete
had been captured Hitler's arrangement of the Balkans had been
completed. In Greece, apart from a Bulgarian occupation of
western Thrace and German control of Athens, Salonika, Crete,

and the Turkish frontier zone, the administration of the country was left to the Italians. Tsolakoglou was rewarded for his treason by the honour of becoming the first Prime Minister of occupied Greece.

The legacy of Greece's unexpected resistance to the Italians was the confirmation of the personal and national virtues which some, especially foreigners, had begun to doubt any longer existed. National honour, for Greeks a crucial quality, had been re-established. In some degree it removed the shame of the disaster in Asia Minor, proving the moral recovery of the nation after the reaction to defeat, the political course and consequences of which we have described. For the success of this campaign there is little doubt that the discipline and relative efficiency of Metaxas' government was an essential ingredient. Without Metaxas the same instant popular enthusiasm to resist Italian aggression and the same will of the people to fight on would no doubt have existed; but the means and organization, and perhaps the necessary courage among some men in government and the High Command, would have been lacking. It is at least unlikely that any political leader, even if he had possessed Metaxas' abilities, could have prepared the country for war working through parliamentary government as this had developed in Greece after the defeat in 1922. The anomaly nevertheless existed that Greece was fighting with the free nations against the totalitarian world in which technically the regime of the Fourth of August was included. Therefore it was necessary rapidly to separate the new-born legend of the Albanian struggle from the embarrassment of its true creator. It was convenient that after his death the defeatism of some senior civilian and military figures of the regime assisted the German attack to its swift conclusion. Personalities of the regime who went into exile with the King survived only briefly in the government; and soon it was permissible to argue that the victory in Albania was due to the courage and endurance of the Greek soldiers, as indeed was the case, but that they had achieved these glories not because of the government of Metaxas but despite it.

VI

Resistance and Revolution: the Nation Divided

The German conquest of Greece in April 1941 left the country without political leadership. A number of the more important Metaxists, and those royalists who felt impelled to fight on, followed the King into exile. But in Athens the majority of the men who had

held positions under the regime of the Fourth of August or had
played any part in the old political world which Metaxas had
suppressed in 1936 shared the generally cautious outlook of the
Athenian bourgeoisie with their duties to family status and property
and their fears for positions in the public service or the commercial
institutions. For themselves and for Greece it was wiser, they
believed, to await the outcome of events. As individuals many
showed the greatest courage in aiding allied soldiers to escape;
but as a class they offered no basis for any movement of popular
resistance. A minority collaborated openly with the Germans,
whether for reasons of personal gain or from a genuine belief that
Germany would win the war and that communism was a more
permanent threat to Greece than the consequences of a probably
temporary occupation; or from a mixture of these motives. Even
the collaborators convinced themselves that their actions were
patriotic.

For those however who were prepared to resist the occupation
forces, the political opportunity was exceptional. This was immediately recognized by the Communist Party (K.K.E.) and somewhat
more tardily by republicans. In the absence of the party organizations destroyed by Metaxas the response of the latter was limited
at first to unproductive debate and individual acts of sabotage.
The position of the Communists was different. Although, as we
have seen, Maniadakis infiltrated the hierarchy of the party with
such effect that under the regime of the Fourth of August its
activities were negligible, sufficient of its membership had survived
underground so that after the release of a number of its imprisoned
leaders during the initial disorder of the Axis occupation, the
party was quick to reorganize cadres, to provoke strikes among
urban workers which embarrassed the authorities, and to hamper
the recruitment of forced labour. It took care, from the outset, to
shelter its identity behind a popular front movement, the National
Liberation Front (E.A.M.), whose military arm, the National
Popular Liberation Army, was known conveniently by the initial
letters E.L.A.S., which almost reproduced the Greek word for
Hellas. Such symbolic identification was invaluable, implying
that E.A.M./E.L.A.S. was a patriotic national movement. The
presence in E.A.M. of socialist and republican groups, unimportant
but impressively named, assisted the illusion. Desperation as well
as patriotism inclined many to turn to any organization which
claimed to resist the Germans. In Athens the winter of 1941–42
brought calamitous conditions close to famine, in a country which
normally imported 45 per cent of its wheat but was now unable to
do so. But although the majority of those enrolled in E.A.M./

E.L.A.S. were not Communists, the ultimate control of the movement which it had originally created was never lost by the K.K.E.
Its own policy was not in doubt: 'to protect the Soviet Union' and
to establish in Greece, by force or political infiltration, a People's
Democracy.

It was only gradually that the Communists understood the
importance of establishing through E.A.M./E.L.A.S. a resistance
movement in the mountains. Since the Axis occupation forces
were limited in number and could guard only the towns and main
lines of communication, two-thirds of the country and half its
population suffered little direct administration. Bands of E.L.A.S.
guerrillas began to appear in the Pindus mountains of southern
and central continental Greece in the late summer of 1942 under
the leadership of Aris Velouchiotis. The disciplined organization
of Communist Party cadres soon made possible a rapid expansion
of their strength. The process draws attention to an important
point. Guerrilla resistance was not a spontaneous response of peasants
to foreign invasion. As patriotic as other Greeks in any expressive
sense, the problem of winning a living for their families from
stony hillsides, and the traditional experience of centuries of
hostile administration by distant governments, whether these were
Greek or not, instinctively encouraged peasants to avoid any
political commitments outside the circle of the family, kinsmen,
and immediate neighbours. Yet when E.A.M./E.L.A.S. had without
consent imposed its rule on village society, it was essential to
appease it by offering the cooperation it demanded. And young
men from the villages, once they were enrolled in the movement,
were not unmoved by its professed ideals of the struggle for a just
and more progressive Greece, just as they welcomed the opportunity
of holding authority, often tyrannically, over other villagers and
of playing the heroic role of a bandoliered *klepht*.

For the leaders of E.A.M., however, resistance to the Germans,
although never abandoned in principle, was always secondary to
the objective of establishing an undisputed political control over
mountain Greece. In the areas dominated by E.L.A.S. a new
Greek state was created which simply by reason of the Axis occupation of towns and lines of communication was centred on the
mountains, bringing to remote areas for the first time in their
political experience the benefits and burdens of detailed and relatively efficient administration in such matters as communications,
taxation, and education. Instead of the indifference of a distant
and centralized bureaucracy whose decisions were taken in the
provincial capital or in Athens, these were often made within the
district under the guerrilla administration. Justice which in criminal

or political cases could be severe, in civil disputes was generally incorrupt. The immediacy of such government was novel and invigorating. It attracted, at first, willing adherents who accepted E.A.M.'s ideal of a new and progressive social order, which indeed in some respects their actions gave hopes of fulfilling. Even during the later stages of the occupation when the communist control of E.A.M. was more widely understood and when forcible recruitment had tempered early enthusiasm, the discipline of E.L.A.S. forces was never seriously threatened.

A corollary of E.A.M.'s political objectives was the need to destroy other resistance movements. In 1942 a number of republicans recruited guerrilla bands. Yet by the middle of 1943 these had been reduced to only two of any significance: a force known by the initials E.D.E.S.[1] under a republican officer, Napoleon Zervas, which controlled an area in the western Pindus, chiefly in Epirus; and a smaller band operating north of Athens known as the 5/42 Regiment, or in its political aspect as E.K.K.A.,[2] led by Colonel Psaros. This reduction in the strength of the non-communist resistance was mainly the consequence of savage aggression by E.L.A.S. In turn each independent band had been assaulted by E.L.A.S. without warning. After the killing, capture, or dispersion of its members it was accused of collaboration with the enemy. In practice many of the men who physically survived these attacks were persuaded to join E.L.A.S., an indication of E.L.A.S.'s confidence in its ability to control new recruits whom it had treated so violently; from the summer of 1943 others, believing that the fight against communism was more important than killing Germans (whose eventual defeat by that time seemed increasingly probable), joined the Security Battalions, formed by the Rallis collaboration government to resist E.L.A.S., and thus justified, if only retrospectively, the accusation that they had cooperated with the enemy.

A dramatic instance of these methods was the destruction of a republican resistance group known by the conventional initials A.A.A. in March 1943. Its leader, General Saraphis, an officer of some distinction, was captured, accused of collaboration, and then offered the position of military commander-in-chief of E.L.A.S. which virtually at pistol point he accepted. For many Greeks at the time the moral force of this exemplary conversion was impressive and reassuring. Yet the appointment was possible only through the tripartite control of E.L.A.S. commands which even at junior levels associated with the military commander a *capetanios* (a

[1] National Republican Greek League.
[2] National and Social Liberation.

politico-military figure) and a political adviser, both of whom were invariably Communists. Under such triumvirates political considerations and principles normally took precedence, indicating clearly the mainly political function of E.L.A.S. Its units could be safely and rapidly expanded for purposes of civil control but it lacked flexibility in military operations. The reverse was generally true of the units of E.D.E.S. which were often well organized for guerrilla warfare under former army officers but were relatively ineffective as instruments of local government.

E.K.K.A. was eventually destroyed by E.L.A.S. in April 1944. E.D.E.S. survived until the end of the occupation only because the British (later, the Allied) Military Mission supported it with money and supplies. The officers of this Mission had originally parachuted into the mountains in 1942 to destroy the railway link between Salonika and Athens which then carried 80 per cent of Rommel's supplies in the period before Alamein. In November the Gorgopotamos viaduct was blown up by a mixed force of guerrillas from E.D.E.S. and E.L.A.S. After this exploit the Mission remained to coordinate the operations of the bands. Its military task however was soon overshadowed by the political problem of preventing E.A.M. from winning an exclusive control over the resistance movement which it did not regard primarily as a military force whose operations should be simply part of the general allied plan. A precarious balance of interests was established between the British Mission and E.A.M. which shifted according to tactical circumstances, the British requiring from E.L.A.S. specific operations against the Germans and a moderation of their hostility to E.D.E.S., E.L.A.S. demanding money, equipment and ammunition, and certain assurances about political arrangements after liberation.

For the K.K.E. the British were a problem. Since the success of E.A.M. depended on its reputation as a patriotic movement it was important both to conceal the degree to which they controlled it and to give every appearance of cooperating with the British. On the other hand, if they were to achieve their ultimate objective of establishing a People's Democracy, it would be necessary both to dominate the resistance movement on the day of liberation so that E.A.M. would exist as an effective provisional government, and to prevent the organization in the Middle East of effective Greek military forces which would support the return of the King as the guarantor of repressive right-wing government devoted to British interests. In its attempt to reconcile temporary expedients with its true objective E.A.M./E.L.A.S. alternated between cooperative gestures and aggression. Thus in July 1943 E.A.M./

M

E.L.A.S. signed a 'National Bands Agreement' under the provisions of which a joint G.H.Q. was established for the resistance forces which at the same time were placed under the operational direction of the Allied Commander in the Middle East. Although these arrangements had little more than a nominal value E.L.A.S. had certainly contributed effectively to the widespread diversionary attacks planned to cover the invasion of Sicily in July by persuading the Germans that a Balkan expedition was intended. But after the Italian capitulation in September E.A.M.'s tactics changed. Convinced that the occupation was about to end and materially strengthened by the equipment they had seized from the Italian Pinerolo Division, E.L.A.S. mounted a violent attack on E.D.E.S. When it became clear, however, that the moment of liberation had not yet arrived and that the British Mission had no intention of allowing Zervas to succumb (although E.D.E.S. was now confined to a limited area in Epirus), a truce was arranged in February 1944.

Checked in its attempt at direct aggression and anxious to recover the popular support which it had lost when the communist loyalties of its leaders and their hostility to other resistance groups became more generally recognized, E.A.M. turned to more subtle methods. On 26 March it established in the mountains a Political Committee of National Liberation (P.E.E.A.) which if not a provisional government in name at least threatened to develop in that sense. In this body E.A.M. invited the participation of radical but non-communist personalities such as Professor Svolos, a respected professor of constitutional law, and other men who had supported E.A.M. without committing themselves to full membership in the movement, but who still naïvely believed that they could guide the impetus of popular revolution into peaceful and revisionist channels. The principal and intended effect of this development was to undermine the position of the exile government of Tsoudheros. After a mutiny in the two Greek brigades in the Middle East in March 1943 this government had been reformed to include a majority of republicans. Its royalist Premier had received a further setback in August of the same year when representatives from both the communist and non-communist resistance on a visit to Cairo had demanded that the King should not return to Greece until the constitutional matter had been submitted to a plebiscite. The establishment of P.E.E.A. in the mountains now offered further grounds for discontented republican officers and politicians in Egypt, probably encouraged by local agents of E.A.M., to pursue their feud against the King, whom they held responsible for the dictatorship of Metaxas and their personal sufferings under it, a feud which they failed to realize had now given place to a more serious division between those who sympathized with the communist-led resistance and those who did not. In April mutiny broke out among the Greek forces in the Middle East, soldiers' committees were formed, and demands were made for a government based on the P.E.E.A. in Greece. And during the same month in Greece, E.A.M., again believing that the occupation was about to end, had allowed its military arm, E.L.A.S., to destroy the bands of E.K.K.A. in southern Roumeli.

For E.A.M. the results of these endeavours were mixed. The British had been forced to disarm the Greek brigades in Egypt and under the impact of these events Tsoudheros had resigned. On the other hand E.A.M. had again miscalculated the timing of the German withdrawal and the British had approved as Prime Minister of the exile government George Papandhreou, no less of an anti-communist than he was a devoted republican. This he proved in May at a skilfully managed conference in the Lebanon attended by representatives of the principal political and resistance movements. Supported by the consensus of republican opinion he manoeuvred the E.A.M. representatives into a position where they were persuaded to sign the Lebanon Charter whose provisions, it was agreed, were to serve as the basis for a government of National Unity in which they were pledged to serve and to whose authority their military forces would be submitted.

Yet although this was an important victory for the anti-communist forces among the Greeks in exile it had little effect in the mountains of occupied Greece. E.A.M. repudiated the signatures of their representatives at the conference and as a condition for their participation in a national government demanded Ministries which Papandhreou would obviously not be willing to concede. Since February E.A.M. had known that only token forces of allied troops would re-enter Greece when the Germans withdrew. In the early summer the plans elaborated in 1943 to seize power in Athens during the critical transition period before the allies arrived were still in readiness. It would be politically difficult, to say the least, for the British Commander, even if he had the necessary forces, to overthrow a 'popular' provisional government already in position. Nevertheless, quite suddenly, E.A.M. conceded the substance of Papandhreou's conditions, accepted on 2 September the six Ministries offered to it in a government of National Unity, none of which in itself gave particular access to power, and in the same month at Caserta in Italy signed a military agreement in common with their only resistance rivals, E.D.E.S., under which these forces were submitted to the authority of the national government of Papandhreou which in turn placed them under the command of General Scobie, the designated British Commander of the allied liberation force.

The event which may have precipitated this fundamental change in policy was the arrival at E.L.A.S. Headquarters in July 1944 of a Soviet Military Mission led by Colonel Popov. He brought unwelcome news of the bargain struck earlier that summer between Churchill and Stalin which reserved Greece as a predominantly British interest. His instructions to the K.K.E. were to avoid open opposition, accept representation in the government, and work indirectly towards their ultimate objective. It is instructive that with the prize of absolute power almost in their hands the communist leaders submitted without audible protest. As the Germans withdrew E.A.M. joined in the general emotional welcome for their British allies. On 18 October amid popular rejoicing the government of Papandhreou arrived in Athens. And until almost the end of November the E.A.M. Ministers worked responsibly and cooperatively with their new colleagues. The opportunity to seize power, it seemed, had passed.

The difference which nevertheless was now to plunge the country into destructive civil war was the problem of disarming guerrilla formations and reforming a national army. It seemed at first that an acceptable formula had been found. The nucleus of a national army would be created from one brigade of E.L.A.S. and one brigade raised from the resources of the troops trained overseas and from E.D.E.S. All other formations were to be demobilized. The logic of their original acceptance of Popov's instructions might have persuaded E.A.M. to adopt a solution based on the principle of parity. But before this fateful decision the K.K.E. were intensely aware that they were about to abandon a military superiority in men and materials which in normal circumstances could not recur. The temptation to revert to the original policy of seizing power by force was strengthened by the discovery that the British forces were even weaker in combat units than they had imagined. It is also probable that Tito offered them moral support in this reappraisal of their position, and that the Russians, while warning them to expect no external assistance or recognition, now relented to the extent of not forbidding them to make the attempt.

The revolution began on 3 December when police fired on demonstrators in Constitution Square. But the decision to fight had been taken several days before by the communist leaders Siantos and Ioannides and already the moderate non-Communists within E.A.M. had been defeated in their attempts to find a compromise, as it was always virtually certain they would be. Bitter and hazardous street fighting between E.L.A.S. and the unprepared British lasted throughout December and into January. From a situation where they had almost lost control of Athens the British gradually restored the position at the cost of transferring two infantry divisions and other units from the Italian theatre. By the end of the first week in January E.L.A.S. began to withdraw from the capital.

The fighting had not prevented political contacts between the two sides. On Christmas Day Churchill and Eden arrived in Athens. But their presence at the opening of a conference on the next day did little to soften the attitude of the communist leader Siantos who made demands, for instance for half the Ministries in the national government, which he must have known would be rejected. The only point of agreement was the establishment of a regency under the Archbishop of Athens, Damaskinos, who took the oath of this office on 31 December. By 10 January, however, E.L.A.S. under severe British pressure were asking for a truce which was arranged with effect from 15 January.

Nevertheless the Varkiza agreement signed on 12 February 1945 which resulted from the peace talks following the truce was not unfavourable to E.A.M. The British wanted a settlement before the Yalta Conference and they knew from the experience of the Germans that with their limited forces they could not effectively subdue E.L.A.S. which still held two-thirds of the country under its control. Moreover, when E.L.A.S. withdrew from Athens they had abducted many thousands of hostages and although the harsh circumstances of forced marches and sometimes summary executions had caused a sharp reaction of public opinion both in Greece and abroad, the fate of these unfortunate people was nevertheless a bargaining counter. As a result the Varkiza agreement permitted the K.K.E. to operate as a legitimate party for its entirely illegal purposes. And although Siantos accepted an amnesty which safeguarded the communist hierarchy from prosecution for political crimes but did less to protect the more humble rank and file, this too was an advantage since the experience or fear of persecution would soon persuade, or oblige, many to take up arms again when the next attempt to seize power was made. For the K.K.E. Varkiza was a necessary respite to regroup their forces. For the British it apparently marked the end of a successful struggle to prevent the Communists from winning power. Although this judgement was soon to be proved illusory, it is true that but for the efforts of the British Military Mission[1] in occupied Greece to protect E.D.E.S.

[1] Commanded at first by Brigadier E. C. W. Myers, and later by Colonel C. M. Woodhouse.

and restrain E.L.A.S. Greece would already have been effectively under the control of the Communist Party on the day of liberation. Even as it was, if the British had not had the resolution to restore the situation in December 1944 in the face of hostile opinion both in England and America it is difficult to see what could have eventually prevented the establishment of a communist state.

Thirty-three days of civil war had cost the Greek people eleven thousand dead and damage to property estimated at 250 million dollars. Yet when Zachariades, the former Secretary-General of K.K.E., returned to Greece on 30 May 1945 from the concentration camp of Dachau to resume his interrupted leadership of the party, he was soon demanding preparations for a new armed conflict to destroy the monarcho-fascist regime.

By the spring of 1946 certain factors might have been thought to justify this call. A succession of caretaker governments had failed to make much impression on the problem of reconstruction and monetary stability. Right-wing excesses were driving those who were suspected of having shown sympathy to E.A.M. to return, often unwillingly, to the communist camp. The prisons which before the December revolution had held collaborators and members of the Security Battalions, were now more populated with men of E.L.A.S. charged with common crimes against life and property. Heroes and villains had changed places to the moral confusion of many. There was, too, a new and critical advantage for the Communists in the northern frontiers with Albania, Yugoslavia, and Bulgaria, countries now within the Soviet sphere of influence. Tito, anxious to extend his influence in Macedonia, offered material support and a military training camp at Boulkes for Greek guerrillas in return for approval of the unification of a greater Macedonia which required territorial concessions from Greece. But these possibilities were as yet unknown outside the hierarchy of the K.K.E. With the British finding it increasingly difficult either to afford their military presence in Greece, or to justify it diplomatically against the public attacks of the Russians, their ability to protect a Greek government against a renewed uprising might be limited.

Attacks on exposed villages in the area of Mount Olympus at the end of March 1946 were an early warning of the new attempt at revolution. Secretly E.L.A.S. had hidden considerable stores of weapons and ammunition and cadres of the more seasoned and devoted fighters had never been dispersed. Throughout the summer a campaign of small-scale guerrilla attacks on villages was continued in northern and central Greece. In Athens the K.K.E., which remained a legitimate party, inveighed against the fascist oppression of democratic citizens defending their liberties in traditional klephtic style. With the appointment on 26 October of Markos Vafiades as military commander-in-chief of the Democratic Army of Greece, as the insurgent forces were now styled, the struggle entered a more intensive phase. Against classic guerrilla hit and run methods the government forces made little progress, handicapped by the unwillingness of terrified villagers to give them information, and tied to a concept of static defence which immobilized large numbers of troops in small detachments vulnerable to the rapid concentration of guerrilla forces.

Despite these successes we can see in retrospect that the insurrection had few hopes of ultimate success. Already in 1946 the political tide was running strongly against it. The Populists won the election in March and the plebiscite in September brought back King George who now became even for republicans a natural focus of anti-communist commitment. The knowledge of the American support for Greece under the Truman doctrine in March 1947 was a critical development. It indicated a limit beyond which the Americans would not tolerate Soviet expansion. On 23 May the U.N. Special Committee on the Balkans (U.N.S.C.O.B.) reported that Albania, Yugoslavia, and Bulgaria had been actively assisting the revolutionary movement. Only the representatives of the U.S.S.R. and Poland disagreed with this majority conclusion. Although it was true that in 1945 repressive reaction after the collapse of the December revolution had confirmed the left-wing loyalties of many Greeks, such persons had not represented a majority. Already many of those whose political position towards the end of the occupation might have been described as republican, radical, and not unsympathetic towards E.A.M., had been alienated by the events of December. Heartened by the moral and practical support Greece was now receiving from the outside world the majority wished only for peace and stability. By 1947 there was no spontaneous popular basis for armed revolution. In areas which they did not dominate at any moment by the intimidation of their physical presence the Democratic Army won few willing recruits except among the small Slavophone minority in Macedonia.

In these circumstances where they could hope for no political demonstration of support among the general public or serious disaffection in the national army, the only hope of further progress was to seize and hold an administrative centre and a continuous stretch of territory which they could claim to govern. Such a policy Markos realized would expose a guerrilla army to the superior numbers and equipment of the national army's conventional forces, but his technical judgement was overruled by Zachariades, the political leader of the K.K.E. The political aspect of this decision to wage this kind of 'conventional' warfare was the establishment on Christmas Eve 1947 of the 'Interim Democratic Government' in the mountains. The response of the royal government was to outlaw, at last, the Communist Party of Greece.

From the outset this new phase of the struggle was unfortunate for the insurgents. After the death of his brother in March 1947 King Paul had proved to be a less controversial figure. With the veteran Liberal politician Sophoulis as his Premier the non-communist political world in Greece was temporarily united behind this partnership. On the other hand the U.S.S.R. failed to give formal recognition to the Interim Democratic Government. Stalin was unwilling to risk a collision with the Americans over the Greek issue and exceedingly irritated with Tito's independent manoeuvres in the Balkans, of which his support of the Democratic Army was a part. Moreover, after Yugoslavia was expelled from the Cominform in June 1948 Tito's gradual change of attitude towards the West brought a corresponding reduction in his aid to the Greek guerrillas.

As Markos had foreseen, without the assistance of a foreign army of conventional forces the policy of attacking and holding larger towns was not a success. The first attempt, against Konitsa during the last days of 1947, was a failure. The longest occupation of a town achieved by the Democratic Army was at Karpenisi which was held from 21 January to 8 February 1949. By that time Markos had been dismissed and Zachariades had assumed strategic as well as political control of the war. Meanwhile during 1948 the national army had received recruits, equipment, and training which greatly increased its effectiveness. It now attacked well defined areas which were encircled by several lines of advancing forces. Operations in any area were relentlessly continued until the last guerrilla detachment had been destroyed or captured. In certain difficult and mountainous areas the entire population was evacuated to deny the enemy the food and intelligence without which he could not survive. Under the leadership of Marshal Papagos, appointed Commander-in-Chief in January 1949, the final major operation of the war was successfully completed on 30 August against the stronghold of the Democratic Army on Mount Grammos, where its forces were trapped and forced to fight a conventional battle against artillery and aircraft in which it could not hope to prevail. Already a critical blow to the insurgents' morale and tactics had been delivered by Tito, who had originally encouraged their hopes in 1946, and now ended them in July 1949 by closing the frontier across which in the intervening years supplies had passed in one direction, and guerrilla units had withdrawn to refit in the other. The 'Third Round', as the civil war of 1946–49 came to be known, was over.

For long periods during the second civil war between 1947 and 1949 Greece was on the brink of collapse. Only massive American support in materials, money, and military advice, had saved her from eventual absorption in the communist world. Dependence on great powers which had characterized Greece's history since the establishment of the modern state was never more evident than in her reliance on the American presence during these years to preserve the Greek version of parliamentary government and a free economy. These institutions were now grievously weakened by the new schism in the nation between those who sympathized with the communist order of society, or were alleged to do so, and those who did not, a division which compromised the position of men who looked for moderate and practical solutions of Greece's moral and economic dilemmas.

PART THREE

Two Aspects of Culture

Chapter 6

The Orthodox Church in Greece

G REECE IS now the only country in the world that is officially an Orthodox Christian country. What does this mean in practice? The answer would seem to have two main aspects. One concerns the whole official and administrative status and organization of the Church in Greece; the other the effect Orthodox Christianity has as a vital force in the lives of the Greek people.

We have already noted[1] how after the Fall of Constantinople in 1453 one of the first acts of the conqueror Mahomet II was to permit the election of a new Patriarch; and it was the Sultan himself who personally invested the chosen candidate, George Scholarios, with the words: 'Be Patriarch, preserve our friendship and receive all the privileges that the Patriarchs, your predecessors, possessed.' In fact, from one point of view the privileges that the new Patriarch received from the Islamic protector of Orthodoxy were far greater than those possessed by his predecessors; for they included not only his own personal inviolability (and, through him, that of all the bishops) and exemption from taxes, but also civil authority over all the Christians of the Ottoman Empire. For in Islamic eyes all the Christian subjects of the Sultan, irrespective of their different confessionals, liturgical practices, or language, constituted a single nation – the nation (*millet*) of the Christians; and this nation, although conquered and bound therefore to acknowledge the Muslim 'ascendancy' and to pay tribute to the Muslim state as a token of its submission, nevertheless according to Islamic sacred law must still be left in charge of its own affairs, administer its justice, levy its taxes, and in other ways continue as a self-governing unit. Moreover, again in Islamic eyes, there was no difference between the civil, or temporal, and the spiritual head of such a nation: the Patriarch, that is, was a kind of Khalif, uniting in himself both civil and ecclesiastical authority, Patriarch and Emperor, and was responsible only to the Sultan. He became an 'ethnarch' (*millet-bashi*), with a power far greater than he possessed prior to the Turkish conquest, a power extending not only over the Christians of his own Patriarchate but also over those of other

[1] See Chapter 1.

Orthodox Patriarchates and even over all non-Orthodox Christians within the Ottoman Empire.

The effect of this extension of power on the Greek hierarchy was of course immense. To start with, the decentralized organization of the Orthodox Churches was centralized; the Patriarch of Constantinople was now regarded as 'head' of the local Churches (in much the same way as the Pope of Rome was regarded in the Latin West), with all temporal and juridical authority vested in his office. The other Patriarchs, those of Alexandria, Antioch, and Jerusalem, although theoretically independent, were in fact reduced to a position of inferiority in relation to the Patriarch of Constantinople, since the latter was the sole intermediary through whom they could communicate with the Porte, and it was he alone who could apply for the *berets* of their nomination. Subaltern Metropolitans in their turn became civil governors responsible for civil jurisdiction, enjoined, in the words of Mahomet II, 'to watch day and night over those entrusted to their guidance, to observe their conduct and to discover and report their lawless action to my government'; and they looked upon, and addressed, the holder of the Oecumenical throne as 'their sovereign, their emperor, and their Patriarch';[1] while in recognition of his new titles the Patriarch wore a mitre in the form of the imperial crown, set his throne upon a carpet bearing the image of the Roman eagle, and let his hair grow in the manner of the Emperor and civil dignitaries of Byzantium. Of his governmental system, the Holy Synod at Constantinople was the supreme administrative body, also a fact which had unhealthy consequences. For not only did it result in a centralization of power that led to bitter antagonism between members of the Synod, with the Patriarch of Constantinople at their head, and the Metropolitans; but also it meant that the highest secular offices of the 'Christian nation' were in the hands of the Church, and were accessible only through the Church, or through the Church admitting lay members to the Synod: in the one case, positions in the higher ranks of the clergy would be sought only because of the temporal possibilities they provided; in the other case, laymen, admitted to the Synod for their administrative capacities – if indeed even for these – were given an opportunity to submit the policy and affairs of the Church to interests completely foreign to its mission. This opportunity was exploited particularly in the eighteenth century, when members of the Phanariot families, with schemes for restoring the Byzantine Empire, were admitted to the Synod in this way.

Another consequence of the new status of the Patriarch of Con-

[1] *Historia patriarchica*, ed. Bonn, p. 177.

stantinople and his subordinate Greek hierarchy was their participation in the system of immense corruption that was inextricably
interwoven with the affairs of the Porte. Although the Patriarch was
theoretically chosen by the Synod, the Turkish government not
only could intervene and depose him on a pretext provided by any
single member of the Synod, but it also required the payment of a
sum of money specified each time in the *beret* of investiture. This
was responsible for the development of an intricate simoniacal
pattern, which began by the Patriarch buying his 'election' from
the Turkish authorities, was extended to include all other episcopal
elections (for all had to be approved by the Sultan's *beret*), and
spread finally through all the ranks of the clergy down to the lay
element of the Christian community itself. 'The Authority,' writes
Sir George Wheler in the seventeenth century, 'which they [the
Greek Patriarchs of Constantinople] thus obtain by Simony, they
maintain by Tyranny: for as soon as they are promoted, they send
to all their Bishops, to contribute to the Sum they have disbursed
for their Preferment; and such as deny, they depose, and send others
to their Charge. Again, the Bishops send to their inferiour Clergy;
who are forced to do the same to the poor people, or to spare it out
of their Wives and Childrens Mouths. But many times they engage
for more than they can perform; and bring the Church so much in
debt to the Turk, that its Ruin is daily threatened thereby.'[1] The
extent to which this system of corruption affected the Patriarchate
may be indicated by the fact that in the eighteenth century, one
of the darkest periods for the Greek hierarchy, forty-eight Patriarchs
occupied the holy office in the space of sixty-three years.

A third consequence of the Patriarch's new role as head of the
'Christian nation' was that it became increasingly difficult for the
hierarchy to distinguish between national interests and strictly
ecclesiastical policy, in the sense that the latter was more and more
influenced by the pressures of the former; and as both Patriarch
and the senior members of the hierarchy, and especially of the Holy
Synod, tended to be Greeks, national interests themselves became
more and more identified with purely Greek interests. This had
unfortunate consequences not only where other ethnic groups of
Christians within the Ottoman Empire and hence under the
jurisdiction of Constantinople were concerned. (A reaction to
nationalistic pressures exercised by the Constantinopolitan Greek
hierarchy during the period of the Turkish occupation of the
Balkans can be seen in the alacrity with which the Churches in
Romania, Bulgaria, and Serbia sought to establish their independence of the Patriarchate of Constantinople as soon as opportunity

[1] *A Journey to Greece*, London (1682), p. 195.

arose in the nineteenth century.) It had unfortunate consequences also where the Greek Church itself was concerned; for it meant that Orthodoxy and Hellenism became more and more entangled. This confusion was made worse both by the proselytizing enterprises of Roman Catholics in Greek lands, and especially of the Jesuits; and by the corresponding attempts of Protestant powers (England, the Low Countries) to win the allegiance of the Patriarch as head of the 'Christian nation' in their political rivalries with Roman Catholic powers (France, Austria). The result, in the theological sphere, was that Orthodox theologians were often led into using the arguments of Protestants against the Roman Catholics, and those of Roman Catholics against the Protestants; while in the ecclesiastical sphere the prophetic action of the Church during the period of the Turkish occupation tended to be concerned less with the new life of the Gospel than with the freeing of the (Greek) fatherland from foreign subjugation. As, in the way we have seen, the revival of the Greek nation was conceived increasingly in terms of a revival of Hellenism, the Church in its nationalistic role found itself in the ironic position of becoming the instrument for the propagation of the fundamentally non-Christian values of this Hellenism. Thus in the seventeenth century it was the Patriarch who appointed Theophyllos Corydaleus, the apostle of the new 'Aristotelian' materialism in Orthodox lands, to the directorship of the Patriarchal Academy at Constantinople; and we have already noted some of the implications of this appointment. Similarly it was the Patriarch who in the eighteenth century, in order to stimulate the spread of Hellenism, established on Mount Athos, the stronghold of Orthodoxy, a college of higher education to the direction of which he appointed the leading Greek representative of western enlightenment and scientific rationalism, Eugenios Boulgaris. (The monks of Athos, conscious perhaps that the purposes of such a college were at odds with their own way of life, set fire to it and destroyed it.)

As a result of all this the position of the Greek hierarchy at the end of the eighteenth century was scarcely less than desperate. Confusing 'Church' and 'nation', 'Orthodoxy' and 'Hellenism'; practically its whole dogmatic literature during the period of the Turkish occupation concerned to point out, often in the most banal terms, the 'errors' and 'heresies' of the Latins, while at the same time in its efforts to resist Protestant infiltration it borrowed arguments and concepts directly from Latin scholasticism; condemning when it was too late the 'new philosophy' of the West which in the name of Hellenism it had been among the first to sponsor; its higher clergy corrupt and in any case penetrated by the lay and 'enlightened' spirit of the Phanariot aristocracy: it is scarcely surprising, in view of all this, that its purely Orthodox character was, to say the least, often compromised. Yet to a considerable extent this situation can be seen as the direct consequence of the dual role, spiritual and temporal, imposed by the Sultan on the Patriarch of Constantinople after the fall of that city to the Turks; for it meant that the Patriarch's loyalties were divided and in a sense irreconcilable. As political head of the Sultan's Christian subjects he was responsible first of all to the Sultan, and any failure here could result in his deposition or worse. As head of the nation of Greek Christians, he had allegiances and responsibilities towards the Greeks in their effort to throw off the Turkish yoke. As the chief Orthodox bishop he was also responsible for the continuity and integrity of the Orthodox Christian tradition, the values of which are certainly not those of Hellenism. Thus as head of the Greek nation, he often found himself using his position to serve interests radically opposed in spirit to his other responsibilities. The lamentable implications of this came to a head first in the execution by the Sultan, on Easter day in April 1821, directly after the outbreak of the Greek war of Independence, of the Patriarch Gregory V, with several other prelates and lay dignitaries, because he had failed to avert (though he had rigorously condemned) the insurrection of the Greek people; and second in the unilateral act by which in 1833 – almost directly, that is to say, after the setting up of the Greek national state – an assembly of Greek bishops demonstrated its regard for the services the Patriarch of Constantinople had rendered the Greek nation during the years of the Turkish occupation (services for which Gregory V had paid with his life) by approving legislation severing the Greek Church from the Patriarch's jurisdiction and proclaiming it autocephalous within the limits of the new state.

It would none the less be unjust to give the impression that the role of the Orthodox Church during the period of the Turkish occupation of Greek lands was largely negative. This is far from being the case. The task alone of preserving the Orthodox tradition through this period was itself an immense one, often requiring great heroism and endurance. For while it is true that the Turkish authorities undertook no direct religious persecution, yet pressures were brought to bear in other ways. The Christians had a place in the Islamic order of society, but it was an inferior place, and their religion was an inferior religion. They had to pay heavy taxes and to wear a distinctive dress. They were subjected to social and economic inducements to change their religion, they were forbidden to marry Muslim women, while to convert a Muslim, or for a

N

Christian who had become a Muslim to revert again to Christianity, was a crime punishable by death. The Turkish period is not the least rich in martyrs for the Christian faith – the New Martyrs, as they have been called. In the face of these pressures what is really surprising is not that certain abuses should have infiltrated into the hierarchy and the administration of the Church, but that the liturgical and dogmatic structure of the Church should have survived at all. As Sir Paul Ricaut wrote in his book, *The Present State of the Greek and Armenian Churches, Anno Christi 1678,*[1] the state of the Greek Church is 'Tragical, the subversion of the Sanctuaries of Religion, the Royal Priesthood expelled their Churches, and those converted into Mosques; the Mysteries of the altar conceal'd in secret and dark places; for such I have seen in Cities and Villages where I have travelled, rather like Vaults or Sepulchres than Churches, having their Roofs almost levelled with the Superficies of the Earth, lest the most ordinary exsurgency of structure should be accused for triumph of Religion, and to stand in competition with the lofty Spires of Mahometan Mosques.' And elsewhere,[2] Ricaut acknowledges the extraordinary tenacity and faith demanded of the Christians in keeping their religion alive at all: 'It is no wonder to human reason that considers the oppression and the contempt that poor Christians are exposed to, and the ignorance in their Churches, occasioned through Poverty in the Clergy, that many should be found who retreat from the Faith; but it is rather a Miracle, and a true verification of those words of Christ, *That the Gates of Hell shall not be able to prevail against his Church*, that there is conserved still amidst so much opposition, and in despite of all Tyranny and Arts contrived against it, an open and public Profession of the Christian Faith.'

For during these years of Turkish occupation the Greek peasant people did remain a dominantly Christian people, living in the light of a Christian interpretation of life. First, the monasteries, most concentrated on the Holy Mountain of Athos, but also existing in great numbers over the whole of the Balkans, were centres for the practice of the strict ascetic tradition of Orthodox spirituality inherited from Byzantium. This tradition had itself undergone a deep inner renewal in the centuries immediately preceding the fall of Constantinople, when the challenge of various rationalizing philosophies, whether from the Latin West or from within Byzantium itself, led to a reappraisal of its doctrinal principles and to an intensification of its spiritual practices in their

[1] 1679, pp. 11–12.
[2] *The History of the Present State of the Ottoman Empire* (1668), 5th ed., 1682, p. 149.

hesychastic form. Of this renewal, figures like St Gregory Palamas and Nicholas Cabasilas were outstanding representatives; and that this hesychastic tradition to which they bore witness in their writings and lives remained fully alive throughout the period of the Turkish occupation is indicated by the publication, at Venice in 1782, of a large collection of spiritual writings, particularly on the subject of prayer, gathered from authors from the fourth to the fifteenth centuries. This anthology, called the *Philokalia*, and compiled by a monk of Athos, St Nicodemus the Hagiorite (1748–1809), with the help of St Macarius, Metropolitan of Corinth, is perhaps the most important Orthodox work published during the last five hundred years or so; its influence has been felt not only among Greek-speaking Christians but also, through translations either whole or partial into languages which include Slavonic, Russian, Romanian, English, and French, throughout the whole Christian world and beyond. St Nicodemus was the author, editor, or translator of several other important spiritual works, some of them derived (though generally with modifications to suit them for Orthodox readers) directly from Roman Catholic writers (Lorenzo Scupoli, Ignatius Loyola). Although original theological works during this period are few, and not in any case of much distinction, the fact that the tradition of monastic life, based upon the spiritual teachings of the great Fathers of the Church, continued to be practised is ultimately of far greater significance.

Then, second, the people of the villages, in any case in close touch with the life of the monasteries and for the most part providing their members, remained linked intimately to the mysteries of the Christian faith through the great liturgical cycle of the Orthodox Church. The Orthodox liturgy is not simply a piece of static ritual or an elaborate but ultimately aesthetic spectacle. On the contrary, it is a theology made visible whose 'mysteries' (the sacraments) constitute the basis of Orthodox spirituality. Into it are woven extracts and reminiscences from the Bible, the theology of the Fathers, the dogmas of the Oecumenical Councils, all transmuted into an intense and moving dramatic form. Moreover, this liturgical poetry and action is not something that the priest performs or recites in isolation from the people; it is itself the work of the people, a drama in which they intimately participate (in fact, no liturgy may take place without the participation of the lay element). Thus through its character at once communal and doctrinal, of great sensual richness and symbolic austerity, dramatic and metaphysic, the liturgy in itself and quite apart from any more academic instruction, has immense didactic qualities. From this point of view it may be understood how the very isolation of the Church in Greek lands during this period, the fact that its role became chiefly one fo preserving the liturgical inheritance of Byzantium, may be seen to have positive aspects of considerable significance; for it meant first that, on the popular level at least, it remained almost totally unaffected by those various movements – struggles between the Papacy and the Conciliar-minded bishops, Reformation, Counter-Reformation, and so on – that so confused religious life in western Christendom; and second that the form of the Christian faith to which Greek-speaking Christians clung so tenaciously was one that enshrined and actualized its mysteries in a most vivid and unadulterated manner. It is above all due to the liturgy, loyally celebrated by simple priests among their village congregations, that the Greek peasant people emerged from the period of Turkish occupation as still dominantly an Orthodox people.

With the setting up of the national Greek state after the war of Independence, the status of the ecclesiastical hierarchy and the whole administrative system of the Church in the new kingdom underwent profound modifications. First of all, as we have remarked, the jurisdiction of the Patriarch of Constantinople over Greek Churches was repudiated, ostensibly on the grounds that it was unfitting for a Patriarchate still situated in Turkish territory to possess the right to intervene in any of the internal affairs of the liberated nation. In 1833, the National Assembly meeting at Nauplion, then still the capital of Greece, passed a resolution decreeing, among other things, that 'the Eastern Orthodox Church of Greece is dependent on no external authority, and spiritually owns no head but the Founder of the Christian Church.' This proclamation of an autocephalous national Church of Greece, made without any reference to the Oecumenical Patriarch or to the other Patriarchs and bishops of the Orthodox Church, was signed by thirty bishops in the new kingdom, and was immediately followed by a 'reform' of the Greek Church on the model of the reforms carried out by Peter the Great in Russia. After vigorous but vain protest the Patriarch recognized the new situation of the Church in Greece in a Patriarchal decree (*tomos*) issued in 1850, though it was stipulated that the Church of Greece should maintain the faith and canons of unity with other Orthodox communities; should refer matters of dogma, or any matters touching the faith, to Constantinople; and should apply to Constantinople for *Myron* (Holy Oil) blessed by the Patriarch. Except for the last, these conditions were of small immediate consequence, for by its new charter the management of church affairs in Greece was placed in practice very much under the control of the state. In effect, by the statute law of 1833 and a subsequent enactment in 1852, the government of the

Church was entrusted to a Holy Synod under the presidency of the Archbishop of Athens, but no decision of the Synod was to be held valid or to be executed unless signed by the government commissioner (procurator). The charter of 1852 further enacts that 'the Eastern Orthodox Church is and will continue to be the religion of the state, and that the state shall also appoint as many bishops and as many priests as necessary. The state will also make provision for their maintenance, and will also undertake the administration of Church property, such as the estates of the monasteries.'

Subsequent charters (1923, 1925, 1931, 1939, 1943) have modified but not substantially changed this position, and the hierarchy still remains very dependent on the state. It is rarely that this dependence is so abused as it was, for instance, during the political upheavals in 1917 and after, when both the Archbishop of Athens and other bishops were deposed and appointed according to whether they were supporters of King Constantine or Venizelos; or as it was during the Venizelist adventure in August 1935, when all members of the Holy Synod were deposed on purely political grounds. But state influence in church affairs is still very real. It was decisively reaffirmed in 1959 during disputes over the election of a new Archbishop of Athens, and even more drastically reaffirmed after the *coup* of April 1967, when the actual Archbishop of Athens was 'retired' and another was elected in his place. The present organization of the Church is in fact largely as laid down in the law of 1931, though this again has been slightly modified by the government that took over after the *coup* of April 1967. The chief hierarch is the Blessed Archbishop of Athens and of all Greece. He is life president of the assembly of bishops and of the permanent Holy Synod. When his throne is vacant, a plenary assembly of bishops chooses three names by ballot, and these are then submitted to the Minister of Religious Affairs who selects the new Archbishop. Much the same system applies for the election of other bishops, only here it is the Holy Synod that sends three names to the Minister. As is evident, the system allows considerable scope for the political 'packing' of episcopal sees by the government, should it so desire.

Technically, the supreme authority in matters ecclesiastical is the ruling bishops assembled in a council that normally meets every three years; but the directing administrative body, exercising full ecclesiastical powers subject to the canons and the bishops, is the permanent Synod. This consists, under the presidency of the Archbishop, of some bishops from the eparchies included in the original new kingdom of Greece and others from sees detached from Constantinople later, as for instance those 'annexed' by the Holy Synod of Athens, in spite of the Patriarch's protest, in the Ionian islands when these were ceded to Greece in 1864, or those similarly annexed after the Russo–Turkish war (1879) in Thessaly and part of Epirus. In addition, sees in other parts of northern Greece (which became part of Greece in 1913), though still nominally dependent on the Patriarch, send representatives to the Synod at Athens. The government procurator must also be present at the meetings of the Synod, though he no longer has the right of veto. In certain internal matters, such as disputes between bishops and clergy, the Synod has direct legal powers, though it can take no direct action against heresy or proselytism, but must rely in this respect on the state. Further, the Synod must cooperate with state arrangements at public functions and at services held at the request of the state, while any encyclicals, or letters, to any state department from the Synod must be submitted through the Ministry of Religious Affairs. No new translation of the Scriptures may appear without the authorization of the Synod – the publication without such authorization of two translations of the New Testament (that of A. A. Pallis in 1901 and that of Queen Olga a few years later) were the occasion of riots in Athens. Finally – and it is here perhaps that the official status of the Church is most strongly felt – no marriage in Greece is legally valid unless celebrated in the Church; and no divorce can be granted unless it is sanctioned by the Church.

The question of the effect of Orthodox Christianity not simply as the official religion of the state but as a spiritual force in the lives of the Greek people itself has two aspects. The first concerns the character of Orthodoxy itself; the second, the extent to which the faith as a faith is practised, and the manner in which it is practised.

We have noted that it was above all on account of the liturgy that the Greek peasant people remained dominantly a Christian people through the period of the Turkish occupation. The liturgy of the Orthodox Church in Greece is the whole complex of rite and worship inherited directly from Byzantium, and still largely involves the same forms and rubrics as those used in Byzantine times. Hence immediately the fact of the enormous historical continuity of the liturgy, and therefore of the spiritual tradition which the liturgy expresses. These liturgical forms may be regarded as a kind of sacred deposit, a guarantee that the 'ways of the Fathers' and 'the faith formerly communicated to the Saints' are not abandoned. This makes the Orthodox suspicious of any modernization, or of drastic reform designed to meet what are called the changing conditions of the world and the needs of the time. On the other hand this loyalty to a formal structure does not, in itself, mean a rigid inflexibility or a blind adherence to externals, though the danger that it will degenerate into this is always present and both individually and collectively excessive formalism may on occasion deaden the living spirit of the tradition. But properly understood and experienced, this formal elaboration of the liturgy is an unfolding and making visible of the inner life of the Church, a manifestation ultimately of the Kingdom of Heaven; and the loyalty with which it is preserved is due in the final analysis to the fact that through it and through the mysteries it enshrines, the worshipper feels himself brought into the presence of the original vision that inspires it.

This perhaps is but another way of saying that the Orthodox people constitute first of all what may be called a community of common worship. Although partly because of the civil role conferred on the Greek hierarchy during the Turkish period, and partly for other reasons, there has arisen a certain degree of separation between priest and congregation, a certain degree of 'clericalism', none the less the liturgy has been and still remains very much the 'work of the people', of which the hierarchy is the voice and instrument. This importance of the lay element is in fact intimately bound up with the whole Orthodox idea of the Church. The Church is the Body of Christ, and the members of this Body are the people of Christ uniting in the local churches. There is nothing similar in the Orthodox tradition to those corporational theories developed by the legal canonists and publicists of the Roman Church in the twelfth and thirteenth centuries, according to which the Church is conceived as a *corpus mysticum* or a *persona mystica* regarded as an abstract juridical entity that must be represented by a single person on earth; nor consequently is there the notion that derives from these theories, that the distinctions between the local communities must be absorbed in the all-inclusiveness of the universal ecclesiastical corporation. The Orthodox Church is very much a communion of local churches, whose universal nature is testified by the unity of its faith; and the guardian of the unity of this faith is ultimately the whole congregation of the faithful. It is the Christian people who are the final authority in the Church on earth: as the Encyclical of the Orthodox Patriarchs issued in 1848 puts it: 'the guardian of Orthodoxy is the body of the Church, i.e. the members themselves'. Neither pope, patriarch, nor council constitutes the final authority; final authority and responsibility rests with the people; it is expressed through the councils of the bishops, but it is still the responsibility of the congregation of the faithful to confirm, check, and if necessary to reject decisions of episcopal councils. Both in local matters and in matters concerning the whole community of the local churches, the peasant may come into conflict with the prelate and it may be the prelate who must admit his error. And where the liturgy is concerned (and it must be remembered that the liturgy unites dogma, worship, and life into a single whole), this fundamentally local and popular character of Orthodoxy is brought out by the fact that the liturgical language is that of the people to whom it is addressed, and is further emphasized by the fact that the majority of priests are married. Thus loyalty to the Holy Tradition of the Church, immutable and obligatory, is matched by the sense that this tradition is not something imposed on the people by some central authority whose task it is to make dogmatic and ecclesiastical decisions; but is on the contrary the creation of the 'liberty of the children of God' whose responsibility it is.

The daily, weekly, annual, and Easter cycles of the liturgy providing in this way the forms of the corporate and social act of common worship, it is clear that the building in which they are celebrated must also be of central importance. The church is regarded as a sacred space, the mirror of the Kingdom of God, or the house of God, and each architectural member has its place in a coordinated symbolic structure. Thus the sanctuary is the image of the spiritual world, of which the altar is the heart. It is separated from the main body of the church – the nave – by a screen or *iconostasis*. Originally this was a fairly low barrier, not more than chest high, but by the fifteenth and sixteenth centuries it had, as a result of various developments all tending to surround the mysteries with a greater secrecy, been elevated considerably, so much so that it is only possible to see the sanctuary through the central, or royal, door, which itself may be, and during certain moments of the liturgy usually is, closed. (This raising of the screen is also a symptom of the improper separation of priest from congregation, and the present tendency is to lower it again to its original height.) But in either moderate or raised form the *iconostasis* has also a symbolic meaning, being regarded as the dividing line between two worlds, the Divine and the human, or the spiritual and the sensible worlds. At the same time it also unites these two worlds into one. The icons which are placed upon it also have this double function, representing as they do the world of the imagination that stands midway between the sensible and the spiritual, separating one from the other and at the same time opening on to both. The main body of the church divided from the sanctuary in this manner – the nave – signifies the eschatological vessel or ark bearing the 'children of God' through the troubled seas of the sensible world. The usual form of the church is a cross-in-square type, surmounted by a central dome, and in this union of dome and cross is seen the union of heaven and earth, or of the two natures of the Incarnate Christ, the theandric mystery of the Church.

Mention has just been made of the icons on the screen or *iconostasis* standing between the sanctuary and the nave; and not only are icons placed on other stands or hung on walls in the church, but also the whole interior wall-surface of the church is often decorated with frescoes. The veneration of holy images is a central aspect of the Orthodox tradition, one intimately connected with its whole spiritual understanding of the relationships between the Divine and the human world. According to this understanding, matter and sensible existence may participate in the life of the spirit; they may be spirit-bearing; and indeed the whole emphasis of Orthodox spirituality is on the transfiguration of human existence and all other created forms through this participation in divine life. Icons are regarded as testimonies to this process of transfiguration, for in them is felt to be present something of the deified reality of the prototypes – Christ, the Mother of God, angels and saints – that they represent and make visible. It was according to this understanding that the VIIth Oecumenical Council (held at Nicaea in 787) promulgated its decisions after a long period during which the veneration of icons had been bitterly attacked. This attack was regarded above all as an attempt to undermine the idea of the participation of material existence in spiritual life, and thus as a challenge to the whole principle of the Incarnation in which the Divine assumes a bodily form; and it was against this dualistic heresy that the Council announced its decrees on the veneration of images: 'We determine that holy images – in colours, mosaics, or other material – be exposed in the holy churches of God, on liturgical vessels and vestments, on walls and furnishings, in houses and in streets: the image of our Lord God and Saviour Jesus Christ [any image of the Father is forbidden], that of our Sovereign, immaculate, and holy Mother of God, that of the venerable angels and those of all holy men. These representations, each time they are contemplated, induce those who regard them to recall and love their prototypes. We determine also that they be kissed and that they are the object of an honouring veneration, but not of adoration, which concerns the Object of our faith and is due to the divine nature alone ... The honour rendered to the image is transferred to the prototype; he who venerates the image venerates in it the reality that it represents.' In making this distinction between veneration and adoration the Fathers of the Council were defending their understanding of the function of the icon from the charge of idolatry: divine worship is reserved for God alone, as the author of all sanctity.

Thus the building of the church, with the symbolic structure of its architecture and its iconographic decoration, is a kind of visible projection of the spiritual world; on entering it, the worshipper feels he enters into the presence of the Divine. At the same time, in spite of this intimacy, or even perhaps because of it, the sense of awe in the face of the overwhelming transcendence of the Divine, of His total Otherness in relation to human life, and His ultimate inaccessibility, is strongly emphasized, both by the half-hidden and shadowed crown of the dome on which the image of the Panto-crator (the Almighty) is often painted, remote, powerful, hieroph-antic, and by the closing off of the altar and the fact that only the priest protected by his sacerdotal vestments may touch it. This sense of the absolute abyss between the Creator and the creature, of the ultimately unsearchable ways of the Divinity, has its psycho-logical counterpart in a sense of total dependence on the Divine: human life and all other life has been brought out of nothing and returns to nothing unless sustained and nourished by the mercy of God. Hence in Orthodox services the frequent repetition of the phrase: Lord, have mercy – *Kyrie eleison.*

It is this sense of the inaccessibility and transcendence of the Divine that gives the celebration of the liturgy, set as it is in the sacred space of the church, its miraculous character. For what it bears witness to, manifests, and actualizes, is the overcoming of the abyss between the Divine and the human through the immense 'condescension', or *philanthropia,* of the Divine in the Incarnation. The liturgy is at once both a recollection, an *anamnesis,* of this event, and its glorification: a recollection and glorification of the 'rending of the veil' of death and corruption that as a consequence of the Fall of Adam had interposed itself between God and man. The Orthodox do not share the idea that life on earth is a kind of punishment for the sin all human individuals have committed in Adam and which they must expiate through the acquisition of merit, the performance of good works, or through obedience to commandments they do not have it in their power to keep. Adam alone is responsible for his transgression, but the consequences of this transgression devolve upon all his descendants. These con-sequences are above all those of corruption and death, and it is through these that evil exercises its usurped influence over human nature. Deliverance from this unnatural state of subjection cannot be achieved by any effort man alone can make. The most man can do is to cooperate in the liberating activity of God. Orthodox tradition maintains a paradoxical sense of the interdependence of the two terms of this divine-human cooperation. On the one hand man is entirely dependent on the grace given; on the other hand without his cooperation in effort and will he cannot receive this grace.

This paradoxical interdependence is signified for the Orthodox in Mary's *fiat* at the Annunciation: without this free acceptance on the part of the human being of the divine *Logos* there could have been no Incarnation. At the same time, without the Incarnation there could have been no deliverance for humanity from its 'fallen' state. This spontaneous cooperation on the part of the human individual is stressed for the Orthodox in their refusal to admit where the birth of Mary is concerned any exemption from the ordinary processes of human conception: there is no immaculate conception of the Virgin in this respect nor any particular exemption from the general condition of mankind implicit in her birth. The only exemption from these processes that Orthodoxy recognizes is in the case of the earthly conception of Christ. It is Christ's exemption from the effects of ancestral sin that all Adam's descendants have inherited which allows Him to 'tear the veil' from between the Creator and the human creature, and to knit their two natures together in a way that is now free from these effects. It is this triumph over death that is at the heart of Orthodoxy. And the great veneration in which Mary the Mother of God is held in the Orthodox Church is due to the fact, first, that she exemplifies the supreme humility which on the human side was – and is – a condition of the Incarnation of the *Logos*, and, second, that it was through her that the *Logos*, in becoming the fruit of her flesh, initiated the process of the sanctification of the material world: her bodily assumption as a consequence of this knitting together of flesh and spirit in her person prefigures the final metamorphosis of the whole of creation.

What the liturgy, then, recapitulates and actualizes is the divine economy of salvation and the metamorphosis of creation that flows from it. Through the liturgy the Kingdom of God descends in the power of the Holy Spirit to take possession of the first fruits of creation, to restore them to their state of grace. In the sacraments, the Spirit 'energizes' divine life in the material elements – in the water, the oil, the wine, and the bread – as He had once energized this life in Mary; and in so doing He forms them in a hidden yet entirely real manner into the glorious body of the resurrected Christ. There is thus a movement of descent and ascent, a double and simultaneous rhythm of invocation and assumption. What in effect the liturgy exhibits – and here reference is particularly to the Sunday liturgy – is the earthly life of the *Logos* in all its phases: 'of all that has been accomplished for us, of the Cross, the sepulchre, the resurrection on the third day, the ascension into heaven, the sitting on the right hand of the Father, and the second and glorious Coming', as one of the liturgical prayers puts it. The first part of the service, known as the liturgy of the catechumens, recapitulates the main phases in the earthly life of Christ prior to the sacrifice: His coming into the world, His initial showing forth, His final manifestation. The second part – the consecration of the gifts (the sacrifice itself) – announces the death, the Resurrection, and the Ascension; while the third part, after the sacrifice, figures the descent of the Spirit on the Apostles, the conversion of the nations through them, and the formation of the 'divine society'. The whole 'mystagogy', as it is termed, is like a single icon of the body of Christ's 'work', making visible the various members of this body in their proper order and harmony. Not only the chants and the readings from the sacred texts, but all the gestures, of priest and congregation, that accompany them, have the same function: all have their present and immediate actuality, but all at the same time symbolize something of the work of Christ, of his actions or sufferings.

Thus the liturgy may be regarded as a 'theophany' in which, in the sacred space of the church, 'holy things' are revealed from 'on high' and in their revelation embrace the whole world of creatures. For underlying the liturgy is the idea of the assumption of the sensible and transitory by the intelligible and eternal. It presupposes, that is to say, that the corporeal humanity of Christ subsists as an intelligible – spiritualized – reality in its integrity, and that through their consecration and 'transmutation' the eucharistic elements – the bread and the wine – become themselves the body and blood of this spiritualized and eternal humanity. It is not that the sacrifice on Calvary is repeated with every Eucharist: this 'happened' once and for all on Calvary and is unrepeatable; it is that the bread and the wine, through the action of the Spirit in their consecration, actually become the sacrificed and resurrected body of Christ. Thus through communing in these spiritualized elements, man himself partakes of the sacred flesh of the divine *Logos*. It is therefore the whole being of man that 'lives' and 'experiences' the liturgy's action, and this also through his organs of sense. There is no spirit-flesh dualism; rather there is an extreme spirit-flesh (or *pneuma-soma*) realism. This reaffirms once again the Orthodox emphasis on the transfiguration of the body, a process that begins here on earth through the spiritualization (not dematerialization) of the bodily senses operated under the dynamic spiritual energies communicated by means of the sacraments. The liturgy sanctifies all the faculties of man, helping them to perceive the invisible through the visible, the Kingdom of God in the mysteries. It is because of this that its performance includes the cooperation of all his faculties, physical and mental: touch, smell, sight, hearing, taste: the icons, the incense, the lights and colours, the chanting, the eucharistic elements: all are involved in the experience of the sacred ritual drama in which the whole creature is saturated with spiritual life.

This is one of the reasons why the cult of the saints plays such an important part in Orthodox worship. For the saints bear for the Orthodox living witness to the fundamental idea of the trans-figuration of the creature which underlies the liturgy: to the fact of the possible sanctification of man. Most – though by no means all – Orthodox saints are monks; and it must be remembered in this connection that the liturgy itself is essentially monastic, and that its parish form is but an adaptation of its total form. Orthodoxy knows only one monastic 'order' or 'monastic society', and this is essentially contemplative. At the same time there are considerable variations within this single order. The monasteries of Mt Athos – the most concentrated group of monasteries in Greek lands, though their territory still has a certain international status – follow mainly the *typikon* (rule) of the Byzantine Constantinopolitan monastery of Stoudios, as it was established by its great abbot, St Theodore; though this in its turn largely derives from the 'rule' of St Basil. Apart from this, each monastery is subject to the surveillance of the bishop in whose district it stands (Mt Athos, being essentially pan-Orthodox – though national Greek pressures have meant a certain loss of this character – is here an exception, for it comes directly under the Patriarch of Constantinople), and its organization may include many local traditions of its own. In any case, the institu-tional form of the monastic life but provides the setting – or, rather, a setting – for what may be only a phase in the spiritual life. For the true purpose of this life is the 'deification' of man through the ac-quisition of the Holy Spirit; and in practice it is found that the eremitic or semi-eremitic life is more suitable than the institutional life of the monastery for the accomplishment of the final phases of this purpose. The hermit in total solitude, or the spiritual father with a small group of disciples, living a life concentrated in prayer: these stand in the Orthodox tradition as the supreme types of spiritual life, in which the Divine penetrates the purified heart and begins that process of metamorphosis of the whole person which is realized by the saint.

Veneration is therefore accorded to the saints for the same reason that it is accorded to the Virgin Mary: because in them the mysteri-ous union of the divine and human natures is accomplished, and their physical forms are filled with divine grace. It is this that makes the holy man even in this life a source of mercy, miracle, and guidance, the healer and deliverer of those who appeal to him; and these acts of compassion he manifests to an even greater extent after his earthly life is over. Appealed to through his image or through his relics (for it is felt that the grace that visits a saint during his earthly life never deserts his mortal remains, and even spills over into the material objects with which he has come into contact), or invoked on his feast-day in churches dedicated to him, the saint, by the very fact that as well as being a spiritualized existence he is also a human being, is felt still to dwell close to earth-bound men and women, to share intimately in their joys and sorrows, to protect them in misfortune, intercede for them, bestow benefits on them, guard their crops, bring safely home sons voyaging on distant seas. All over Greece, on mountain top or lonely headland over-looking the sea, are shrines and small chapels dedicated to the most popular saints of the Greek Orthodox world: St Nicholas, St John the Baptist, the Prophet Ilias, St George, St Demetrius, and many others. In many cases the churches in which their relics are kept or that house one of their miracle-working icons have become veritable cult centres to which thousands of pilgrims may flock yearly: such is the church of St John the Russian at Procopion on the island of Euboea, or the church of St Spyridon on Corfu, or above all the church on the island of Tenos with the miraculous icon of the Holy Virgin where on 15 August, on the feast of the *Dormition of the Mother of God*, the faithful gather in great crowds in expectation of help and healing. Indeed, one may say that still today the communal character of Greek village life is manifested above all on the feast-days of the saints, celebrated not only with the liturgy but also with music and banquet, wine and dance.

Centring, then, round the veneration of the saints and the twelve major feasts of the Christian year – the Annunciation, the Nativity, the Presentation in the Temple, the Baptism, the Transfiguration, the Raising of Lazarus, the Entry into Jerusalem, the Crucifixion, the *Anastasis* (Descent into Hades), the Ascension, the Pentecost, and the *Koimisis* (the *Dormition of the Mother of God*) – the liturgical cycles unfold. Their order is fixed by the *Typikon* (Rule), a monastic order deriving ultimately from the *typikon* of the Palestinian monast-ery of St Savvas. The whole annual cycle is in three main parts: the cycle of the *Ochtoechos*, in which, from the second week after Easter till the Thursday before Palm Sunday, an eight-week cycle is repeated, each of which employs one of the eight ecclesiastical 'tones' and is made up of seven offices, one each day; the cycle of fixed feasts; and, thirdly, the paschal cycle, which covers the ten weeks prior to Easter. Six of these weeks are a fast period. (Other long fasts are that which precedes Christmas, beginning on 15 November, the last two weeks of June, before the feast of the Apostles Peter and Paul, and the two first weeks of August before the feast of the *Dormition*; in addition each Wednesday and Friday is a fast day.) Easter itself is the culmination of the liturgical year. In fact, Holy Week, the 'Week of weeks', orientated towards, and receiving its fulfilment in, the Resurrection, concentrates in itself the whole central meaning of the Christian message for the Orthodox: the sacrifice of the Incarnate God and the victory over death and darkness that is achieved through this: 'Christ is risen from the dead, by death he has vanquished death. To those in the tombs he has given life' – such are the words sung at the triumph of the Resurrection. 'The night of Easter', an Orthodox writer has said, 'its joy, its exaltation, transports us into the life of the world to come, into new joy, the joy of joys, the joy without end.'

To what extent is this liturgical pattern of Orthodox Christianity lived and experienced by the Greek people? The question of course is impossible to answer in any but the most approximate terms; in fact, all that can be done is to point to a few external signs that may indicate the strength of Orthodoxy as a living force in Greece. And here perhaps the first thing to recall is that the Greek hierarchy, although maintaining the ritual forms of the Church, had already very much compromised its intellectual integrity from the first years after the war of Independence – indeed, as we have seen, in many ways even from before this war itself. For in severing its connection with the Patriarchate of Constantinople and in setting itself up as an autocephalous national institution, the Greek hierarchy, whatever reasons it ostensibly gave for its act, was in fact simply accommodating itself to the dictates of propagandists like Korais and to the pressures of the civil state whose form was largely determined by the secular ideas Korais represented. This meant that the hierarchy, apart from its immediate sacramental functions, became very much dependent on the state, supporting the latter in its task of shaping modern Greek society in terms of that urban and middle-class liberalism whose ideals it had adopted. In addition, as the hierarchy, because of its role through the time of the Turkish occupation, had in any case lost to a considerable degree its capacity to distinguish between Orthodoxy and Hellenism – two totally incompatible ways of thought – it found itself involved in the purely national aspirations for a 'greater Greece' pursued by the 'hellenizers'; and although racialism was officially condemned by the Council of Constantinople in 1872, in practice the legacy of the confusion of roles established under the Turks still makes it difficult for the hierarchy to maintain its strictly Orthodox principles when an ethnic Greek question is at stake.

This intellectual, or theological, failure of the Greek hierarchy to maintain Orthodox standards except in its strictly liturgical functions – and one must remember that its social and prophetic functions were forcibly restricted during the Turkish period –, has naturally had a corresponding effect on the whole Orthodox community in Greece. To begin with, it has seriously affected the attitude to, and consequently the concern for, what has traditionally been the most central and fundamental element of the Church: its monastic life. Men like Korais and other 'enlightened' spirits of the time were, under the influence of the secular humanism of the eighteenth century, bitterly hostile to monasticism, and regarded monks and their prayers as entirely useless to society; and in following the lead given by these intellectuals one of the first anti-monastic steps in the new Greek state was the closing of a large number of monasteries in the territory under its jurisdiction, with the confiscation of their wealth for purely civil purposes. With the failure of the hierarchy to promote the ideals of monasticism or the ascetic life based upon them, and with the indifference or hostility of the educated classes to both, Greek monasticism has declined drastically over the last century and a half. Many historic houses have been closed altogether, and many more are inhabited only by a few monks, sometimes even by but a single elderly monk. Given the central place that monasticism has always occupied in the spiritual life of Orthodox Christians, its decline in Greece may be seen as directly reflecting a loss of spiritual consciousness among the Greek people.

Moreover, in accepting in a similar spirit the ideals of an urban liberalism where the formation of modern Greek society is concerned, the hierarchy has been compelled to renounce, when not actively to oppose, the Orthodox pattern of social organization which had been practised on the village level during the Turkish period and of which the monastic form was the most complete example: that of the coenobitic life based on the social equality and brotherhood of man before God. In thus abandoning its social legacy from Byzantium, and in supporting the creation of a completely non-Christian form of society, the hierarchy at once lost its capacity to act as an independent social force. This has meant that its social and prophetic role as a transfiguring influence not only on individual and isolated human souls but on the whole social-political organism of its flock – a role that it cannot abandon without also abandoning its Orthodox doctrine that the Incarnation is related to the whole of creation – has been enormously weakened and may even be said to be practically ineffective. This in its turn has meant that the deeply engrained sense among the Greek people, inherited from their Orthodox tradition and in particular from their monasticism, of equality and brotherhood expressing itself in the communal and economic forms of society, is led to seek expression in an entirely non-Christian form. It is not an accident that the first communist country was also an Orthodox country.

This loss of spiritual leadership on the part of the hierarchy, with its corresponding loss of Christian values and the way of life based upon them among the Greek people as a whole – reflected in the sparse attendance at church, the neglect of fasting, the lapse of local religious festivals – does not however mean that Greece has entirely forfeited its right to claim that it is an Orthodox Christian country. To begin with, few Greeks are active non-believers, even when they maintain social and political ideals of a non-Christian nature. Then many village priests and many individual bishops have maintained both in their liturgical practice and in their capacity as shepherds of their people standards of the highest order, often against the greatest odds and with truly heroic self-sacrifice. Moreover, the hierarchy as a whole is now beginning to take stock of some of the abnormalities to which it has found itself committed in the past. There are signs of a renewal of many features of liturgical life that had been neglected or misapplied. In church architecture, in the chanting, in iconography, there is a return to more strict Orthodox models. Iconography in particular has been the subject of a considerable renaissance, largely due in the first place to the immense labour of the iconographer Photis Kontoglou. The Home Mission of the Greek Church – the *Apostoliki Diakonia* –, founded in 1930, has made great efforts to revive a liturgical consciousness among the Greek people and to promote through its publications the study of the Fathers of the Orthodox tradition. Parallel to this are the activities of certain other non-official or semi-official organizations directed to the same end. The most influential of these organizations is the *Zoë* (Life) brotherhood founded in 1911 by Father Eusebius Matthopoulos, a kind of monastic order in the world. Holding the three traditional monastic virtues, its members – over a hundred in all, most of them with degrees in theology, and about a quarter of them priests – live in common in the parent house of the brotherhood for one month of the year; for the rest of the time they travel to different parts of Greece, preaching, teaching at catechetical schools, and directing various missionary or educational organizations. They are also anxious to overcome that 'clericalism' which partly as a result of the Turkish occupation and the need for secrecy has crept into the celebration of the liturgy, the sense that the liturgy is something performed by the priest for the people rather than that it is a communal work in which priest and congregation cooperate. (We have noted that the raised iconostasis between the sanctuary and the main body of the church is a symptom of this clericalism, emphasizing the isolated role of the priest.) To this end too they advocate frequent communion, as opposed to the general practice of communion three or four times a year, if that. Their numerous publications; their dominant influence if not control over a number of subsidiary organizations; their efforts to stimulate a consciousness of the Orthodox tradition among students and urban workers – all this may help to overcome the somewhat static ritualism with which the liturgical life tends to become identified. On the other hand, the militant and institutional character of this brotherhood, as well as the great emphasis on social action, may be fundamentally more dangerous for the life of the Church than the reforms aimed at would seem to suggest.

Another factor that must be included among those working for a renewal of concern for their Orthodox tradition among the Greeks – and in this case particularly among the educated Greeks, the class, that is, which since the war of Independence has done more perhaps than any other to undermine Greece's Orthodox heritage – is the great awakening in the West of interest in what till recently had been the despised field of Byzantine studies. Just as it was the West that taught Greek intellectuals to scorn and to seek to suppress their Byzantine heritage by infecting them with its own extraordinary enthusiasm for the classical world, so now the rehabilitation of the mediaeval European Christian world in the western cultural consciousness, and the extension of this to include Byzantium, is making their Byzantine heritage once more a respectable asset to educated Greeks themselves. This so far has mostly had its effect in such activities as the restoration and preservation of Byzantine monuments or as purely academic research into the many Byzantine sources available in Greek lands. But it has also meant, if more indirectly, an increased respect for, and estimation of, the Orthodox tradition itself, as the dynamic and creative force of the great artistic and intellectual achievements of the Byzantine world.

But whatever reforms, revivals, or awakenings of interest are taking place where the Orthodox Church in Greece is concerned, these will not touch the heart of things unless they are accompanied by, and develop from, the practice of the central tradition of Orthodox spirituality, that which in the last years of Byzantium was expressed by the great hesychastic masters and which has its roots in the depths of Christianity itself. That this tradition is fundamentally monastic and ascetic does not mean that its practice is necessarily confined to monasteries, though it may mean that there it is lived with most intensity. We have already noted evidence for its continuation during the Turkish period in the activity and work of such figures as St Nicodemus of the Holy Mountain; and it was chiefly under his spiritual guidance that a group, known as the Kollyvades, originally formed on Mt Athos but later spreading through the islands of the Archipelago and eventually even reaching the capital, came into existence. (It was under the lasting influence of this group that the writer Papadiamantis came early in life.) In the latter half of the nineteenth century also the great compilation of spiritual writings embodying this tradition, the *Philokalia*, was reprinted three times; and a further edition has recently been published in five volumes in Athens. Other works representative of the same tradition have also recently been republished, works like *The Gerontikon or Sayings of the Holy Fathers*; *The Lausiac History*; the *Homilies* of Macarius; the *Book of Barsanuphius and John*; and several others. The fact of the publication and of the relatively wide sale of these works among the laity are a sign that beneath the surface of modern Greek life the current of the tradition of which they speak has not ceased to flow.

As for the monasteries themselves, though the overall condition is still one of decline, there are also exceptions to this. Not only on Athos itself are still to be found powerful representatives of the monastic tradition – two in particular who through their writings have made their voice heard outside Athos are Father Gabriel, Abbot of the Monastery of Dionysiou, and Father Theoklitos, author among other things of a remarkable study of the monastic life entitled *Between Heaven and Earth*; but also monasteries outside Athos – the Monastery of Longovarda on the island of Paros under the direction of the venerable Father Philotheos is an example – still form living communities. But more significant is the revival during recent years of monastic life among women. During the period of the Turkish occupation monasticism for women, unlike monasticism for men, was made practically impossible and the number of convents dwindled away almost entirely. The only great figure among women in this connection during this period is St Philothei who in the sixteenth century founded in Athens the first active order for women in the Greek Church, turning her home into a convent for the purpose; her activities brought her into disfavour with the Turks, and she was persecuted and finally put to death. After the war of Independence however a slow revival began, and this has increased markedly during the present century. In 1904 St Nektarios Kephalas (1846–1920), Metropolitan of Pentapolis, founded on the island of Aegina the Convent of the Holy Trinity.

At Keratea in Attica the Convent of Our Lady was founded in 1925 by the Old Calendarists,[1] and now houses between two and three hundred members. In 1928 the Convent of Our Lady of Help was founded on Chios. Since the Second World war, this revival, in spite of certain opposition from sections of the clergy and elsewhere, has further developed: in 1945, for instance, the Convent of the Annunciation was founded on Patmos by Father Amphilokios, one of the great spiritual directors of contemporary Greece; and two daughter houses – on Rhodes and Kalymnos – have since been founded. The Convent of the Apparition (*Panayas Phaneromenis*) on Salamis, the Convent of the Taxiarchs near Nauplion, and that of Our Lady on the island of Icaria (one of the refuges of the Kollyvades), are three further houses, among several others, that bear witness to the growing strength of monastic life among women in Greece.

In view of all this, what can be said of the influence of the Orthodox Church in Greece as a whole? In terms of numbers the picture is not very encouraging. Those seeking to live according to the principles of the great patristic and hesychastic tradition of Orthodox spirituality, whether inside or outside monasteries, are likely to be few; and even regular participation in the liturgical life of the Church is no longer common—it has been said that not more than 2 per cent of the total population are regular 'church-goers'. Moreover, since the *coup* of 21 April 1967, the two great dangers already noted in this chapter to the life of the Church appear to have grown considerably. The first is the danger of state intervention in the Church's internal affairs. The deposition of the Archbishop of Athens, Chrysostomos, and the election of the new Archbishop, Jerome Kotsonis, in his place was a direct consequence of government action, and the question of the legality of these proceedings is still, at the time of writing, a matter of debate. In addition to this, Archbishop Kotsonis has been an active member of the *Zoë* brotherhood mentioned above, and his acceptability to the government has largely been due to the fact that it sees in him a possible ally in implementing its programme of national and religious revival based on an aggressive anti-communism and on the ideals of what it calls Greco-Christian civilization. We have already noted some of the disastrous consequences of the confusion between 'Church' and 'nation', 'Orthodoxy' and 'Hellenism'; and this latest alliance between Church and state, should it develop, threatens to make this confusion far worse. What may be expected is a reform, carried out by a 'spiritual' and intellectual élite who are either members of the

[1] Those who still adhere to the Julian calendar; the Greek Church, together with the Romanian Church, adopted the Gregorian calendar in 1920.

Zoë brotherhood (or its companion organization, *Sotir*) or strong sympathizers, and directed at strengthening the social, missionary, and moral aspects of the Church at the expense of its liturgical and mystical life. In other words, what may be expected is a kind of 'westernization' of the Church on the basis of neo-humanist Greco-Christian ideals. This would of course have the effect of widening the already existing gulf between the 'official' Church and the people, especially if this reform were to be carried out with the support of a military, anti-communist government. But it must be remembered that this reform, should it be brought about, does not necessarily mean any direct attack on Orthodox spirituality as such, or destroy the conditions in which it can be lived. And it must further be remembered that from the Orthodox viewpoint the life of the Church and the life of the soul are one: it is never numbers that count, and a single holy person realizing the spiritual life in its plenitude makes present and active the full life of the Church, radiating its influence through the whole environment. It is because of this that though the faith of the Greek people has been, and is, undermined and threatened in so many ways, none the less the impact and vitality of the Church may still be extremely real.

Chapter 7

Modern Greek Literature

The Poetry

I T IS OFTEN said that the Greeks are a nation of bards, and it is true that if there is one form of expression which particularly distinguishes their creative life it is their poetry. A knowledge of the poetry of the ancient Greek world has from the time of the Renaissance until recently been a *sine qua non* of western education and culture, and even today lip-service is still paid to such great names as Homer and Aeschylus, Sappho and Theocritus. But the poetry of the ancient world by no means exhausts the Greeks' poetic heritage. There is, first, the immense wealth of poetry written in Greek during the Byzantine period – a poetry whose recognition in the West has been delayed, because of its specifically religious form and content, even longer than that of its counterpart, Byzantine pictorial art: only recently have the works of one of the chief Byzantine poets – Romanos the Melodist (sixth century) – been fully edited. A great deal of this Byzantine religious poetry – or, as it would be better to call it, liturgical poetry – is still in use in the offices of the Orthodox Church and hence is still intimately familiar to the modern Greeks and of direct influence on contemporary poetic productions: one of the most ambitious poems recently published in Greece – the *Axion Esti* of Odysseus Elytis, published in 1960 – deliberately reflects in its tone, diction, and structure the traditional liturgy of the Orthodox Church, itself a Byzantine creation.

Then, in addition to this liturgical poetry, there is the vast body of popular ballads and folk poetry built up over the centuries and particularly during the time of the Turkish occupation, which again is intimately and directly related to the lives of the Greek people. Indeed, one of the features of Greek poetry, and something which goes a long way to support the nation's claim to bardic election, is its essentially popular nature: whether it is the highly intricate and profoundly intellectual poetry of the liturgy or the direct un-sophisticated spontaneity of the ballad or folk-song, the Greek people as a whole share in and are affected by the creative genius of their poets. And this is still true today: the words of one of the most popular songs in recent years are those of a short lyric by the distinguished modern poet, George Seferis; and on the back of every strip-off leaf which proclaims the day and date, as well as the names of the chief saints whose feast it is, in the little block calendars that hang on the wall of every Greek house, cottage, or flat, are printed rhyming couplets, on erotic or gnomic themes, taken from the ballads or from the seventeenth-century Cretan epic, the *Erotocritos*, by Vizentzos Kornaros, large sections or even all of whose 10,052 verses are in Crete still recited by heart by peasants who in other ways might be termed illiterate.

As where many other aspects of contemporary Greek life and culture are concerned, an appreciation of the nature and quality of modern Greek poetry is impossible without a certain degree of retrospection. In this connection we have already indicated the importance of liturgical poetry and the ballad and folk-song tradition, though it is from this latter demotic tradition that modern Greek poetry itself more directly stems. The origins of the Greek ballads and folk-songs, like the origins of the popular poetry of other countries, are difficult to trace. In one sense they may be said to go back to Homer, and even beyond, for all ballad literature makes use of certain universal images and deals with certain universal themes and experiences. More specifically though it may be said that their metre – the 'δεκαπεντασύλλαβος', a line of fifteen syllables with a caesura after the eighth syllable and two main accents, one on the fourteenth and one on the sixth or eighth syllable – was already in use in Byzantine times. It is the metre in which much popular and satirical verse was written, as well as that of some of the finest mystical poetry of the Byzantine period – the poetry of St Symeon the New Theologian (949–1022). More significant from the point of view of the later demotic poetry, it was the metre of the epic, *Digenis Acritas*, and of the cycle of folk-songs connected with the legendary hero whose exploits it commemorates. This epic seems to have taken shape in the tenth century on the eastern frontiers of the Byzantine Empire, in the district of the Tigris and the Euphrates, far from the sophisticated and formalized atmosphere of the Byzantine capital and its court. Here the leaders of the border-fighters – *Acritas* means border-fighter – were relatively free from direct imperial control, while the Arab emirs who were their main opponents had also taken advantage of the weakness of the Caliphate to set themselves up as independent princes. In this self-assertive and strongly individualistic world of almost continual border warfare a military aristocracy grew up whose heroic exploits in love and battle had much in common with those of which Homer writes.

The warrior life, the life of the hero, of the hunter and fighter, of the man who lives violently and dies valiantly, boasts the beauty of his women and the strength of his children – this life is indeed one that Greek poetry has celebrated from the earliest times. Throughout the poetry of this life runs the breath of strong masculine vitality and independence. The Acritic poems are of this type. Digenis himself is one of those characters close to the popular heart of Greece, the epic hero who at the same time has qualities of a sage or a saint. In fact, one of the main forms of the popular literature of Byzantium as of the Greek world in the period of the Turkish occupation was the lives of the saints; and among the most loved saints, of whom there is a great number, are the military saints. Some of these military saints were leaders of a group of companions, like St Maurice, St Probus, St Tarachus, St Andronicus, St Sergius, and St Bacchus; others were isolated figures like St Artemius, St Menas, and St Aretha; though by far the best known of either type are St George and St Demetrius. It is the qualities of these military saints as mirrored in popular literature that combine with older recollections of pagan times to form the character of such an epic hero as Digenis Acritas. Epic heroes are saints and saints are epic heroes. Sometimes these hero-saints are the defenders of a national faith, and sometimes of a religious faith. Sometimes the two faiths are so intertwined as to be inseparable in the popular consciousness, so that these military leaders are then defenders of both at once. Digenis thus combines elements of an Achilles or an Odysseus with those of a St George or a St Demetrius. In this way he foreshadows the type who was to become the hero of the ballads – the klephtic ballads – that came into being during the Turkish occupation of Greek lands: the mountain chieftain who personified the Greek Christian nation in its struggle against the Islamic Turks. From the point of view, then, both of metre and of content the epic cycle of the Acritic ballads is of direct significance for the whole later demotic tradition of poetry.

In many respects this later demotic poetry is much like the folk-poetry of other countries: it records, that is to say, in simple direct language the hopes and fears, joys and sorrows, of the peasant's life in its natural setting. But on the other hand it is distinguished by this epic quality of which we have been speaking. It is a dominantly masculine poetry and the virtues it exalts are above all the virtues of manliness. Its ideal heroic type – and this poetry is not concerned with subjective individual features but only with the delineation of the ideal type – is the noble fighter alone or with his band among his enemies, high up in the mountains or in the lonely passes: the type whose historical actualization was to take place in the heroes of the Greek war of Independence, in figures like Kolokotronis, Androutsos, Makriyannis, Mavromichalis. From this point of view it may be said that it was this ideal portrait of manliness represented in the epic Acritic poetry and in the later klephtic ballads which created the heroes of the Greek war of Independence, providing the image or model towards which the individual worthy of respect must aspire and which he must as far as humanly possible embody in his life. There is nothing of the city in this poetry, nothing of urban culture or civilization, nothing sophisticated or feminine. Instead there is a burning, almost archaic, sense of life and freedom; of life, that is, as it is lived in time and experiences through the senses. It is not that this sense of life is materialistic or godless. On the contrary, it is that life itself is regarded as an absolute reality and as such as sacred. Both nature and the life of man in nature are felt to be a mode of existence of the Divinity; they are hierophanies; and for the klephtic poet the mythical hero of the ballads and his actions are means for revealing this sacred sense of life and the values that go with it. To the living of this life, all settled ties, all constraint, all merely utilitarian preoccupations, are felt to be an impediment. The true significance of life, its sacredness, is felt to be revealed in certain instants of heroic joy and liberation when the normal bonds and trivialities of existence are overcome and the essential dignity of the human being is asserted.

Freedom therefore may be said to be the keynote of this poetry, a freedom which man and nature share and experience as it were in terms of each other. That is why the elements and creatures appear in this poetry in so personal a way: they are intimately involved in the struggle for freedom in which man, their crowning glory, is engaged. There is a vital, almost organic, connection between man and the natural world surrounding him. It is as if man's whole emotional sphere is animated by his attachment to the earth on which he is born. Thus man's freedom demands the corresponding freedom of his natural world, of this earth on which he treads. The klephtic ballads were not originally patriotic in any chauvinistic or nationalist sense, though in the eighteenth century, and particularly in the latter half of that century, they were affected by the intense nationalist propaganda then pouring into Greece through various channels. Before this though such nationalist bias was entirely absent: 'patriotism', where the klephtic ballads are concerned, sprang from the hero's need to have a free 'sphere of action' in the world in which he lived, for not to possess this was the emotional equivalent to personal slavery and frustration – was to be deprived of the means of expressing the sacred values of his life; and this need was manifested in purely individual terms, in terms of the hero's independence, together with that of his band if he had one, and not in terms of any collective or nationalist purpose. What is in question is individual freedom, and it is in the struggle for this that birds, mountains, rivers, woods, and wild beasts, all participate in the hero's activity. They are as aware of the humiliation that any constraining powers, whether foreign invaders or the normal forces of law and order, impose on him as he is; they assist him in his battles, rejoice with him in his victories, mourn for him in defeat or overthrow. Only in one respect are they set apart from him, only one of his experiences – and this perhaps the deepest – they do not seem to share or at least to share with the same finality; and this is his experience of death. 'Lucky mountains, lucky fields', goes one short poem:

> Lucky mountains, lucky fields,
> They have no fear of Death.
> They don't expect the Murderer,
> They only wait for lovely spring,
> For summer to make the mountains green,
> To strew the fields with flowers.

Death is the one experience which sets man radically apart from the rest of nature; it is the one experience too that appears to set a limit to his aspirations to freedom. The sense of death – of the transitoriness of life, particularly of human life – is always strong among peoples with long histories and old memories. They have seen too many things pass away to believe too much in the stability or permanence of anything. They are acutely aware of the brevity and precariousness of their own mortal existence. This sense is perhaps more intense where, as was the case with the Greeks, so much of man's personal fulfilment is felt to be bound up with the fate of the earth on which he treads. The contrast then, indicated in the lines of the poem cited above, between the endless renewal of nature and man's 'once and for all' appearance on earth is realized with particular intensity, for this irrevocable breaking at death of his links with nature, with the world with which his life has been so indistinguishably identified, seems to mark in one blow the total end and annihilation of his existence, to sever the vital thread of his being; and yet at the same time this 'other', the natural world, the earth which has borne him and with which he has shared so much of his life, continues on its way as though he had never been. Death, far from being anything natural, in this manner presents itself to man as the most unnatural thing there is.

This awareness however of the 'injustice' and unnaturalness of death does not rob man of the sense of the importance of living.

On the contrary, it increases his sense of life and his determination to live it, and to live it on his own terms and not on any terms proposed or imposed by anybody else. It polarizes and concentrates his longing for freedom, so that death appears in his consciousness as but the final and most absolute of those unnatural and vicious enemies with which his life is surrounded and whose presence is felt to be incompatible with human life and the dignity which is, or should be, its natural birthright. So great is this resentment against the unjust interference of death with man's freedom, that the hero of the ballads, the *pallikari*, is often pictured as fighting with Death itself – a fight in which man's courage and longing for freedom are thrown into intense relief and at the same time are revealed as the most absolute of human values by the fact that they are not to be surrendered even though in fighting for them man knows he will be defeated. In one of these ballads the fight takes place on the 'marble threshing-floor': Death addresses the young man, and the young man in his turn replies:

> 'Take off your clothes, young man,
> Lay down your arms, and fold
> Your hands across your breast,
> So I take your soul away.'
> 'I'll not take off my clothes,
> Lay down my arms or fold
> My hands across my breast,
> For you to take my soul away.
> We're men and both are brave,
> So let us fight it out
> On the marble threshing-floor,
> Where we won't shake the mountains
> Or terrify the village.'
> They went away and wrestled
> On the marble threshing-floor.
> Nine times the youth threw Death,
> And the ninth time Death was hurt.
> He seized the young man's hair,
> He forced him to his knees.
> 'Death, leave my hair, grasp me
> About the waist, and then
> You'll see how young men fight.'
> 'By the hair I seize them,
> Men young and old, and girls,
> And children with their mothers.'

It was, then, from this stream of demotic poetry that modern

Greek poetry, in the full literary sense of the word, developed. It took over or, rather, inherited not only the metres of this poetry – which naturally it was to adapt with time to its own purposes – but also its central preoccupations and themes: those of man's essential freedom and his determination not to surrender it; of his relationships and sense of reciprocity with the natural world and the earth on which he is born; and, related intimately to the first two themes, the consciousness of the ever-present and appalling fact of death, which seems both a negation of his freedom and a total severance of those ties which link him so strongly to his natural world that he finds it difficult to conceive of human life in any other terms that would make it worth living. As the basic metre of the demotic songs – the fifteen-syllable line – was to be modified in accordance with new needs, so the perspective in which these central preoccupations and themes were to be viewed by the major poets of modern Greece was also to vary according to the changing circumstances of life and to the differences of perception that go with an intelligence and sensibility more highly elaborated than that of the peasant; and clearly the fact that these later poets were to be increasingly affected by the complexities and sophistications of an urban education and culture on the western pattern was to play an important part here, for it meant a certain independence of and detachment from the peasant's intimate and inescapable involvement in the rooted world of his earth. But this being said, it still remains true that these themes and preoccupations, transposed as they may be to a new level of understanding, continued and still continue to be those that above all distinguish the communication of modern Greek poetry.

This can be clearly seen in the works of the poet Dionysios Solomos (1798–1857), the poet who ranks *par excellence* as the national poet of modern Greece. (Among other things, he is the author of the words of the Greek national anthem.) Solomos, as two of his contemporary fellow-poets, Ugo Foscolo and Andreas Kalvos, was born on the small island of Zante (Zakynthos), one of the Ionian islands, or Seven Islands (*Heptanisa*), lying off the west coast of Greece. It was no accident that it should have been the Ionian islands that produced the first major literary poets of modern Greece. For some three hundred years these islands had been under the rule of the Venetian Republic, and a local aristocracy had been formed whose culture was largely a reflection of that of Italy, and whose standard of living was with few exceptions greatly superior to that of mainland Greece. Solomos himself was educated at Venice and, later, at the university of Padua, and his first literary language, and that of his first poems, was Italian.

Moreover, in the seventeenth century, after the capture of Candia, chief city of Crete, and the subsequent occupation of the island (1669) by the Turks, a number of Cretan refugees had settled in the Ionian islands. Crete itself had for some four and a half centuries previous to this (1204–1669) also been under Venetian rule, and similarly had come under the influence of Italian culture and civilization. This influence had not only expressed itself in the formation of a local aristocracy, or indirectly in the works of a painter like the Cretan El Greco (Domenicos Theotocopoulos), but it had also stimulated the creation of dramatic and epic poetry. The dramatic literature includes such plays as *Abraham's Sacrifice*, a religious work, and the *Erophile*, a bloodthirsty tragedy in which all the main characters are killed or kill themselves. But the master-piece of this Cretan literature is the epic already referred to, the *Erotocritos* by Vizentzos Kornaros, a work in the chivalrous genre telling of the love of Aretousa, the daughter of a king, and the valiant Erotocritos. This work, written in the fifteen-syllable metre, though with rhyming distichs, and incorporating much of the im-agery and spirit of the demotic tradition, became, in spite of its literary and sophisticated character, immensely popular throughout the Greek world, great parts and sometimes even all of it being learnt by heart like any other demotic poem. When the Cretans settled in the Ionian islands they brought this literature with them; and indeed the old ballad-singer whom, it is said, the young poet Solomos, Italian educated and still writing in Italian, heard singing in a street in Zante one evening and whose ballad – it was about setting fire to the Holy Sepulchre at Jerusalem – made Solomos suddenly aware of his true vocation as a Greek poet, using the common language of the Greek people, may well have been a Cretan.

Be that as it may, Solomos did begin to write in Greek – and in demotic Greek, not in the 'mixed' Atticizing language proposed by Korais; and we do find those themes we have singled out as char-acteristic of demotic poetry to be the ones with which he is most concerned. But Solomos was not a peasant; he was an aristocrat with a lofty and proud intellect. Dante was his model of the true poet; and he himself was a religious poet, who regarded his function to be that of a kind of hierophant with the task of leading his people into the way of truth. He saw man's situation in relation to freedom, nature, and death, in the light of a spiritual vision which might be described as Augustinian in quality, though strongly influenced by the idealism of contemporary German philosophers and in partic-ular of Schiller. Thus, freedom and death are still the opposites that polarize man's inner life, though death is now regarded not as the term of human life but as the 'last enemy' that man has to overcome on his path to ultimate liberation. Because of this shifting in emphasis, this shifting of the dividing line between the unreal and the real, so that now death is seen as opening on to reality, the attitude to nature and the physical world correspondingly changes. Solomos was acutely aware of the beauty of the natural world and wrote of it in some exquisite lyrical passages. But instead of nature being the norm in harmony with which man's life must be lived and from which he is only separated by the 'unnatural' experience of death, it now in some way represents, in spite of its beauty, a kind of illusory or unreal power, one whose spell man must also break if he is to achieve true freedom.

This spiritual vision that Solomos brought to bear on his consideration of those basic themes of freedom, death, and nature, he sought to express in all his later poetry – poetry that for the most part remains a series of splendid fragments; and in what was to be his major poetic endeavour, a long unfinished poem called *The Free Besieged*, he attempted to give it a dramatic and symbolic setting. One of the most stirring incidents of the Greek war of Independence was the siege of Mesolonghi by the Turks. This small town, where Byron had died, was besieged by such an overwhelming enemy force that there was no doubt of its final capture. Yet in spite of this the Greeks did not surrender, and it was only when those who were still in a physical state to do so had made a last desperate attempt to force a passage through the besieger's lines, while those who were left behind – the aged, the wounded, the sick, the women and children too weak to follow – blew themselves up by firing barrels of gunpowder, that the Turks were able to enter the ruined and deserted town. It was this incident, with all its dramatic possibilities, that Solomos chose to write his poem about. Mesolonghi was a kind of marble threshing-floor, a microcosm in which could be mirrored this struggle of man to achieve his essential freedom even to the point of fighting against death itself. But now, as we saw, the idea of freedom is given a new content. It is not simply a matter of fighting with Stoic fortitude against forces which in the nature of things are bound to overwhelm and defeat one in the end. It is also a matter of deliberately and consciously striving to realize, through a process of inner transformation that requires the overcoming of all attachments to the natural world and even of death, a state of absolute and supernatural freedom: a state which is that of what Solomos calls 'the intellectual and moral Paradise'. We have, that is to say, passed beyond the sphere to which the idea of freedom is limited in the heroic world of the epic and the ballad – the natural and historical sphere – and have entered the sphere of metaphysical

realities. The struggle of the soul to free itself from the brute forces
of matter, from the weaknesses of the flesh and the enticements of
the senses, is now the theme. Only when all has been surrendered;
only when all which binds man to mortal life and when all he has
borrowed from the world of time and place has been given up, and
when he faces his own nothingness and death without fear or hope
– only then is his soul's true nature and magnificence revealed.
Solomos sums up the process of this psychic drama through which
man passes on his way to freedom in two lines from the poem:

> From depth to depth he fell until there was no other:
> Thence he issued invincible . . .

As we remarked, *The Free Besieged* was never finished, and in the
state in which Solomos left it it is hardly more than a series of
densely-charged fragments consisting of verses from three independent drafts of the poem. These, together with a series of notes that
Solomos made in connection with the poem, make it possible to
piece the action of the drama together. There is the picture of the
besieged enduring hunger and deprivation, the death of children,
the mockery of the superior and well-supplied enemy. Their hopes
of relief are raised by the sight of a fleet approaching, only to be
dashed to the ground again when it is discovered that it too belongs
to the enemy. In some lovely lines the beauty of spring spreading
over the earth is described, though now this beauty also represents
a temptation, threatening to waken in the besieged so much the
love of life that their courage is enfeebled:

> Blond April dances with Eros, and nature knows
> Her best and richest hour. In the swelling
> Shade which closes coolness and fragrance, un-
> Heard of birdsong trembles. Clear lovely waters,
> Sweet waters, spill through scented caverns,
> Steal the scent, leave their coolness, and,
> Showing to the sun the treasures of their source,
> Hither and thither dash and sing like nightingales.
> Life throbs through earth, through wave and sky.
> But over the clear and dead-calm lake,
> Dead-calm, clear down to the depths, the butterfly
> That had perfumed her sleep within the wild lily
> Was playing with a small unknown shadow.
> Light-shadowed seer, what did you see last night?
> Miraculous night, night sown with magic!
> With neither earth nor sea nor sky breathing
> Even as the bee close to the little flower,

The moon round something motionless that
Shimmered on the lake alone was pulsing;
And beautiful a young girl came out in her light.

Finally, the last night comes. The besieged have decided to make
a bid to break through the encircling enemy or, as is most likely, to
die in the attempt. They gather in the church to pray. Incense rises.
All is silent. Not even a dog barks. It is as if life has stopped. In this
last moment, now that the decision to face death has been reached
and they are as it were stripped naked, no longer attached to any
material form or fortune, hope or desire, they feel strangely united.
Only, after the final prayer, the women become frightened a little
and weep. This is the last 'temptation' they have to overcome and
they manage to survive it. Then, as dawn breaks, they make their
sortie, to issue free, either beyond the circle of besiegers, or beyond
death. For in this final moment of self-sacrifice, the barriers of life
and death, as well as the limitations of the purely natural world,
are transcended, and man achieves a new state of complete inner
freedom.

Andreas Kalvos (1792–1869) was the second important poet
from Zante who was also writing at the same time as Solomos. He
too came very much under the influence of Italian culture, and like
Solomos wrote his first poems in Italian. Indeed, if anything this
Italian influence was more pronounced where Kalvos was concerned; he not only lived in Italy for a certain period of his life but,
under the direction of his fellow-countryman, the poet Ugo Foscolo,
he also came to accept the then fashionable western views about
ancient Greece and the glories of the classical world of which we
have spoken elsewhere. This, combined with the fact that a few
years before the outbreak of the Greek war of Independence he
came into contact with enthusiastic philhellene circles in Switzerland, strongly affected his attitude to his country's destiny, and this
is reflected in the twenty odes – his total poetic production in Greek
– that he wrote on and soon after the outbreak of the war of Independence. These twenty odes form one long hymn to Greece and
to Greek freedom. But Kalvos' Greece was not that of the demotic
tradition, nor did he share Solomos' majestic spiritual vision.
Kalvos' Greece was, rather, the Greece of the romantic western
philhellenes, still haunted by the glorious beings of the golden age,
as it was too for Byron:

The very gale their names seemed sighing;
The waters murmured of their name;
The woods are peopled with their fame;

1. War of Independence. Fighting Priest and guerrillas, by Panayiotis Zographos (d. 1839)

2. Theodore Kolokotronis
(1770–1843)

3. Charilaos Tricoupis
(1832–96)

4. King Constantine I (1868–1922) during the Balkan wars. On his right Metaxas as a young staff officer

5. Eleutherios Venizelos (1864–1936)
6. Asia Minor refugees with their icons, 1922

7.   Crown Prince Paul (later King; 1901–64), King George II
(1890–1947), and General Metaxas (1871–1941)

8.   The Italian war, 1940

9. Markos, the communist leader during the Civil War,
and Zachariades

10.   The victims who are not forgotten. Civil War, Athens, January 1945

11. Constantine Karamanlis, Prime Minister 1955–63.
A new man for the new Greece

12.   George Papandhreou

13. The poet George Seferis (Seferiades), Greek ambassador in London 1957–62

14. The village of Portaria in the Pelion range

15.   Constitution Square, Athens. The Acropolis in the background

16.   The Old Palace, Athens, since 1935 seat of the Greek parliament

17.   The port of Piraeus

18. A wedding procession at Heracleion, Crete

19.   The wife of a potter at Archangelos, Rhodes

20.   An old man of Heracleion

21. The church of Moulki on Salamis

The silent pillar, lone and grey,
Claimed kindred with their sacred clay;
Their spirits wrapped the dusky mountain,
Their memory sparkled o'er the fountain;
The meanest rill, the mightiest river
Rolled mingling with their fame for ever.
Despite of every yoke she bears,
That land is Glory's still and theirs!
                              (*The Siege of Corinth*, XV, pp. 407 ff.)

For Kalvos then, as for so many others, the significance of the struggle in which modern Greeks were now engaged lay in the fact that it was thought to mark the historical regeneration of the ancient Greek world. Kalvos therefore, in spite of the fact that he was himself a Greek, had little awareness of the true realities and potential ities of the contemporary Greek situation. In the introduction to the second volume of his *Odes*, published in 1826 and dedicated to General Lafayette, he speaks of returning to Greece to 'exposer un coeur de plus au feu de Musulmans'; and when he left Switzerland for Greece he had no doubt hoped to find men who were a reincarnation of the heroes of Marathon and Salamis – men who would be ready to welcome him as his country's new Tyrtaios. Instead he found himself unknown, and the appearance of his fighting compatriots must have been as disillusioning and alarming for him as the appearance of the strange and terrible Greek sailors to the philhellene Shelley. Realizing that he had in fact no real contact with the Greek people or with the war whose ideals he had sung with such fervour, Kalvos chose to retreat. He fled to Corfu, to the welcome of, among others, Lord Guilford of the Ionian Academy. There he found an atmosphere more congenial to his temperament. But the poet in him seems to have suffered some injury beyond cure. Kalvos died, in England, in 1869. During the forty-three years between 1826 – when he published the second volume of *Odes* – and the day of his death, he did not as far as is known write a single further line of poetry.

If Kalvos' *Odes* did no more than reflect the ideals and attitudes of a romantic philhellenism they would not be of much significance in the development of modern Greek poetry. Fortunately, though, the Kalvos who thought of himself as an impersonal public figure with a conscious historical role, even as a maker of history, is only half the story; and behind the patriotic exhortation and the pedantic classicism is something at once more real and more truly responsive to the contradictions and ambiguities of human existence. And here once again we are able to recognize in the living aspects of this

P

poetry precisely those features we have noted as particularly characteristic of the Greek poetic tradition. There is first of all a sense of the almost pristine beauty of the natural world. Throughout the *Odes* occur lines of a wonderful freshness and spontaneity describing the Greek landscape in terms of a kind of primitive innocence reminiscent of Traherne's childhood vision, lines like:

> The scented lips of day
> Kiss
> The earth's rested forehead.

Or those which describe the sun that:

> Shows on the horizon
> Like the idea of joy.

But alongside this keen sense of natural beauty and innocence is an equally keen sense of mortality and doom, of the loss of everything, expressed in lines such as the following that describe the passage of time:

> As from the sun the hours
> Like drops of fire
> Fall into the sea of time
> And vanish for ever.

Or:

> Ah, the hopes of man
> Dissolve
> As the light dreams of a child;
> They sink as fine shot
> To the sea's fathomless depth.

In no poem however is this experience of the loss of life and of the transitory and doomed nature of human existence so vividly expressed as in the *Ode to Death*. Once again we are brought back to that fundamental theme of man's confrontation with death which we found in the folk ballad of the young man wrestling with Death on the threshing-floor and in Solomos' *The Free Besieged*. In Kalvos' poem the confrontation takes place in a graveyard at night, with its tombs and cold moons and phantoms:

> Here in this church
> Of the first Christians
> How came I,
> Kneeling?
> Silent, frozen,

The vast wings of midnight
Cover the earth.
Quiet here; relics
Of the saints sleep;
Quite quiet: do not disturb
The sacred rest of the dead.
I hear the wind
Raging furiously, and
Windows of the church open,
Torn to pieces;
While from the sky
Where black-winged clouds sail
The moon
Casts her cold silver,
And floods with light
A silent tombstone . . .

From this grave a phantom rises. It is the poet's mother, and she addresses her son:

Do not search out
The inexpressible
Mystery of death . . .
What do you weep for? You don't know
My soul's state,
And in the grave my body rests from pain.
Yes, life is unbearable pain;
Hopes and fears,
The world's pleasures
Torment you.
We the dead enjoy
Eternal peace,
A sleep without fear,
Without sorrow or dreams;
While you, cowards, tremble
Hearing the name of death – death
No one can escape.
There's but a single road
And it leads
Straight to the tomb . . .
My son, you knew me when I was alive:
The sun
Revolving like a spider
Enfolded me ceaselessly
With light and death.

The spirit which gave me life
Was God's breath
And has returned to God;
My body was earth and lies here in the grave . . .

At this point the vision vanishes, leaving the poet 'in thick darkness'. But this encounter with his dead mother, with death itself, has allowed him to overcome his fear of mortality which made him a slave to the things of this passing world; and in overcoming this fear he achieves that freedom of which he had previously been deprived:

Now my lips can kiss
The knees of death,
Now I can crown his skull.
Where are the roses? Fetch
The fadeless wreaths and the lyre.
Sing.
The terrible enemy has become a friend.
Can Death that embraced frail woman
Put fear
Into the heart of man?
Who is in danger?
Now that I face Death with courage
I hold
The anchor of salvation.

We have spoken particularly of these two poets, Dionysios Solomos and Andreas Kalvos, because, standing as they do at the beginning of the whole later literary development of modern Greek poetry, they gave the essential direction to this development, setting its course and in a considerable measure determining its character. They ensured that the themes which had been at the roots of the consciousness of the Greek people as this is reflected in their demotic poetry, as well as the direct language of this poetry, passed over into the poetic consciousness and diction of modern Greece. In fact some three-quarters of a century – years of assimilation and experimentation where Greek poetry is concerned – had to pass before other Greek poets arose capable of taking up and continuing this 'dialogue of the spirit' at the level at which Solomos and Kalvos left it. But during this present century one poet after another – Palamas, Kavafy, Sikelianos, Kazantzakis, Seferis, Elytis – to mention but the most important of them – has contributed to the richness of the emerging tradition in a manner fully worthy of the example set by his predecessors.

In one particular respect however these later poets seem to differ from the two earlier poets and indeed from the anonymous ballad-makers, and this is in their sense of, and attitude to, the ancient pre-Christian, or at least non-Christian, Greek world. In the ballads there is scarcely an echo from or allusion to this ancient world: the whole attention is directed to the immediacies of living existence. Where Solomos' poetry is concerned, what is important again are living men and women and their heroic and tragic struggles in the contemporary world: and there are few direct references to Greek antiquity. In the case of Kalvos, it is true, the classical influence is far stronger and more explicit; but even so it scarcely amounts to more than the figure-painting in neo-classical style of a kind of primitive Arcadian landscape, an earthly paradise; and in his *Ode to Death*, his major poem, even this classicizing is, as we have seen, entirely absent. Where these later poets are concerned however the sense of this ancient past, and the use of material and myths borrowed directly from the storehouse of the classical world, is far more pervasive – so pervasive that at times it seems to over-shadow and all but eliminate the present and its realities, which then appear by contrast to be but empty and largely negative affairs. Whether it is Palamas speaking of the 'people of relics' living and reigning among the temples and olives of the Attic landscape and contrasting their presence with that of the modern crowd which is like a caterpillar crawling sluggishly over a white flower; or Kavafy evoking some scene – ironic or erotic – of Hellen-istic Alexandria; or Sikelianos endeavouring to resurrect the whole pantheon of the ancient gods and to be a hierophant to their mysteries; or Seferis seeking for the archaic King of Asine – the true man – and finding but the unsubstantial emptiness of contemporary human existence: whichever it is, the impression is that the ancient world in one phase or another of its history has become of deep concern for these poets, as if they had been caught up in it in such a way that the modern scene appears hazy and unreal, a series of meaningless gestures and uncoordinated sounds. The statues have taken over from the living.

This sense of Greece's ancient past could hardly not have devel-oped in the country which had once provided the physical setting for the whole mythological and historical drama of Greek antiquity. Moreover, the latter half of the nineteenth century and the opening years of the twentieth century marked a period of great archaeo-logical discovery in Greek lands. It was during this period that many of the major centres of the ancient Greek world – Olympia, Delphi, Mycenae, Knossos, and so on – were excavated. Everywhere in Greece reminders of this ancient world began to leap to the eye and stimulate the imagination:

Scattered drums of a Doric column
Razed by unexpected earthquakes
To the ground. . . .

as Sikelianos puts it; or as Seferis writes: 'fragments of a life which was once complete, disturbing fragments, close to us, ours for one moment, and then mysterious and unapproachable as the lines of a stone licked smooth by the wave or of a shell in the sea's depths.' In addition to this, with the spread of education on the western European pattern in Greece, many more Greeks themselves, and particularly the cultivated Greeks, now accepted that idealized version of Greek antiquity which, as we have seen, had so captured the mind of educated Europeans in the post-Renaissance period. These factors alone are sufficient to account for the overshadowing place that the classical past began to assume in the modern Greek poetic consciousness.

   This reorientation of consciousness had however certain vital consequences. The actual living traditions of modern Greece at the time of the Greek war of Independence were still, in spite of the partial alienation of the mercantile middle classes, those of Orthodox Christianity and of the demotic heritage, both coming down from Byzantium, both intimately connected one with another, and both sharing reciprocal values. But the values of Hellenism are not those either of Christian Orthodoxy or of the demotic tradition. Their acceptance therefore on the part of the educated classes of Greece and of the poets could only be at the expense both of Orthodoxy and of the demotic tradition. Hellenism, it might be said, has done more than anything else to displace the values of Orthodox Christianity and the people's tradition in the modern Greek consciousness. Moreover, because it had no living roots in Greece, its acceptance has gone with the same idealization of the ancient world that had already taken place in the West. Not only, that is to say, is the ancient Greek world now felt to represent a past phase of the history of the modern Greek people (whether or not this is literally true is of no consequence here); it is also felt to represent a phase in which human life was lived with a degree of completion and perfection that has never been attained since, one that therefore presents the perpetual ideal against which later ages, and in particular the modern age, must measure the integrity, or lack of integrity, of its own beliefs and activities. 'Dionysos is a *judge*! Am I understood?' Thus Nietzsche; and the sense that this ancient world, the archaic world of the natural simplicities of the vine and olive (still a physical presence in Greece), and of the beauty of ritual gesture and naked dance, is a kind of norm; and that its god Dionysos is the judge of the values of the modern Greek world and its aspirations, is implicit again and again in the poetry of modern Greece:

> And behold
> You, Plato, image of Dionysos on earth:
> The end of your journey
> Has become my beginning.
> Word
> Where Athenian thought for ages rested
> To flower in my own struggle:
> 'The only method is death!'

writes Sikelianos; and in a more minor key Seferis questions from substantially the same point of view:

> Because we know so well this our destiny
> Circling round among broken stones, three or
> six thousand years,
> Searching in wrecked buildings which were
> perhaps our own home,
> Trying to remember dates and heroic deeds . . .
> Shall we now be able to die properly?

What has happened in effect is that an ideal of man living in a world of extraordinary natural and artistic beauty, at peace with himself and in harmony with his gods by virtue of myths of a pure simplicity and clarity mirrored in a ritual worship of equal simplicity and clarity – the 'peaceful limbs of the great Dionysos' (Sikelianos) – this ideal has taken the place of or been substituted for a Christ-centred vision of life with the Cross at its centre: the kind of vision that inspired Solomos' *The Free Besieged*. And because this ideal is of the past and has no actual potentialities of concrete realization in the modern Greek world, the situation in which the poet finds himself can only be one of intense and increasing anguish, not to say despair. For not only does the modern world stand condemned by this ideal, but there is no possibility of it even remotely recovering the conditions of the ancient world in which the life of man is alone considered to have achieved ultimate value and significance. Sikelianos, it is true, seems to have thought that some such recovery might have been possible. He thought it might be possible to establish at Delphi a centre of education, or rather of spiritual regeneration, in which the principles and practices – and particularly the artistic practices – of the religious and cultural tradition of ancient Greece might be represented to the people of modern Greece and, through them, to the whole world; and in this spirit he initiated a movement he called 'The Delphic Idea' which had as its immediate consequences two Delphic Festivals, one in 1927 and the other in 1930. The movement failed, as it was bound to fail; and other poets more realist if less heroic than Sikelianos, or more heroically resigned, have been content to express their sense of exile from the 'true life', to record the pain of the human situation in a world that has betrayed its proper significance: Palamas speaking of 'the painful, lofty, and tragic reality' of man who, 'bound with the golden chain of verse, lives incapable of grasping any solid creations, and advances embracing only phantasies'; Kavafy, sick guest of a city he can never escape from, contemplating in the mirror of his art some incident of folly, tenderness, or ironic frailty set in the Hellenistic world and which, so contemplated, can relieve him for a moment not of the disease of being alive at all, but of the deeper disease that makes it impossible to bear living; or Seferis finding a startled bat where once the man of the golden age had bred his noble children and anchored his proud ships; while elsewhere, in this nightmare of the present, men, the human masses – for there is no man in the proper sense in this modern world – whirl past like eddies of meaningless dust, frantic and incomprehensible:

> I don't understand these faces, I don't understand them,
> Sometimes they imitate death and then again
> They gleam with the small life of a glow-worm
> With a limited effort, hopeless,
> Squeezed between two wrinkles
> Between two stained café tables.
> They kill each other, grow smaller,
> Stick like postage stamps on glass –
> Faces of the other tribe.
> We walked together, shared bread and sleep,
> Tasted the same bitterness of departure,
> Built with what stones we had our houses,
> Set out in ships, were exiled, returned,
> Found our women waiting:
> They scarcely knew us, no one knew us.
> And the companions wore statues, wore the naked
> Empty chairs of autumn, and the companions
> Destroyed their own faces. I don't understand them.

In these circumstances, what has happened to the three themes we singled out as particularly characteristic of modern Greek poetry? Have they been abandoned or at least attenuated? In this context another aspect of the attitude of these poets to the past must be indicated. The past for them – the past of lost gods and godlike men – is not simply the norm against which the significance of the present may be measured; it does not only represent a refuge or an escape from the horrors and complexities of contemporary existence; it is also, and perhaps above all, something that must be *reappropriated*, must be integrated to and find its proper place in the total consciousness of the Greek people, as part of their repossession of their natural world. This has come about in a curious way. Rightly or wrongly the attitude of a great deal of Christian thought to the ancient Greek world and its culture has been negative and even destructive: the ancient Greeks were victims of the false gods, had whored after vain superstitions, been duped by absurd myths, had 'worshipped creation rather than the Creator' as the endlessly reiterated Pauline phrase had it. This in its turn had produced a double reaction where the mediaeval Christian tradition was concerned (and above all in this context where eastern Christendom was concerned); or, rather, it had produced a reaction which expressed itself in two main ways: first, in an almost total denial of any positive value in the pre-Christian Greek world; and, second – because the worship of false gods was inseparably associated with the idea of worshipping creation rather than the Creator – in a kind of ascetic suspicion of and hostility to the natural world – a suspicion and hostility which in their turn amounted also to a certain devaluation of the positive content of creation. Thus the devaluation of the ancient Greek world came to be associated very intimately with a certain devaluation of the natural world; so that, correspondingly, a reappropriation of the positive content and significance of the natural world, of creation, was from this angle bound to have its counterpart in a reappropriation of the positive content and significance of the ancient Greek world: in an overcoming of the sense of guilt distilled by the destructive and negative attitude of much Christian thought to that world through a realization that the 'false gods', although they may have degenerated into idols in the late 'pagan' era, were, in their pristine manifestations, really supernatural or divine powers active in nature itself, attestations of the original springs of life. In other words, the break, amounting almost to total cleavage, established in the consciousness between the pagan and the Christian worlds, which had its counterpart in this devaluation of creation, has meant that the affirmation of the beauty and significance of creation – this repossessing by the Greek of his natural world – has both taken in some measure a non-Christian form and involved this reappropriation of the positive content of the pagan past. From this point of view it may be said that behind the intense preoccupation of modern Greek poets with the pagan past lies an intense affirmation of the beauty and significance of creation. That a similar affirmation – as we show else-where – lies at the heart of Orthodox Christian doctrine does not alter the fact that for the historical and psychological reasons we have indicated this affirmation in the modern Greek consciousness had nevertheless initially, though perhaps not eventually, to take a non-Christian form.

In this way then these later poets of modern Greece resume the theme of man's reciprocity with the natural world that was ex-pressed in the ballads (though here, and in what follows, it must be said that Kavafy is the exception that proves the rule): there is a great affirmation of the natural world, of all life's most various and contradictory manifestations. 'Of nothing am I ashamed,' writes Palamas, 'nothing do I silence, nothing do I despise, for all with purpose, both the world's priceless things and what the world rejects, are by law established, determined by fate, and you cannot alter them or deny them. Everything of man is holy, everything deserves sympathy . . .' In Sikelianos' poetry this relationship with the natural world is felt almost as an organic relationship. The stream of life that runs through the poet's veins is felt to be one with that which runs through all nature, through stones and grass, leaves and flowers, and the stars. Man's body and blood are part of this same dance and rhythm of life. From direct, living, sensual contact with every living thing, man draws in the vital nourishment of his own life and spiritual development:

> Tighten well
> The girdle, that you grow
> Light-footed, and all nature round you,
> Luminous to your desire,
> Will come with youthful vigour
> To attire your flesh;
> And the body will grow strong
> In thought . . .
> And when your grasp is firm
> Upon the sacred earth,
> In triumph and deliverance
> Will I forge wings for you
> Which the sun cannot destroy . . .

Yet this vision of the 'sacred earth', of the holiness of all life's expressions, is not a simple pantheism. The affirmation of creation is matched by a sense of its transience and evanescence; of the transience and evanescence of man in history; it is matched also by the sense that both the natural world and man in history may lack any real substantial identity beyond that contained in their immediate appearance, as if their expression in a natural or historical form exhausted their potentialities. This may appear contradictory; and yet it is in a certain sense a consequence of that psychological compulsion which associated in the modern Greek poetic conscious- ness the affirmation of the significance and beauty of creation with a reappropriation of the pagan past. For however much the gods of this pagan world may once have been venerated as living realities, forces active in nature itself, and however much the deepest intuition of the modern Greek poets may be of this presence in nature and in this world of what one can only call spiritual qualities, so that the cleavage between the world of the senses and the world of the spirit is overcome in a celebration of the holiness of 'everything that lives': however much this may be so, yet these gods themselves cannot for the contemporary consciousness really be gods, onto- logical realities that man may worship through ritual and prayer as the generators and sustainers of his own and nature's existence; and there is bound to be something artificial about presenting them as figures mythologically valid for the present age. The consequence is that while there is felt to be a spiritual quality in nature, there is not so readily felt to be any substantial or ontological reality behind nature, giving it any enduring or more-than-temporal significance. It is as if creation and man's life in creation lack all ontological basis; as if beneath their existence is a void: the funeral mask (the mask of human existence) sounds hollow as a dry jar in the light (so writes Seferis); and in the sensible world all that is left to worship is the stagnant emptiness of a few cisterns, image *par excellence* of this vacuity that seems to lie beneath the tantalizing appearance of things.

The second of those themes we noted as characteristic of modern Greek poetry – the theme of death – tends thus to express itself in the work of these later poets as a haunting sense of the void that lies behind the visible forms of this world – that lies 'beyond the statues', as Seferis puts it; and the struggle with death, that con- frontation on the threshing-floor, takes shape as a struggle to grasp the significance of this void in its full dimensions, and to overcome the negation and despair with which it threatens to overwhelm man's creative effort. Nor is this struggle to penetrate into this void, this silence that opens beyond the borders of the natural world and man's life in history, itself simply a heroic but ultimately pointless defiance of death and the forces of annihilation. It is on the contrary felt to be the most positive of movements, something even on which the possibility of man's real fulfilment depends. For if the 'gods are dead' in the sense that they cannot in their ancient forms now be the objects of human worship, none the less, if those ancient forms were the expression of genuine ontological realities, those realities must still be what they always have been: the hidden source of all things. So that the void out of which the ancient gods were born and which their 'death' has as it were exposed in all its dark intensity may also be envisaged as the ultimate generative ground of everything, of gods and men and all creation: as life itself in the deepest and fullest sense. This at least is how Sikelianos envisaged it, writing of this experience:

> And again I know
> That in this Silence
> I must go forward,
> Forgetting the Word's ferment within me,
> Silent, as though fearing to wake someone,
> To see the world's face,
> The whole world's,
> From the beginning:
> The face of all creatures,
> Of all peoples, all ages, from the beginning.

At the same time – and here the creative orientation of these poets reunites with the more consciously Christian orientation of the Solomos of *The Free Besieged* – realization of the void – or, as Elytis puts it in the poem, *Axion Esti*, already mentioned, of the Voids – requires that kind of self-sacrifice which the heroes of Missolonghi had to face: the stripping bare or dispossession of all attachments to the habitual world. In this way the struggle to realize the nature of the void – this struggle with death – is also a struggle of the human soul to free itself from the ties that keep it in subjection to the ordinary round and run of things: to free itself from the weaknesses of mind and body, from the enticement of the senses, from ultimately all its familiar and passing preoccupations. Freedom, the struggle for freedom in this sense is still therefore the keynote of Greek poetry; for it is felt that only through such freedom can human existence find its fulfilment; can the One – the Source of life Who makes the shadows of the void His dwelling-place – enter into and complete the one who is the individual person, the subject of life as we first know and experience it. 'And the One I really was' – the lines are again from Elytis' *Axion Esti*:

> And the One I really was, the One of many centuries ago,
> The One still verdant in the midst of fire, the One
>   still bound to heaven
>   entered into me, became
>   the one I am

At three o'clock in the morning
  above the shacks, distant
             the first cock crowed
For a second I saw the upright Pillars, the Metope of
  Powerful Beasts and Men bringing knowledge of God
The Sun assumed its face, eternal Archangel, on my right
          THIS I then
        and the world so small, so great.

A short survey such as this cannot do more than indicate some of the dominant features of modern Greek poetry. But it by no means exhausts its richness and variety. It says nothing of the numberless minor poets writing in the demotic language each of whom has contributed to its development. It says nothing of the poets who have chosen to write in the purist language, the *katharevousa*, and particularly of those who formed the first literary group – known later as the Old School of Athens – of the modern Greek state and whose founder and leading spirit was Alexander Soutsos (1803–63). It says nothing of the foreign influences that have affected in one way or another both form and theme: that of the Italian romantics, of Germans like Schiller, of Byron, on the Ionian School; of French romantics (Lamartine, de Musset, Victor Hugo) on the Old School of Athens in the first half of the nineteenth century; of the French Parnassians on what is known as the New School of Athens, with Kostis Palamas at its centre, in the latter half of the same century; of English poets, and particularly of T. S. Eliot, on poets like Seferis. It says nothing of modern Greek poetesses, though they have been few, or of satirical and dramatic poetry, though there is little here of distinction. But in spite of this it is within the perspectives established by its major representatives, past and present, that the wealth of modern Greek poetry may best be appreciated. For though such an account as is given here must necessarily reduce its endlessly changing imaginative and emotional patterns to what appear to be their basic elements, this but serves to indicate what may constitute one of the main secrets of its strength: that through ever fresh and spontaneous forms of expression it remains always at one with itself, repeating through the ages the same fundamental attitudes to human life, to its pain and joy, its love and death.

The Novel

The modern Greek novel takes second place to the poetry. This is not simply because as a general rule the development of poetry precedes that of prose, or that in any case poetry is the proper and primary literary vehicle for the communication of the great imaginative truths. It is also, where Greece is concerned, due to the fact that prior to the war of Independence there was no tradition at all of novel-writing in Greece, and hence nothing from which the genre could develop; while poetry, as we have seen, had behind it the immensely rich demotic tradition as well as the more sophisticated poetry of the Cretan school. The Greek novels, such as they were, of the Hellenistic and Byzantine periods were too remote in every way to serve as models, and the popular lives of the saints were not of a form that could be adopted for fiction. Thus the modern Greek novel had to begin from nothing where local tradition was concerned; and in order to make a start novel-writers were compelled to rely entirely on western models both in the matter of technique and for the ideas of what constituted suitable thematic material. This further meant that the Greeks who were first stimulated to write novels were those familiar with literary developments in western Europe, and in the event these for the most part were Greeks who lived outside Greece, in the cultural centres of western Europe. A consequence of this was that not only did early Greek novels derive from western prototypes in the matter of technique and general choice of subject, but that also early Greek novelists had very little contact with or knowledge of the contemporary Greek scene. In this way they were doubly alienated from any local Greek tradition.

Moreover, the novel had scarcely even in western Europe achieved the status of a respectable literary genre, and in Greece its pursuit was still something that no serious-minded writer would give his time to: if one was concerned with works of the imagination or sentiment one turned to poetry; if one was concerned to communicate other matters the proper medium was the pamphlet, the treatise, or straightforward memoirs. Fiction in prose was but a rather frivolous form of philology, suitable perhaps for young ladies. In addition, even supposing those who were tempted to write novels had been familiar with the Greek scene, here they would have encountered further difficulties. The form of the novel seems to require a certain corresponding stability in the forms of the society it portrays; there have to be certain more or less defined and accepted modes of personal behaviour, certain more or less defined patterns of class, interest, or activity. All this was lacking in the Greek scene immediately after the war of Independence; here everything was unsettled, in flux, undefined. Village life had been disrupted and often reduced to shambles during the long years of struggle; and city life was still embryonic and unformed, indeed often the scene of the most total confusion (and it must be remembered that such towns as there were in any case were scarcely more than overgrown villages). It is true that it might be assumed that the war of Independence would itself provide plenty of material for the novel; but this material was already being presented in the form of war memoirs, some of which, particularly those of General Makriyannis, still constitute what are among the most vivid and significant prose-works of modern Greek literature.

In these circumstances it is hardly surprising that the Greek novel made a slow start, and that its earliest ventures are not very rewarding. Mostly these – they began to appear already in the first half of the nineteenth century – reflect at second-hand the novels of Walter Scott or to a lesser extent those of de Staël, Dumas *père*, or Goethe (the Goethe of *Werther*). That is to say, they are historical novels, with scenes and characters taken from the past; or sentimental and romantic, full of dark sorrows, brooding and desperate loves, and a general rejection of life often amounting to suicide or near suicide; or a mixture of the two; and in any case the final products are hardly of great interest except as being the forerunners of later and more successful works.

These began to appear in the latter half of the nineteenth century, and their new character can in part be attributed to three distinct factors. The first is the most external of the three, and consists in the number of translations into Greek of some of the great European novels of the nineteenth century, particularly of the Russians, and of French realists like Emile Zola, the translation of whose *Nana* in 1880 made a deep impression on several contemporary Greek novelists. The effect of these novels was to indicate to Greek novelists possibilities of theme and treatment other than those exploited in the historical and romantic novels they had so far produced. It led them to look for themes in their own immediate environment, and to approach them in a direct, unromantic, and realist manner. The second factor was that a period of relative peace in Greece was reflected in the reforming and comparative stability of Greek village life in terms of its traditional age-old patterns. This meant that novelists could now find in Greece that relatively defined area of behaviour and interest which had previously been lacking.

Moreover – and this is the third factor – the pattern of this traditional village life had itself become of great concern to the more thoughtful minds of Greece. It was increasingly realized that many of the ideals in the name of which the Greek war of Independence had been fought, and many of the forms of life which as a consequence had been adopted by the new Greek state, were alien importations, or at best relevant only to the 'westernized' middle classes; they had no roots in or relationship to the life of the local Greek people, the people of the villages who after all still composed by far the greater part of the population. The life of these people on the contrary seemed to be based on other values and to express itself in other forms; and it was the growing awareness of this that began to lead these more thoughtful minds of Greece to turn towards the people, their forms and traditions, in order to search for truer, more native foundations of their national life; in order to search for the genuine sources of neo-Hellenism and for the living roots of their culture. The result was the inauguration in Greece of what we now call folk-lore studies – studies in the traditions, customs, values, language, and artistic expressions of the Greek village people. The great pioneer in these studies was Nikolas Politis, whose monumental *Neo-hellenic Mythology* was published in 1871. His work had an immense influence on contemporary and later novelists, already for reasons we have noted themselves beginning to turn towards the Greece of their immediate environment for their themes. As one of these novelists, George Drosinis, was later to write of Politis: 'He led us to the still unexplored treasure of traditions, legends, perceptions, customs of the Greek people, and incited us to study our national heirlooms and to use them each one of us according to his art.'

In fact there had been one or two earlier and isolated attempts to explore the realities of the contemporary Greek scene. The first of these was a novel called *Thános Vlekas* by the jurist Pávlos Kalligás (1814–96). This book was published in 1855 and attempts to portray, through the lives of two brothers, a kind of comprehensive view of the Greek world in the time of the reign of Otho, contrasting the relatively just but extremely poor life of the simple peasant with the immense and growing corruption of the new urban and official circles. A second attempt in the same direction was a novel called *Loukís Láras* by Dimitrios Vikélas (1835–1909), published in 1879 and concerned, rather from the external and picturesque point of view, with the life of the peasant people during the time of the war of Independence. But the real emergence of a particular type of novel – and short story – as a result of the factors we have mentioned came only towards the end of the century and in the opening years of the twentieth century in the works of authors such as Andreas Karkavitsas, Alexandros Papadiamantis, Yannis Kondylákis, and Konstantine Theotókis. These authors – and there were others as well – produced a series of novels and short stories that are not only distinctively and, one might say, uniquely Greek, but are also genuine creative achievements. All of them – collectively they form what has been called an ethographic genre – are devoted to the faithful description of the morals, customs, habits, and other characteristics of village and rural life, and they often achieve this in a way that is dramatic, completely unsentimental, and even ruthless in its uncompromising realism. Two novels in particular stand out in this latter respect. The first, *The Beggar*, by Karkavitsas, described the life and fantastic cruelties of a community of professional beggarmen, the area of whose activities extends over the whole Balkans and into Russia; and the second, *The Life and Death of Karavelas*, by Theotókis, tells of the remorseless hunting down and destruction by a neighbour and eventually by the whole village community of an elderly widower.

One writer of this group, while belonging to it, also stands somewhat apart from it. This is Alexandros Papadiamantis. His work is not simply descriptive, any more than for instance Dostoievsky's work is simply descriptive. In fact he was not really concerned with fiction as such. His great concern was to present in his work the world of Greek Orthodox Christianity that he saw in danger of being destroyed by the hopeless and haphazard pursuit of modern ideas, modes, and practices, on the part of the urban and so-called educated classes, particularly in Athens. He himself – he came from Skiathos, one of the islands of the northern Sporades – came very much from this Christian world, and in his youth was greatly influenced by the group known as the Kollyvades, whose members regarded with dismay the growing secularization of the Greek Church, and sought a return to the founts of the Orthodox Christian tradition, particularly in its hesychastic and monastic or semi-monastic form. Papadiamantis himself did not become a monk but lived 'in the world' on his island as a monk, and the practice of his faith always took precedence over his activity as a writer, although the two in fact were never separated for him. 'As for me,' he wrote, 'as long as I live and breathe and am in possession of my faculties I shall not cease from praising Christ with reverence, from lovingly describing nature, and from portraying with tenderness the true Greek world.' For him this world, nature and man, of which he wrote in his stories, was illumined and bathed in the light of God and the divine judgement and had existence only because behind it and within it he perceived its deep spiritual roots. These roots he saw embodied in the Orthodox Christian tradition that modern Greece had inherited from Byzantium, in its liturgy, music, architecture, and spiritual life; and he was appalled and dismayed by the spectacle of modern Greeks, especially in the cities, abandoning this tradition in the name of classical Hellenism and the values and practices of the modern West.

Novels describing life in the new city world of Greece were not written, for reasons at which we have glanced, during the greater

Q

part of the nineteenth century. But towards the end of the century there was a change and novelists began to turn their attention to the urban scene and its problems. One of the precursors in this respect was Yannis Psycharis. Psycharis, an expatriate Greek descended from a Chian family and living in Paris,[1] is in fact better known for the part he played in the 'language question' of modern Greece. We saw that Korais had first attempted a language reform, proposing a language that should be a kind of mixture of the ancient language and the language of the new middle classes. The acceptance of this language had disastrous consequences and prepared the way for a complete split in linguistic usage in Greece. On the one hand the people of Greece spoke and wrote a language – the demotic language – which was a natural organic development from the Greek of the Byzantine period, very much as modern English is a natural and organic development from Chaucerian English; and it was this language – the language of the ballads and the Cretan plays and epics – that Solomos had 'consecrated' for modern Greek poetry in adopting it for his own work. On the other hand, the official language of the state – the language of civil servants, of the professional classes (lawyers in particular), of university professors and schoolmasters, newspapers, and so on – followed the pattern proposed by Korais, and even veered more completely towards a hybrid Atticism. This meant that there were virtually two languages in Greece, one the living and spoken language, the other a dead artificial construction that had to be learnt but which became a status-symbol indicating the social and intellectual superiority of those who could use it. The early novelists, unlike Solomos and his followers, used this latter purist (*katharevousa*) language. But when they began to explore and write about the life of the village people of Greece they had to use, anyhow for dialogue, the language of the people, even though they might keep the purist language for narrative passages. Thus, for instance, Papadiamantis used his island language for dialogue, but preserved, not in his case the purist language, but rather the traditional ecclesiastical language for the rest of his writing.

Psycharis, a professional philologist, became an ardent champion of the demotic language, and in 1888 published what was virtually the manifesto of the demoticists, *My Journey*. It is difficult to envisage the passions aroused by the publication of this book and by the subsequent struggles of the demoticists to establish the demotic language as the proper language for creative writing, whether poetry or prose. Perhaps something of their intensity can be understood when it is remembered that it was precisely the users and

He held posts at the philological school in the University.

advocates of the purist language who were most fully affected by the myth of their 'Hellenic' descent and for whom a proof of this descent was the similarity of their language to the ancient language: they therefore naturally wished to pretend both to themselves and to the outside world that the modern Greek language was in fact this hybrid Atticizing mixture they had adopted in the steps of Korais; for the demotic language, while preserving a certain resemblance to the ancient language, was too remote from it to be a very convincing demonstration of their case. Thus, attacks on the purist language appeared to them, quite wrongly, to be attacks on the whole myth of their Hellenic origins, and they retaliated with the fury of those who feel their *raison d'être* is threatened with destruction. What subsequently complicated matters in this struggle (in which the demoticists triumphed as far as the literary language is concerned, but not as far as the official language of the state, university, newspapers, and so on, is concerned) was first the fact that Psicharis himself, the publication of whose *My Journey* marked a decisive phase in the battle, had never lived in Greece and had little living contact with the Greek people and their language, so that the demotic language he proposed was in its turn a somewhat stilted and artificial *demotikē* worked out in the Parisian study of the professional philologist; and second the fact that as the purist language maintained its status as a symbol of social and intellectual superiority and as in addition it was spread, in one form or another, among the people through schoolmasters and newspapers, the people themselves began to lose their sense of their own traditional language, and to absorb into it elements of a demoticized purism. Thus, one of the by-products of the Hellenic myth in modern Greece has been an ever-worsening confusion of language, a confusion which it is now impossible to resolve in terms of either of its original components, purist or demotic.

Apart however from his important place in the language question in Greece, Psicharis also has a place as a precursor of the Greek novel dealing with city life. His own novels – there are several – are set for the most part in the cities of western Europe; but his example encouraged other Greek novelists who followed him in his championing of the demotic language to follow him also in writing of city life. Moreover, city life in Greece, and particularly in Athens, had by the end of the nineteenth century achieved a coherence sufficient for it to provide theme and background for the novel. The result has been that the last sixty years has seen a succession of novels all more or less centred on the city world – in fact all more or less centred on Athens – of which perhaps the most distinguished are those by Gregorios Xenopoulos, K. Politis, and George Theotokas.

The last named in particular, in his novels *Argo*, *The Daemon*, *Leonis*, and more recently in what is perhaps his greatest work *Invalids and Wayfarers*, has sought to grapple with the actualities of Greek life as these presented themselves after the First World war and the subsequent Asia Minor disaster in 1922 in which the idea of the 'Greater Greece' was finally shattered. In his work Athens is no longer a parochial setting for idyllic love affairs but a growing Mediterranean metropolis in which the destinies of the modern Greek nation are being hammered out. One might say that for Theotokas, as for Nikos Kazantzakis of *Zorba*, *Christ Recrucified*, and other works published in the years after the Second World war, the novel becomes a medium for the dramatization in terms of living people of what are basically philosophical themes: themes concerned with man's destiny in the world, with the meaning of freedom, love, and sacrifice, with the mysteries of life and death.

This new scope given to the modern Greek novel does not mean however that the preoccupations we have noted as those of the ethographic novelists have been abandoned. Rather they have been deepened and seen in terms of a new complexity of relationships. First, the Asia Minor disaster itself and the displacement of the Ionian Greek population exposed a whole new vein of traditional Greek life; and this has been exploited by novelists like Ilias Venezis and Stratis Myrivilis, both of whom, in novels such as *Aeolian Earth* and *The Mermaid Madonna*, have written of aspects of the Greek world of the Anatolian seaboard and the islands of the eastern Aegean with a clarity in which poignancy, charm, and bitter realism blend. Then the growing ordeals, ugliness, frustrations, and sense of ultimate purposelessness in modern Greek city life itself are producing a reaction in which those traditional values that had been the concern of the ethographic novelists, and particularly of Papadiamantis, are again sought for in a philosophical quest for the meaning of man's life, above all of Greek life, in the modern world; and of this reaction novels like *The Sun of Death* and the subsequent *The Medusa's Head* and *Bread of Angels* by Pandelis Prevelakis, are products. The result is that the contemporary Greek novelist is now in a position to create works which, while remaining true to the positive aspects of local Greek tradition itself, are yet of a more universal significance; and in this creation he is able to build upon the achievements of his predecessors of the last hundred years and more.

PART FOUR

Contemporary Greece

Chapter 8

Political Events since the Civil War

I

THE EMERGENCE of Greece from the chaos of the civil war and its immediate aftermath, and the beginnings of reconstruction, were symbolized in the appearance of Marshal Papagos on the political scene. In May 1951 Papagos renounced all his military appointments, and two months later announced that he intended to contest the forthcoming general elections with a new national party, the Greek Rally. The fact that he had previously avoided all political intervention, and the prestige he enjoyed as victor in Albania and in the civil war, not only lent a dramatic quality to the announcement, but also enabled him to project the Rally as a patriotic movement rather than a political party. Thus with the support of those Greeks who were disenchanted with the traditional parties, and with the adherence of influential politicians such as Kanellopoulos, Stephanopoulos, and eventually Papandhreou, Papagos succeeded, in November 1952, in winning a majority large enough to allow him to initiate a vigorous programme of reform and reconstruction.

The Greek Rally broke a deadlock in which the traditional parties had proved unable to produce a government that was both stable and representative. At the first post-war elections, of 31 March 1946, the conservative coalition of nationalists (mainly Populists) won 206 out of the 354 seats contested. The decisiveness of this victory of the Right however was qualified by the abstention of Communists and some Liberals as a protest against alleged conditions of 'white terror'. And the 156 Populists, the core of the coalition, were not enough to provide an enduring and effective government.

Ten political parties were represented in the parliament of 1946–50. This fragmentation, and in particular the disarray and division of the old Liberal Party, are attributed by many commentators to the suppression of political life by Metaxas. The period of dictatorship and the experience of the occupation undoubtedly had a disruptive effect; but there were other, perhaps equally important, divisive factors. First, the system of proportional representation adopted in the 1946 elections encouraged the tendency

247

towards fission in Greek political life where loyalties were to personalities rather than the corporate party. Secondly, the division between those who supported or sympathized with the communist position and those who preferred the traditional regime of parliamentary parties – in these years the significant division in Greek politics – did not coincide with the older schism between republicans and monarchists; and this worked against the unity and strength of the liberal and republican forces to the advantage of the communist Left and the monarchist Right. The old-fashioned monarchist could be assumed to be anti-communist. The old-fashioned liberal or republican was drawn by his republicanism towards the communist position, and by his fear of extremism towards the anti-communist Right. The fear of extremism and the commitment to the parliamentary regime, usually proved the stronger attraction.

The confrontation between communist Left and bourgeois Right favoured the monarchy, which claimed to be the symbol of anti-communism and the protector of constitutional stability. Immediately after the 1946 elections, with the threat of renewed civil war very evident, Sophocles Venizelos, Papandhreou and Kanello-poulos, men of resolute republican convictions before the war, were prepared to accept the return of the King if a plebiscite should result in his favour. The deteriorating internal situation strengthened the insistent arguments of Tsaldaris, the Populist leader, for advancing the date of the plebiscite from 1948 to 1946. The British acceded to this request, and on 1 September 1946, 68 per cent of the Greek voters declared themselves in favour of King George's return.

One problem was thus settled. But the return of the King did not signify the return of stability. In the absence of any opposition from the Left (for the Communist Party was banned in 1947), and as a result of the mutual suspicion between Liberals and Populists and the internal division of the Liberals, there were no less than ten governments during the 1946–50 parliament. Only American insistence after their assumption of responsibility for Greece through the Truman doctrine announced in March 1947, and the brutal realities of the civil war, forced the Liberals and Populists into a coalition under the veteran Liberal Sophoulis on 7 September 1947. With periodic adjustments this alliance of old enemies held together during the critical period of the civil war, giving public expression to bourgeois unity, and preventing the government from falling too obviously into the hands of right-wing personalities tainted with collaboration during the occupation, or service under Metaxas. The unity however was precarious. After popular discontent over the inconclusive prosecution of the war in January 1949 Sophoulis was unable to reconstruct his government until King Paul threatened to find 'another solution' if a government of national salvation did not emerge within twenty-four hours. The final Sophoulis government, although based on the same alliance of Populists and Liberals, included Markezinis, an energetic and original leader of younger right-wing action, and appointed Marshal Papagos as Commander-in-Chief. Under these arrangements the government was in sight of victory when Sophoulis died on 24 June 1949.

Quite apart from the physical reconstruction Greece had to face after the civil war, political reconciliation was by itself a problem of great complexity. There was the disconcerting anomaly that those who had fought during the occupation in the left-wing resistance movement were now villains and their opponents in the collaborating security battalions, heroes. Many of the former because they had suffered at the hands of security forces or right-wing organizations after the Varkiza agreement, or because they had believed they were compromised by their resistance record, joined the Democratic Army. Others had been forced into its ranks simply through the misfortune of geography. Under the governments of the 1946–50 parliament, all of which depended ultimately on Populist support, rebels or their supposed sympathizers had suffered severe penalties. The too enthusiastic activity of General Zervas when he was Minister of Public Order in 1947 led to a government crisis. Again in 1948 after the murder of Ladas, the Minister of Justice, executions and arrests increased. Between 1 June 1946 and October 1949, 3,150 persons had been sentenced to death of whom 1,223 had actually been executed; and many thousands remained in preventive detention. In this atmosphere of denunciation and fear when the report of quite trivial suspicions might result in arrest, concern about the excesses of the Right was very real.

The results of the general election held on 5 March 1950, again under a system of proportional representation, reflected these apprehensions. The Populists lost a great part of their strength, winning 62 seats in an Assembly reduced to 250 deputies. Parties with an apparent relation to the Centre increased their numbers but their forces were divided: the Liberal Party now led by Sophocles Venizelos won 56 seats, a new grouping under Plastiras, the National Progressive Union of the Centre (E.P.E.K.), 45 seats, and the party of George Papandhreou thirty-five. Since the Communist Party had been banned, the Left was represented by an electoral coalition known as the Democratic Front. It polled 9·7 per cent of the vote and won 18 seats. Once more the electoral system emphasized and contributed to the fragmentation of the country's political forces. Forty-four parties fought the election and ten obtained representation in parliament. With the immediate external threat of the war removed, the new Assembly produced in the eighteen months of its life five weak and unstable coalition governments, four led by Venizelos and one by Plastiras. A stern warning from the American ambassador that aid would be withdrawn if the Assembly failed to form a stable government temporarily brought together the three centre parties under the leadership of Plastiras during the spring and summer of 1950. Yet within a short time the coalition was in difficulty over the Plastiras policy of clemency to the rebels still held in detention, an issue which had earlier persuaded electors to favour the centre parties rather than the Right. With the outbreak of war in Korea in June the opponents of leniency became more militant. In August Venizelos withdrew the Liberals from the government, demonstrating once more the essentially conservative attitudes of some parties supposedly standing between the Populists and the socialist or communist Left.

With little hope of arranging any enduring government from the resources of the existing parliament, new elections were announced for 9 September 1951. It was to fight these elections that Papagos formed the Greek Rally, thus further weakening the prospects of the centre parties. From the first Papagos was supported and influenced by Markezinis. In August, Kanellopoulos and Stephanopoulos joined the Rally with their followers. In the same month the communist Left and their sympathizers also drew up their forces, forming the 'United Democratic Left' (E.D.A.), a legitimate party through which, despite the banning of the Communist Party, they could present their policies and organize their adherents.

The electoral results revealed that under a modified system of proportional representation designed to favour the larger parties and restrict the representation of the Left, the Rally Party with 114 seats out of 258 had annihilated the Populists who won only two seats in the new chamber. In the centre both E.P.E.K. under Plastiras and the Liberals under Venizelos increased their vote and could together command the Assembly with 131 seats by a very narrow margin. There had been some concentration of the country's political forces since only nine parties contested the elections and eventually only six won representation. But with the purposeful refusal of Papagos to take part in any coalition Plastiras' majority of four was too slender for resolute government. Although Plastiras achieved some of the measures of pacification he considered so essential, in the abbreviation of sentences for many of the 20,000 rebels in detention and the commuting of most death sentences to life imprisonment, and although his government led Greece into N.A.T.O., it could make little headway with the intractable problems of monetary instability. The necessity for stable government over reasonable periods of time could not be disputed. Papagos insistently demanded elections on a majority system and in March 1952 the American ambassador Peurifoy intervened to state publicly that his government believed the simple proportional system of election prevented the effective use of American aid. This considered interference in Greece's domestic affairs provoked a protest from the government. Nevertheless in spite of resistance from his colleagues and the effects of debilitating sickness Plastiras passed a bill providing for elections under a simple majority rule.

With this single measure Plastiras contributed to an extraordinary simplification of the political scene; and incidentally to stable government, and the removal of centre parties from power for the next decade. In the elections of November 1952 the Rally Party polled 49 per cent of the vote and won 247 out of the 300 seats: the coalition of centre parties polled 34 per cent of the vote and won 51 seats. Apart from the return of two independents the four other parties which fought the election, including E.D.A. and the Populists, were left without representation. In its successful advance the Rally had concentrated the forces of the Right and made perceptible gains among supporters of the centre parties including the capture of a number of political personalities whose adherence may have owed more to opportunism than conviction. George Papandhreou whose personal party had been destroyed at the previous election was among this number. Apart from the traditional supporters of the Populist Party, those who voted for Papagos were influenced by renewed fears of communist sedition. A wide network of communist espionage in Greece had lately been uncovered. And before the election the desertion of Plastiras deputies to the ranks of the Rally had endangered the government's majority to the point where its enemies could claim that a supposedly nationalist government was kept in power by the support of two deputies who had defected from E.D.A. A reliably anti-communist government, it was implied, must be founded firmly to the right of suspect centre coalitions.

The first problems which faced the Papagos government were primarily those of political and economic confidence. Electoral victory by a very handsome majority, for a leader whose prestige in the country was considerable enough to overawe the majority of the political personalities serving under him, made it probable that Greece would be governed for a number of years by a stable right-wing government supported by a loyal and efficient army. Citizens whose professed opinions were not too liberal could turn with some security to restoring farms, properties, and businesses. And without too much concern for its ephemeral popularity the government was now able to introduce a measure of decentralization into local administration and to consider a rationalization of the public service whose hypertrophied growth was a form of relief which the country could not afford. Civil servants were made to work in the afternoons and recruitment was suspended. It is true that such measures were often less successful than published intentions had indicated. Decentralization was formal rather than effective; reorganization in the public service tended to mean the removal of persons judged to be politically unreliable from positions of importance. Nevertheless in the announcement of reforms and by busy attention to the building of roads and other essential public works the government succeeded in creating a novel atmosphere of resolution and purpose.

This assisted a slow return of confidence and activity in commerce and manufacturing. In a sense the Right was fortunate in coming to power at a point where time and immense sums of American money and material had already repaired the physical damage of the war. Nevertheless in 1952 entrepreneurs were still acutely sensitive to rising prices and increasing inflation, wealth was secure only in property or gold sovereigns, and consequently Greeks were reluctant to invest money in productive enterprise. The general course of the Greek economy since the end of the civil war will be described in the chapter which follows. Here it will suffice to say that Markezinis, Papagos' Minister of Coordination, laid the foundations of economic recovery by a skilful devaluation of the drachma by 50 per cent, and by lifting most of the controls which prevented the free importation of foreign goods. The latter move was an incentive to commercial activity, and a concession appreciated by an important section of the Rally's supporters. Thus gradually over the next two or three years, political stability was converted into economic confidence. Gold was dishoarded and bank deposits rose.

Although Markezinis resigned from the government on 3 April 1954, his policies continued to guide his successors, both in the Rally and in the subsequent governments of Karamanlis. He judged that the quickest path to prosperity was through a free market economy and the importation of foreign investment capital. To allow private enterprise to flourish government administration must be efficient, economic, and unobtrusive, and in this sense Greece could not at the present stage of her development disperse her resources in too great a concern for social welfare. The policy was approved by the Americans and was consistent with Papagos' association with the western alliance; and to the extent that aid and foreign investment capital were needed to expand and modernize manufacturing industry, and that the same funds would assist the balance of payments, it was indeed dependent on western support.

The Americans played an important and not uncriticized part in bringing Papagos to power. Since their purpose was to contain the influence and expansion of communism they let it be known that they disapproved of coalition governments. The implication was that America would continue to give material support more readily to a single party government with a secure majority. Not only by the definition of its divisions was the Centre unable to do this but due to the heterogeneous opinions of its adherents, including a leavening of socialist radicals among its predominantly conservative membership, its commitment to N.A.T.O. was less unconditional than that of the royalist Right. It was less attached to the King and more suspicious of the domestic role of the Greek army which supported him. And in the face of any reduction of American aid it was ready to make proportionate cuts in Greek military expenditure. For Papagos the reverse was true. With his supporters he was adamantly opposed to communism, and even to liberalism which might too easily tolerate its growth. Since the army was his most secure support he could reduce expenditure on its equipment less easily. At the time of the 1952 campaign it was still electorally valuable to emphasize the communist threat and claim that the Rally was more acceptable to the Americans than other parties. It was true that association with the western alliance impaired the integrity of Greek sovereignty. This was debated with some bitterness after the signing of a military agreement between Greece and the United States on 12 October 1953. It allowed the Americans to use the country's roads and railways, to build and operate military bases, and to quarter their personnel in Greece with rights which amounted to extraterritoriality. But three years after the end of the civil war this seemed to the Papagos government a reasonable price to pay for the assurance that the allies would resist any attack on Greece across her long northern frontier, a danger then mainly represented by the Bulgarians. Also the N.A.T.O. alliance offered a convenient framework for military and economic collaboration with Turkey which Papagos and Markezinis considered a necessary ingredient of their policies. An extension of this relationship in the form of a tripartite five-year pact of friendship between Greece, Yugoslavia, and Turkey was signed in Ankara on 28 February, and more significantly was converted, a year later, into a military alliance signed at Bled in Yugoslavia on 9 August 1954, in which an act of aggression against one of the signatories would be regarded as an act of aggression against all three. Within this system of alliances Greece appeared to have found a reasonable balance with her neighbours and to have made satisfactory provision for economic and military assistance. Yet scarcely had this been achieved than events in Cyprus threatened the whole basis of this arrangement.

II

According to the 1946 census 80 per cent of the Cypriote population were Greek in language, religion and sentiment, 18 per cent were Turkish and Muslim. Agitation in the island of Cyprus for *enosis*, or union with Greece, which by 1954 was becoming an international issue, had existed before the island became a British preoccupation in 1878. By the Cyprus convention of that year Britain was allowed to administer the island in return for a guarantee of protection for Turkey against Russian aggression. Nominally it remained Ottoman territory, but when Turkey entered the First World war the island was annexed by Britain, a status which was later confirmed by the Treaty of Lausanne in 1923. Popular demonstrations and riots in favour of *enosis* in 1931 led to the abolition of the Legislative Council.

The first attempt after the Second World war to reintroduce representative government was a failure. A constitution was proposed in 1948 in which Greek elected representatives would have been, for the first time, in an absolute majority over the official and Turkish members. But it did not provide for self-government. After Britain had withdrawn in 1947 from the role of protecting power in Greece there was less reason, so it seemed, for the Greek government to restrain its support for *enosis* and therefore less reason for the Cypriotes to settle for the terms of the proposed constitution of 1948. The indications of Britain's economic exhaustion and her inability to play the part of the dominant power in the eastern Mediterranean appeared to offer new prospects for *enosis*.

As was often the case in Greek communities in the Ottoman Empire, popular political leadership in Cyprus was assumed by the dignitaries of the Orthodox Church. In 1950 a new 'ethnarch', Archbishop Makarios, was elected. This astute churchman had already played some part in organizing in January 1950 an unofficial plebiscite on the question of *enosis* which, it was claimed, showed that 96 per cent of the voters were in favour of union with Greece. In 1951 Makarios met Grivas, a Greek army officer of Cypriote birth. Grivas had already earned some notoriety as the leader of an extreme royalist organization, 'X', in Greece at the time of the liberation. He now proposed to build a movement for sabotage and guerrilla attacks in Cyprus. Makarios had doubts about 'armed action' but he was prepared to join Grivas on a revolutionary committee.

To both these men Papagos had given some assurance that he would actively support the Cypriote cause if the Rally came to power. In his attempt to create a genuinely national party that would make an appeal to the adherents of the Centre as well as those of the traditional Right the atavistic attractions of a national question seemed electorally convenient. They might, indeed, compensate for a foreign policy which was otherwise so closely tied to the policies of America and the western alliance. No doubt like most of the other participants in the developing tragedy he did not foresee the scale of the struggle. Far from recognizing the eventual incompatibility of the Cypriote question with Greece's membership in N.A.T.O. he may have believed that through this membership judicious pressure on other members of the alliance and direct negotiations with Britain would lead to some acceptable compromise such as full self-government. Certainly, after the election victory of November 1952, when Makarios reminded him of his earlier undertaking and asked that Greece should raise the question at the United Nations, Papagos, with the responsibilities of office now upon him, was counselling prudence and insisted that a direct approach should first be made by him to the British. In the autumn of 1953 a convalescent cruise by Eden in the Mediterranean provided an opportunity for a meeting. The result was a brusque refusal to discuss *enosis* then, or in the future.

The events of 1954 did not increase the probability of a peaceful outcome. In March and October, Grivas smuggled in two shiploads of arms. In June it was announced in advance of the withdrawal of British troops from the Suez Canal zone that Middle East Land and Air Headquarters would be moved to Cyprus. At the end of July the Minister of State for the Colonies, Henry Hopkinson, offered a new constitution which now provided for only a minority of elected members in the legislature. He explained that there were some territories which because of particular circumstances could never expect to be fully independent. The use of the word 'never', and the 'particular circumstances' which referred to the increased military significance of the island after the withdrawal from Egypt, caused indignation and some apprehension in Greece and Cyprus. And the year closed with the shelving of the Greek resolution on self-determination at the United Nations.

After the failure of the appeal to the United Nations it became difficult for Makarios to resist Grivas' determination to use force. Papagos, now a sick man facing increasing popular criticism that his policy of restraint had produced no result, and personally affronted that the British had not responded to his reasonableness, did not prevent Grivas from developing his plans. On 1 April 1955 bombs were exploded in government offices and police stations in many areas of Cyprus and the National Organization of Cypriote Fighters (E.O.K.A.) under its leader Dighenis, Grivas' pseudonym, publicly announced its existence.

The British response was to invite Greece and Turkey to a conference in London. Both countries accepted, although the Greeks protested at length over the exclusion of the Cypriotes and the presence of the Turks. At this meeting which opened on 28 August the British hoped to show that irreconcilable differences separated the two invited powers. Hitherto the Turks had been content to treat the dispute as a British concern but the possibility that the British might give ground in the new and more acute phase of the struggle drew them actively into the debate. Moreover, the signing of the Baghdad Pact in March 1955 between Britain, Turkey, Iraq, Iran, and Pakistan, which was for Britain as much an instrument for maintaining her authority in the Middle East as a means for containing the Russians, both increased the supposed value of Cyprus as a base, and enhanced the significance of Turkish views on the island's future status. The Turks were not slow to sense their new importance and the British were pleased to argue that Turkish objections were an impediment to *enosis*. Apart from considerations of national pride, which certainly existed, security was the problem which chiefly concerned the Turks. Already enclosed by Greek islands along the western coast of Asia Minor, Turkey did not wish to add to this ring a large island 40 miles from her southern coast in which communist trade unions were strongly organized. To the Turks, at least, the possibility of a left-wing government in Athens was not so remote. At the conference, the Turkish Foreign Minister countered the Greek claim for self-determination by the proposition that if Britain gave up sovereignty over the island it should revert to Turkey.

Between these extremes Harold Macmillan, the Foreign Secretary, on 6 September, attempted to present Britain's 'reasonable' proposals: limited constitutional self-government, with British sovereignty unimpaired, and a standing committee of the three powers which would watch over the constitution's proper functioning. The introduction of Turkey as an interested party would in any event have made it difficult for Greece to accept this solution. But on the very same day the conference learned of serious anti-Greek riots in Istanbul, the looting of property, and the desecration of churches. The next day the conference was suspended and in Cyprus there were more bomb attacks.

Although the Turkish government apologized to Greece and offered compensation, the ferocity of the riots and well-founded suspicions of deliberate instigation made collaboration between the two countries within N.A.T.O. or the Balkan Treaty impossible. Greek N.A.T.O. staff officers were withdrawn from Smyrna. In Greece the opposition insistently demanded that the country should withdraw from N.A.T.O. The receipt by both the Greek and Turkish governments of an admonitory telegram from the American Secretary of State Dulles, which failed to recognize the provocation suffered by the Greeks but baldly suggested that both powers should 'mend their fences', was bitterly resented. And on the next day, 21 September, the General Committee of the United Nations voted against the inclusion of the Cyprus question on the agenda for the coming session of the General Assembly. Five of the seven negative votes were cast by N.A.T.O. nations. The alliance with the western powers on which Papagos had so firmly based his policy was in jeopardy; that with Turkey was for the time being unworkable. Neither was compatible with an unconditional commitment to the Cypriote cause but in Greece nothing less than this could appease the popular indignation. In these circumstances on 5 October 1955 Papagos died.

The motives which then prompted King Paul to overlook the Foreign Minister Stephanopoulos whom Papagos had indicated as his successor, and to invite instead Constantine Karamanlis, the Minister of Public Works, remain uncertain. Karamanlis at the time was a politician of secondary importance with some reputation as an efficient administrator in the technical concerns of his Ministry. His responsibility for public works had brought him into close association with American aid officials who judged him to be energetic and a convinced advocate of the western alliance.

For the King, acceptability to the Americans was a necessary credential since their presence in Greece was an ultimate assurance of the throne and of the material strength of the army which supported it. It followed that a new Prime Minister must be prepared to negotiate a settlement of the Cyprus issue which threatened to disrupt the alliance. It followed, too, that a Prime Minister raised from relative obscurity by royal patronage would be vulnerable in times of difficulty. In the tradition of Greek political life it was inevitable that Stephanopoulos having been rejected for the leadership should leave the party. Twenty-nine deputies followed him. But the remainder of the party were ready to support the man who had the confidence of the King and the tacit approval of the Americans. The full resources of state publicity were used to project Karamanlis as a young and dynamic statesman, equipped to lead his country in the new technological age. In January the Rally Party was dissolved and a 'new' party, the National Radical

R

Union (E.R.E.), almost indistinguishable from its predecessor, was formed, representing yet another renaissance of political life from the corruption of the 'traditional' parties. In fact the fundamentals of economic, social, and foreign policy established by the Rally Party hardly changed. Popular indignation over Cyprus, the less strained atmosphere in relations between Russia and the West, and simply the need to have a policy different from the government's had led the opposition press to question vehemently the value of the N.A.T.O. alliance. Karamanlis held firmly to the view that unrealistic policies based on ambiguous notions of equal friendship with East and West could result only in the country's isolation. A qualifying statement that Greece's position might have to be 'revised' if her allies continued to obstruct the just demands of the Cypriotes neither altered the underlying attitude nor carried much conviction.

With this pragmatic but hardly popular policy, and after the loss of Markezinis and Stephanopoulos, Karamanlis was not sufficiently confident to trust his fate to a simple majority system in the elections arranged for 16 February 1956. A bill was passed which introduced a hybrid system in which in smaller constituencies a simple majority decided the issue, but in larger constituencies with more than three seats at stake some were allocated by a form of proportional representation. Apart from this contrived advantage which benefited the local distribution of E.R.E. support, Karamanlis was assisted by the customary fragmentation of the Centre and the personal competition between Venizelos and Papandhreou. For purely electoral advantages and with the declared purpose, in the event of victory, of holding fresh elections with proportional representation, the opposition parties of the Centre and the Left banded together in a 'Democratic Union' which included E.D.A. Such an opportunist alliance of communist sympathizers with the rest, inspired little confidence in the moderate bourgeoisie, or among a peasantry on whose lives a relative prosperity had lately dawned. Karamanlis and E.R.E. were returned with 47·3 per cent of the vote and 165 out of the 300 seats.

Karamanlis now faced a grave deterioration in the Cyprus dispute. After the breakdown of the London conference Field Marshal Sir John Harding had been appointed to govern the island. Despite the conditions of rebellion Harding continued to negotiate with Makarios for a settlement on the basis of a wide measure of self-government. In January 1956 Harding made a concession in declaring that it was not the British view that self-determination should never be applicable to Cyprus but merely that in present conditions in the eastern Mediterranean it was impracticable.

Agreement was close. Makarios was willing to accept internal self-government if there was a guarantee of eventual self-determination. Karamanlis urged the Archbishop to accept the Harding proposals but these probably fell short of the minimum that E.O.K.A. would agree to accept. It is possible, too, that Harding had gone further than his instructions allowed, for Eden, apart from his prejudice, was influenced by his commitment to the Baghdad Pact and the sensitivity of his back-benchers to further British withdrawals in the Middle East. Thus at the end of February 1956 talks between Makarios and the Colonial Secretary, Lennox-Boyd, were broken off after only one meeting and less than two weeks later Makarios and the Bishop of Kyrenia were exiled to the Seychelles islands.

It was fortunate for E.R.E. that this occurred just after and not before the elections in Greece. Disillusionment with the N.A.T.O. alliance, and indeed with the United Nations where Greece's appeals in 1956 and 1957 had been without effect, was now widespread and naturally found its most vocal expression in speeches of opposition politicians and the articles of their press. The open impatience of N.A.T.O. countries with Greece, the burden of military expenditure, the national indignity of Greece's subordination to American policy were repeatedly mentioned. Neutrality, 'equal friendship', improved relations with Russia, Romania, and Bulgaria, were suggested substitutes. The Romanian President's invitation to Greece to a conference to consider a Balkan non-aggression pact fitted well with this mood. Older difficulties and anxieties with Bulgaria over the settlement of war reparations and the policy of a 'Macedonian People's Republic' were discounted. And there was speculation about the formation of a Belgrade–Athens–Cairo axis of uncommitted nations. Greeks in all political parties were now genuinely confused about the proper orientation of the country's foreign relations, a debate which became even more concerned when at a N.A.T.O. conference in December 1957 the possibility of installing intermediate range ballistic missiles was discussed. Critics were quick to suggest that Greece was being used to attract nuclear attacks from more important targets in the event of war. Through these storms Karamanlis steered a consistent course. He would not desert an alliance on which Greece's security and prosperity depended. This did not prevent him from condemning Britain and Turkey for their unjust and irresponsible attitudes. But these two powers would be under greater pressure to settle the dispute if Greece remained loyally within the alliance than if she did not.

The legislature elected in 1956 did not run its four-year course. In February 1958 the government resigned after fifteen deputies including two Ministers had deserted over a bill which proposed yet once more to alter the electoral system, preferring for this contest 'reinforced' proportional representation which penalized electoral coalitions and would give Karamanlis more control over rivals in his own party. The bill was later passed by a caretaker government and elections were held on 11 May 1958 in which E.R.E. held its majority with 171 seats out of a total of 300 and on the basis of only 41 per cent of the popular vote.

The victim of this contest was the Liberal Party which stood alone, uneasily directed by the joint leadership of Papandhreou and Venizelos and unable to persuade other centre parties to join with it in a union rather than a coalition. Its strength was reduced to 36 seats in a parliament where it had to give precedence to E.D.A. (79 seats) which now for the first time became the official opposition. In explaining this remarkable and, to the majority of Greeks, alarming reversal of position between the Centre and the Left, a factor of importance is that although E.R.E. won 6 per cent less of the popular vote than in 1956 the solidarity of the party showed no sign of weakening after the rebellion which had precipitated the election. The patronage which Karamanlis had to offer was still very substantial. Within the limits imposed by the economy's structural weaknesses and due to the cumulative effects of eight years of reconstruction with American aid, sections of the community were prosperous. The inflationary tendencies in the economy had been checked by 1956, bank deposits had increased, and between 1956 and 1958 prices showed an exemplary stability. Such conditions had been rare in Greek economic experience and conservative voters were anxious not to give up the recipe for success. Not only was it the case objectively that the Right still held the great majority of its supporters, but after six years of continuous rule by right-wing governments its clients were everywhere in control of the public services and the armed forces. In Greece this capture of the state is psychologically crucial. People generally did not believe it was possible for Karamanlis to lose.

Nevertheless there was much dissatisfaction. The unbalanced prosperity was conspicuously evident in the cities in the display of imported luxury goods which the majority of citizens could not afford. There was urban unemployment and underemployment and in some industries very depressed wage rates. In the countryside despite improvements in income and production the difference between average incomes in the cities and those in the countryside became wider. This, among other factors, considerably increased the rate of migration from the countryside which created problems of depression in severely depopulated areas and difficulties of employment and housing in the cities. But beyond these practical discontents there was the Cyprus issue which, for almost 60 per cent of the electorate who voted against E.R.E., was a cause for the collective expression of dissatisfaction with the government in terms of deeply emotional and patriotic values. In the weeks before the election E.O.K.A. had been active and the opposition press had written at length about the perfidy of allies and the commercial and political advantages lost by not improving relations with the eastern bloc. It seems that many voters convinced that, in any event, Karamanlis would win, but disillusioned by the fragmentation of the Centre and the disputatious tendencies of its leaders, decided that it would be an altogether more dramatic gesture of protest to vote for E.D.A.

Almost one-quarter of the electorate had voted for a party openly sympathetic to communist policy. This reaction against the established western alliance and the free market economic system associated with it reinforced E.R.E.'s belief in the dangers which it had been so often accused of exaggerating. Security checks on the political reliability of public servants became more exacting. By whatever means, it was now essential that E.R.E. should remain in power. And the importance of the western alliance as a guarantee of internal security required a settlement of the Cyprus dispute.

Since 1956 the inevitable multiplication of bomb episodes, murders, and executions embittered the relations of the contestants. The proposals of the Radcliffe constitution in December 1956 which made no concessions over the question of self-determination or British control of internal security were rejected. After Suez, with Macmillan as Prime Minister, British attitudes became less inflexible. Although forbidden to return to Cyprus, Makarios was released from detention in April 1957. And later in the year Harding was replaced as governor by Sir Hugh Foot, a colonial civil servant of liberal views. But in other respects the problem appeared to be more intractable than ever. The Turkish government was now stubbornly devoted to a sophistry, in which they were originally encouraged by the British, that the Turkish Cypriotes, as a community, were equally entitled to the right of self-determination which could be satisfied only by partition. The British 'partnership' proposals of 19 June 1958 which suggested that for seven years the island should be governed by a council consisting of the British governor, representatives of the Greek and Turkish governments, and four Greek and two Turkish Cypriote Ministers elected by separate Greek and Turkish assemblies, were rejected by the Greek government and Makarios as a proof of the Anglo–Turkish intention to impose partition. Following the breakdown more than a hundred

Greek and Turkish Cypriotes were killed in bitter fighting between the two communities.

Yet towards the end of 1958 events and certain changes in attitude contributed to a settlement. The Greek government partly attributed the new strength of E.D.A. to demagogic exploitation of the Cypriote question. Makarios, believing that no effective action would result from further appeals to the United Nations and sensing that even supporters in the British Labour Party were becoming less ardent, feared that the British would lose patience and enforce partition. The British no longer believed that sovereignty over the whole island was necessary for the security of their bases; rather the reverse was now obviously true. And since, following the overthrow of Nuri Said in Iraq in July 1958, that country was no longer an effective member of the Baghdad Pact, an important reason for a British show of strength in the Middle East had ceased to exist. The Americans, too, confronted with Russian threats over Berlin, renewed their arguments for ending the schism in N.A.T.O. The Turkish position was fundamentally unchanged: an implacable opposition to *enosis*. The one solution which did not conflict with the immediate policies of these interested powers was independence without *enosis*.

Encouraged by the British, the Greek and Turkish Foreign Ministers began direct negotiations. The two Prime Ministers, Karamanlis and Menderes, met at Zurich on 5 February 1959 to draw up an outline agreement, and again in London on 17 February where the agreed formula was presented by the three governments to Archbishop Makarios and Dr Kutchuk, the Greek and Turkish Cypriote representatives. After some hesitation on Makarios' side the agreement was initialled on 19 February 1959.

Under this, Cyprus was to become an independent republic in which Britain was to have an air base at Akrotiri and a military base at Dhekelia over which she would retain sovereign rights. Greece and Turkey were also to maintain small contingents of troops on the island and the three powers guaranteed the independence of, and respect for the constitution of, the new republic. Both *enosis* and partition were forbidden. In the event of a breach of the treaty the three powers undertook to consult together, but if there was disagreement each reserved the right to take action to defend the arrangements intended by the treaty. The form of government was to be presidential, the President to be a Greek, the Vice-President a Turk. They were to be assisted by ten Ministers, seven Greek and three Turkish. The President and the Vice-President would each have the right of veto over foreign affairs, defence, and questions of internal security. The House of Representatives was to have 50 members, 35 Greek and 15 Turkish, elected on separate rolls. In the case of changes in the electoral law or in questions of taxation separate majorities would be required from Greek and Turkish members. Such, then, was the settlement. Its terms reflected, inevitably, the positions and arguments of the contestants. In retrospect the recognition of specifically separated rights for the Turkish Cypriote community and the continuing role of the three powers as guarantors of the settlement probably pre-determined the later resumption of the struggle between the two communities. But for a time there was relief and on 16 August 1960, with Makarios as the first President, Cyprus became an independent state.

III

The end of hostilities in Cyprus, although it relieved the Greek government of its most acute embarrassment, won it little domestic credit. Indeed the surrender of *enosis* which had made the settlement possible was represented as a surrender to the West. We must remember that during these years the government was under almost continuous attack in parliament from a crypto-communist opposition whose numerical strength in the Assembly was provocative and alarming.

In June 1959 the fear of commercial isolation between the two groupings of industrial nations, E.E.C. and E.F.T.A., decided the government to apply for associate membership in the Common Market. But the possibility of negotiating such an agreement was also opportune in other ways, since it would link Greece with another powerful western institution whose members, already related in the N.A.T.O. alliance, would have an additional interest in the political and financial security of the country. At a time when further American aid was doubtful, and the intractable character of the balance of payments problem was better understood, this was important. As a result of the negotiations which were eventually concluded with the agreement signed at Athens on 10 July 1961, Greece obtained, among other benefits, $125 million of financial aid and a reduction of the tariff on the vulnerable tobacco crop which contributed so disproportionately to the country's exports.

As we indicate in another chapter, the strictly economic con-sequences of the Treaty of Athens may eventually prove to be unpalatable. But in the short run the political advantage for E.R.E. was considerable. In the popular imagination attachment to this group of nations dominated by France and West Germany, at this time enjoying a particular prestige in Greece, offered an attractive political alternative to the past indignities of Anglo–American domination; and it would further enmesh Greece in a complex of obligations and alliances in western Europe which it would be difficult for any succeeding government with neutralist beliefs to unravel or reverse. Economically, it seemed to hold out the promise that in cooperation with such inventive and advanced partners the country could not fail to ride to an assured prosperity.

Between the relatively stable and disciplined parliamentary forces of E.D.A. and E.R.E. the fragmented formations of the Centre found it difficult to recover from the defeat of 1958. In November of that year Papandhreou ended his joint leadership of the Liberal Party with Venizelos by forming his own Liberal Democratic group. A year later General Grivas attempted to found a new political party, 'The Movement of National Regeneration', which was supported by Venizelos and his followers in protest against governmental corruption and the desertion of the *enosis* principle in the Cyprus settlement. But the opportunism of a group of centre deputies led by a personality with a notoriously extreme right-wing history, and the General's own limited political ability, gradually lost the movement what little impetus it ever had.

Eventually however the political leaders of the Centre accepted that if they persisted in competing individually for adherents, the Centre would cease to play any effective part in political life. Between February and September 1961, and after laborious negotiation, Papandhreou succeeded in uniting in a single Centre Union Party the disparate groups from Tsirimokos' followers, of whom the majority, like their leader, had been for a time in the ranks of E.D.A., to the right-wing Liberals of Venizelos who differed little from the more moderate followers of Karamanlis. This process of fusion had been obliquely encouraged by officials of the State Department who had implied that the new Kennedy administration would not be ill-disposed towards a centre government if it showed unity and resolution.

The end of October seemed to Karamanlis a favourable time for new elections. International tension over Berlin, rumours and alleged discoveries of communist plots, countered the propaganda of the E.D.A. opposition which in conformity with the earlier Russian peace offensive had been urging for many months the establishment of a neutral Balkan zone without bases or nuclear weapons. The recent signature of the Common Market agreement in July balanced, if it did not silence, the critical arguments of both E.D.A. and the Centre Union Party against the burden of military expenditure which they claimed was preventing a proper development of the economy. And it appeared more prudent to fight the contest before the Centre Union's campaign against the arbitrary actions of the government's agents had gathered too much force.

The result was a clear majority for E.R.E. in the new House with 176 seats out of 300 and 50·8 per cent of the vote. The Centre Union in coalition with Markezinis' small Progressive Party won a respectable 100 seats but E.D.A. in coalition with Agrarians lost the ground it had gained in the 1958 election and carried only 24 seats.

In the aftermath of defeat the Centre Union did not break up. Its solidarity was maintained by the fury and persistence of the attacks which Papandhreou now mounted on the political morality of the Right. The voters, it was alleged, had been the victims of an electoral *coup d'état* carried through by the agents of E.R.E. who after nine years of right-wing government dominated every function of the state apparatus. The 'non-political' caretaker cabinet under General Dovas, head of the King's military household, had viewed these illegal acts with approval, or at least indifference. In Athens, Papandhreou estimated, there had been 100,000 false electoral inscriptions; in the countryside the police and the paramilitary security battalions of territorials (T.E.A.) had everywhere intimidated impressionable peasants. Probably the scale of these anomalies was exaggerated. It is equally certain that E.R.E. was ruthlessly determined to remain in office. The weakness and incipient neutralism of the centre parties, and the success of E.D.A. in 1958, had revived the fears of communism. Thus the justification of national security was a temptation, especially in the personal antagonisms of local politics, for the use of strong-arm methods. With some adroitness Papandhreou widened the area of conflict by accusing the Army General Staff of conspiracy with E.R.E. and by demanding that the King should dissolve parliament and hold new elections. When the King did not respond to this exhortation he was accused of unconstitutional partiality. By the pressure of his 'relentless struggle' which was accentuated by the immoderate commentaries of the Greek press Papandhreou very effectively created an atmosphere of crisis and corruption in which the government showed a loss of nerve and judgement.

The resignation of Karamanlis on 11 June 1963 was almost certainly not only due to a difference of opinion with King Paul over the timing of a state visit to Britain. On a private visit to London in April Queen Frederika had been molested by a demonstrator protesting against the detention of political prisoners, and particularly of Ambatielos whose wife was an Englishwoman. In fear of demonstrations which might be the occasion for tendentious protests against the lack of political freedom in Greece, which in the circumstances could not fail to enjoy wide publicity, Karamanlis advised the King to postpone the visit. The King did not wish to accept this advice.

But behind this 'difference' were matters of more substance. Under the psychological pressure of Papandhreou's attacks the government was not always in control of its agents. In breaking up an E.D.A. peace rally in Salonika in May 1963, right-wing bravos staged an absurd and sinister attack on Lambrakis, a popular deputy of the Left, by running him down with a motor cycle. Lambrakis died from his injuries. The assassination of a man who happened also to have been an international pre-war athlete, and was now a respected physician and teacher at the university of Salonika, produced a reaction of popular horror which was not appeased by the suspension of the commanding officer of the Gendarmerie in northern Greece, an action which was interpreted as an admission of official guilt.

As well as the dramatic events of the campaign against electoral and administrative corruption and the killing of Lambrakis, there were economic difficulties. In 1963 the country had the largest trade deficit since 1950, balanced only by invisible receipts that considerably depended on the remittances of migrants. The number of workers leaving the country began to affect the production of labour intensive agricultural export crops, particularly cotton. In 1962 Greece entered the Common Market as an associate member but ceased to receive substantial American economic aid. More was now heard of the structural weakness of the economy in this new competitive environment, and the wasteful extravagance of much public investment in the past. Suddenly Karamanlis appeared tired, vulnerable, and beset with criticism on all sides.

It may be that Karamanlis chose the neutral issue of the state visit as a means of withdrawal from an awkward situation, believing that he could later regain the nation's confidence at the election. But it is not unlikely that the initiative came from the King. Papandhreou had accused King Paul of acting virtually as the political leader of the Right. Many had been persuaded that the King was in collusion with Karamanlis; he had appointed him originally, and he had not rejected him after the fraudulent elections of 1961. A new Prime Minister would disembarrass the Palace of an imputed connection which was bringing the monarchy into disrepute. On this interpretation Karamanlis was the victim of the same forces which had originally raised him up. It has also been said that King Paul hoped that eventually a new political formation would emerge joining conservative Liberals under Venizelos with the less reactionary members of E.R.E., and that the army and the Americans approved of this conception.

Meanwhile the King turned to Pipinelis, an E.R.E. Minister and a convinced royalist, to form an interim government of non-political personalities. Papandhreou's threat to abstain from elections if they were not conducted by a caretaker government with a neutral Prime Minister had its effect. Mavromichalis, a supreme court judge, formed a government on 28 September and under his firm and impartial supervision the elections took place on 3 November 1963.

The result was indecisive. The Centre Union won 138 seats, six more than E.R.E.; E.D.A. with 28 and the Progressive Party of Markezinis with two seats held the remainder. Nevertheless E.R.E. had been defeated. The cumulative dissatisfaction of personal grievances and unrealized hopes of patronage which in Greece inevitably erodes the popularity of a party long in power, the unvaried critical rhetoric of Papandhreou and his promises of social reform, seemed enough reason for a change of heart to many voters. The pledge to make education free at all levels was particularly influential since this was the traditional path to success for the children of peasants and labourers. There is no doubt that the charges of fraud and undemocratic behaviour had their effect. Apart from the events of the 1961 elections it was unfortunate for E.R.E. that earlier in 1963, when they were still in power, they had published proposals for constitutional reform which included suggestions for strengthening the powers of the executive and checks on the right to strike, and on the abuse of its liberty by the press. In the existing mood of relative international calm which followed the Kennedy–Khrushchev *détente*, the conservative philosophy of 'disciplined liberty', and vigilance against liberal attitudes which permit communist infiltration, seemed not so much wrong as out of date. The more dignified and independent foreign policy which the Centre Party and the Left had been advocating, each with its particular emphasis, might, after all, be practicable. Indeed E.R.E.'s own act of leading Greece into the Common Market was already facing the government with the problem of balancing and maintaining equally amicable relations with America and France.

Papandhreou formed a government and remained in power for fifty-five days. To prove that the Centre Union was a party which honoured its pledges, and to prepare the ground for a new election on which, it seems, Papandhreou had already determined, the government passed legislation for its education programme, wage and salary increases were approved, and political prisoners were released. On Christmas Eve 1963 he resigned, asking the King to call a new election which would provide a government able to legislate without the support of E.D.A. Before resorting to this solution the King called on Kanellopoulos (who after Karamanlis' departure for Paris and withdrawal from political life following the November election was now the leader of E.R.E.) to explore the chances of forming an E.R.E.–Centre Union coalition. This possibility was at once rejected by Papandhreou, but more importantly Kanellopoulos found no dissident faction within the Centre Union to support him.

The Centre Union faced new elections on 16 February 1964 with some confidence, its earlier electoral promises in part fulfilled and doubts about its ability to remain united apparently unfounded. This confidence was justified. In a political system where the notion of patronage is traditional many vote for the party which they believe will win. (Modiano, an experienced observer, puts the percentage as high as 25 per cent.) The Centre Union was expected to win. In fact the party polled 52·7 per cent of the vote and won 173 seats out of 300; E.R.E. in coalition with the Progressive Party took 105 seats and E.D.A. 22. The Centre Union had made gains on both its wings.

IV

The immediate problem for the new government was Cyprus. The constitutional machinery set up at the 1959 settlement failed because of a fundamental mistrust made particularly bitter by the communal killings of 1958. Neither side regarded the agreements of Zurich and London as permanent. The Greeks, initially at least, regarded them as a step on the road to *enosis*. The Turkish community hoped to defeat this aim by the intervention of the Turkish government and an eventual agreement on partition. The arrangements for checks and vetoes in the executive and legislative processes, and the statutory ethnic ratios for the recruitment of the army, police, and civil service, which had been included to convince the Turkish Cypriote minority that its rights were secure, were used by both sides for their ulterior purposes; by the Greeks to show that only a unitary system of government could work; by the Turks to hold up government business whenever they judged that their rights were infringed or the needs of the Turkish community were not equitably met, especially in the matter of development funds and the recognition of separate Turkish and Greek municipalities in the five largest towns. During 1963 the Greek Cypriotes became increasingly insistent that the constitution must be revised. Although Cyprus was not a leading issue during the Greek election campaign of November 1963 the Centre Union Party did imply that they would support *enosis* for the Cypriotes. It fitted well with their intention to inaugurate a less servile foreign policy. Makarios, encouraged by this attitude and the resignation of the government which had taken part in the Zurich and London discussions, presented to Dr Kutchuk a memorandum setting out thirteen proposals including the abolition of the President's and Vice-President's veto and the unification of the municipalities. These were rejected by the Turkish government on 16 December 1963 and five days later the shooting began.

On Christmas Day 1963 Britain, Greece, and Turkey called for a cease-fire. Turkey threatened that if it was not obeyed she would take unilateral action and on the same day Turkish jet fighters flew over Nicosia. In its turn the Greek government stated that a Turkish invasion would be resisted by Greece. This pattern of events indicated the essence of the struggle. Both sides were armed but the Greek Cypriotes were more numerous; yet whenever they promised to overwhelm the Turkish Cypriotes Turkey threatened to intervene. Turkey, it must be remembered, is only 40 miles from Cyprus but Greece is 500.

The thankless task of peace-keeping was undertaken in this emergency by the British. In January a conference in London led nowhere. The Greek Cypriotes demanded unfettered sovereignty, the Turkish Cypriotes insisted on their rights under the Zurich constitution. In the middle of February there was more serious fighting in Limassol and in the same month Britain brought the problem before the Security Council where a resolution was eventually passed which set up a U.N. peace-keeping force, and the office of U.N. mediator. This force by its presence made it easier to control haphazard outbreaks of violence. Nevertheless both sides were prepared to disregard its appeals if it suited their strategy: the Turks when they wished to provoke an incident which proved the maltreatment they suffered; the Greeks when they believed that local military superiority gave them the opportunity to engulf a Turkish enclave.

The most serious fighting of the year began on 6 August. In June Makarios had introduced military conscription and in retaliation the Turks had brought in arms and volunteers. The Greek attack which now developed was planned to obliterate the important village of Kokkina through which Turkish supplies were passed. It was mounted with great ferocity and the use of heavy equipment including 25-pounder guns. Only attacks by Turkish government fighter-bombers on Greek Cypriote positions which inflicted severe casualties saved the Kokkina enclave. With the threat of a wider war between Greece and Turkey, the promise of support for Makarios from Russia, and the effect of an earlier warning from President

Johnson against precipitate action, no invasion followed the air attacks and the crisis fortunately subsided. After this experience both sides apparently realized that neither could prevail by force without serious international complications. The Turks consolidated their enclaves into which about half their population was concentrated. In these areas a *de facto* administrative partition now existed. Makarios passed legislation which established a unitary state and abolished specifically Turkish rights and institutions. An uneasy balance was established with the U.N. force holding the ring. But the possibility of a solution was remote. The U.N. mediator's report in March 1965 proposed that the island should remain independent, demilitarized, and unpartitioned with a U.N. guarantee for the rights of the Turkish minority. These proposals were rejected both by Turkey and the Greek Cypriotes.

For Papandhreou's government the development of the Cyprus crisis was diplomatically embarrassing. Since Makarios wished to revise the Zurich constitution he was opposed to the wishes of Britain and Turkey. Turning away from the western powers he put his trust in the threat of the increasing military superiority of the Greek Cypriotes over the Turkish Cypriotes and the support of the Afro–Asian nations at the United Nations. He bought arms from Czechoslovakia, appealed to Soviet Russia when threatened with Turkish invasions, and courted the favours of Nasser. This was an independence of western opinion which for Papandhreou went disconcertingly far. Sometimes Greeks outside Cyprus had to bear the consequences of Makarios' actions. In Constantinople the Patriarchate was harassed and Greek citizens were expelled when the Greek Cypriotes established an economic blockade of Turkish enclaves on the island in July 1964. On the other hand the Greeks could not admit how incomplete their control of Makarios had become. Ironically at a time when the Americans, in fear of Cyprus becoming a Mediterranean Cuba, had begun to advocate a form of *enosis* which would allow the Turks to lease a military base on the island, there were signs that Makarios and a substantial section of his following were in fact favouring independence with neutrality, but without *enosis*. For evident reasons this was the approach which the Cypriote Communists also approved. The cumulative effect of these developments on Greece's position was one of diplomatic isolation. The Greeks were even induced in June 1964 to agree to the return of Grivas to Cyprus to check the Archbishop's manoeuvres. The General was at least anti-Russian, distrustful of Makarios, and pro-*enosis*. But even for the immediate purposes of the Greeks this was a doubtful expedient.

Inevitably, the Cyprus crisis damaged the domestic economy.

Although higher revenue from taxation, due to an immoderate increase in imports, offset the cost of the men and materials sent to Cyprus, the possibility of war with Turkey weakened the resolve of foreign investors and discouraged tourists at a time when these transfers and receipts crucially affected the balance of payments. At home confidence was uncertain, bank deposits did not increase, and to check a renewed tendency to hoard gold the Bank of Greece was forced into expensive selling operations.

Unfortunately, in addition to the serious impact of these developments, the unbalanced economy was subject to the inflationary effects of Papandhreou's social and economic policies. He promised to accelerate the rate of industrial growth and at the same time to concern himself with problems of welfare and social equity. In this he differed from the E.R.E. leaders who believed that monetary stability, in their view the necessary basis for any effective expansion, must always have priority over programmes of education or relief. Although many of the measures taken by the government of Papandhreou, for instance the extension of free compulsory education to include three years of secondary education, pay rises for public servants, a policy of leniency towards farmers who had not repaid agricultural loans, were responses to a supposed need or a genuine hardship, which in principle it might be difficult to argue against, they were also inflationary in tendency. Other policies of the government were harder to justify. The pre-election promises of higher minimum prices for wheat-growers resulted in a surplus of 500,000 tons of wheat which the government bought from the producers at a price 80 per cent above the international level. The method of financing these subsidies and the existence of the increased demand of farmers' incomes made their contribution to the pressure on price levels which by the end of 1964 had shown an advance of 3·5 per cent, greater than in any year under E.R.E. government. It was therefore especially inappropriate that from 1 January 1965 income tax was cut by 10 per cent. More generally the policy of encouraging the commercial banks to lend more freely to industry and to persons, and the finance of the deficit on the public investment budget by foreign loans were dangerously inflationary agents in the new economic situation.

The Papandhreou government had at its disposal a number of talented economic advisers including the Prime Minister's son Andreas, an economist of some academic distinction, who had taught at Berkeley. It did not propose to leave the economy to the free play of market forces and existing institutions. A supreme consultative board for economic development was set up which included representatives from banks and industrial and agricultural organizations. Two existing institutions which financed industrial development were merged into a new investment bank. The restrictive regulations governing the issue of credit to industry were changed. As is commonly the case in Greece such measures were published with satisfaction as if the announcement by itself had achieved its purpose. Unhappily, due to administrative weakness in the public service and obstruction by some interested persons and institutions, the projections of the planners were not often realized as they had been intended. For instance, changes in credit regulations designed to assist smaller enterprises which had been denied long-term assistance, mainly resulted in larger firms borrowing more money from the commercial banks with which they had long been associated.

By the middle of 1965 the effects of Papandhreou's expansionist and inflationary policies were being felt, and the economy was beginning to face critical difficulties. The visible trade gap had widened alarmingly. Reserves of gold and foreign exchange, which had fallen by $11·6 million in 1964 despite a very satisfactory inflow of foreign loans and private investment funds, declined by a further $31 million in 1965. The disastrous policy of wheat subsidies had discouraged the planting of the valuable export crop of cotton. Cotton and other agricultural products had also been affected by the scarcity of seasonal farm labour, and the government had to attempt to check the emigration of workers to Europe despite the contribution which their remittances made to the receipts of foreign exchange.

Despite these economic difficulties Papandhreou's political position, at least in the earlier months of his premiership, was unassailable. The triumph of his 'relentless struggle' was a personal success which invested him with a moral authority that did not only depend on the inducements of patronage. It was also confirmed by the deaths in February and March 1964 of Sophocles Venizelos and King Paul. The former left no successor as leader of the right-wing Liberals who could immediately challenge the position of the Prime Minister. And the accession to the throne of young Constantine apparently offered Papandhreou the chance of amicable relations with a King uncommitted to past controversies. His control of the Centre Union Party was boldly indicated in his reaction to the revolt, immediately after the February election, of Tsirimokos and Papapolitis, leaders of left-wing groups who were discontented with the ministerial positions offered to them. In spite of protestations of loyalty both men were immediately expelled from the party, although later they were permitted to return. In a different context Papandhreou's ability to advance his son Andreas firstly as Minister in charge of the Prime Minister's department and later as deputy Minister of Coordination, and to support him in his frequent differences with other Ministers, demonstrated his dominance. Nevertheless this supposed grooming of Andreas for a dynastic succession to the party leadership accentuated the existing divisions and rivalries in the party.

As we now know, the often predicted dissolution of the party came about rapidly as soon as Papandhreou resigned from office in July 1965 and it became clear that he was not acceptable to the King. This reversal of political fortune was not due to any loss of personal popularity among the supporters of the Centre Union who had brought him to power. From the earliest days of the Papan-dhreou regime both E.R.E. and the military establishment were genuinely apprehensive about a supposed leftward and permissive orientation of its policies. In the case of E.R.E. its role in opposition naturally led it to insist on these dangers. The Centre Union had benefited in the February election from the support of E.D.A. in those constituencies where the latter party had no realistic hopes of success. Although the assistance was probably unsolicited the charge of collusion was difficult to refute. The remarkable successes of E.D.A. in the local elections in April 1964, when the party won 30 per cent of the total vote in Athens, suggested to the Right that Papandhreou had received more communist support in the national election than he was willing to admit and that in consequence he must continue to make concessions in that direction.

It was not difficult to interpret the diplomatic and commercial activities of the government in this light. An agreement with Bulgaria initialled on 28 June 1964 which settled the long out-standing problems of war reparations and Bulgarian access to Salonika, the appeal for Yugoslavia's support in the Cyprus dispute when Russia appeared to transfer her diplomatic support from Makarios to the Turkish government, and the general diplomatic isolation from the N.A.T.O. powers which Papandhreou's attitude to the Cyprus question involved, indicated both the intentions and dangers of his policy of equal friendship with East and West. And the attempts to negotiate bilateral trading agreements with coun-tries of the eastern bloc and Yugoslavia, which E.R.E. itself had initiated, were now seen to bind the country to perilous contracts which restricted its freedom in international relations. Under a new five-year agreement with Russia that country would buy consider-able quantities of tobacco and more than half Greece's bauxite, cotton, and citrus fruit.

It was however on questions of national security, in its widest interpretation, that the Right was most suspicious of Papandhreou's

S

intentions. The threat to reduce expenditure on the armed forces was one of these. National frontiers, internal order, and professional careers at once seemed vulnerable. Intimations of inflation were another, for monetary instability was a classic condition for communist success. A third was the release of political prisoners, 421 of whom were set free in April 1964. In the eyes of those who wished to see disaster in these policies the evidence was sufficient. It mattered little that Papandhreou had refused to recognize the legality of the Greek Communist Party; or that he repeatedly accepted that Greece must remain in the N.A.T.O. alliance.

The suspicions of Papandhreou's enemies outside the party were shared by some leaders of moderate and right-wing opinion in the Centre Union. In this the situation of Andreas Papandhreou had its significance. Arriving late upon the political scene, the parachutist of politics as his rivals derisively named him, he found his radical views and the possibility of winning personal adherents drew him to the left of the party. Inevitably it was in the interests of rivals further to the right, such as Mitsotakis and Stephanopoulos, to confuse the positions of father and son although in fact they were often far from coincident. The impetus of relentless opposition, which had united men out of office, was lost in government and the hopes of profit and privilege had either been attained or frustrated. By the early months of 1965 with the fruit of inflationary policies already beginning to ripen, the mutual tolerance of the assorted groups within the Union had become frail.

In May the alleged conspiracy of a left-wing officers' group, known as 'Aspida' (Shield), was revealed. Its scope and intentions were obscure. Its slogans advocated social justice and rule by the worthy. No doubt like right-wing societies of the same kind, which have always existed in the Greek army, its chief function was the protection and promotion of its members. In this case the political significance of the discovery was the embarrassment which it caused the two Papandhreous, since members of 'Aspida' were said to regard Andreas as the future leader of Greece and it was alleged that the society was fostered by the Greek Central Intelligence Agency, an organization directly responsible to the Prime Minister which, it was claimed, he used to keep the right-wing officers of the General Staff, and indeed his own political colleagues, under surveillance – among other devices, by tapping their telephones.

The independence of the predominantly right-wing officers of the General Staff had become intolerable. The Prime Minister and his son had been represented as presumed conspirators. Information about controversial military questions was regularly passed to the opposition press. Pressure for a purge of officers who were patently disloyal to the Centre Union grew within the party. To these demands, when they were presented by the Prime Minister, Garoufalias, the Minister of Defence and a man in the King's confidence, refused to agree. Ironically his appointment had been a concession to Constantine, an earnest that the policies of a centre government did not threaten the integrity of the armed forces or national security. These were the values which Garoufalias now felt he must defend. He declined to make the appointments, or to resign even after the Centre Union Party had expelled him. On 15 July Papandhreou asked the King to sign a decree dismissing Garoufalias and to accept his own appointment as the new Minister of Defence. This transaction the King would not agree to confirm although he offered to replace Garoufalias with another acceptable colleague. He argued that it would be improper for Papandhreou to have personal control of the Ministry when his son's involvement in the 'Aspida' affair was still under examination. No doubt it is true that Papandhreou wished to have direct access to the investigation; as much to prevent the fabrication of evidence by his son's enemies, as to arrange for its suppression. But the deeper fear in the minds of the King and his advisers was the infiltration into senior staff appointments and army commands of officers who for personal advancement might be prepared to break with the conservative and monarchist commitment which had generally characterized the army since 1935.

It is possible that Papandhreou welcomed this crisis. He probably believed that in view of his own extraordinary popularity in the country very few deputies of the Centre Union would have the courage to defect and that consequently no government could be formed without his support. Having established his case with the people by the liberality of his policies, it was an advantage to fight the next election before the incipient monetary crisis, which was its consequence, became too acute. Moreover, Papandhreou might reasonably hope, through the careful endorsement of Centre Union candidates loyal to him personally and the magnitude of his expected victory, that his following within the party would be sufficiently strengthened to ensure the succession of Andreas.

The values of Greek society and its institutions do not encourage responsibility in its politicians. The danger of Papandhreou's rhetorical power and his ability in declamatory Greek to present an issue with epigrammatic simplicity was apparent in his response to his disagreement with the King. The special circumstances of the King's sensitivity about the position of the army were, of course, well known to Papandhreou. He equally understood the probable consequences of a constitutional crisis in a country whose precarious

economy crucially depended on political stability. But with impending difficulties in the economy, in Cyprus, and over the future
leadership of the party, he chose to allow the crisis to develop, for
he saw too clearly the political value of the simple issue which would
inevitably emerge. Did a twenty-five year old hereditary King rule
in Greece, or the government supported by the majority of the
people's elected representatives? Continually Papandhreou reminded them that they had returned him to power with 53 per cent
of their votes. The King had not only humiliated him, but them.
He had outraged their honour as well as his. Presented in this light
the quarrel between the King and the Prime Minister ceased to be
a matter of merely constitutional principle.

V

Papandhreou was initially right in thinking that an upsurge of
popular sentiment would protect the solidarity of his party. It was
clearly the King's strategy not to resort to elections if he could
avoid them. Within an hour of Papandhreou's resignation Athanasiades-Novas, the President of Parliament and a Centre Union
personality with moderate views, had accepted a commission to
form a government. But Novas could collect only some twenty
supporters in his own party. Even with the support of E.R.E. and
the Progressive Party these were not enough. In the hope of dis-
rupting the left wing of the party, the King then offered the task to
Tsirimokos. This attempt met with more support but on 29 August
was finally defeated by the opposition of Markezinis and his seven
Progressive Party deputies, who declined to vote for a left-wing
Prime Minister supported by right-wing conservatives. It was not
until late in September that the King was ultimately successful in
his manoeuvre to avoid elections. On this occasion with a leading
figure from the right of the party, Stephanopoulos, a government
was formed by 45 dissidents of the Centre Union, supported by
E.R.E. and the Progressive Party, each of which was represented
in the government by a Minister without portfolio. In parliament
on 24 September this symbolic coalition won a precarious vote of
confidence by 152 votes to 148.

The formation of a government of Centre Union dissidents, albeit
with some difficulty, indicated the underlying fragility of the party
which never possessed the homogeneity of E.R.E. The high-handed
and despotic control of George Papandhreou had been suffered
partly because his chief collaborators feared his popularity among
the electors, partly because they believed he must soon retire on
account of his age. Unlike the electors many deputies did not

identify their fate or honour with his, and at the first check, and with
the lure of a Ministry or an under-secretaryship which in normal
circumstances most of them could not have expected, a number
were prepared to break with their leader. Nevertheless, especially
in the weeks immediately after the resignation of Papandhreou, this
act of severance required a strong sense of courage or greed. Some
deputies who wished to desert to the new government were restrained by the fury of popular passion in their constituencies against
the King for his dismissal of Papandhreou. In a number of instances
they received anonymous threats of death if they betrayed him.
This partly explains why the remainder of the party remained
faithful to its leader. Indeed, the terms of trade were precise: a
deputy became a dissident only when he was offered a position in
the government.

In unpromising circumstances the government of Stephanopoulso
survived until December 1966. With a slender majority on which it
could rely only from day to day it was possible to attempt few
innovations of policy. From a bill drafted to check the inflationary
pressures on the economy it was compelled to withdraw measures
of austerity including a 10 per cent increase in income tax. It was
not until September 1966 that it raised the interest rate on bank
deposits by a half per cent and added one per cent to loan charges
for domestic and import trade in an effort to restrain consumption.
Fortunately the economy was already recovering from the more
acute symptoms of instability, partly because political uncertainties
deterred merchants and manufacturers from the expansion of their
businesses. Thus the demand for bank credit slackened. It was also
opportune that for similar reasons many import orders were can-
celled. Nevertheless the trade gap continued to widen. Only by
increasing public borrowing abroad to £90 million in comparison
with £53 million in the previous year was it possible to protect the
meagre reserves of foreign exchange. With increasing sums to be
repaid on earlier loans and growing service charges, and despite
the continuous growth of the national income, the problems of the
balance of payments seemed insoluble.

Within the limits that his parliamentary position allowed
Stephanopoulos' measures were courageous and unexpected, particularly if we remember his reputation for indecision and the
undoubted opportunism of many of his followers. To discourage the
gold hoarding to which political uncertainty customarily drives
anxious or cautious savers in Greece, it was made illegal to buy and
sell gold sovereigns on the free market. To check, at least, the
demand of farmers for consumption goods which the industrial
economy could not satisfy the price of wheat was lowered. At the

same time to improve the balance of the farming economy increased subsidies were offered for fodder crops and beef cattle. Inducements and penalties were devised to persuade the commercial banks to give medium- and long-term loans for the expansion of small manufacturing firms. In its own spending the government did what it could to make economies and hold back the rise in prices, and in public investment it proceeded cautiously with those parts of the existing programme of which it most approved, education and the development of new industrial zones, the first of which was planned at Volos.

For his success in checking the country's course towards a calamitous economic crisis Stephanopoulos received little credit. Quite apart from the interest groups offended by particular measures E.R.E. and the Centre Union were each naturally intent on fixing the blame on the other for the unpleasant political curiosity of a splinter party government kept in power by the former opposition. E.R.E. hoped that under a government of centre dissidents the ardour of Papandhreou's supporters would grow cooler while they observed the division of their original party, and learned the lessons of the 'Aspida' revelations. And no doubt many voters who had changed their loyalties in 1964 were now prepared to return to the security of E.R.E.

For Papandhreou a policy of continuous attack and harassment suited his temperament and offered the best hope of holding together the remains of his party. Against the allegedly corrupt and opportunist clique in office and those who kept them there he declared a second 'relentless struggle', for constitutional rights, for the unconditional right of a Prime Minister with a parliamentary majority to choose his Ministers without interference from the Crown, for the right of the people to stand as guardians of the constitution as the 114th article directs. With this obligation in mind he did not hesitate to organize the expression of public indignation in strikes and street demonstrations on a scale and with a persistence which set a new style in the manipulation of political opinion in urban Greece.

The strikes for wage increases which became frequent in the later months of 1965 were generally justified by the considerable rise in prices for which Papandhreou's own policies were mainly responsible. The unions capable of effective national demonstrations were particularly those whose members worked for the government or public institutions and utilities. Among those who went on strike were bank employees, postal workers, teachers, telecommunication technicians, civil servants, and hospital staff. These were categories of the working population among which the supporters of the Centre Union were strongly represented. In most instances they were also workers over whose services the government could, and did, issue civil mobilization orders in their attempt to maintain order and essential services, and to resist the full demands of inflationary wage increases. These were situations and responses not always engineered by Papandhreou but invariably exploited with his customary skill. The vociferous and unflagging demonstration of their grievances by convinced supporters of the Centre and the Left reached a climax in July 1966. On the anniversary of the happenings in 1965 many thousands of devotees passed in a mass motorcade before the floodlit balcony of the leader at Kastri, near Athens. It was an intimidating expression of solidarity. Athenian workers, shop assistants, and clerks in their narrow circumstances and social frustrations sensed a personal identification with a leader who had himself been unjustly rejected by a King whom they regarded as alien and privileged.

In this campaign for popular political indignation there was inevitably what later proved to be a fatal conjunction of interest between Papandhreou and E.D.A. which the former almost certainly did not welcome. E.D.A. supporters were present at all demonstrations to take what profit they could. In some, for instance the farmers' demonstration at Salonika against the 10 per cent reduction in the wheat subsidy, they were prominent and violent. The development of this *de facto* popular front, in which communist activities and recruitment were covered by Papandhreou's campaign for constitutional rights, began to alarm the Right; it strengthened the resolutions of E.R.E. to support the Centre Union dissidents and prevent elections; and it so alarmed the opinion of senior army officers that speculation about a military *coup d'état* became increasingly common.

Events and personalities joined in 1966 to discredit Greek political life. The King by refusing to dissolve parliament, and manipulating the divisions in the Centre Union and the personal ambitions of its leaders, destroyed the parliamentary strength of the Centre Union with such humiliating ease that the prevalence of personal expediency over common moral purpose was seen to be far greater than even a cynical observer might have suspected. The lengthy investigations and trials of those implicated in the manslaughter of Lambrakis or the 'Aspida' affair (which at times were proceeding simultaneously), were opportunities for scandalous and often perjured revelations. Although the dissidents in the government might take comfort at the embarrassment of both left-wing opponents and their own temporary friends of the Right, it was known that Ministers had been forced into a wholesale dispensation of personal favours, not only to their constituents, but to allies in

E.R.E. and, by way of reinsurance, even to ex-colleagues in the Centre Union. No doubt the extent of these transactions was exaggerated but the air of corruption which now compromised the regime of parties generally, was entirely real, and was to be a justification not without its effect for the military *coup* in 1967.

A censure debate in April 1966 over the government's handling of the Cyprus question offers a revealing example of political relations at this time. Makarios had taken advantage of Stephanopoulos' hazardous position to make his attempt to recover control of the Cypriote National Guard from General Grivas, his autonomous defence chief and in some degree the unofficial agent of the Athens government. Makarios claimed that it was important to counter the Turkish allegations that the island was under *de facto* Greek occupation by indicating clearly that the Cypriotes controlled their own forces. With some adroitness he proposed to replace Grivas by General Gennimatas, the former chief of the Greek General Staff whom Papandhreou had wished to remove in 1965 and therefore a man of unexceptionable right-wing sentiments. His demand for Grivas' removal was also based more personally on his belief that the General was preparing at least a *coup d'état* to remove him from power and possibly an attempt on his life. In support of these fears he produced a letter from Grivas to Sossidis, Stephanopoulos' private secretary, which on one interpretation suggested an embarrassing involvement of the government in this plot. Under these well contrived pressures the government was ready to accede to Makarios' view when Markezinis threatened to withdraw the support of the Progressive Party if Grivas, whom he believed to be the only sure guardian of the *enosis* principle, was dismissed.

In the circumstances Grivas had to remain. And when Tsirimokos, the Foreign Minister and the principal advocate of Makarios in the cabinet, chose to resign over this issue, taking with him two political associates, the government had little difficulty in drawing from the deputies of the Centre Union two replacement Ministers who secured its majority by 151 votes to 148. But during this debate the national audience was enlightened by the evidence of two other deputies of the Centre Union who claimed that each had been offered a cabinet post and £60,000 to defect to the government's ranks. Deputies used their fists and the President of the Chamber had to invite policemen to restore order.

By the end of the year many in E.R.E. were no longer certain that Papandhreou would win an overwhelming electoral victory. It was clear, also, that normal parliamentary politics could not be resumed until elections had been held; but for evident reasons it was essential for the Right that before the contest the Centre Union should desist from attacks on the King and undertake not to present its case in the form of a plebiscite on the monarchy. These in fact were the principles of an agreement accepted by Kanellopoulos and Papandhreou. E.R.E. withdrew its support of the Stephanopoulos government and on 23 December a non-political caretaker cabinet under the banker Paraskevopoulos was formed depending on the votes of E.R.E. and the Centre Union for its mandate to prepare the country for elections at the end of May.

This imaginative but inherently unstable agreement aroused varying reactions. For Kanellopoulos an election might confirm his leadership of the party, some of whose more extreme members had been pressing for the return of Karamanlis. The elder Papandhreou wished only to hold elections, which he believed his party must certainly win. Stephanopoulos' party, the victim of the compact, was understandably opposed to it. Both E.D.A. and the entourage of Andreas Papandhreou also opposed the arrangement, believing that it was a palace plot to destroy George Papandhreou. Andreas, whose appeal in the parliamentary party and the electorate was made particularly to those with radical and anti-monarchist opinions, was not prepared to give up his criticism of the King's constitutional deviations or his public assessments of their probable consequences. For a time his group of deputies, over thirty in number, would not attend party caucus meetings and lived under a threat of expulsion from the party.

Late in March the 'Aspida' affair was again the occasion of a new crisis. After the trial of the officers had ended on 16 March with fifteen convictions, the courts began proceedings against the civilians involved. The Public Prosecutor requested that the parliamentary immunity of Andreas Papandhreou and Vardinoyannis, another ex-Minister, should be lifted. The Centre Union responded by tabling an amendment to the electoral bill extending the immunity of deputies to cover the period between the dissolution of parliament and election day during which it would otherwise lapse. This was rejected by Kanellopoulos as unconstitutional. A compromise based on the suggestion that Paraskevopoulos would guarantee that no arrests would be made before the day of the elections was not accepted by Papandhreou. On 30 March Paraskevopoulos resigned.

Having apparently approved of the December agreement between Kanellopoulos and Papandhreou the King had no practical and constitutional alternative but to satisfy the demand for elections. The most he could now hope for was to control the violence and exuberance of left-wing and centre anti-monarchist demonstrations in the coming weeks. His first attempted solution was to invite Papandhreou on 2 April to accept responsibility by leading a government in which all parties would be represented. This was rejected. The King was not then prepared to establish a non-political caretaker cabinet whose authority and will to control the excesses of the Left and the Centre Union demonstrators in the pre-electoral period might prove to be wanting; for it was now improbable that Papandhreou would deny himself the advantage of using the constitutional issue.

The final constitutional resort was a right-wing E.R.E. government under Kanellopoulos which was sworn in on 3 April. It was hoped that the electoral bill proposing a system of simple proportional representation could be passed with the assistance of the smaller parties whose chances it favoured, and that consequently, at worst, the Centre Union's majority would not be absolute or sufficient to support any conclusions about the people's attitude to the monarchy. In the event Kanellopoulos could not find the support he needed. No legitimate course then remained except to dissolve the parliament and await the result of the election. The only consolation was that possibly the Right would gain some psychological advantage from its control of the army and the administration.

VI

Papandhreou's initial reaction to the appointment of Kanellopoulos as Prime Minister was threatening. But after some play with the traditional response of boycotting the elections it seems that in truth he was well pleased to have achieved his aim of consulting the electorate; and in circumstances which many of his party would interpret as releasing them from any constraint not to discuss their opposition to the King. In the first week of April student riots in Athens and Salonika were an example of the violence which had become the customary accompaniment of political meetings and demonstrations in Greece, and a foretaste of what might be expected during the electoral period.

We now know that a circle of relatively junior officers in command of units of infantry and armour had for some time been considering the need to assume the powers of government. The immediate danger which, as they claim, moved them to take pre-emptive action was the probability of disorder and bloodshed at a rally of 100,000 Centre Union supporters at Salonika planned for Palm Sunday. A threat of popular revolution if elections were postponed was the message expected from the leader. The choice of date associating Papandhreou's political rejection by the King with the events celebrated in Holy Week, was no doubt intentional. According to one right-wing speculation Papandhreou's followers intended to lead him on a white donkey along a path carpeted with palms. In the press of the crowd Communists disguised as policemen then planned to assassinate him, a murder which would be attributed to the agents of repression.

The motives of the officers were more fundamental than limited problems of public order. They had decided that if Papandhreou were returned to power the consequences would be at least a revision of the King's constitutional powers to prevent his resisting a massive retirement of officers, destruction of the politically homogeneous royalist and anti-communist character of the officer corps, and the end of many personal careers. It would set the nation, as it had done in 1964, on the road to an unsound expansion of the economy in the interests of political popularity, to a neutralist foreign policy and withdrawal from N.A.T.O., and to permissive treatment of disruptive left-wing front organizations and youth movements. In the wake of economic and administrative failure, and with an army weakened by the promotion of self-seeking and politically unreliable officers, they believed that some form of left-wing regime would be an inevitable sequel. The contemplation, even, of this possibility, to satisfy abstract constitutional principles, was an intellectual indulgence no patriot could justify. Fear of the unstable brilliance of both Papandhreous perhaps strengthened the conspirators' resolution; fear of the effect of the father's hypnotic rhetoric on his audiences and on himself; apprehension about the radicalism and professional economic skills of the son, whose political actions after his long absence from Greece seemed hard to predict or control.

During the early hours of the morning of 21 April the conspirators moved their forces into position, principally the tanks of Brigadier Pattakos and special security units of infantry under Colonel Papadopoulos. Key positions were taken and the communications network seized. Members of the Kanellopoulos government and the leading personalities of other political parties were arrested before dawn. There was no resistance. A characteristic of the *coup d'état* was its use in Athens of relatively small but highly trained units with overwhelming fire-power. This incidental consequence of American equipment and training made it possible for a restricted circle of relatively junior commanders of élite units to seize the state.

As in any *coup d'état* strikes, demonstrations, and gatherings for whatever purpose became illegal. It was necessary also to arrest all those who might publicly disapprove of the military action or clandestinely organize opposition to it. Six thousand detainees were sent to the Aegean island of Yioura, many others were detained on the mainland or restricted to their homes. The methods of Greek policemen, especially towards political prisoners, are not temperate at any time, but there were no summary executions apart from the arbitrary killing of a communist prisoner by a junior officer. Nor, as in Turkey, have there yet been any impeachments of politicians for corrupt administration or treasonable actions if we except the case of Andreas Papandhreou whose impending trial with ten other civilians involved in the 'Aspida' affair was announced in August.

In the event this showpiece trial was never staged, presumably for lack of convincing evidence, but it is unlikely that death sentences were intended. In the middle of January 1968 Andreas Papandhreou was allowed to leave the country. The majority of the less important prisoners were gradually released on signature of promises to refrain from political activities and in April 1968 the regime was claiming that only 2,500 political prisoners remained in detention, mainly hard-core Communists imprisoned on the islands of Yioura and Leros. Yet it is true that the military leaders are prepared to imprison indefinitely without warrant or trial any person suspected of intended opposition.

At the moment of the *coup* only two centres of possible and serious resistance threatened its leaders once the capital city was in their hands. The Third Army Corps massed along the country's northern frontiers contained the principal armoured units; but its commander, General Zoitakis, had already agreed to support the revolution. The second possibility was the opposition of the King who might, with some hope of success in view of the junior rank of the revolutionaries and their arbitrary actions, demand their submission and the support of other formations to effect it.

It seems certain that the King was not forewarned of the *coup*, and that had he known of it he would not have been a party to it. This did not prevent the revolutionaries from acting in his name. At 7 a.m. the Greek radio broadcast a royal decree suspending eleven articles of the constitution, which it claimed had been signed by the King, the Prime Minister, and the entire cabinet.

The King's choice was not an easy one. The officers could not withdraw from their act of revolution in which they had invested their professional careers and perhaps their lives. As we have suggested, the King might have appealed to the army. The Colonels had broken the principle of seniority in taking matters into their own hands and the forced retirement of certain generals after the *coup* indicated that not all of them approved of it. But with the communications system in the hands of the revolutionaries it would have been difficult for the King to organize his opposition, and the civil war which might have followed would in all probability have destroyed the monarchy. Another possible course would have been to leave Greece in protest. But apart from the question whether this was physically possible at that time, the uncertain chance of returning to his throne once he had abandoned it, must have ruled it out.

The more practicable policy was to show the regime a limited tolerance on the understanding that the country moved progressively back to parliamentary rule and that the revolutionary government was not exclusively military in character. At a meeting on 21 April a compromise along these lines was accepted by the King and the Junta. Kollias, a strict and conservative jurist, became Prime Minister and other civilian Ministers were introduced. The King took an early opportunity to express publicly his wish that the country should return as quickly as possible to parliamentary government. He was careful, at first, to show little personal enthusiasm for the new leaders while he awaited developments. In these he may have been disappointed by the ambiguous response of the Americans to the new situation. Yet undoubtedly he was relieved that he did not have to fear the outcome of elections on 28 May. The probability is that Constantine was torn between a private sympathy for the motives, but not the methods, of the officers, and his understanding that any protracted identification with a dictatorial regime might end the monarchy in Greece.

The diffuse impression made by the collective leadership of the military revolution was that they were determined but intellectually limited men genuinely convinced by the narrow philosophy of their profession. It was assumed that Colonel Papadopoulos, a specialist in intelligence and political warfare, was the senior member of the group. His intolerant demeanour and obsession with communist subversion offered little hope, at first, that he would personally accept a return to democratic processes. As Minister in charge of the Prime Minister's department he guided the government's programme and took personal responsibility for reform of the constitution and changes in the civil service. Two other officers became well known to the public: Brigadier Pattakos, a ruthless but not always humourless puritan who commanded the tanks which dominated Athens on 21 April and then assumed the office of Minister of the Interior; and Colonel Makarezos, the Minister of Economic Coordination, whose problems were among the most critical which the regime had to face.

Yet the regime produced no national leader. This was an important if negative feature of its position. A lack of any moral authority was a problem for junior officers without national reputations or obvious capacities for managing an increasingly complex state. The *coup* not only overthrew the legal government but also, by the use of an existing N.A.T.O. contingency plan, the hierarchy of rank in the army itself. Therefore when the King demanded a civilian Premier the Colonels were prepared to accept Kollias and to use the services of General Spandidakis who, after he was persuaded that the *coup* had been successful beyond reasonable doubt, agreed to serve as deputy Prime Minister. As Army Chief of Staff his adhesion was important since it partly regularized the relations of the military members of the government with their professional superiors. But although the Colonels welcomed the collaboration of nationally known personalities there was little surrender of effective power. The more important members of the revolutionary council of thirty-eight officers met informally each evening to decide questions of policy. Since the council had its own representatives observing the work of different Ministries it happened that important instructions were sometimes passed without the knowledge or agreement of the department's civilian Ministers. Inevitably relations between the Junta and the civilians who offered them some shreds of respectability became uncomfortable. By September it was reported that there was disagreement within the Junta between those who wished to retain the civilian Ministers and those who did not. As domestic problems and international pressures mounted in number and intensity some officers found it difficult to risk or tolerate in senior positions in government any whose loyalty was not directly pledged to them.

For similar reasons they wished to remove from the armed forces officers who were loyal to the King but whose attachment to the regime was suspiciously inexplicit. When Constantine returned in September from his visit to America the government submitted a list of 400 'unreliable' officers whose retirement was requested. Strengthened by his discussions in Washington and in the knowledge that the Americans had not yet decided to continue the shipment of heavy arms, the King refused. Early in October a shorter list of 140 officers were in fact placed on the retired list, one must suppose without the King's permission.

By the autumn of 1967 inherent weaknesses in the regime's position became apparent; particularly the isolation of the Colonels within the wider structure of government which their attempt to keep in their own hands the right of making decisions partly created; and the tensions in their own circle which this isolation and sense of living under siege produced. Public gestures of resistance or displeasure began to come from the Right where the regime could least afford to tolerate them; from the King, from Mrs Helen Vlachou who resolutely refused to publish her right-wing newspaper *Kathimerini*, from Kanellopoulos who on 27 September denounced the military government to foreign correspondents and had the temerity to repeat his views three days later.

Events in Cyprus brought a more dramatic setback. After the *coup* negotiations between Athens and Ankara had been resumed unhandicapped by the exploitation of this emotional issue in the party press. At first there was some prospect of a solution on the basis of a disguised partition in which the greater part of the island would be united with Greece while a base, initially under N.A.T.O. control, would hold a Turkish garrison and population. The scheme was eventually rejected by Turkey and was always skilfully opposed by Archbishop Makarios who disliked both the complexion of the regime in Athens and the contemplation of losing his role in an independent Cyprus. *Enosis* was an ideal the exact political form of which had to be carefully negotiated. For the present he preferred to work for better communal relations in an integrated and independent Cypriote state. In this endeavour he was opposed by General Grivas, the advocate of immediate *enosis*, in command of the Greek Cypriote National Guard and the illicit Greek forces which supported it. On the last day of October the capture, and later the release, of the militant Turkish Cypriote leader Denktash by Greek Cypriotes, and violations of Greek air space by Turkish planes on 2 and 4 November, had created an atmosphere of tension both in Cyprus and between Greece and Turkey which Grivas was prepared to exploit, perhaps in the first instance with the tacit approval of the Athens government. A dispute about patrols in the area of the villages of Ayios Theodoros and Kophinou was adopted as a pretext for a violent assault on local Turkish communities in which twenty-seven villagers were killed. If Grivas had demonstrated once more the preponderant power of the Greek Cypriotes on the island, Turkey lost no time in reminding Greece and Greek Cypriotes of the ultimate sanction of her military strength. Probably encouraged by the success enjoyed by the Israelis through bold military measures and understanding the weak international position of the Greek dictatorship, Turkey sought to shift the balance of power in the Cyprus problem by demanding the immediate dismissal of Grivas and the withdrawal of all Greek troops in excess of the 950 allowed by treaty. Threatened by an air strike on Cyprus, the landing of Turkish forces on the island, and hostilities on the Thracian frontier, the Greeks temporized until some face-saving formula could be found. On 19 November General Grivas was recalled to Athens for 'consultation'. On the next day Pipinelis, the first important political figure to join the Colonels, was sworn in as Foreign Minister in a desperate effort to introduce order into the regime's external relations. With the good offices of President Johnson's negotiator, Cyrus Vance, and a United Nations proposal which disguised the Greek defeat by balancing the dismantling of Turkey's war preparations against the withdrawal of 9,000 Greek soldiers from Cyprus, the substance of Turkey's more important demands was conceded and once more the island returned to its uneasy peace.

Despite censorship it was hardly possible to disguise the fact that Greece had suffered a humiliating defeat. It was made worse by the interview given by the former Prime Minister Karamanlis in Paris to the paper *Le Monde* in which he attributed the responsibility for this grave reverse entirely to the dictatorship. The effect of these difficulties on the regime was to strengthen the arguments of the more extreme officers in the ruling circle for an undisguised military government and a definitive purge in the armed forces of those officers whose first loyalty was not explicitly to the Junta. It was in these circumstances that the Colonels apparently demanded from the King the dismissal of his civilian Premier Kollias and the retirement of senior officers. The same difficulties which had prompted these demands probably persuaded Constantine that it was a not unfavourable moment to oppose them. Moreover, if he hesitated to take action on this occasion the opportunity would not recur after his supporters had been removed. The issue was control of the army. On 13 December, assured of the support of the commander of the Third Army Corps which was concentrated in Thrace and eastern Macedonia, King Constantine broadcast in a recorded statement from a disused radio station in Larissa his decision to assume the government of the country and the active command of its armed forces. Before this was heard the King and his family were already flying to Kavalla to join the Third Army Corps. But there, after apparent success, the plan went rapidly astray. Senior officers including the corps commander, Lieutenant-General Peridis, had been entirely deceived about the loyalties of their junior officers who were in effective control of infantry battalions and tank units. The few senior officers who had declared for the King found their orders disregarded and themselves under arrest. The operation demonstrated that the monarchism of the younger generation of army officers had rested on the identification of the throne with authoritarian principles of firm government and anti-communism and not on personal loyalties to the King. Intimidated by the threat of retirement, seduced by promises of promotion, and assured that the Junta's ideological attitudes were their own, they had no hesitation in abandoning him when the choice was presented. Almost without a shot fired the rebellion collapsed and the King with his family left by air for Rome. From this chosen place of exile Constantine made few public statements other than dignified affirmations that he was ready to return when it was plain that a return to democratic government was intended. For their part the Colonels spoke abstractly of inviting him to return after parliamentary elections had been held.

In Greece the end of the unsatisfactory compromise with the King and his supporters allowed the regime to improve its control over the whole machinery of government. Lieutenant-General Zoitakis was appointed regent in Constantine's absence and Papadopoulos became Prime Minister with Pattakos as his deputy. Although Papadopoulos, Pattakos, and Makarezos resigned from the army and henceforth appeared always in mufti, there was no resignation of control over the armed forces. Officers implicated in the King's *coup* were dismissed but not prosecuted. On 26 January a list of the names of eighteen generals and fifteen colonels who had been dishonourably discharged for their part in the *coup* was published in the Gazette. In February senior naval and air force officers suffered the same penalty. Although rumours in the middle of January that a conspiratorial circle of dissatisfied officers had been uncovered indicated the damaging effects of purges on discipline, the regime pursued its single-minded search for supporters and opponents, dismissing the latter and placing the former in key positions especially in Athens and on its approaches. In Attica the Prime Minister's brother commanded a strategically positioned battalion of infantry.

In the public service the regime apparently met no resistance. The traditional dependence of Greek civil servants on political favour has never encouraged much independence of attitude in that quarter. Military representatives of the Junta in each Ministry were consulted by the senior civil servants on all matters except those of simple routine. Any misleading recommendation by an official, it had been said, would be treated as sabotage. In these circumstances even senior officials hesitated to take an initiative, and no action was decided on without the confirmation and assurance of many signatures. The fear of dismissal was now added to the normal political hazard of an uncongenial posting. In keeping with the practices of political governments the regime placed its own men in important positions in the public services. But its power, the ease of arbitrary legislation, and its reformist intentions, encouraged it to accompany changes in personnel with other measures. Since it was not embarrassed by a clientele of political supporters claiming their rewards, the new government dismissed, and did not replace, a great number of temporary public servants and advisers who had

T

been introduced by Papandhreou and Stephanopoulos. And they summarily withdrew the right of tenure from permanent civil servants and placed them on probation. Particularly after the King's unsuccessful *coup* the political opinions of officials were carefully examined. At the beginning of March 1968 nine hundred disloyal civil servants were dismissed.

With the diligence and loyalty of their agents to some extent assured the government hoped to improve relations between administrators and the public. But although directives required that the public should be assisted promptly, with courtesy, and their correspondence answered within forty-eight hours, and while the authoritarian structure of the regime frees the administrative machine from the excesses of political patronage, the gain in efficiency is to some measure offset by the increased centralization of a bureaucracy already handicapped by that defect. Moreover, the regime in its anxiety to prevent the growth of political opposition in towns and villages dismissed the elected representatives of municipalities and communes from local government. Their own appointees had less interest than their predecessors to plead for local needs and difficulties when they conflicted with national policies. The flexibility of patronage was replaced by a discipline, or a repression, the inefficiencies of which might be as great. Ordinary people failed to register their objections to administrative acts which harmed their interests because they feared to raise the suspicions of the police. Although the systematic exchange of political favours was no longer possible citizens continued to compete for the favour of those with any authority. This demonstration of dependence was acceptable both as a reassurance of political security and as a mark of social prestige. Less admirably the rivalry between individuals, or even simply their mutual distrust, resulted in the laying of false information. For the psychological insecurity of the military government, and its own constitution, were such that it found it difficult to ignore any charges however unconvincing the evidence.

It would be an injustice to the officers to suggest that only questions of personal security or advancement motivated their rebellion. Like Metaxas, although without his sophistication, they hold a simple political philosophy which is a curious blend of paternalistic military discipline, Orthodox Christian morality, and the traditional values of Greek community life. Factional politics are evil because they interrupt the direct relationship between the people and those who govern them. Thus the concern for the polite and rapid transaction of citizens' business in the Ministries is less a question of justice or efficiency than of solidarity and discipline. Delay and indifference in administration, and finding the means to circumvent them, are the preconditions of patronage in politics which concentrate interest on personal and party benefits to the detriment of national unity. At another level aberrations in dress and sexual morality reflect a challenge to the authority of parents and seniors and to patriotic and disciplined sentiments in political attitudes. It is therefore the mission of the Orthodox Church and the national schools to hand on to the younger generation the inherited values of Hellenic and Christian civilization. There is, also, some ambivalence towards private capital as the necessary means for the development of the economy. Its inherent tendency to exploit and divide should be regulated just as the power of industry to attract peasants from the villages, where the strength and virtue of traditional Greece supposedly reside, must be checked.

Communism is the antithesis of this moral order. 'Communism is a miasma,' King Constantine has said, 'born outside Greece and directed from abroad. Its ethic is lying and treachery. It corrupts and turns into an unforgivable enemy of the fatherland everyone who comes into contact with it.' With this definition the leaders of the *coup* would agree. And because the anarchy of party interests under the parliamentary system had again exposed the nation to communist subversion the army, as the guardian of the country's integrity, had intervened. Its mission, according to Colonel Papadopoulos, was to organize the state during a period of intense social training. When individuals understood their responsibility to society it would be possible, perhaps, to return to democratic government.

The practice of this philosophy has been marked by attempts at moral regulation which particularly outside Greece seem both bizarre and naïve. More prayers in school, obligatory church attendance by school children, and instructions to civil servants to attend church as an example to the community; a prohibition on mini-skirts for girls and long hair for boys in high schools, and discouragement of extreme expressions of this kind in the rest of the population; a regulation that no salary shall exceed that of the Prime Minister, fixed at £536 a month; and a threatening exhortation that conduct must conform to the ideal of service to the nation.

Such curiosities are matched by the exaggerated repression of apparently trivial faults or violations of regulations. Courts-martial dispense heavy sentences of several years on those who distribute leaflets critical of the regime, write slogans on walls, or simply discuss the political situation. Until the regulation was suspended in September 1967 no meeting or social gathering of more than five persons could be held indoors without police permission since presumably it was either frivolous or conspiratorial. Several well known persons suffered under this attempt to legislate away Athenian social life. Among them Karamanlis' Foreign Minister, Averof, was sentenced to five years imprisonment for holding a small cocktail party in his home. It is reported that the severity of this sentence, which was quickly moderated by the issue of a free pardon, was due to the insistence of junior officers on the tribunal. Such verdicts owe something to fear. But they illustrate more clearly the inflexible idealism of many Greek army officers who genuinely believe that by honest precept and sharp exemplary punishments they can change the disrespectful ways of their countrymen.

Since reformers cannot easily tolerate criticism of themselves or allow others to offer truths which differ from their own, it was necessary to censor the press which in the past had been undeniably irresponsible and untruthful. At first the newspapers which continued in circulation printed only political material passed to them by the government. Later they were permitted to add their own emphasis to this but the penalties for false reports, criticism of the regime, or its personalities, were punitive. Under these conditions, as we have already mentioned, Mrs Vlachou, the owner of the leading newspaper *Kathimerini*, has steadily refused to publish. The consequence of her irritating opposition was her arrest on 28 September for insulting the regime in an article which appeared in an Italian journal. Its culmination was her escape from house-arrest on 15 December 1967 to exile abroad in London. Later, in May 1968, in an effort to disarm foreign criticism the government allowed certain trusted newspapers and journals to publish without submitting their material to the censors. But the understood limits for free comment were narrow and the penalties for trespassing beyond them heavy.

Literature, drama, cinema, and more significantly education, have not escaped this zeal for censorship and direction. The books of left-wing authors have disappeared from the shops. The popular songs of the left-wing composer Theodorakis may not be performed. Plays and films, classical or modern, which offend against the regime, traditional morality, or God, are not presented. University professors and their assistants with known radical opinions have been relieved of their positions; despite the shortage of staff some schoolteachers, too, have suffered similar treatment. As in other spheres the search for disloyalty was particularly intense after the events of December 1967. In January forty-nine university professors were dismissed. Text-books and curricula, also, have been examined and reformed. And the dead hand of the *katharevousa* language again fell on secondary education and even on the senior grades in primary schools. Education is not, one must be clear, an intellectual training for open minds; it is an education in the acceptance of a particular moral order, the validity of which cannot be disputed.

In their direction of the economy the Colonels hoped to demonstrate the practical benefits of patriotic and honest administration uninfluenced by political interests. With the advantage of legislation by decree they altered the system of wheat subsidies which had seemed to both political parties a necessary electoral incentive despite the burden it imposed on the budget, and the uneconomic crop structure it encouraged. In their place direct land grants were offered for the improvement of farms, a measure which advisers had often suggested but political governments had resisted in the belief that its electoral cost was too great. Yet for this regime, too, the contentment of countrymen was important. For this they increased by 70 per cent the admittedly low rates of benefit for agricultural pensions and insurance. And in March 1968 came an even more substantial gesture of concern when Papadopoulos relieved Greek farmers of their outstanding debts on 21 April 1967, amounting to £105 million. Practically and symbolically this would enable farmers to redeem themselves from the corrupt past. 'You are the clear heads and the soul of the nation,' he told them.

The problems of the industrial economy however were less tractable. Before the *coup* there had already been a marked slackening in economic activity. Greek entrepreneurs lacked confidence for the extension of plant or for new undertakings. With higher costs of construction and relatively low returns from rents, activity and profits in the building industry had begun to fall away, with corresponding effects in the industries supplying materials. Colonel Makarezos could do no more than offer favourable credit terms to builders, and hope for an improvement. In the departments of direct administration the military government could legislate enforceable changes within the hour. But accepting the principles of private initiative and a free market it was considerably dependent in economic matters on the confidence and cooperation of its otherwise disenfranchised citizens who were not immediately convinced of the prospects for business under its guardianship. The year 1967 was one of recession. The regime's attempt to reverse this trend by offering credits to industry, increasing salaries and pensions, and especially in 1968 by cancelling farmers' debts, had only limited success. In Greece as in other 'developing' countries national prestige and governmental success have been increasingly measured by the amount of annual increases in industrial production and employment. In the context of this obsession with economic growth the soldiers' concern with moral interdictions, patriotism, and discipline, considerations which do not appear, at least directly, in the gross national product, seemed disproportionate and even irrelevant.

Nor was the regime less vulnerable in relation to the balance of payments. Any general disinclination, abroad, to buy her exports, or invest capital in Greece, might be disastrous. Colonel Makarezos had rapidly resurrected and signed a contract with the American firm of Litton which undertook to raise $800 million of foreign capital over twelve years for the development of the western Peloponnese and Crete mainly in respect of tourism and improved agriculture. This contract originally proposed by the Stephanopoulos government in 1966 had been withdrawn because of criticism in the Greek parliament of its financial terms and the indignity of national development by sub-contract; and because the Greek government was uncertain that it could sufficiently control the details of planning. Its swift renegotiation after the *coup* with an improvement of the financial terms seemed to speak for the efficiency of extra-parliamentary government. Yet by the middle of 1968 Litton had not attracted any of the foreign capital it contracted to find. And while it is not obliged to do so before May 1969, the immediate value of the contract for present payments problems is negligible. The Colonel also presided over the completion of other applications for investment from abroad including a $12 million Goodyear tyre plant. However, negotiations for most of these investments preceded the *coup* and in the absence of convincing accounting since that time there has been no evidence of the continuing inflow of capital needed to offset the deficit on the current account, particularly in 1967 when political uncertainty in Greece and the Middle East seriously affected receipts from tourism. Moreover, the Greeks have not received $57 million remaining from the $125 million which the European Investment Bank was authorized to loan to Greece under a protocol of the agreement for her association with the Common Market. Although it is true that the economic recession benefited the balance of payments through a reduction in imports, 1967 ended with a net payments deficit of $39 million. The liquidity in the economy, largely in the form of private hoards of bank-notes, threatens a serious inflation as soon as any quickening of economic activity becomes apparent. Already an increased payments deficit in 1968 is probable. Yet if a payments crisis develops one must not underestimate the regime's will to face these troubles by the imposition of physical controls, for instance by restricting the importation of luxury consumer goods.

If in Greek domestic development and foreign trade the country's dependence on foreign resources was acutely embarrassing for the regime, in foreign policy it was, at first, less uncongenial. This was firmly oriented towards N.A.T.O. and America. It was partly to prove this allegiance that in September 1967 the Junta held talks with the Turks to find a realistic solution of the Cyprus question. Relations with communist neighbours, particularly Bulgaria, became more distant. While the Americans initially expressed some public distress at the form of the regime, privately they put it on probation. If the alternative were an unstable Centre Union government subject to left-wing pressure a limited period of authoritarian rule and reform might be the lesser evil. From the regime's point of view American support seemed crucial, for the equipment of the army and as a source of foreign exchange whether through loans, the surplus grain programme, or private investment. Unfortunately for the Colonels American policy, at least in its public expression, became less tolerant. In September President Johnson told the new Greek ambassador that military aid might depend on a return to some form of representative government. The President may have been influenced not only by his own political preferences and the embarrassment of supporting yet another illiberal regime but also after six months of military government by practical doubts that the soldiers could remain in power, or that, if they did, they could rule effectively. Although the personal leadership and authority of Papadopoulos were greatly strengthened by Constantine's defeat in December and his ability to smother domestic opposition could no longer be doubted, this consolidation of power probably added to his difficulties abroad by increasing the anxieties of those opposed to the regime. The Americans withheld certain deliveries of heavy military equipment. There were problems in Greece's relations with her partners in E.E.C. The Council of Europe threatened Greece with expulsion if by September 1968 the stages of a return to democratic government were not clearly outlined. Generally the dictatorship was severely criticized in the foreign press particularly in connection with allegations of physical torture on political prisoners. Such a climate discouraged the foreign tourists who were an important prop to an unbalanced economy. More seriously, political uncertainty as to how the dictatorship would evolve held up the flow of foreign investment capital.

After the *coup* of 21 April 1967 the military leaders quickly appreciated the need to calm the moral anxieties of western governments by declaring their intention to return eventually to a form of democratic government. On 8 May 1967 Brigadier Pattakos announced that the Greek people would be asked to approve constitutional reforms by a plebiscite before the next parliamentary elections. The date of these, however, might be some years in the future. After a long experience of selfishness and corruption social re-education was not a process which could be accomplished in months. But as time passed and the pressure on their position increased the Colonels were led gradually to make a number of imprecise promises. In this traditional procedure they showed some skill and won for themselves some relief from foreign harassment. In July 1967 a commission of twenty leading jurists began their work on a draft for a revised constitution which it was required to submit to the government by 15 December. The draft constitution after its amendment by the regime would be submitted to a plebiscite sometime in 1968, it was said. For the present the labours of the commission conveniently presented the illusion of a promise of democratic elections which in fact had not been made. By January 1968 the main provisions of the draft were known, in March they were published in Greece. In the same month Mr Papadopoulos promised that proposals for a new constitution would be submitted to a plebiscite in September, although the date for the eventual elections remained distant and vague, in 1970 or beyond. In the meantime he invited the opinions of his countrymen on the published draft. According to the government five hundred thousand of these were received on postcards during the weeks which followed.

The draft constitution of the jurists proved to be a piecemeal revision of the 1952 forms suggested by the crises of the past. Thus although the King retained the right to appoint or dismiss his Prime Minister, he could choose or dismiss Ministers only on the latter's recommendation. The draft also provided for a new institution, a Constitutional Tribunal, which was empowered to dissolve all parties whose aims, or the activities of whose members, were openly or covertly opposed to the existing social order. Many of the draft's detailed provisions were in the spirit of article 23 which forbade the abusive exercise of individual rights and liberties for the purpose of overthrowing the principles of the regime and the social order. In parliament the number of deputies was reduced from 300 to 200 and provision was made for the election of one-fifth of the chamber in a separate ballot for lists of names drawn up by each party. The aim of this proposal was to draw into parliament the talents of those who were normally unwilling to submit themselves to the indignities of electioneering.

The draft was not the instrument which the Colonels sought. They allowed it to be criticized as 'anachronistic'. The supposed consultation of the people's opinion by postcard not only gained more valuable time but also offered a convenient justification for the regime's amendments to the jurists' constitution which from an unofficial account at the time this book went to press virtually amount to a new draft. The King's powers are much reduced. He no longer appoints the Prime Minister. It is possible that the final draft will recommend his election by direct ballot by the people. The government proposes that the number of deputies should be reduced to 150 and that they should be elected in wider constituencies to break the narrow circle of personal allegiances on which a deputy's election has depended in the past. Moreover, to disrupt the personal oligarchies of the old parties it is intended that no candidate may have served in four successive post-war parliamentary terms. In effect this means that few members of the last parliament would survive in politics. The regime proposes also to disqualify deputies from becoming cabinet Ministers. The latter would be extra-parliamentary experts. These suggestions amount to an attempt to sever the relations of patronage and clientship between the voter and his deputy, between the deputy and the Minister, on which the cohesion of the bourgeois parties uncertainly depended in the past. Its justification is the elimination of corruption and the support of fearless government undeterred by electoral consequences. For the Left there are no prospects. Communism would remain under its ban, and a 'Constitutional Tribunal' similar to that proposed in the jurists' draft would judge when other parties departed from their professed principles. In these proposals, and from other sources, there are indications that Mr Papadopoulos might in certain circumstances withdraw from dictatorship to a form of guided democracy in which he would be almost assured of one parliamentary period of power after the first elections under the new constitution. The virtual destruction under the suggested regulations of the existing system of essentially personal parties would be one step in that direction. And the popular character of recent legislation, particularly the cancelling of farmers' debts, lends some substance to the speculation that the Colonels are laying the foundation of their own political party to replace those which they hope to have destroyed.

While the blessings of democratic government in Greece have never been considerable, their surrender has been a high price for an improved punctuality and efficiency in administration. The cost has generally been greater for those who were politically active, either men with influence in the system of bourgeois parties who benefited from its undemocratic malfunctioning, or Communists and their collaborators whose interference with the liberties of the citizen would be at least as unacceptable as the Colonels'. Yet military government does not offer any lasting solution to the problems of Greek political life other than the continuance of its own forms. It teaches the majority that it is prudent to obey regulations and avoid the attentions of the police, but apart from unheeded exhortations it can do little to create that minimum of civic conscience which the practice of parliamentary government requires. And it is likely to persuade those who from temperament or conviction have the will to resist that the commitments of the Left are more effective than the reasonable and more passive resistance of the Centre.

From the evidence which is available resistance has been slight. Most supporters of E.R.E. and Markezinis were uneasily content that they had been saved from strikes, civil disorder, and communism. A yearning for stability and honest administration after the repeated demonstration of individual corruption among deputies of both the Centre and the Right prepared many others with less conservative views to accept with some relief the crude certainties of military rule. If, inevitably, these people have had their hopes disappointed and find the restrictions on their freedom of expression distressing, many of them remain unconvinced that the path forward is a return to Greek parliamentary politics. And whatever the potential of communist reaction a year of intense persecution has decimated the now illegal organization of E.D.A. There are the communist-led 'Patriotic Front' resistance movement and 'Democratic Defence', the most effective among a number of clandestine Centre-Left organizations. More recently the existence of a monarchist resistance movement, 'Torch', has been reported. At present the effectiveness of such groups may be little more than the propaganda value of their existence. Certainly after fifteen months of dictatorship there have been no demonstrations of effective resistance. The regime holds too many hostages in detention. Of those who disapprove of the regime we cannot know how many are ready to accept the risks of clandestine resistance when informers are active and many families depend on the state for work, loans, and crop subsidies. As long as the petty tyranny of regulation does not personally affect the interests and dignity of too many, their number may not be large. Nor is it likely that armed resistance, or mass demonstrations, even if they could be organized, would be successful against the efficiency and fire-power of the army.

Change is more likely to come in a less heroic style; through discontent and disunity in the army where the precedent of self-help has been set and the principle of seniority broken; through economic embarrassments particularly in the balance of payments; or through the policies of other countries, especially America, which can deny the Greeks arms, loans, and private investment funds. In the field of Greek politics prophecy is unwise. It is, at least, not improbable that Greece may live for a period of years under authoritarian rule, with or without parliamentary institutions of limited democracy.

Chapter 9

Economic Dilemmas

THE FORM OF the Greek economy is affected by simple but important limits. Although the country has an area of 130,900 square kilometres, large areas of the mainland and the Peloponnese are covered by intricate and formidable ranges of mountains and only 37,000 square kilometres are cultivated. Arable land is scarce and its fertility is often indifferent. Yet farming absorbs half the active male population and still produces one-quarter of the country's gross domestic product. Wheat is the most important crop and is grown on 31 per cent of the cultivated area. By the use of better strains of seed, fertilizers, and more scientific methods of rotation, Greek farmers succeeded in 1957, for the first time, in growing enough wheat for the nation's bread.[1] But Greece depends on her agricultural production for more than subsistence in grains; the crops of tobacco, cotton, and fruit (dried and fresh) are the basis of the country's exports, accounting in 1966 for 51 per cent of their value.

The structure of Greek industry, on the other hand, is deficient. From small beginnings manufacturing industry grew steadily between the two world wars, but its orientation was to the small domestic market protected by high tariffs. Its scale of production was small, it could afford to be inefficient, and since domestic costs were high it was little concerned with production for export. The legacy of this development remains today, for manufactured goods contributed only 3.4 per cent in 1963, and 11.6 per cent in 1966, to the value of the country's exports. Against this has to be set the import of a very wide range of manufactured consumer and capital goods. Therefore, despite the increase in agricultural productivity which has removed some of the need to import grain, Greece suffers a serious and apparently structural deficit on the balance of her visible trade. Whether in any year this can be offset depends on invisible earnings from emigrants, tourists, and shipping, and on the inflow of foreign investment capital or loans. The problem of balancing payments has been a recurrent theme in many

---

[1] Population at the 1961 census was 8,389,000.

of the crises in Greece's modern history, and its contribution to her fated dependence on other powers has not been small.

I

In Greece war did not end until 1950. The problems which faced the government were those of elementary subsistence. Seven hundred thousand people awaited resettlement. Almost a third of the population were dependent in some degree on its support. Production of foodstuffs at home was inadequate, hyper-inflation virtually eliminated credit facilities, and a large deficit in the balance of payments was checked only by import and foreign exchange controls of great severity. Impressive amounts of American aid had been received but this had been spent on defence and the maintenance of essential services.

The simple form of the Greek economy made the initial stage of recovery relatively rapid. The peasants sowed their fields again with some security, and in manufacturing, which mainly consisted of small factories and artisan workshops, relatively little plant had been removed or destroyed during the wars and occupation.

Despite inflation the rate of growth was impressive, but in 1951 overvaluation of the drachma forced the government to check its spending and to control credit. About the same time the Americans sharply reduced their aid; partly because they felt the Greeks had not made sufficient efforts to put their house in order, partly because of commitments elsewhere. Ultimately in 1953 a solution was found which seemed to be effective. The drachma was devalued by 50 per cent and the currency was renominated from 30,000 drachmas to the dollar to a rate of 30 drachmas to the dollar. During the ten years which followed, and particularly after 1956, prices remained comparatively stable and confidence in the currency and domestic savings increased.

Markezinis, the Minister mainly responsible for the new direction of economic policy, preferred an open and free economy compatible with the interests of his political supporters and the American allies. Devaluation was only half of this policy. At the same time he withdrew controls on imports. Checked at first by the increase in domestic prices which followed devaluation the bill for imports grew from $333 million in 1950 to $547 million in 1958. Devaluation affected exports in the opposite sense. At first their price gave them some comparative advantage and they increased from $105 million in 1950 to $259 million in 1958. Since then inelastic demand for the agricultural crops on which exports still heavily depend, and rising costs at home, have hampered their advance. By 1966 imports had advanced to $1,104 million, exports to only $404 million. With a trade imbalance for which no remedy has been found, the balance of payments deficit has been contained within limits only through the remarkable improvement in invisible receipts from emigrants' remittances, the earnings of Greek ships, and tourism, which rose from $27 million in 1950 to $229 million in 1960, and $481 million in 1966, an amount now considerably greater than the value of commodity exports.

The ever widening deficit in the balance of visible trade remains the central problem of Greek commercial policy. In 1963, for instance, ten years after the 1953 devaluation, years of relative monetary stability during which the country's manufacturing output doubled and the generating capacity for electric power was increased by three times, the structure of exports still remained fundamentally unchanged. Agricultural produce accounted for 81 per cent of the total value of exports during this year, manufactured and handicraft products for only 3.4 per cent. Among the agricultural exports tobacco represented 43.2 per cent of the country's total exports, currants and fruit 16.7 per cent, and cotton 11.5 per cent. But Greek tobacco, although it now benefits from important tariff concessions in Common Market countries, begins to suffer from the declining popularity of oriental tobaccos. And although Greece produces a quarter of the world's output of currants and raisins the demand for these is unlikely to increase. Only in the cases of citrus fruit and cotton has there been some progress. Important amounts of both these crops, and of the tobacco, are sold through bilateral clearing arrangements with communist states, especially the U.S.S.R. and Yugoslavia. Indeed, Greece has a higher export dependence on Comecon than any other member of O.E.C.D. These commercial links are also valued because they create channels for normal relations across difficult frontiers; but for this reason, too, they are politically precarious.

The balance of Greek agriculture may yet be improved by reducing the area put down to wheat and by increasing production of livestock, sugar, fruits, vegetables, rice, and cotton. It has been the policy of successive governments to encourage the labour-intensive use of land. An acre of land under fruit or vegetables requires six times as much labour and provides six times as much income as an acre of cereals. In this way there would be the possibility of reducing agricultural underemployment and, if the produce were processed, of increasing exports. But during recent years the cumulative effects of an exodus of workers from the countryside, which is believed to have averaged 100,000 annually during the period 1960 to 1965, have in fact created local shortages of seasonal labour in the villages. In 1964 and 1965 such shortages contributed to increases in agricultural wages of about 20 per cent in each year, and these, complemented by the political policy of support prices for wheat, have prevented the proper development of valuable labour-intensive export crops, especially that of cotton. Nor, until 1966 under the Stephanopoulos government, had any effective incentives been offered to farmers to meet an increasing demand at home for meat, by producing more fodder crops and livestock. Since agricultural production is subject to the physical conformation of small fragmented holdings and to considerations of a family's subsistence needs and labour resources as much as to simply commercial interests and responses, it neither answers existing market demand effectively nor realizes its potential productive capacity. But whatever future progress is made in agriculture it is clear that it cannot by itself alter the serious imbalance of visible trade. Moreover, as they exist today, agricultural exports are neither sufficiently secure nor varied.

We have said that manufactured goods contribute little to the value of exports. This is so despite 400 million dollars of investment in industry between 1950 and 1960. A particular difficulty lies in the environment surrounding Greek industry. Until 1953 tariffs and severe import controls blocked competition from abroad. There was little incentive for Greek manufacturers in small family businesses to improve their methods: prices were high. Although after devaluation import quotas were removed, the tariffs remained and credit regulations worked in the favour of goods produced in Greece. In an economy with growing incomes, and effective protection, domestic enterprise inevitably offered a much higher return on capital than exports. It is true that there is now a growing sector of large-scale industry created with the aid of foreign capital. Recently constructed industrial complexes, particularly Esso–Papas and Péchiney, have added new exports of aluminium, nickel, iron products, and liquid fuel which have helped to raise the share of industry in the country's total exports from 3·4 per cent in 1963 to 11·6 per cent in 1966. Yet the great majority of firms remain as small family businesses. Since their true purpose is often to provide the members of a family with executive positions and social status, opportunities for expansion may be rejected because they would affect the family's control. The quality and cost of their goods generally limit their market to a local clientele whose loyalty is increasingly strained by the competition of more attractive or efficient imported goods. Thus although Greek industry now produces a greater percentage of the gross domestic product than agriculture, not only does it contribute relatively little to exports but with protective tariffs selectively lowered towards the Common Market many inefficient sections of traditional industry are in difficulty.

Since 1953 the rate of expansion in the value of imports has far outreached the indifferent showing of export receipts. The liberal policy on importation was proposed in the belief that foreign competition, despite the risk it might involve for domestic development, would ultimately provide the incentive for modernizing industry. But also the commercial interests of important persons and institutions in the importing business, with their numerous clientele of lesser retailers, influenced the policy. It incidentally developed tastes among richer Greeks for foreign luxury consumer goods. In a socially competitive community where differences in income are great, conspicuous consumption of things like cars, refrigerators, and clothes is easily converted into political indignation among those who must continually see and hear advertisement of these goods but have little hope of possessing them. Comfort had been drawn in recent years from the substantial share in total imports of capital goods needed to equip industry with modern tools and transport. But this trend was reversed in 1966: consumer goods increased from 11 per cent to 24 per cent of total imports while capital goods fell to 11 per cent from 26 per cent in 1965. In other respects, it is true, the structure of imports has improved since 1953. With increases in agricultural production and the establishment of two oil refineries, grain, fuels, and lubricants represent a smaller percentage of total imports. Nevertheless the value of total imports is more than twice that of exports and this relation is possible only through the country's ability to import capital and through the remarkable expansion of invisible earnings.

These receipts, to which shipping, emigrants' remittances, and tourists are the major contributors, were in some measure the reward for the relative monetary stability that was preserved after 1953. The surplus on invisible payments rose progressively, and without check; in 1963 it contributed $356·4 million which paid for 50·3 per cent of the country's imports. In 1966, as we have already recorded, it amounted to $481 million; but by then the annual rate of increase had become less abrupt. Hesitations in the economic expansion of West Germany checked the growth of remittances from abroad while receipts from tourism and shipping have been periodically affected by loss of foreign confidence due to conflict or tension in Cyprus, the Middle East, and domestic politics. Earlier the increase in these payments was assisted by the almost continuous growth of the international economy. Had this not been the case there would have been fewer Greeks working abroad, fewer tourists, and the earnings of Greek ships would have been less. Yet, even in 1963, a capital inflow of $56·1 million was necessary to reach an exact balance of incoming and outgoing payments; and by 1966 the gap had widened to $219 million. In these circumstances a relatively mild recession in international business is sufficient to disorganize a balance of payments dependent on the sensitivities and preferences of foreign capital, invisible receipts liable to fluctuation, and the export of a few agricultural products for which the demand can fall away distressingly under difficult conditions. For the comfort of Greeks, and the confidence of foreigners, there are too many factors in the situation which escape control.

Since confidence in the economy both inside and outside Greece has been precarious, symptoms of inflation and instability cannot be disregarded. At the same time every Greek government must affect to give priority to economic development. Unhappily prudent finance, economic growth, and the competitive, but not always responsible, programmes of the political parties were seldom compatible. If there is to be monetary stability, a balanced budget is a prerequisite since the relatively inflexible economy cannot react to the extra purchasing power, which deficit financing implies, without developing inflationary pressures. Yet the economy cannot grow as it ought to, unless a sound infrastructure exists. In particular deficient public administration in Greece and inadequate or non-existent technical education handicap most forms of development. But unless other sectors of the economy are subjected to an unhealthy restriction, public expenditure, already burdened by defence costs which pre-empt about one-fifth of the ordinary budget, and by subsidies which have protected the incomes of farmers by a variety of methods cannot be greatly increased without risk. External aid to cover budgetary deficits offers one solution of this dilemma. And until 1951 the budget deficit and considerable sums of public investment expenditure were in fact covered by American aid. Between 1951 and 1957 the reduction of this aid produced forced economies. Public investment was severely cut back and eventually in 1957 the budget deficit was replaced by a small surplus. One effect of this careful retrenchment was that by 1956 private savings which had been kept outside the banking system were tempted out of gold hoards and into bank deposits. Increasingly these funds were used to finance the private sector of the economy while the growing surplus on the ordinary budget was available for public investment. In Greece a steady development of the economy depends upon reasonable monetary stability; but these two factors are compatible only if the emphasis on either is not too emphatic.

In an economically undeveloped country which had both the institutions of parliamentary democracy and a payments problem, the difficulty was that whenever a position of some stability and incipient prosperity has been reached, opposition forces demanded a rate of advance which was perilously rapid; although, clearly, it might be justifiable on many other grounds. Between 1957 and 1963 the annual average of investment expenditure on the Greek education system, whose archaic inefficiencies are not easily exaggerated, was 2·1 per cent of the total of public investment. The importance of education not only for national economic development but for the progress of the individual to personal security and social status, made it an issue of great significance in the elections of 1963 and 1964. But the promises for reform and expansion in this, as in other areas of national life, were beyond the monetary and technical means which the new Papandhreou government had at its disposal. It is almost inevitable that an opposition party overbids its hand in this way, particularly when it has been long out of power. In this instance the attempt to put its policies into practice led back to budgetary deficits and inflation.

The period of conservative rule (1952–63) under the governments of Papagos and Karamanlis which preceded Papandhreou's victory began during a period of political and monetary instability and was, in one sense, an outcome of it. Monetary stability and political firmness was the dogma which the business and political interests of the party favoured. But during the years of conservative rule inflationary pressure continued. This was unavoidable in a country straining for economic growth at a level of investment expenditure which exceeded available domestic savings. Defence costs, agricultural price support, and credits to farmers issued through the Agricultural Bank, contributed to monetary expansion. And, as is generally the case in developing countries, international comparison and advertisement encouraged people to press for a level of consumption beyond the existing productive capacity of the country, Instalment credit, which makes it possible to discount future income, assisted this tendency. But also a very substantial fraction of business profits went into luxury consumption rather than reinvestment.

Inflationary tendencies in other currencies, and the increase in invisible receipts, did something to offset this monetary expansion and the rising bill for imports. Even so, the struggle for stability was continuous. The Currency Committee of the government, which watched over fiscal and monetary policy, had first to face the task of persuading people to put savings in the commercial banks and not into gold or private money-lending. Until 1955 when deposits began to increase the Bank of Greece had financed credit through

v

inflation of the note-issue. Attractive rates of interest and growing confidence in the currency, which followed the 1953 devaluation, and the new political stability, solved this problem. Thereafter, within the framework of a free economy, the Committee countered inflationary pressures through credit controls and fiscal measures. These were generally selective, not global. It was essential that resources should be applied where they would give the best return for the development of the economy rather than quick profits for speculative ingenuity. For instance, credit facilities for the importation of capital goods which would assist development were more liberal than for consumption goods, and the extension of credit to industry by the commercial banks was examined more carefully after 1958 when it became obvious that there had been a serious leak of credit to the importation of consumer goods and the finance of sales by instalment. In an effort to force funds into productive investment the Currency Committee required the commercial banks to use 10 per cent (the level was later raised to 15 per cent) of their total deposits for medium- and long-term loans. The rates of interest on this kind of loan were lowered and in many cases there was the unusual phenomenon of rates on long-term lending lower than those on short-term credit. Nevertheless the unwillingness both of banks to give long-term loans to small businesses, and of more substantial concerns to make full use of the industrial credit which was available, continued to hold back the economy's development.

Taxation, also, had an important place in the government's strategy. Whether to avoid a budget deficit or to accumulate a surplus which could contribute to public investment, increased revenue was needed. It was hardly possible to satisfy the popular passion for a lighter, or even a more equitably divided, burden of taxation. At the same time, it was necessary not to discourage business interests by unduly taxing their gains. Income tax was considerable on higher incomes but its practical incidence was uncertain because of the capricious and inefficient methods of assessment and collection, and because salaries were more vulnerable than business profits in a community devoted to tax evasion. At the same time, many concessions were made to encourage certain kinds of enterprise. To persuade shipowners to register their ships under the national flag the earnings of shipping were very leniently treated; and foreign capital invested in industry was protected and favoured. Domestic businesses which saved, or earned, foreign exchange, and industries established outside the province of Attica, qualified for similar facilities. After 1959 further concessions were added; for example, half the net profits of industrial and handicraft firms were exempted from taxation if they were re-invested in new plant. Since the very great majority of Greek enterprises are owned by families, the relative advantage of the merchant or entrepreneur over the professional or salaried man is again obvious. But a characteristic feature of Greek taxation is that revenue from indirect taxes is between three and four times as great as that from direct taxation. This is so for various reasons; almost all incomes from agriculture are exempted from income tax; and income distribution and tax evasion reduce the return from those which are liable. It is true that much indirect taxation is designed to restrict the consumption of luxury goods. Nevertheless in most instances the burden of indirect taxation is proportionately greater for the lower-income groups. In such a system this is perhaps inevitable. But opposition politicians were naturally prepared to exploit the circumstances.

Thus in the political battle the popularity of the Karamanlis government was slowly eroded both by its use of selective credit control which alienated those whose interests were not helped and by the unjust incidence of taxation which was the result of the government having to accommodate the need for revenue, incentives to expand production, the inefficiencies of tax collection, demands for social justice. At the same time in public expenditure it could not rival the promises of those who were not yet in power, unless it abdicated all sense of responsibility. That in most matters it did not do so, must be partly attributed to the restraining influence of American officials whose sometimes open support was believed to be, until the election of 1963, the touchstone of electoral success. Yet the commercial policies of this American connection, cautious monetary habits, and a trading policy which accepted the need for exports to communist countries only when a satisfactory outlet was lacking in the West, eventually contributed to its defeat.

In the previous chapter we have already described the more important measures of Papandhreou's economic policy. He had made his electoral appeal to the country on policies of social justice and the planned expansion of the economy. To this programme he was committed not only by his promises but more seriously by the pressure of radical deputies in a party whose unity was uncertain. In 1964 and 1965 there were notable increases in production. The gross national product grew by 8·7 per cent in 1964 and 7·3 per cent in 1965, and for the first time in the country's history the value of industrial production exceeded that of agriculture. Although these increases were mainly the outcome of earlier investments, they owed something to an increase in the use of existing capacity encouraged by the atmosphere of commercial optimism which Papandhreou at first created. But the economy's productive capacity as a whole could not contain the inflationary effects of the consumers' demand which the higher incomes of farmers, wage increases, and government expenditure on education and other items of its ordinary budget, provoked. In 1964 and 1965 the general level of prices rose each year by 3·5 per cent in comparison with the annual average of 1·9 per cent preserved by E.R.E. during its last five years in office. Wages and salaries followed a similar trend assisted by political pressures in a more liberal environment and by local and seasonal shortages of labour in the countryside and in industry. In 1964 wages rose by 10.7 per cent in comparison with 6·3 per cent in 1963 and 3·5 per cent in 1962. In keeping with these developments the supply of money in 1964 increased by 21 per cent, due mainly to the considerable expansion of public sector financing which Papandhreou's social policies required. In the circumstances it was perhaps fortunate that in the summer of 1964 a further period of crisis in Cyprus resulted in a revival in private buying of gold. Bank deposits advanced only modestly and therefore the increase in credit to the economy, especially in the private sector, was slightly less than in 1963.

It might be thought that this degree of instability was a not unreasonable price for measures of social justice and a brisk rate of economic growth, but in the context of the Greek economy there were particular difficulties. Increases in the national product were accompanied by proportionately greater increases in the amount of goods imported. (Over ten years the average of this elasticity was 1.8.) Any growth in internal demand is partly satisfied by additional imports of foreign goods which increases in the value of exported goods cannot balance. In 1964 this was dramatically evident; imports increased by $123 million, exports by $13 million. The adverse balance of current transactions increased disastrously from $57 million in 1963 to $172 million in 1964. Only a net inflow of foreign capital of $141 million protected the reserves which nevertheless fell by $11·2 million. The uncertainties of a continuous quest for foreign funds on such a scale hardly need to be stressed.

In the domestic economy Papandhreou's policies created other problems. Crop subsidies, larger pensions for farmers, free schooling, and the raising of the school-leaving age among other measures claimed a percentage of the revenue of the ordinary budget which left little or no surplus to finance public investment. In 1964 the surplus was $13·4 million only; in 1965 there was a deficit of $2·3 million. With reasonable demands for projects of every kind still unsatisfied a proper rate of public investment could not be financed only by foreign loans without seriously adding to inflationary pressures. Too great a reliance on long-term internal borrowing presented other disadvantages. The burden on the ordinary budget for the servicing of the Public Debt increased by 11 per cent in 1964 and 31·5 per cent in 1965. Yet although the economic arguments for public saving by budgetary surpluses were plain, Papandhreou, for reasons already mentioned, was bound to act by political criteria offering the electorate the tokens of social justice which he had promised them and receiving in return the popularity of the moment. Yet however indisputable the need to increase the farmers' incomes or improve national education, the financing of the first by methods which resulted in only limited investment in farm improvements but added considerably to the economy's inflation, and the attempt to achieve the second by modifying and extending an existing but inefficient system rather than by creating new facilities for technical and vocational training, merely made worse the problems they were intended to solve.

In 1966 domestic demand again increased considerably, by 9·4 per cent in value. The additional demand was partly met by an important increase in the volume of production estimated at 8·2 per cent, but also by a further rise in the general price level. Although the Stephanopoulos government remained precariously in office from September 1965 until December 1966 its dependence on E.R.E. and the importunities of its less principled members prevented it from carrying through any austere revision of economic policy. It is true that this government had the courage to check the inflationary financing of crop subsidies, and to improve the qualitative regulation of credit, and that although prevented from increasing personal income tax it arranged its ordinary budget to provide a substantial surplus of $63·3 million for public investment. But despite this sensible fiscal and administrative husbandry it could do little to relieve the annual rigours of the payments crisis.

Although the marked deterioration of the current balance of payments in 1964 and 1965 was in fact somewhat arrested in 1966, the reasons for this relative improvement and the fact that nevertheless the deficit on current account widened further, only underlined the economic predicament. The decline in the proportion of capital goods to the total value of imports reflected not only the completion of major investments supported by foreign capital, but the relative unwillingness of Greek entrepreneurs to invest in their own industry when they believed that greater and more immediate profits could be made in commercial rather than productive enterprise. Behind the considerable increase in exports which rose by 22 per cent in 1966 in comparison to an annual average of 10 per cent between 1960 and 1965 there were other discouraging considerations. Twenty-eight million dollars of the $70 million increase were contributed by the sale, at a considerable loss, of surplus wheat stocks accumulated over a period of three years. The unsatisfactory structure of agricultural production to which this refers had already had its effects in a sharp rise in 1965 in the quantities of imported foodstuffs, particularly meat. The entry into production of such new complexes as Esso–Papas and Péchiney contributed another $13 million of the increase and helped to raise the share of manufactured goods to 11·6 per cent of total exports in 1966. Such an annual increment to exporting capacity is unlikely to recur at least for some years, yet the relative importance of manufactured goods remains small and their limited advance represents the results of many years of struggle and exhortation, and a considerable effort of investment. Despite this, tobacco, currants, cotton, and fruit, continue to dominate the export trade.

Our account would be unbalanced if we suggested that the achievements of Greek economic endeavour over the past fourteen years had been negligible. The country's infrastructure has been improved. There has been come diversification of agricultural exports with the production of cotton and citrus fruit; and with planting of rice and sugar beet imports of such commodities have been reduced. Under favourable terms foreign capital has been drawn into the country to create a number of modern industrial complexes. The facilities of the tourist trade have been improved and extended. And, until 1963, the management of monetary policy has been remarkably effective, contriving a difficult balance between economic growth, price stability, and a manageable balance of payments.

Fundamentally however the country's economic structure is not compatible with the development which is believed to be necessary. Its weaknesses are inherent in existing institutions and for this reason were not easily corrected by parliamentary legislation. The possibilities of improving agricultural production are limited by the size and fragmentation of farm holdings which are the result of earlier demographic conditions and particular rules of inheritance and dowry. And the flow of migrants from these unprofitable surroundings now threatens hopes for an increased diversification of agricultural products, which the political expedient of wheat support prices, liberally used by parliamentary governments, also impeded. In industry, as we have said, a multiplicity of small family firms contribute the greater part of the national production. Unwilling or unable to obtain long-term credit to modernize their methods and reduce their costs, bound to a local circle of clients, and protected from foreign competition, they are not equipped to sell their products abroad. Only a relatively narrow sector of industry is concerned with exports, just as only a very small fraction of the total area of arable land is used for the few export crops which nevertheless dominate Greek foreign trade. In these circumstances incomes and the demand for imported consumer goods are likely to increase without any necessary expansion of exports, thus ironically linking apparent prosperity with deterioration in the balance of payments.

It has been beyond the ability of parliamentary governments to alter the conditions which underlie this structural imbalance. In industry and agriculture there were too many small proprietors whose interests could not be safely disregarded for the radical measures which would be demanded. And in handling the public investment budget governments have paid too much attention to seducing the electorate by initiating new projects before the existing programmes were completed; so that in 1966 uncompleted public works represented investments six times the value of the investment budget for that year. The result of many projects being temporarily abandoned was not only the cost of physical deterioration but a slow and haphazard improvement of the infrastructure on which the growth of industry with an export potential might be built.

Although these are the failings of Greek parliamentary government in economic policy there is no evidence that the present extra-parliamentary regime has attempted any imaginative reform apart from a sensible policy of land subsidies. It cannot control the confidence of foreign investors or indeed its own entrepreneurs. This is due in the first instance to uncertainty that the military government will continue in power and to fear of the uncertainties which may succeed it; and secondly to doubts about the effects of foreign disapproval. At the end of 1966 official reserves stood at only $273 million. After the inflationary consequences of Papandhreou's policies in 1964 an annual deficit on current account of more than $200 million must be balanced by an inflow of foreign funds of an equivalent amount. Apart from the final negotiation of capital inflow which had been originally discussed under previous governments the military regime appears to have had little, if any, success in drawing foreign capital to Greece. It has failed, even, to persuade the European Investment Bank to release a portion of the $57 million remaining from the $125 million loan negotiated at the time of Greece's admission to E.E.C. as an associate member. Quite apart however from the difficulties which the present government faces in its international relations, it is difficult to believe that annual capital inflows of the substantial amount which Greece now requires, will be indefinitely available to any Greek government, however acceptable.

II

Throughout the post-war period American influence, aid, and technical advice have affected the course and rhythm of economic recovery. Between 1946 and 1963 Greece received $3,285·5 million; of this 54·7 per cent represented economic aid and loans and the remaining 45·3 per cent was received as military materials or grants for their purchase. In the beginning assistance was mainly in the form of food shipments under the U.N.R.R.A. programme. Inevitably between 1947 and 1949 the use of resources was dominated by the civil war. But in the years which followed the defeat of the Democratic Army funds and supplies from the United States were used to re-establish the economy and its infrastructure. Road construction, land reclamation, agricultural investment, food processing, power projects, and the replacement of equipment in factories and mines, where this was necessary, indicate the range of concern. In the early stages aid in money contributed the operating capital to encourage production and employment. For American action was influenced by a political consideration of the importance of unemployment, labour conditions, and housing. And without doubt the transfer of dollar funds and their circulation through the Greek economy both made possible a rate of economic growth[1] that was very respectable despite the low base, and enabled an economy beset with grave structural weaknesses to meet its external payments problem despite a very adverse balance of visible trade. Had Greece not received this aid it is hardly speculative to suggest that her future course would have been very different, whether leading her to a people's democracy or an earlier dictatorship. But in the situation as it existed in 1950, America was more or less compelled to continue her support of the Greek state and Greece had little choice but to accept it.

Naturally, this acceptance had its less pleasant consequences. Before 1947 the British influence in Greece had worked more indirectly and discreetly than the American power which replaced it. It was less ruffling to national pride but also less effective. American aid was overwhelmingly greater both in currency and in materials. Its amount, the aims of the foreign policy which required it, and the uncertain control of the Greek public service over national resources led the American officials to demand a voice in its administration. In military affairs through a joint staff during the civil war, and in later years through the institutions of N.A.T.O.,

---

[1] Between 1948 and 1962 the gross domestic product expanded at an average annual rate of 6·75 per cent; for the period between 1955 and 1962 the average rate was 6 per cent each year.

American officers exercised a very real influence over the Greek army. Once equipped with American weapons and vehicles the Greeks became dependent on their ally for spare parts, replacements, and technical advice. And, inevitably, in the absorbing contest for promotion the quality of being acceptable to the Americans encouraged in ambitious officers dual, and sometimes conflicting, loyalties. American influence was no less marked in economic affairs. Through the attachment of officials and technical missions and experts to different Ministries, particularly to the Ministry of Coordination, Americans affected in detail the making of economic policies.

The disadvantages of such close dependence are evident enough in international relations. Karamanlis, whose government had supported the principle of *enosis* in the Cyprus dispute, was eventually persuaded to accept the Zurich agreement which produced a quite different solution. But in another and less dramatic matter the American attachment had economic and political consequences which were ultimately more serious. The flow of dollar funds and materials to Greece has assisted a defective economy to expand steadily without however causing it radically to alter its structure. In particular it helped to cover, and encourage, a considerable trading deficit with the United States and an adverse balance of payments. And while aid made it possible for most Greeks to enjoy increased personal incomes, the importation of foreign consumer goods contributed to a bourgeois style of life and conspicuous expenditure practised by a minority of affluent families living at levels above those which the country, unaided, could have afforded.

The acceptance of aid however is also necessarily followed by the problem of its ending. As we have seen, during the decade after 1950 the trade gap widened and only the remarkable increase in invisible receipts from shipping, tourism, and emigrants' remittances approximately offset the deficit. Even so, the reduced amounts of American aid after 1952 were necessary to bring ingoing and outgoing payments into balance. Moreover, the sources of invisible receipts were vulnerable to economic conditions and political actions beyond the control of the Greeks. Before American direct economic aid ended in 1962 the Greek government was already negotiating for the alternative supplies of foreign exchange which it would require if the incomes and standards of living enjoyed under American economic protection were to be preserved. These supplies might be assured in two ways: through external public loans and through the attraction of foreign private investment funds to Greece.

In relation to the payments problem the transfer of funds raised through external loans offers the same immediate advantages as direct grants. But unless these are effectively invested to improve the level of exports the original benefit is soon undone through the loss of foreign exchange funds needed for interest and amortization payments. The circular maladies of external borrowing by poor nations are not new. Since the raising of new loans depends on the credit standing of a country abroad, the Greek government had been compelled to pay some interest again on the pre-war foreign debt of some $250 million. In the post-war period to 1966 loans from the United States, and more recently from western Europe, have increased the public external debt by $377 million. It is true that $92 million of American loans are repayable in drachmas. Yet the fact that in the three years 1964 to 1966 the government, denied the support of American direct economic aid and unable to check the rapid growth of imports, incurred a net addition to foreign borrowing of $147 million indicates the serious and increasing rate of external indebtedness. At the end of 1963 the service of internal and external debts was absorbing 7 per cent of the budget revenue; and 8 per cent of the foreign exchange earnings were used to service public external debt and private loans and investments from abroad. These percentages were likely to increase in the future as the aggregate of amortization payments on loans increased.

Since the running down of American aid, however, it is mainly through the attraction of foreign investment capital to Greece that the government has hoped to relate a favourable balance of payments to economic growth. This anxiety is clear in the measures passed to protect the security of foreign capital. Article 112 of the revised constitution of 1952 declared that 'An Act once and for all shall regulate the protection of capital imported from abroad to be invested in the country'. The Act foreseen in the constitution was passed as decree 2687 in 1953. Among other irrevocable provisions it permitted the repatriation of capital at the rate of 10 per cent a year, beginning one year from the date of first production. Profits could be transferred abroad each year up to 12 per cent of the amount of outstanding imported capital. To these conditions were added considerable tax concessions to businesses which mainly exported their products or whose operations resulted in substantial savings of foreign exchange. Despite a generosity not appreciated by many Greeks these measures did not draw the amounts of capital that were needed. Additional legislation was therefore passed in 1961 and 1962 to make the conditions for foreign investment funds even more favourable. Foreign capital and its earnings might now be repatriated at higher rates, with the only qualification that the total of foreign exchange required for this must not exceed 70 per cent of the exchange imported into the country for the goods exported by the business.

There are objections to development by the importation of private investment capital. Generally foreign firms have come to Greece because they hope to exploit the wider domestic profit margins in a protected and monopolistic market. Almost all the important investments under law 2687 have been made by firms producing goods not previously manufactured in Greece. This import substitution has saved foreign exchange but prices to Greek consumers are not necessarily lower. Polystyrene, the raw material of plastics, is made and sold in Greece by the Dow Chemical Company at a price of over $600 a ton c.i.f. But the international price c.i.f. per ton is $370. Again, some firms exist only because of high protection; for example, those which make refrigerators with imported compressors and steelsheet were originally supported by a 56 per cent duty on imported refrigerators. With the lowering of tariffs under the Common Market agreement it is possible that these businesses may withdraw their capital.

Although the tax and credit concessions offered to the producers of export goods are important and justifiable, the emphasis on import substitution has not provided competition or stimulus within the more traditional sectors of Greek industry. The danger exists of an industrial schism. The government must provide the infrastructure for the new industries in which foreign investors have important interests. It is left with few resources to assist the older, smaller, and less efficient Greek firms other than the negative protection of tariffs which only perpetuates a faulty structure. And this support will, in any case, soon have to be abandoned under the provisions of the Common Market agreement, a corrective which some economists fear will have the extreme and opposite effect of destroying, instead of renovating, a large part of Greek industry.

The amount of the flow of foreign development capital into Greece has not been great in absolute terms. Between 1954 and 1963 applications for investments amounting to $398·5 million were authorized, but of this sum only $110·1 million in fact entered the country. Nevertheless this investment is very significant in relation to the narrow base of Greek industry in which, according to one estimate, the total investment in 1963 was $628 million. Between 1963 and 1966 a further $160 million of foreign investment capital entered the country under the provisions of law 2687. The critical role of these funds in the balance of payments has already been discussed. And since, in the foreseeable future, the servicing and amortization of external loans and the repatriation of capital and profits on existing foreign investments in Greece must be balanced in part by a regenerating flow of foreign funds, the government must fervently hope that foreigners will continue to invest an ever increasing amount of capital in the Greek economy. The alternative is a regime of austerity that would be politically unacceptable under a parliamentary government and might force the present Junta to measures of even more severe repression.

Politically, a price has to be paid for these benefits. It means that the country's most modern industrial plant is largely owned by foreign entrepreneurs who, precisely because they have made investments beyond the capacity or interest of native industrialists, are in a position of monopolistic strength. The Esso–Papas complex of oil refinery and steelworks in which Standard Oil of New Jersey have an important interest, the French Péchiney aluminium plant using bauxite mined in Greece, the Italian Pirelli tyre factory, are examples of such undertakings and among the largest. The American government naturally encourages American investment as an extension of its influence. Many of the loans, which are made to Greek and American firms from drachmas received from the sale of surplus American grain, have been granted to petrol distribution agencies which assist American control of the market. But, also, since their own investment and loans are no longer sufficient to support the Greek economy, the Americans have looked with no disfavour at the rate of West German investment which has lately increased and now supports the Bonn government's position as Greece's most active trading partner both in exports and imports.

In such ways as these the growing complexity of the economy and its increasing dependence on foreign money and technology have led to some loss of control by the Greeks over their own industrial affairs. Outwardly this is evident in the influence of some western powers, especially America, on Greek policies and actions; before the *coup* were, Ministers exposed to the corrupting incentives of presents to individuals and of promised political aid to parties made by foreign concerns or governments. The actual extent of this is difficult to know; but hardly less important, before the imposition of censorship by the present regime, was the atmosphere of indignation which it created through the regular revelations of the press. And these 'discoveries' supported the existing popular suspicion of capital, whatever its provenance, and of the motives of foreigners, especially those from the West. If political animosity, or collective prejudice, lay behind much of the opposition to particular authorizations of foreign investment, it is nevertheless not difficult to find grounds for more objective doubts. For instance the Esso–Papas contract completes a process of concession which means that the

Greek petroleum market is dominated by the International companies, that prices have been fixed at a level which may handicap industry, and that the government is free to purchase only limited quantities of the cheaper Soviet products. Although Papandhreou altered to some extent the terms of the original contract, the same objections to it remain. In the case of the establishment of the Péchiney aluminium plant the Greek government bore the cost of very large hydro-electric installations which provide the quantities of electric current consumed by it. These are great. They will amount, perhaps, to one-third of the Public Electricity Corporation's capacity in 1963. Not only will the rest of Greek industry hardly benefit from the additional energy produced by the new installations but Péchiney will pay for electric current at a concessional rate which is markedly lower than the ordinary commercial charge.

To doubts concerning the equity of such contracts there is added the objection that development by direct foreign investment leaves the future structure of Greek industry essentially to the judgements of foreign entrepreneurs by criteria which may not be consistent with the growth of a balanced economy. There is, too, an implicit contradiction in the argument that foreign capital must be persuaded to come to Greece if the general standard of living is to be raised, while at the same time this capital is in fact attracted through low labour costs and the illiberal regulation of trade union activities.

If it is necessary to rehearse the objections and consequences of the general investment policy followed both by Karamanlis and the centre governments which have succeeded him, it would be unrealistic to suppose that they could have been, or even should have been, deflected from it. Investments create employment and in the manufacture of import substitutes, or goods for export, foreign exchange is saved or earned in the struggle to correct the structural weaknesses in Greece's balance of payments. And there is the immediate gain when foreign funds are first imported. It must be hoped, too, that in the long run the level of technical skills in Greece will be raised through the presence of foreign firms. Lack of resources, information, entrepreneurs, technologists, an educated labour force, and under parliamentary government the demanding expectations of an impatient electorate, have confronted planners too often with a prospect that resembles the landscape of Wonderland. They are naturally pleased to retreat to the formula that foreign investment will be the catalyst for the good life. Thus the announcement of a proposal for some spectacular investment by a foreign concern is reported by the government as an indication of international recognition, not as evidence of local incapacity. Foreign investment and membership of the Common Market will together effect the social and economic transformation that will cure all present ills. This at least is the hope.

III

By 1961 after almost a decade of effort to cure the economy of its underlying weaknesses the Karamanlis government could claim no real success. With the support of very large sums of American aid the economic infrastructure had been improved. Production and incomes had increased steadily. But private investment in manufacturing industry was inadequate and after some expansion between 1953 and 1958 exports were again relatively stagnant and still predominantly composed of agricultural products. The balance on visible trade was obstinately and increasingly adverse. The sales of Greece's vulnerable agricultural exports to western Europe had fallen away and the government had been driven to find alternative markets in eastern Europe, especially the U.S.S.R. and Yugoslavia. This was a trend that was hardly welcomed by America although the strain over the Cyprus dispute and the diminishing amount of her own aid to Greece made it difficult to object too insistently. But the new commercial orientation also conflicted with the Karamanlis government's own foreign policy of alliance with the West through N.A.T.O., and its domestic counterpart of repressing or harassing left-wing movements. For these reasons a form of association with the Common Market countries of western Europe appeared to offer certain advantages.

The negotiations proved that in the short run, at least, there would be practical benefits in this shift of dependence. The technical terms of association were favourable. The Common Market countries undertook to reduce the duties on the two important agricultural export crops of currants and tobacco by 50 per cent from the day the agreement came into force and to abolish them entirely by the end of 1967. And over the first five years of the agreement they would make loans to Greece amounting to $125 million. The general aim of the Athens treaty which came into force on 1 November 1962 is to remove the tariffs and restrictions on trade between Greece and the E.E.C. countries so that within a period of twenty-two years these will entirely disappear. By 1966 Greek industrial exports were already subject to 70 per cent lower duties and these, too, will disappear with the eventual elimination of all such duties between the market members. On the other hand duties on imported industrial goods from the E.E.C., which are also made in Greece, will only be gradually removed over a period of twenty-two years. For goods not manufactured in Greece the duties will be removed within twelve years. But in a case where, at a later date, Greece begins to produce goods which were not previously manufactured in the country, it will be open to the government to protect the new industry by a limited tariff of 25 per cent *ad valorem*. Ultimately however by 1984 all duties must be removed.

The terms, we have said, were favourable. It is also clear that because of structural weaknesses in the economy many of the problems now so emphatically presented by the agreement of association would in any case have had to be faced if acceptable standards of life, in political terms, were to be secured. But for Karamanlis there were other considerations. This new alignment would offset the previous reliance on American aid which political opponents had criticized with some effect as excessive and nationally humiliating. Dependence on one country was to be exchanged for association with a powerful and extensive economic alliance which in the popular imagination had brought immense prosperity and prestige to its members. The agreement of association was signed on 9 July 1961 and a general election was held on 29 October 1961. The conjunction of these dates is perhaps significant.

The question is whether the cure prescribed for the Greek sickness was too radical. An early and inevitable effect was that the importation of durable consumer goods which already represented one-third of the import total would continue to rise. For, when tariffs drop, the quality of foreign products attracts more buyers as price differences become less. To compete successfully Greek manufacturers now have to cut their costs and increase their quality. With a dearth of modern equipment and managerial ability, and many external diseconomies in high transport and fuel costs, this is asking much. Although some manufacturers are unaffected where local taste is paramount or heavy transport costs give natural protection, the effects of this competition are already painfully evident. It seems that many small and inefficient businesses will have to merge their interests to find economies of scale, or disappear. And in some cases the monopoly or oligopoly power of larger firms may be broken up.

A successful adaptation to the new circumstances depends on whether industries with some comparative cost advantage for exports to E.E.C. countries can be developed. Before the agreement was signed agricultural exports to the Common Market were losing ground. In the case of citrus fruit, for instance, packing and quality were inferior and considerable quantities of Greek fruit were sold under bilateral arrangements to countries in eastern Europe. As we have seen, manufactured exports have entered little into Greek external trade. To create export industry and to expect an annual increment of 6 per cent to the gross national product one must assume that there will be a decisive increase in private investment in industry; that much of this money will come from abroad; and that capital output rates will not deteriorate. These are questionable assumptions, especially since the military *coup*.[1] Even before this event forecasts for private fixed investment showed no appreciable growth, only a little more than one per cent. Fluctuations in the growth of private productive investment depend almost entirely on the periodical enterprise of foreigners. There are few signs of any productive use of domestic savings and the establishment of large enterprises by Greek initiative. The uncertainties for industry under unaccustomed competitive pressure rather than the opportunities of an immense new market have dominated Greek entrepreneurs and the capital market. The diseconomies of a faulty infrastructure, particularly as this is reflected in a poorly educated labour force, and the discouragement of the generally low profitability of most existing firms, persuade men with money to look for investments in other directions. Information about market opportunities for Greek goods in European centres is often lacking, while the possibilities for investment of money abroad are too well known. And mobility of labour and capital, which are aims of the E.E.C., is likely to result over a period of time in higher wages in Greece, and perhaps an outflow of private capital if full convertibility is effected.

It is true, as every tourist may see with his own eyes, that in some respects development in Greece has been remarkable. But this has been mainly in aspects of the infrastructure such as transport and road construction financed by public investment, and accompanied by a frenetic boom in private building to which too great a percentage of domestic savings has been committed. The industrial, or even agricultural, basis for self-sustaining growth does not yet exist.

With associate membership in the Common Market accepted the sensible strategy for an economic policy is reliance on foreign capital and technological knowledge. Autarkic planning based on the elimination of imports is no longer possible. Greece must select the goods she believes she can produce and sell under open competition in the wider market. But success will depend on important factors quite beyond her control: the flow of foreign investment, full employment, and growing consumer demand in the other Common Market countries which must insure the receipts from emigrants' remittances and also absorb Greece's productive capacity. The time allowed for Greece to create a modern trading economy is short. The approach of integration is relentless and it follows therefore that only social needs of paramount importance ought to take preference

---

[1] The course of the Greek economy since the *coup* of 21 April 1967 has been briefly described in Section VI of Chapter 8.

over the needs of productive efficiency. Nothing in the past history of Greece under democratic institutions suggests that such political self-discipline is possible; and while a prudent austerity might be imposed by an extra-parliamentary regime, clearly the military government believes that it cannot survive except by a repressive administration which has already damaged the country's ability to find the foreign monetary support without which the economy cannot exist in its present form.

Chapter 10

The Greek Countryside

I

IN GREECE the country people generally live in compact hamlets or villages and not on their farms. A great number of
these settlements are very small. The 1961 census found
11,516 settlements or urban 'agglomerations': 5,677 had fewer than
200 inhabitants, 5,500 held between 200 and 2,000, and together
these categories accounted for 43·1 per cent of the population. There
is a great dispersion of population in the countryside but at a figure
of sixty-four persons per sq. km. the population density is considerable in relation to the country's resources.

National statistics of this kind are not without value; but they
obscure the emphasis of regional and local variations. Although
there is little unoccupied territory in Greece the wide areas of
mountain are very thinly populated. The peasant of contemporary
Greece is not typically a highlander, indeed only one in five of
countrymen lives at a height of over 500 metres. It is, of course, the
upland village in rough uneven country with poor soil and difficult
communication, where improved methods of cultivation cannot
produce commensurate returns, which loses population beyond the
limit permitting a vigorous community life. Political events after
the First World war had earlier affected the distribution of population between the mountains and the plains. The settlement of the
refugees from Asia Minor after 1922 had accelerated the division
into small cultivated holdings of large estates in the plains which had
previously been mainly grassland pasture. This in turn restricted the
transhumant grazing economy of many mountain villages and semi-
nomad groups of Koutsovlach and Sarakatsan shepherds who
brought their flocks of sheep and goats to pasture in the plain each
winter. Before and after the Second World war the completion of
drainage and irrigation works allowed the intensive cultivation of
rich alluvial land, and malaria no longer debilitated the plainsmen
and discouraged colonization. Today the tobacco-growing plains
of Thrace, Macedonia, and Aetolia, and the wheat lands of
Thessaly, are closely settled. Most areas of Crete and the Ionian
islands are well populated. But the Aegean islands, as a rule,
are sparsely peopled. The highlands of the Pindus range and

the Macedonian and Thracian mountains have few inhabitants. Central Greece apart from the metropolitan area and the Attic peninsula is not closely populated. The Peloponnese is well peopled along its coastline but by contrast the interior is relatively empty.

If these local variations in rural population produce no exact pattern, it is possible to identify an area extending from Attica north to Macedonia as a zone of real demographic and productive increase where in many districts, despite internal migration, there has been no net loss of population. In these plains, particularly, the mechanization of agriculture has been possible and profitable. With deeper ploughing, weed control, and greater use of fertilizers, yields have increased. In many villages of this more fertile area the cultivated area per head of the country population is greater than elsewhere; and fragmentation of farm holdings, although only slightly less considerable than in other areas, is less crippling in the conditions of flat plainland.

To variations in relief and population density which characterize different areas of Greece, we must add differences of climate and soil. A true Mediterranean climate with a hot, dry, cloudless summer, frequent north winds, and a mild, rainy, cloudy winter, affects only part of Greece, the eastern Peloponnese, central Greece, Euboea, Crete, and the Aegean islands. The western coastal plains of the Peloponnese and continental Greece have more rain; and the climate of lands north and east of central Greece in Thessaly, Macedonia, and Thrace is the modified continental kind with cold winters and hot, usually dry, summers. These variations are reflected in the preference given to particular crops in the agricultural economy of different provinces.

Wheat, which is adaptable to a wide variety of climatic conditions, is now grown in most areas of Greece, but is particularly concentrated in the flat plains of Thessaly and Macedonia where with tractor ploughing, fertilizers, and improved cultivation its yield is vastly superior to the return from the thin soils of many highland villages where wheat growing is in fact an unsuitable choice. Government policy encouraged the planting of this traditional cereal grain by subsidizing the price of bread, and by guaranteeing the farmer a minimum price for his crop with a differential for the small producer. In 1957, for the first time in its recent history, the country was self-sufficient in wheat and 31 per cent of the cultivated area was under this one crop. The policy of increasing wheat production both as a contribution to the saving of foreign exchange and as a support to the farming population was willingly accepted by the peasants who required increased cash incomes but also felt instinctively more secure when they were directly producing their own bread. Moreover, from the farmer's point of view wheat has the advantage of requiring relatively little labour. Although there is seasonal underemployment in most country areas, there is also a shortage of agricultural labour in many places at the periods of peak activity, and consequently the government's attemps to encourage the cultivation of labour intensive crops with an export potential were not always successful since, at least until the advent of the Colonels' regime, it was politically difficult to abandon the support of wheat. Other cereal grains are grown in Greece, but in quantities which are small in comparison with wheat; and generally they are now used only for feeding livestock. Maize and barley each occupy about 5 per cent of the cultivated area; maize is found particularly in northern and western Greece where it has the necessary moisture; barley is popular in the Aegean islands. Rye and oats in rather smaller quantities are grown on high ground with poorer soils, often in the villages of the western Pindus. But a development of some importance since the war has been the profitable cultivation of rice, although it is restricted to areas of reclaimed marshes in western Greece and Macedonia. And everywhere in Greece a variety of vegetable crops are grown mainly for the local urban population, but in some instances small amounts are exported. This is the case with tomatoes and peppers. With more processing plants and more efficient packing and grading, the labour intensive cultivation of vegetables has some export prospects. Potatoes, also, have increased in importance since the war, although the Greek climate is scarcely ideal.

The olive tree is sensitive to cold and flourishes best in the true Mediterranean climate, particularly along the coastline of southern continental Greece, the Peloponnese, and the islands. With wheat and vines, olives are the basis of traditional Greek agriculture. Modern developments and the acquisition of lands in the north have changed this emphasis, but with 79 million trees Greece remains the third or fourth largest grower in the world. Eleven per cent of the cultivated area is given to compact olive groves, although these are often intercropped with wheat and vines on the better soils. It is an advantage that the peak labour demand in its cultivation comes in late autumn and the early winter. Olive trees also have the ability to grow on the stony soils of broken sloping land. This is a great benefit both for the peasants who own them and for the nation which satisfies its annual consumption of fats and oil almost exclusively from the olive crop.

It must be said that their cultivation is far from efficient. Where the spring rain is slight the practice of intercropping reduces the yield. The use made of organic manure is infrequent and the nitrogen deficiency in the soil is not repaired by the application of fertilizer. Weed control and cultivation is insufficient, pruning imperfect, and pest control inadequate. Thus yields are often low and generally the crop is subject to wide seasonal fluctuation. Variable export surpluses and uneven demand in foreign markets have caused exports of olive oil to vary considerably and their average contribution to the value of exports does not exceed 2 per cent. But domestically, as we have said, this is an important crop. And in a poor season the effects are reflected throughout the economy in higher prices for oil, the reduced spending power of many farmers, and their inability to pay debts.

Of the other important tree crops, oranges and lemons were long ago grown in the Peloponnese but it is since the Second World war that citrus fruits have been seriously cultivated and exported. Although orchards occupy only 0·9 per cent of the cultivated area, production is now about ten-fold more than it was before the war. Orchards are generally young and even if no further planting takes place their yield can be expected to increase. If packing and marketing were improved, they might contribute more to the value of exports. Citrus trees, particularly lemons, are sensitive to cold, and the areas most favoured for planting have been the northern coast of the Peloponnese, Epirus, central Greece, and some islands, especially western Crete. Further north in the colder climate of Macedonia the systematic cultivation of deciduous fruit trees such as peach, apple, and pear has also increased since the war. Domestic consumption has grown with the effective refrigeration storage which extends the marketing season, and exports of fresh and processed fruit have given the growers some encouragement.

Yet, of the edible products of Greek agriculture, currants and raisins remain in the field of exports the most important. The derivation of the word 'currant' from 'Corinth' is itself an indication of the antiquity of the industry. Vineyards in this highly specialized and labour intensive trade are mainly in the northern Peloponnese and Crete, and although the area now devoted to it is only 65 per cent of its pre-war extent, production remains about the same, and in 1964 contributed 11 per cent of the total value of exports. Of this the traditional British market still absorbs about 70 per cent, despite competition from American and Australian raisins. Most of the balance is taken by West Germany. West Germany is also the outlet for about 15 per cent of a growing production of table grapes, a high value crop which makes some demand on labour. In local vineyards throughout the land farmers make their own wine for home consumption. Some wine is exported (almost exclusively for blending) but today this is not an important item.

The other export crops of importance in Greek agriculture are tobacco and cotton. Tobacco, indeed, although it occupies only 2·8 per cent of the cultivated area of the country, has produced in recent years about 35 per cent of the value of total exports; and it supports large numbers of agricultural and industrial workers. Because of the importance of this crop to the national economy the government supervises closely the quality and the area sown each year. The risk entailed for the balance of payments in relying so heavily on the earnings of a single crop has been very evident since the war with the decline in popularity of oriental tobacco.

The cultivation of tobacco mainly developed after 1922. Districts of the new lands in the north combined the climatic and low humus soil requirements needed for the production of high-grade tobacco. At the same time tobacco growing suited the needs of the refugees returning from Asia Minor since they brought with them the necessary skills, and the cultivation of the crop required intense family labour on small areas generally without irrigation but heavily fertilized. After the leaves have been picked they must be manipulated, and this has given further employment to the tobacco workers in Kavalla, Drama, and Salonika. Today tobacco growing is fairly widely dispersed in Greece, but there is a marked concentration in Thrace, Macedonia, and Aetolia–Acarnania.

Cotton assumed its present importance more recently. The amount grown is now three times greater than in 1938, and it contributed 12 per cent of the value of exports in 1963. In comparison to wheat on an equivalent area it earns double the income but needs considerably more labour. Thus, it is a crop which adds to farm incomes and assists with the problem of seasonal under-employment in the countryside where this still exists. But its extension is limited by water requirements (and more recently by higher agricultural wages and a shortage of cotton-pickers). Irrigated land is the most suitable; where it is grown elsewhere the land must have natural sub-irrigation. Its cultivation is mainly found in Thrace and Macedonia which produce the short-staple variety, and in central Greece in the area around Lamia and Lake Copais where a longer stapled cotton is grown. Cotton seed is a by-product of the crop which is increasingly used by sheep owners as winter feed for the ewes before they lamb and while they are still in milk.

The principles of modern animal husbandry are little practised in Greece. With the continuous expansion of the cultivated area[1] natural pastures, except those at higher elevations, are usually a

---

[1] But, recently, in some areas of rapid depopulation in north-western Greece transhumant shepherds have rented land from villagers who were unable to cultivate it.

residual category of land, unfit for other purposes and with little grass, where frequently only goats can feed from the sparse and thorny shrubs. Even this inadequate land is deteriorating through over-grazing. We have already said that the disappearance of winter pasture in the plain has restricted the transhumant movement of sheep and goats on which traditionally the economy of many mountain villages depended. But throughout Greece most villagers own a few sheep and goats, small-boned animals, adapted to the difficult struggle of living on very little. They provide milk for the children, cheese for the family, wool for homespun cloth and blankets, and very occasionally, at important religious and family celebrations, meat. Where the size of the flock permits, milk, wool, and most of the male lambs and kids bring in some additional income. The cattle population of the country is relatively small. Numbers are greatest in the plains of Thessaly, Macedonia, and Thrace.

Some fortunate upland villages have forests which give employment and incomes which are more rewarding than those offered by the subsistence cultivation of small stony fields and the shepherding of sheep and goats. But centuries of grazing by goats, soil erosion, and ruthless cutting, have not left many extensive areas of true forest. Where it does exist, fir, pines, oaks, and beeches predominate. Its survival, as in the Pindus mountains, generally owes something to inaccessibility, and this, with inadequate saw-mills and few plants for pulp and hardboard, reduces the possibility of using these resources effectively.

These are the elements of Greek agricultural production. Naturally the combination of crops varies from one village to another; and even more radically in different provinces. The crops which typically dominate Greek agriculture, wheat, tobacco, olives, have an annual cycle and even when they are combined in a suitably complementary fashion it is inevitable that there is some seasonal underemployment; for, as yet, advanced agricultural practices such as dairy farming are of little importance. Under existing conditions villages in the Peloponnese which typically cultivate grapes, olives, wheat, and vegetables show some diversification and farms are reasonably busy throughout the four seasons. But in areas of Thessaly devoted almost exclusively to mechanized farming of wheat and other cereal crops seasonal underemployment is considerable (25 per cent in winter, 37 per cent in summer) and even at the period of peak activity there is 7 per cent of surplus labour. Another pattern which is found both in the intensive cultivation of tobacco near Drama and in prosperous villages near Edessa with a varied economy that includes many orchards of apple, pear, and peach trees, is one of considerable seasonal under-employment in the winter accompanied by a seasonal shortage of labour during the months of peak activity.

Under a static regime of subsistence agriculture and traditional social values, underemployment in the economic sense is scarcely relevant. But in a nation now everywhere dedicated to 'progress' and growing incomes the increase of agricultural exports, the production of foodstuffs at reasonable cost for those who live in the cities, and hence the efficient organization of rural labour, whether to avoid underemployment or shortages at particular seasons, are problems of importance whose solution is not in the least obvious.

A factor which affects every projection is the rate of emigration from the countryside. In the five years from 1956 to 1960, some 250,000 persons left the countryside to go to towns of more than 10,000 inhabitants (and 80 per cent of these people went to Athens). This does not take into account the very heavy emigration to West Germany which in recent years has afflicted particularly the provinces of northern Greece. In 1963, 64 per cent of 100,072 departing Greeks went to West Germany. Not all were migrants and of these we cannot know exactly how many were farmers. But the obvious effects of emigrants' remittances on the villages of northern Greece have been noticed. Some families invest these sums in house building. But others use at least part of the money to buy a wider range of goods than they did before. The 'demonstration effect' of these purchases in small competitive communities persuades some of those who still remain that they too must follow. There is a sudden revelation that life in the traditional manner, and at the material level which they had accepted as part of their fate, is now deprived of the value it once held.

We said that the outflow of population from the countryside has left relatively untouched the areas of mechanized or intensive cultivation in Thessaly, Macedonia, and Thrace. These are areas where improvement has been perceptible and *per capita* incomes are above the national agricultural average. But even some villages in more prosperous districts begin to be affected. And in less fortunate communities, which are not however farming on marginal land, the contagious effect of seeing people go has already reduced their human resources below the level required to maintain output.

It might be thought that the use of more machines could replace the manpower which is deserting the villages. But the government's insistence that the country's salvation lies in a massive investment in industry implies that the capital available for agriculture will continue to be inadequate and below the point which would permit a programme of rapid mechanization. And under existing conditions of cultivation and land tenure, although there is certainly scope for the use of small tools, the benefit from introducing more tractors may not be great since the number of these machines is already approaching the considered optimum of 30,000. Investment in industry, of course, affects the problem more directly, for it is avowedly creating industrial employment which will accelerate the attraction of men from the land. At the same time the government encourages farmers to cultivate more labour-intensive crops of cotton, fruit, and vegetables which, they hope, will increase the value of agricultural exports. The contradictions in policy are many and possibly unavoidable.

Yet, in the end, every effort at rational economic planning in agriculture is blocked by the very considerable fragmentation of land holdings. Not only is the average Greek farm small in its total extent, 30·75 *stremmata*, but it is divided into 6·5 plots of only 4·7 *stremmata* each. Naturally an average of this kind covers many more acute instances; farms divided into as many as nineteen plots and a considerable percentage of plots smaller than one *stremma*. But the variation between provincial averages is small and fragmentation today is virtually ubiquitous. Multiple causes have produced this result. By custom sons have equal inheritance rights and daughters on marriage exercise an equivalent right in the form of dowry. For those children who remain in the countryside the family asset which must generally be divided is land. Since land comes into a family with daughters-in-law but leaves it with daughters, the combination of inheritance and dowry customs tends to produce farms of dispersed plots. And this effect has been heightened through time by the growth of population during the past hundred years and the present absolute shortage of cultivable land. To this process land reform has made its own contribution.

The distributions of smallholdings to landless peasants from national lands, and subsequently from expropriated estates, were made both before and after the First World war. The return of refugees from Asia Minor after 1922 increased the urgency of this operation. But through too delicate a concern that the peasants receiving new farms should benefit equally from a share in the better land of the district even these original allotments of land were usually made in four to six plots of land in different areas. Thus before the Second World war the division of the fertile parts of the country into an intricate pattern of small farms fragmented into smaller dispersed plots had been completed.

The technical and social consequences of these conditions are very marked. In the first place much of the working day is spent simply travelling with implements to and from dispersed plots situated generally in different directions from the village home at distances often greater than 10 kilometres. A man may have to make a round trip of 20 kilometres to carry out a spraying operation which takes only 15 minutes. Where land is considerably fragmented the use of modern machinery is difficult. Fields are small and irregularly shaped and often enclosed by other fields with no direct access. Without the cooperation of neighbours it may be impossible to turn implements. Even where goodwill exists, if it happens that neighbours are growing different crops, it may only be possible to cultivate restricted fields with hand tools.[1] It is clear, too, that the introduction of crops which require constant attention faces some obvious difficulties. Irrigation, crop rotation, spraying, weed control, and measures to avoid soil erosion, may be discouraged or prevented. Another disadvantage is that animals cannot be systematically grazed on small, dispersed, and unfenced plots. Invaluable manure is lost and livestock are generally relegated to the community pasture land which is poor and overgrazed. The enormous extent of unfenced and often imprecise boundary lines is a source of disputes and litigation, whether these arise from disagreement about where the boundary is, from damage by straying animals, or the passage of equipment when a farmer has to reach an enclosed field.

From the point of view simply of rational agricultural production and practice no system of land tenure could be more exactly designed for the dissipation of physical effort and mechanical resources. Legislation for voluntary land consolidation exists where the majority of the inhabitants of a community wish it. Yet after eighteen years only about 2 per cent of the cultivated area has been affected. Meanwhile the process of increasing fragmentation continues. In one village, after thirty-five years, although the average size of farms remains about the same, each now consists of twice as many plots and in some instances heirs must remain the multiple owners of midget fields.

Apart from farm fragmentation Greek agriculture has other general deficiencies. A combination of population pressure and inappropriate farming methods has produced soil erosion. And in many areas the practice of continually planting cereal crops instead of using proper rotations has exhausted the soil. Except in limited areas of advanced farming the use of chemical fertilizers is insufficient or wrongly applied. And generally the ratio of current expenditure on farms to the gross value of the product is too low. In Greece it is only 9 per cent in comparison with 22 per cent in France and

[1] In Thessaly with the development of mechanized wheat farming, a solution to this problem is found by ploughing the 'inside' plots first and harvesting them last. Even so, the delays involved often lead to damaged crops in the 'inside' fields.

40 per cent in the Netherlands. It is not only that there is not enough capital available for investment in agriculture but traditional investment habits, and the need to find dowry land for daughters, generally persuade the prosperous farmer to keep his savings intact, or invest them in land. He seldom applies them to the improvement of his existing plots. For the little he may do in this respect he relies on loans from the Agricultural Bank. Generally, there is a lack of technical knowledge and of capital; and neither land nor labour is as productive as it ought to be. In these circular difficulties land fragmentation is, of course, an important factor and impediment to progress. It makes the use of machinery difficult, as we have already pointed out, and even the application of fertilizer becomes un-necessarily burdensome for men and animals. And it partly dis-guises the effects of underemployment by dissipating the time and energy of farmworkers over geographical limits which from an economic point of view are absurdly wide.

The structure of Greek farms and the use that is made of land are elements in the pattern of institutions and values that characterizes the countryside. So long as this pattern persists it is doubtful if the productivity of agriculture can be more than modestly improved. About one-half of the rapid increase in production achieved since the late thirties can be attributed to the extension of the cultivated area, made at the expense of pasture and forest and through the virtual elimination of fallow land. Neither of these processes offers much further scope. The other half of the increase has been due to improvements in yield through irrigation, better seed, and the spreading of fertilizer. Fertilizer and improved strains of seed are extensively used already in the more fertile plains. And although it is true that in many upland districts farmers have yet to be proper-ly instructed and persuaded into better methods of cultivation, the quality of the land limits the increment to production that can be expected.

Irrigation could increase yields. At the present time it affects about 13 per cent of the cultivated area, but new works would be progressively more expensive and they would have to compete with industry for the limited amounts of investment capital. A more immediate advance might be possible through the efficient use of already irrigated lands, by educating farmers to understand better the requirements of different crops and particularly to prepare their land more thoroughly. But for this drainage ditches would be needed, which is not economic with the present pattern of land holding. Once again the fragmentation of farms is the barrier to technical improvement.

Under present conditions, then, we can expect no remarkable

increase in the volume of agricultural production. Nor is it always easy to persuade a farmer to grow a proper combination and rotation of crops. We have already mentioned this problem in relation to seasonal underemployment in the countryside, and also to soil exhaustion where correct rotations are not followed. But there are other aspects of this question. For a number of years since the war the government has guaranteed a minimum price for wheat. This has both saved foreign exchange and increased farmers' incomes. The latter have been an important factor in stimulating the demand for consumption goods which has contributed in its turn to higher incomes throughout the economy. As we mentioned in the previous chapter, one reflection of these changes has been a considerably higher demand for meat and dairy products which is not satisfied by Greek farming as it is presently organized. Neither enough livestock is kept nor are sufficient fodder crops grown. And knowledge about animal husbandry is deficient. The result is that imports of these products increase the adverse balance of trade.

Meanwhile the production of wheat advanced far beyond domestic needs. The probability is that Greece's requirements could have been grown on three-fifths of the land in fact devoted to it in 1965. At the end of that season the government had on its hands a million tons of wheat which had to be stocked and disposed of at the state's expense. And the total cost of growing this crop was approximately double the world price. This excessive expansion of wheat production had been encouraged by the maintenance of price support for mainly political reasons, but it also had other more disturbing causes. The exodus of migrant workers in the sixties, especially from northern Greece, as well as the continuing internal migration to the towns, created acute local shortages of labour at the seasonal peaks of farming activity. The wages of farm labourers increased, inevitably, by as much as 20 per cent in a year. These were additional costs not easily borne by an industry as relatively unmechanized as Greek farming. Thus some farmers were compelled to regress to sowing wheat and other cereal crops, which demanded little labour, instead of the labour intensive crops such as cotton, fruit, and vegetables to which, ironically, the government had been asking them to turn. The figures for the production of wheat and cotton indicate this development quite dramatically: wheat, in 1963, 1,387,000 tons; in 1964, 2,169,000: cotton, in 1963, 266,000 tons; in 1964, 184,000 tons. And this happened despite the emergence, in recent years, of cotton as an important export crop.

The government refused to pay subsidies in the season 1965–6 for wheat sown on irrigated land and it seems that the area put under wheat was substantially less. Yet, as we have seen, the problems of agricultural production are deeper and more complex than the manipulation of subsidies, even if this is done selectively and with political courage. Theoretically it is easy to say that there should be more livestock more efficiently managed; and more labour intensive crops with export prospects. But faced with the objective conditions of small dispersed plots and increasing labour costs, and suffering the diffusion of energy and interest which matches the fragmentation of his land, the farmer is only ready to adopt new techniques with enthusiasm when they offer a quick return and when they appear immediately practical under existing conditions.

These conditions are intimately connected with institutions of land tenure, inheritance, family, and community which originally existed to support a family honourably and frugally by the crops it grew, or the services it gave, within a world with local boundaries and agreed values. What are now economic anomalies were then particular facets of a relatively closed social system of neighbouring villages. The interests of villages now transcend both local and provincial boundaries, and the introduction of city ways and goods into the villages has changed the quality of life. Yet some elements of the rural social structure are finally not compatible with intensive agriculture as a form of rational industry. For this in effect is what is required of the countryside by the changing demand structure of urban preferences and by the exigencies of export opportunities and import substitution. Radical legislation for compulsory land consolidation, the regulation of inheritance and dowry practices, and land sales more generally, would be minimum requirements to make this possible in the short run; and with some confidence one can say that it is unlikely to be attempted even by a military regime.

II

Despite the variety of climate, relief, and crop patterns in different parts of the Greek countryside, and although, clearly, the quality and detail of social life is different, for instance, in a declining hill village in Epirus from conditions in a wheat-growing village in the Thessaly plain, there are still certain institutions and aspects of village life which are sufficiently widespread to justify a generalized description.

On paths and roads leading into many villages one first comes on a stone pillar with a recess for an icon and a simple oil lamp, or sometimes a small chapel, which both guards and marks off the boundary of the community from the outside world. On the outskirts, too, will be the cemetery, generally with a chapel beside it. At the centre of most villages is the *mesochori*, a public place or square, sometimes paved, around which the buildings concerned with village public life are clustered: the church where the liturgy is celebrated each Sunday, the community office in which the mayor and council carry on their administrative functions, and one or two coffee-shops which generally serve as both tavern and general store. The schoolhouse, too, may be close to the square.

Behind or surrounding the square are the family homes. Styles of architecture show considerable regional variation but stone houses with two floors are common, generally with a balcony and an external staircase. Ideally a house has a courtyard with a tree, a separate storehouse, perhaps an outside oven, and some kind of enclosure, preferably a high stone wall. Houses may have become semi-detached through division on inheritance but where this is so each household is self-contained. Every family, in its domestic life, wishes to live to itself closely and secretly. The houses themselves are seldom aligned in a regular manner. They face in different directions, emplacements may be of irregular shape, some walled and some not, interconnected by a maze of twisting paths. Whether by design or not the effect of this kind of distribution is to make it difficult for one family to keep under observation the activities of more than two or three neighbouring households. Reliable information about the domestic affairs of others is difficult to obtain, and for this reason is highly prized. Speculation based on slander and inference, on the other hand, is perpetually at work, but the thoughts which it prompts cannot be too loudly broadcast without arousing enmity. And to be found listening against the wall of another's house is humiliating and dishonouring.

We have emphasized the historical importance of the family institution in the social structure of Greek communities. In the uncertainty and changes of contemporary country life this remains true. A man's categorical obligations are still, in most situations, to his family. Outside his family he may have other roles. He may be mayor of the village or President of the Cooperative, a member of the village or church council, secretary to the village council, or an agricultural field guard. Yet where there is conflict between loyalty to the family and duty to another group or service, the former has precedence. The family has a multiform character. It is not only a domestic group concerned with the care and upbringing of children. It is also an economic enterprise and a religious community. This quality underlies the exclusive solidarity of the family and its isolation.

We have mentioned earlier the reference of family roles to the holy figures of God, the Virgin Mother of Christ, and Christ

Himself. On a shelf or in a niche in the corner of one room in the house are the icons before which members of the household will cross themselves and perhaps add a simple prayer at night and in the morning, asking for protection and good luck. The simple acts of worship are frankly pragmatic and manipulative. Men understand that the family depends on the beneficence of God for rain, for the fertility of land and women, and in the struggle to preserve social reputation. Through the intercession of the saints, and particularly the Mother of Christ, there is hope that God will hear their prayers, for the family institution, its values, and the duties which the individual has within it, are sanctioned by Him. Appropriately, the wedding crowns used in church on the day of the marriage are often kept with the icons, and sometimes the bed used by the married pair is beside the corner where the icons stand. Those acts which a Greek villager is disposed to regard as sin are very largely confined to transgressions which injure the harmony of the family's internal relations, diminish its prestige, or put its material welfare at risk. Striking a parent, grossly inefficient farming, or reckless gambling might all be so described. On the other hand a measure of exploitation and dishonesty in dealings with people who are not kinsmen or neighbours may be tolerated or forgiven by God in the narrow circumstances which most families confront.

As the members of the family stand together before God, so together they work the land. Men and women have their segregated tasks but they are a complementary team and when it is necessary they will work together at the same task. In wheat growing the ploughing is done by the men, the hoeing and weeding generally by the women. This is also the case in the cotton fields but here the hoeing is particularly arduous and the men will sometimes help. Irrigation of cotton and other crops is men's work. In tobacco cultivation men again do the ploughing but women tend the small plants which must be handled delicately while they are still growing in the frames. And where crops must be hand-picked women do the collecting while the men weigh, lift sacks onto trucks or mules, and supervise. The division of labour appears to follow a simple sexual symbolism. Men do the tasks which require organization and strength: women the work where nurturing and care are needed. For this reason, too, men have no part in domestic work or carrying water, which indeed would be dishonouring.

The unit of economic enterprise is invariably the family and the fields it owns. Each family resents the lands held by other families and envies them any success which is above its own. The fragmentations of farms and the multiplication of boundaries provide a flow of disputes over the movement of equipment and the depredations of animals which ensures that mutual opposition, and the notion that the existence of other families limits one's own resources, are a permanent factor in men's attitudes. But in those important areas of the plains where there is now a relatively intense cultivation of cash crops the requirements of commercial farming qualify these circumstances. It may only be economic for individuals to invest in tractors, pumps, and other mechanical equipment if they offer these machines for hire to other farmers. This is commonly the case and it presupposes standards of behaviour which make such contracts possible. Similarly for the picking of crops of cotton and olives, for instance, hired women workers may be needed, of whom some will come from the less employed families in the village and others from outside. The spirit of cooperation created by the need for such arrangements must not be exaggerated. Indeed they sometimes serve only to indicate how little of this spirit exists. Yet the economic interdependence which such contractual agreements produce suggests a social structure of a different quality from that of the mountain village with an economy nearer to the subsistence type. Cooperative needs may there be satisfied by the limited assistance of kinsmen or neighbours and villagers are free to express without inhibition their opposition to those with whom they have no positive relationship of blood or common interest.

The main concern of the family is the marriage and honourable establishment of the children. Traditionally this particularly depended on the preservation of a girl's reputation and virginity and the courage of her brothers which protected her from physical attack or slander. Sexual misdemeanours still gravely compromise the prestige of a family, but since the end of the civil war urban and western values which appear to question the civilized propriety and practical sense of fixing upon virginity as a main criterion of feminine uprightness have greatly weakened the certainty of retribution in cases where a girl's honour is in question. And the doubt which they have introduced has increased the frequency of clandestine premarital affairs without however legitimizing any custom of open courtship. This change introduces anxiety and frustration, and no doubt contributes to the general wish of young people to leave the villages. With the greatly accelerated rhythm of migration to the towns, improved communications, and the more commercial economy of many villages, the efforts of families to establish their children are now more oriented to prestige values of the world beyond the village whether this takes the form of educating a son for a position in the town, finding a town bridegroom for a daughter, or merely the purchase of clothes, radios, and household goods of modern style for the family and for the dowries of its daughters.

For these aims the family resources of whatever kind, land, houses, flocks and money, and the produce and income from them, are a general stock from which different members of the group are endowed according to their needs, and as equitably as possible. If it is possible, fathers do not wish to divide again a small and already fragmented farm, and they attempt to find a position for a second son in the town. The money expended on this son's secondary education, which may cause the family considerable hardship for a number of years, will be taken into account when his share in the patrimony is considered. Where traditionally manliness in its literal sense, influence, and independence of others might be claimed by a man supported by four or five sons, such a family today may be regarded as rather too much fortune for one man, and the product of sexual intemperance which makes it difficult to give each son the means to establish a respectable position in society.

The honourable settlement of daughters however is the greater test of social effectiveness. For respectable marriage a girl requires health, a reputation for modest behaviour, and dowry. Any physical, moral, or material deficiency in these respects reflects on the whole family. In village society marriage is normally forbidden within the kindred, the body of recognized kinsmen related through the mother or the father generally to the collateral degree of second cousin. In villages of modest size a consequence of this customary regulation is that although marriage within the village is favoured, a bride may have to be found elsewhere; in that case the two families contracting the marriage will be 'strangers' to one another in two respects, unrelated by kinship (except in the marginal instance of marriage between the children of second cousins) and not associated by the ties which fellow villagers share. The arrangements are, in most cases, a negotiation between families not individuals, an evaluation of future intentions and present prestige not personal sentiments, in which each side proceeds with caution and suspicion using the services of an intermediary so that a withdrawal will not bring public humiliation for the other side. It is true that the views of the future partners must be consulted, and that in recent years there have been more instances where a secret liaison has precipitated families into contracting alliances which were never intended; yet as long as collective prestige and dowry are concerned in the choice of a marriage partner, the attempt to arrange these contracts by families rather than individuals will continue.

A girl inherits through her dowry which may include in varying proportions the value of her trousseau, furniture for her new house, money, and land. Through dowries a family demonstrates its ability to care for its more dependent members. A dowry complements

X

the bridegroom's potential patrimony. For two families are contributing one of their members and a certain amount of wealth to establish a new family in which both will have a balanced interest. Both village custom and the Greek Civil Code emphasize that dower property is given in trust for the yet unborn children of the new family. The wife's parents and siblings have a right to be consulted before the alienation of any part of this property and by law a wife must sign a form of agreement to any such transaction.

The actual amount of dowry has always been an instrument for the adjustment of difference in family status and personal qualities of the bride and bridegroom. A girl marrying into a family of greater social standing, or a girl whose health or virtue is suspect, will contribute more dowry. Where such deficiencies are in the bridegroom she will pay less. But the current extension of villagers' ambitions to the search for town bridegrooms, both for reasons of prestige and to save their daughters from the hardships of village housekeeping and work in the fields, and the intention of young farmers in prosperous families to build a 'modern' village house, has led to an inflation of dowry values which has accompanied increases in agricultural incomes and easier credit facilities, and is no longer merely a question of adjustment. These are developments which reflect the growing importance for villagers of standards external to the traditional village culture. But it has also incidental economic effects which impoverish agriculture, in the sense that the town bridegroom is not interested in dowry in the traditional form of land but asks for considerable sums of money, or a house in the town built by instalments and paid for out of the farmer's savings and borrowings. Savings which ought to be reinvested to increase the productivity and efficiency of the farm are drawn off into the financing of private dwellings in towns and cities which are, for the requirements of the national economy, the least desirable and productive forms of urban investment.

Through the institutions of equal inheritance and dowry there is a redistribution of property at each generation. And parallel to this redistribution there is also, through marriage, a rearrangement of authority and social obligation. The fundamental and categorical value in the nexus of family ties is the strength of the obligations of parents to their children which include their honourable establishment in society through the institutions we have just discussed. Children have reciprocal duties to their parents, obedience at least until they are married, respect at all times, and provisions for their mother and father in old age. But marriage, and the birth of his own children which should shortly follow, at once involve a man in the same obligations to his growing children which his own parents had to him. The contingent quality which now enters his relations with his family of birth is particularly marked in his dealings with his brothers and sisters. An unmarried brother is the natural avenger of a murdered brother or a dishonoured sister. The moral pressure to fulfil this obligation is still very great despite the uncertainty which the values of urban life have introduced. And just as the reputations of unmarried brothers and sisters are interdependent, so in a common solidarity their attitude to rights in family property or their share of the work on the family farm is relatively uncalculating. But whatever may have been his sentimental attachments, the differentiation of social personality effected by his marriage and the duties of parenthood in a competitive community with limited resources soon accustom a man to make a precise assessment of his rights, even in trivial matters, and while he may still be living in a joint household with his parents and brothers. For this reason it is generally considered right that brothers should delay their marriages until their sisters have been settled, so that they have champions to protect their virtue and a united household to accumulate their dowry. In this way two important sets of obligations in a man's life, the one to his sisters, the other to his children, do not conflict. These developments in the life cycle of a family indicate the quality of its solidarity and the corresponding isolation of this group, opposed to other families with which it is not related by blood or an alliance of marriage or common interest, and only conditionally supported by those with which it is.

The members of a family are united in the face of a hostile world. Yet internally relations between parents and children are complex, tense, and at the same time constrained by the need for a minimum of material and emotional security which is only to be found in the family. Children during the first four years of life are enormously indulged by their parents and told incessantly by all their relations how remarkable they are. The mother, who in her person is the moral and expressive centre of the family life, continues throughout her life to pour an almost unconditional affection and admiration upon her children, especially her sons, in contrast with (and perhaps in compensation for) the often pragmatic relations with her husband. But as a means to control her children a mother also resorts to stratagems of deceit and promised rewards which are rarely delivered. Although the transparent dishonesty of these appeals is soon appreciated by an intelligent child, his dependence forces him to accept the terms and the idiom of this behaviour. Thus attitudes of suspicion and cunning which in later life are to be so appropriate in dealings with unrelated persons are in fact learned within the context of the relationship that stands for the quintessence of love and confidence. In the case of the father, after years of praise and indulgence he is somewhat abruptly transformed to an authoritarian figure some time before the child begins school at the age of six or seven. This is necessary both to sanction lessons of loyalty and conventional behaviour, failure in which brings the family into disrepute, and to prove indisputably that the father is master in his house, since any lack of respect to a father shown by older children at once diminishes his prestige. The child is alternatively indulged and commanded. Later, in adolescence and early manhood, a son in his attempts to develop his social personality in the prescribed pattern of self-assertive confidence inevitably comes into conflict with his father. This ambivalence in a son's relations with his father mirrors the contrast between the remarkable potentialities of his nature which he has been encouraged to believe in and the straitened circumstances in which he now realizes he must live. These relationships throw some light on the villager's quickly provoked intolerance with its latent threat of violence, his excesses of hope and despair, and the distance between the elevated character of personal and national ideals and the limits of achievement.

Opposition and distrust between families in a village is more often negatively expressed in the difficulty of organizing any wide cooperative initiative unless it is imposed from outside, or of bringing a dispute to any conclusion except by the decision of a court. Physical violence is not generally approved unless it arises in specific questions of honour, such as seduction, adultery, or insupportable insult. But secrecy is a very general index of these attitudes. For if others know of a man's movements and intentions it is felt that in some respect his independence is compromised. The information denied may in itself be trivial. A woman will not disclose what she is cooking. A man about to pay a routine visit to the nearby town makes his preparations inside his house and appears at the very moment the bus moves off. He has not had to fence with curious enquirers and this is a small tactical triumph. Conversation between women at the well or between men in the coffee-shop is in part a contest to gain information without conceding it.

These attitudes are expressed even more suggestively in the concept of the Evil Eye. In a limited world a man desires objects or qualities which he admires but does not himself possess. Through the eyes, his envy creates (although unconsciously) an alarming and pervasive force of wickedness which may destroy or injure the person or object which he desires or envies. To this evil force a family may attribute most of its misfortunes, for its effective range is wide, causing disease in animals, illness in children, or the breakdown of a tractor. Women with a known ability for exorcizing the Evil Eye may themselves sometimes be suspected of using their powers malevolently to bewitch their fellows. Fear of others' envy, whether its destructive effect is consciously directed or not, is a further reason for secrecy.

It is not however a simple destructive opposition which particularly characterizes social relations in a Greek village. Where emigration has not drained a community of vitality, these are dominated by competition for social reputation, especially in the sense of surviving the continuous questioning of motives and behaviour. Life is a struggle, shepherds say. 'We are struggling'. The Boeotian peasant gives this standard response in reply to a polite enquiry about his work. Partly the struggle is against nature. But this is the common lot of men and there is God's mercy and protection. In the contest for reputation, which never ceases and is never won, families and individuals depend on the judgement of a community which in its majority is hostile to their interests. There will be as many assessments of a man's prestige as there are families in a village. But the very ambiguity and uncertainty about the ordering of reputations in a community ensures that competition is anxious and intense.

In the first chapter we have already described the traditional notions of honour. Today, even in villages with an economy of mechanized farming, this code still retains some force as a traditional and respected pattern. But in practice the interpretation of conduct changes and the severity and certainty of sanctions weaken. Maidens must still be modest and virginal but in fact their eyes are bold where before they were downcast, their arms bare where they were covered; cotton dresses set off their figures which, previously, homespun clothing was designed to conceal, so that the danger of their sexuality to their own honour and to the honour of those who protected them might be controlled. The violator of a girl, if he is not immediately arrested, is still today in mortal danger from her brother. If she is merely seduced and then abandoned the outcome is less certain. For her weakness the girl and her family lose honour and she has little hope of a respectable marriage in the district, but it cannot be said that the brother's reputation is fatally and permanently compromised if he takes no action against the girl or her seducer. In these circumstances much depends on the wisdom of the philanderer in avoiding his victim's family. The ease with which a violator of honour can now leave his village to live and work elsewhere assists in this, as it also tends to weaken the sanctions of the code. Moreover, the public reaction to an act of vengeance is now ambiguous: some praise the killer but others are affected by the barbarity of the act particularly if the girl's life is taken by her brother.

From these remarks it must not be supposed that sex-linked stereotypes of approved behaviour are no longer important. Men must be brave, vigorous, and assertive; wives, modest, faithful, obedient, and dedicated to their children. But in the ideal self-image which men attempt to realize there is an increasing urbanity. Within the existing notions of what is possible men wish to be efficient farmers, heads of family who are independent economically and able to provide respectable patrimonies for their sons, and dowries for their daughters, with alliances through marriage or patronage with persons of influence in the provincial town. A man requires an articulate wit to excel in the competitive debates of the coffee-shop and cunning in his manipulative manoeuvres and negotiations with merchants and authorities. His sense of honour (*philotimo*), of what is due to the integrity of his social personality, is acute; but it is better defended by the evidence of prosperity, a properly ordered household, and verbal effectiveness than by resorts to physical violence. It is against these standards that the qualities of individuals and families are judged. Criticism is comprehensive since the social roles which men and women may play are relatively few and their requirements, or even the ambiguities which changing conditions and values have introduced, are precisely understood, just as the personal circumstances of each inhabitant are also well known. The members of a family must carefully guard their reputation for proper conduct in their social relations and reasonable efficiency in working the farm. Other families will miss no opportunity for ridicule or scandalous speculation at their expense. The moral pressure of this hostility draws together the members of a family in defence of their common reputation and it follows, too, that each member, even a child of five or six years old, bears an exacting responsibility when he appears in public.

Villagers tend to look on their local world as a closed economy of fixed resources. The success of one man implies the failure of another, and vice versa. Good arable land is scarce, grazing is scarce, irrigation water is limited. What is owned by, or allocated to, one family is denied to another. In the moral field a similar attitude prevails. To discover and broadcast the failings or dishonour of another family in a sense confirms by contrast the integrity of the gossiper's own family. Since the force of familial attachment is so strong it is a man's duty to exploit other men and families where he can find advantage and profit for his own. One should not press too far a close neighbour or a man much poorer than oneself; there is a prudential consideration in the first limitation, and a sense of *hubris* about the second since the family is an institution protected by God. These are ill-defined limits and it is often difficult for a man to know exactly where he ought to draw the line, but much easier to predict on which side of it his error will fall.

Yet, because villagers rely on one another for that recognition of their social personalities which they crave, they compete with and oppose one another in terms of values which they cannot ignore. A man cannot compete with his fellows unless he associates with them. A man who avoids the coffee-shop, or sits unspeaking, is unnatural or unmanly. The intense and competitive fellowship of men in the coffee-shop is based on the sharing of wine, company, and conversation, and this is an important recognition of a man's social personality in terms of equality and opposition. Altruistic acceptance of others, men believe, with regret, to be incompatible with the conditions of their life in this world. Formally, the punctilious exchanges of greetings, when villagers meet, express concern for the health, wellbeing, and good luck of others. And at religious festivals, and particularly Easter, there is enjoined goodwill, the houses of the village are visited in turn, and in some communities food is given to those who are too poor to provide their own. Such events interrupt the flow of profane life and mark the sense of religious community, yet by their symbolic reversal of customary attitudes the particular and limited obligations of ordinary life are confirmed.

It follows that the free and sentimental commitments of personal friendship are hardly consistent with the exclusive family loyalties we have described. With cronies of the moment, who may or may not be kinsmen, a villager from time to time exchanges small services, the loan of tools, help with some task in the fields. These men are 'his friends'. Despite differences in wealth and prestige which in a cash economy increasing competition for goods with status value accentuates, the style of life for most families in a village is very similar. Friendship, conceptually at least, exists between equals. It begins with the acceptance of a favour by one man from another. The giver asserts that he expects no return. It would be insulting to suggest that his friendship had any motivation. It is however the very altruism of the act, whether this is simulated or not, which demands a counter-favour. If this is returned, the question then is whether it is equivalent; or even greater in value than the original favour requiring a further act or gift from the man who first prompted the relationship. In the atmosphere of distrust, where *philotimo* demands that a man must not appear to be worsted or exploited, it is unlikely that the judgements of the two sides will always coincide. Thus accusations of ingratitude are not uncommon and the pattern of friendship relations is shifting and unstable.

Similarly a man has enemies. Quarrels have many growing points: the breakdown of former friendships, differences between brothers over inheritance, the flow of disputes which arises from the fragmentation of property and the absence of fencing, the verbal defeat or disparagement of another in public debate, the collapse of negotiations for a marriage, are some of these. Generally quarrels are controlled by mutual avoidance and in time the majority are resolved in the sense that by tacit consent normal relations are gradually resumed; but some may remain as lasting enmities. As with friendships the particular pattern does not endure. In both instances this instability is due to the exclusive solidarity and isolation of the family group. Once a man has manfully and effectively asserted his rights, and providing the original cause was not too grave, it is not in his interest permanently to estrange the other family and its allies in a community where position and reputation depend on public judgement. Although in aggregate the links of friendship and hostility in a village are many, they generally exist with any intensity only between the two families principally concerned in a dispute, and their force and effect are isolated. This tends to prevent the growth of any widely based cooperation within the community, or its division into permanent factions with well-defined loyalties and memberships. Only where the formal structure of agricultural cooperation or the organization of national political parties are imposed from outside the village do such bodies have any permanence. And, predictably, the administration of cooperatives is handicapped by pervasive distrust and the stability of political groups by the shifting allegiances of families.

A village with a primary school and a population of more than 500, and in practice often a village with a smaller population, constitutes an administrative 'community' (*koinotis*) which enjoys a measure of local self-government through the election of a council of five members.[1] The elections, held every four years, are contested between groups which are not necessarily extensions of the national parties, although some loose affiliation generally exists. The victorious faction gains four seats on the council but the fifth is reserved for the candidate of the minority party with the greatest number of votes. The five councillors then meet to elect one of their number as the village mayor. The council institutes local by-laws; it prepares local taxation registers for which information about land, its produce, and numbers of livestock is required; it fixes within statutory limits grazing dues on community land; and it prepares

[1] Under the military regime, as under the Metaxas dictatorship, the officials of local government are appointed by the central administration. However, we leave this account, optimistically, in the present tense.

each year the community budget which includes the costs of its own administration and its programme of works. In a formal sense, and considering the parochial nature of its affairs, the powers of the council are relatively wide, but the Nomarch (the provincial representative of the central government) has a veto over budgetary and taxation decisions and in practice can effectively suppress any measure which displeases him.

The mayor is the executive officer of the council. Assisted by a permanent and salaried secretary he attends to the daily business of village administration and represents the community in its relations with the central government; and he is himself used as a final link in the hierarchy of the central administration by the Nomarch (Prefect) and officials of various Ministries. Through him instructions are passed, and information is gathered about different aspects of village life and economy, and sometimes about the circumstances, character, and political reliability of individual villagers.

The mayor's position in these administrative exchanges gives him the ability to hinder or help, whether legally or not, the affairs of his fellow villagers. Applications for credit, social welfare assistance, or other facilities may require the certification of information by the mayor. Or in the matter of local levies he may enter a sale of produce or the amount of a dowry at a figure which is less than the true value. If a mayor is to hold on to the support of his more influential friends in the village he must generally grant them some favours the legality of which is doubtful. But through the accepted evaluation of his role simple routine duties of his office are also converted into favours. Since his obligations as a head of family have priority over the duties of his office, it cannot be taken for granted that a mayor will exert himself in any way over the affairs of a person with whom his only tie is that of common citizenship in the same village. If he made a habit of signing documents with expedition and without considering the applicant's attitude and services to himself, this would indicate a lack of confidence and self-respect. If the applicant's relationship with the mayor is unsatisfactory a document may be signed eventually, but only after a humiliating and perhaps damaging delay. For the favour or service he has received, or hopes that he is about to receive, the villager must reply with gifts or the promise of social and political support for the mayor. This reciprocity takes place in the context of friendship between equals in the village. The mayor insists that he helps a man because it is right to protect one's friends. The villager responds in whatever way he can, but claims that he does this not in fear of the mayor's disfavour, but because he ought to show his esteem for a good and honourable man who is his friend. In fact, within these

conventions, friendship between the mayor, leading village personalities, and their friends and clients, is a network of local political
patronage. Through it a man may find some protection when he is
in difficulty with local administration or when he is the victim of
some hostility. It may be difficult for the mayor, or another village
notable, to victimize a man of less importance since the latter is very
probably the friend and client of one of his own friends, or of a
personality whom it would be impolitic to provoke. Once a man is
recognized as the friend, and in some sense the client, of a more
important villager, any attack on the client is also an attack on his
friend's influence and *philotimo*.

Men with wealth, dependent 'friends' in the village, and important patrons outside it, often hold no local office and are among the
undisputed leaders of the community. But of others who hold offices
and follow occupations which confer a certain status, the secretary
has influence because he has access to documents; the president of
the agricultural cooperative because he arranges applications for
credit; the owner of the coffee-shop because he, too, supports on a
smaller scale an intricate nexus of debt relations. The authority of
the ordinary members of the village council depends on whether
they are independent figures with a following of their own, which
must be appeased by the mayor if he is to control his council, or
whether they are more properly clients of the mayor who owe their
election to his support. The agricultural guard or policeman belongs
to a government service but in practice is often subject to direction
by the mayor who may request his transfer if he shows too great an
independence of spirit. If he is a native of the village he enjoys no
increased status from his office but his duty to prosecute those
whose animals trespass and damage crops, gives him the power to
make a farmer's life anxious and less profitable.

The positions of the schoolmaster and the priest are somewhat
different. The former is normally not a son of the village. He is a
stranger and his pretensions to higher education, his work, and his
clothes set him apart. He is respected as a repository of abstract
knowledge whose treasures he is only too willing to display, but his
often radical opinions about politics and progressive farming may
be ignored. Although he probably grew up in a village he is in some
sense the local representative of the educated town life now so
generally desired. Yet despite his education he has not succeeded in
escaping to the town, and today there will be families in the village
whose sons or kinsmen have done better. Mingled with the traditional respect for the school teacher, particularly as the instructor in
the proper expression of national sentiments, there is now an element
of faint contempt.

The priest is more often a native of the village and he is unlikely to be estranged from other villagers by superior education. He may have a wife, family, and fields of his own. But inevitably his ambiguous occupation as an intermediary between the community and God gives him a separate and ambivalent status. Villagers are disturbed by the contradiction that to make his own living he must charge, in addition to the salary paid to him by the Church, something for the blessings, liturgies, exorcisms, baptisms by which men draw upon the Grace and protection of God. In earlier times, before 1909, the priest was directly supported by his village through contributions of grain in a transaction which seemed more fitting and uncommercial. There is doubt, too, about the motives of a man who becomes a priest; on the one hand his office protects him from the competitive tests of manliness that other men must face; yet, on the other, he manipulates the symbols and forces of the spiritual life without himself having any marked ascetic obligations (the village clergy, for instance, are married), or personal virtues which distinguish him from ordinary men. Therefore the suspicion that priests may abuse their spiritual trust or social position persists; it is unlucky to meet one on a path, and scurrilous stories of adulterous priests are legion. A man reserves his respect for some old monk whose reputation for holiness is known, 'who reads all day the Holy Book', and it is to such a man that villagers may make their confession before the one or two occasions each year when they receive communion. They say they would not willingly do so to a village priest, and he in any case is only very rarely licensed by his bishop to hear confessions. Despite these ambiguities the villagers generally respect the office even if they are dissatisfied with the incumbent, and in those instances where a priest is upright and authoritative his influence in the village outside his strictly liturgical and sacramental role may be considerable.

In villages which serve as administrative centres for a district there will be other functionaries, a sergeant or an officer of the Gendarmerie, the district agronomist, and the Justice of the Peace who presides over a 'Court of First Instance'. There may also be a doctor. But although these men and their families live in the village their relation with it is essentially external and they consider themselves as a group of unfortunate and unwilling exiles. The more humble offices and occupations we have mentioned, including with some qualification those of schoolmaster and priest, are held by people who belong to village society. The values of this world are changing, affected by urban and western ideals of material progress and acquisition. But although these developments create uncertainty about standards of behaviour and reveal the growing doubts about the value of life in a village under any conditions, nevertheless village notables live within the community and depend on it for the recognition they seek. This the elders of the leading families and the priest may achieve by upholding traditional values while the prestige of younger office-holders and the school teacher derives more obviously from the claim to technical knowledge and the effectiveness of their contracts with persons of importance in the wider world. Many traditional values persist alongside urban and commercial attitudes. Each set of values is more generally appropriate for a different age group and different offices. But although the one is virtually the inversion of the other, both may be invoked and manipulated by the same man according to the needs of the situation. What remains common to any situation and its assessment is the priority of the family commitment which qualifies any duty or requirement of an office, occupation, or membership in another social group.

III

Increasingly the relations which exist between a village and the rest of Greek society are multiple and complex. The majority of rural communities may now be reached by road and a great number of these are connected by daily bus services with the local market town and administrative centre. Visits by villagers to the town and by officials to the village are frequent. And at times of festival villagers or their descendants who live elsewhere return for a few days to the ancestral home. There is movement also between neighbouring villages. For, as we have seen, men must often marry women from other communities, thus acquiring relatives by marriage and dowry property outside their villages. And the more intensive commercial pattern of agriculture also leads to some mobility of rural labour at the peaks of seasonal activity.

As the government administration of a planned economy extends the scope of its interest and interference into village affairs, as (until recently) political parties attempted to improve their local organization, and as farmers require more credit and better marketing facilities, many relations which pass the boundary of the village may either threaten the interests of an individual farmer or offer him new and important facilities. The villager's problem is that he does not expect consideration from the officials or merchants with whom he must deal. Even between men of the same village who are not kinsmen or friends social obligations, as we have seen, are merely negative and prudential. From the official who is neither kinsman nor fellow villager, whose position is marked by differences of status and probably of education, a villager is morally isolated. Since from his own experience he is aware that a man's status depends upon the prosperity and prestige of his family he knows that the official must cultivate his 'own interests' and support those who support him. Nepotism is an obligation not a moral fault, and honour is opposed to the canon of honesty; particularly when an official must compete on a meagre salary to confirm his position in the stratum of the middle class to which he belongs by wearing the clothes and possessing the domestic prestige symbols that are appropriate. It is entirely logical that with some indignation, but also resignation, the villager categorizes all such persons as 'eaters'. Related to these attitudes is the general belief, which is not confined to countrymen, that the 'state' (*to kratos*) is a body which takes away from the family and returns very little, a body from which ordinary Greeks are excluded, something threatening and almost malevolent which stands, therefore, in opposition to the nation (*to ethnos*), the community of Hellenism for which every Greek feels a deep and natural devotion.

Since it is foolish to expect any official of whatever rank or service to act for one's benefit without some inducement, the practical problem is one of finding suitable means of persuasion. Gifts of farm produce for policemen or the agronomist resident in the district, small money bribes for ushers or junior clerks at government offices in the town, given to ensure that an application is filed at all, are thought to be necessary and acceptable. But when a question is of any importance or complexity it may be necessary to influence a senior official who is not easily or effectively approached by a simple villager without a personal introduction. The civil servant marks his position in the service through the display of severity and pride and by indicating the social distance between the administrators and the administered; not by implementing any ethic of public service, or through the treatment of each case on its merits. Some intermediary, then, must be found to bridge this absence of moral concern and difference of status. The persons who fill this role are people who, on the one hand, by occupation or profession, have village clients, and, on the other, are able to number higher civil servants and other persons of importance among their friends in the local provincial élite. These may be merchants, doctors, and particularly lawyers. Naturally, if a villager has an influential kinsman he will turn to him for help; indeed part of the reasoning behind the countryman's ambition to educate his son is the need to find protection. The villager pledges not only his professional or commercial custom to the patron but also his political and social support; in return the patron protects his client, so far as he is able, in all his affairs and particularly by bringing any case of hardship to the notice of a friend in the government service who is able to deal with it. The civil servant may effect this not because he is impressed by the justice of the villager's grievance, but because the political support which the villager's patron is able to command makes him a person of some importance on the political scene able to affect the civil servant's promotion or posting; or more simply because the patron is a friend who does more strictly professional or social favours for the official or for his kinsmen and friends. The more clients the patron has, the greater, of course, his political influence and social prestige; and the more effective the protection he is able to offer. Through such relationships the villager is protected in some degree from uncomprehending administrators and from regulations which were framed without consideration or knowledge of the local difficulties of particular communities. And it is not only in difficulties with the administration that a patron may be able to assist his client. A money loan on reasonable terms, admission to hospital, a place at university, employment in the town for a son or nephew, are examples of other problems which may be influenced by the recommendations of a patron. For little can be achieved by a poor man without influence.

Frequently the villager will ask a patron, or a man whose attitude he hopes to influence, if he will baptize his child. The relationship of spiritual kinship requires that the godfather should show a general concern for the spiritual and worldly wellbeing of his god-child which would be damaged if relations between the child's spiritual father and natural father were not cooperative and friendly. Any dishonourable act committed by the one or the other 'destroys the oil' with which the child was anointed and, consequently, his right relation to God. If a man accepts an invitation to enter this relationship the duties are categorical and binding in a way that the less defined obligations of an ordinary patron towards his client are not.

The form and function of patronage connections are essentially related to the precedence which obligations to the family are generally accorded both in village and town life. Differences of status and community only accentuate the distrust which villagers feel for those outsiders whose power or influence affects their lives. In effect, patronage converts impersonal and ephemeral connections into permanent and personal relationships which have their own moral quality. The role of patron is to give benefits; that of the client is to support the social position and prestige of the patron by openly accepting dependence. In a world of limited resources the villager has no confidence that concessions are to be gained on a wide front for the whole community but only as particular dispensations to favoured families. Moreover, in the competitive struggle for prosperity and prestige within the community the protection which a man enjoys because he has a powerful patron is not to be shared with other unrelated men who envy him this advantage. It may be extended vicariously to kinsmen and 'friends', since their dependence is a mark of strength, not weakness. But, in general, to share an advantage is to lose it. An effect of this is that while patronage relates the community in a certain sense to the wider society, it does so along lines of personal obligation and not as a corporate group capable of attempting an infinitely more effective resistance to the authority of the state.

Although the individual's pattern of patronage relations may often change, in principle the political and social obligations between patron and client are seen as having a permanent quality. This type of social relationship has its analogue in commercial life where the existence of different kinds of debt and contract between wholesale merchants and farmers introduces some stability and a certain balance of expectations between the two parties. This balance however is not generally equitable. And it is less often necessary for the merchant to show his benevolence and concern for his client's problems unless these affect, in one way or another, the profitability of his interest in their relationship.

The people of Greater Athens and Salonika, who today number 2,226,000, purchase the greater part of the surplus of agricultural produce which is not consumed in the villages themselves and the small towns which serve them. On the amount of income which the countrymen receive from this source depend their ability to emulate in some of its material aspects the city style of life which they admire, and the quality of education and the kind of marriage which they hope to arrange for their sons and daughters, questions which intimately affect their self-esteem. As in many peasant societies where village communities climb with difficulty beyond the level of a simple subsistence economy, and each increase in real income is overtaken by new wants before it is realized, the practice of selling crops in advance to traders is inevitable. For his part the merchant is assured of a source of supply at a somewhat depressed price, and to keep the farmer indefinitely in debt and bound to him he may be willing to offer additional loans in excess of the crop's worth. But this credit does not usually suffice. Farmers also borrow from the Agricultural Bank through short-term loans of three to nine months which must be repaid on due dates before they can be renewed. They may also borrow small sums from patrons or money-lenders, and they normally have running debts with village and town shops where they are regular customers. These debts to patrons, merchants, shops, and the bank, are mutually supporting; as one is renewed, or increased, another is repaid. At any time the manipulation of these debts and relationships represents in aggregate the amount of credit which a farmer can command, and this is a critical factor in the evaluation of his social position and prestige.

Yet a characteristic of the farmer's relation with the merchant is his weakness and dependence. This is particularly evident when the produce to be sold is perishable, as is the case in the market for fruit and vegetables. In this instance most wholesalers prefer to sell on commission at their own discretion, subsequently remitting the sum which they allegedly received, less expenses and percentage. Disagreement and distrust are rarely absent from these negotiations. The main causes of friction are the amount of box tare; the real gross weight of the product (as a result of imprecise weighing methods); the fact that merchants are often selling on their own account as well as on commission; and the sale price. The last of these is the most serious. The producer believes that sale prices are understated since the price differential between the producer and the consumer is often greater than the legal profit margins at wholesale and retail levels in fact allow. False reporting on sales slips is apparently common practice and since all agreements are verbal the farmer has no legal recourse. Moreover, in this market it is the retailers who enjoy liberal credit facilities from the wholesale merchants since they buy their produce and ensure their market outlet. Yet even under conditions such as these the farmer may prefer to attach his fortunes to a particular merchant, allowing himself to be systematically defrauded in the belief, which is often misplaced, that this gives him the right to greater consideration in the eyes of the merchant and some security in selling a perishable crop. How far the merchant will agree to go in admitting the existence of any kind of obligation is, of course, another matter. But at least he may not press the farmer as far as the strength of his bargaining position would in fact permit. There is the physical problem of reaching producers which is not always easy in Greece with its mountainous relief and unsatisfactory communications. There are economies in time, energy, and money if he can establish more or less permanent commercial relations with particular producers. Naturally, it is always in the interest of the farmer to draw the merchant into a relationship which resembles the complementary interests of patron and client. And the merchant may allow this to develop in the case where a client is an influential producer, or where he is willing to undermine local prices by appearing to sell his crop cheaply.

The producer in Greece, whatever his crop, is usually a small farmer. If he is faced in a narrow local market with offers which are unsatisfactory (or if he has no confidence in the honesty of merchants selling on commission in Athens) he is also discouraged by inexperience and his lack of contacts in urban markets, and sometimes by poor communications and the difficulties of transport, from attempting to eliminate the intermediaries and sell directly to retailers. Moreover, such operations, even on a very modest scale, require working capital which a farmer seldom possesses and is generally unwilling to borrow at high rates of interest to add to his existing indebtedness. It might be thought that the agricultural cooperative movement would prove to be the corporate organization in Greek country life which could meet many of the farmers' difficulties and overcome the fragmentation of effort and interests which exclusive family loyalties produce. Its development from the original legislation in 1915 was assisted by successive governments as a means to improving the production and marketing of crops from the small-holdings which, after the division of large estates and the influx of refugees from Asia Minor, increasingly characterized the country's agriculture. But the resources of a village cooperative are slender. In a majority of cases the membership of a village cooperative is less than one hundred and the average contribution to the share capital is about £12 which the farmer may be allowed to pay over a period of five years. It is inadequate for the purposes of the cooperative, yet in relation to the income of the less prosperous farmer it is considerable enough to be resented. The one effective service which, unaided, the village cooperative is usually able to offer its members is the arrangement and guarantee of short-term loans from the Agricultural Bank, the importance of which for the farmer's credit position we have already remarked. By this service it saves the farmer a number of journeys to the branch of the bank and the need to persuade the village mayor to certify that the information in his application is correct. In this it does little more than act as a local office for the bank. But it is a reflection of cooperative weakness and endemic attitudes of independence that a third of the country's farmers prefer not to belong to a cooperative and arrange their loans by a personal application to the bank.

In other activities the role of the village cooperative is even less significant and it acts simply as a formal link between its members and the regional and national cooperative bodies where the power of the movement lies. Six thousand three hundred and fifty of the 7,543 village cooperatives in Greece belong to 131 Regional Cooperative Unions, each village cooperative depositing with the Regional Union a certain percentage of its share capital. Through the Regional Union the farmers of the village cooperative obtain, on credit, their supplies of fertilizer for which the Agricultural Bank holds the import and distribution monopoly. Similarly the Regional Union sells for the Cooperative Supplies Company at, or slightly below, the usual retail prices household supplies such as sugar and olive oil of a guaranteed quality. Yet the extent of this trade is limited. Many farmers are bound to the long established credits they have with the owner of the village coffee-shop and to the complex of 'friendship' relations which would be endangered if they withdrew their custom.

These essentially 'consumption' services (short-term loans, fertilizers, household supplies) characterize the main activities of about 60 per cent of the village cooperatives. Gradually however more effort is being devoted to cooperative collection, processing, and marketing of produce. Since the capital resources of village cooperatives are small and their credit standing with the Agri-cultural Bank is unsatisfactory, these operations are almost exclus-ively in the hands of Regional Unions. They own cereal storage space, cotton ginning mills, olive oil presses, canneries, milk pasteur-ization equipment, fruit packing depots, and so on. But with the exception of cereal storage these installations are generally small, local, and few in relation to cooperative needs.

Individual Regional Unions market products such as olive oil, raisins, dairy products, and citrus fruit. But they may also act as agents and intermediaries for specialized central cooperative marketing organizations which handle olives and olive oil, dried figs, sultanas, cotton, tobacco, and wheat. Three-quarters of the country's wheat is handled by the 'Central Unions Pool' (K.Y.D.E.P.). But the strength of this organization is due to its position as the state's agent for the collection of a crop to which price support is given. It is significant that in the case of other important crops only relatively small percentages of the total pro-duction are entrusted to the cooperative institutions. S.E.K.E. is a company, controlled by cooperative interests, which is the most considerable purchaser and exporter of tobacco in Greece, but in a very competitive market its purchases account for only 10 per cent of the total production.

The market operations of cooperative bodies have some effect in keeping agricultural prices at a more equitable level. But, as we might expect with the social attitudes and loyalties we have been examining, it is limited by a lack of cooperative discipline. The social aspirations of countrymen become more expensive and no less compelling in the present conditions of social and economic change, and it is certainly not less difficult for the farmer to resist the advance sale of his crop to a merchant. However small, or simply illusory, the benefit, the farmer feels more secure and successful in this direct and personal negotiation. There is a tendency to offer the better grades of produce to the merchant and to give what is left to the cooperative. Only when it is able to pay ten to fifteen per cent more than the price offered by the trade, is the cooperative confident that it can compete on reasonable terms.

Perhaps inevitably, the cooperative institutions and activities which have any significance lie outside the village. Through lack of funds and technical skills it can achieve little by itself. The salaried and professional officials of Regional Unions, and other national cooperative bodies, in many situations appear to the villagers to be little different from administrators in the government services. And since the Agricultural Bank is the guardian of the cooperative movement, providing its institutions with the greater part of their funds which the Agricultural Bank itself draws mainly from the Bank of Greece, this view is not simply one of prejudice. The very professional officials of the bank are prepared to give development loans to Regional Unions but are seldom willing to trust a village cooperative further than the collection and guarantee of the details required from its members for short-term loans. For longer term loans farmers must make individual applications to the bank. In these circumstances the presidency of the village cooperative offers little scope for personal initiative and power; nor does membership in the cooperative demand a loyalty, or offer a functional alternative, which could in any way replace the family as the unit of economic enterprise, or qualify the duty to seek its advantage at almost any cost. Certainly the villager regards the more inclusive institutions of the cooperative movement as extensions of the state apparatus. Since they exist and offer certain advantages, he is willing to exploit them where he can, but he does this in terms of the immediate advantage to his family and not of belief in any cooperative commitment. The general characteristics of the cooperative movement, then, differ little from the structure of the rural society in which it functions. A central administration controls weak and dispersed local communities or organizations, whose participation in their own government, and confidence in the central authority, are both limited.

IV

It is difficult to characterize briefly the change from traditional to modern attitudes in Greek village life. Before national independence villages were neither socially and politically independent, nor entirely self-sufficient economically, and they gradually became somewhat less so after the foundation of the Greek state. But the relative autonomy conferred in the village both by Ottoman policy and Greek cultural resistance gave its life a certain coherence and made it the frame for a man's life. Although there were competitive tensions in a community which set simple but demanding ideals for men to follow, the self-regarding values of honour and reputation were sanctioned and disciplined by collective opinion. The village gathered about its church represented a microcosm of the Christian Oecumene, a space blessed by God and protected by His Grace against natural and demonic forces outside its boundaries which though not intrinsically evil were dangerous to men and might be invoked and used by the Devil, especially against the innocent or spiritually unprepared. The traditional village was not obsessed by piety or concerned about the orthodox morality of the Christian ethic which, indeed, was at odds with the premises of notions of honour and pride. But it was fundamentally a religious community in the sense that men believed that their fate ultimately depended on God's will. Men, individually, asked for His protection through their own prayers, the intercessions of the priest, and offerings and devotions to the icons of the saints they favoured. The women of the family would also seek protection against dangerous forces through magic rites which however made use of religious symbols, signs, and words. The decorative and artistic expression of this peasant world in its material culture, in weaving, patterns of embroidery, and wood-carving, the mythical and imaginative themes of folk stories and songs, the rhythms and movements of the dancing, illuminated or reflected the institutions and beliefs of the society, a way of life that was inescapable and required no justification outside itself.

We have spoken of these traditional features of village life in the past tense. Certain of these have, of course, survived, although now qualified by elements of alien and western origin. The gradual process of erosion began early under Capodistrias' presidential rule, when instead of local communities despatching their appointed representatives to a regional assembly as had been the custom in the Peloponnese under the later Ottoman rule, local authorities were appointed by the central government through whom a growing number of administrative regulations and taxation demands were passed. Faced with the indiscipline of competing local notables and guerrilla leaders Capodistrias inevitably applied with some vigour the administrative philosophy of a western centralized bureaucracy that a homogeneous and ordered nation state is the product of a detailed and meticulous arrangement of local affairs which checks the growth of local power and particularism. This process continued with increasing effect during the first hundred years of the life of the Greek state. Under Ottoman rule the secular and religious affairs of the village were scarcely separated. Village business might be discussed in the church immediately after the liturgy was celebrated and in this the priest had an important voice. Under the new dispensation secular business was clearly separated and often conducted in a village office apart from the church. The priest gradually played a less important role. The government also discouraged the life of the monasteries which had offered a model for corporate life and discipline. Moreover, the pressure of administrative interference, and after 1843 the introduction of a democratic franchise, encouraged the growth of patronage relationships which further weakened the corporate spirit of village life. Since the decisions which affected village life were taken in Athens the fact of political subordination bred a sense of inferiority about the quality of life in the village. Political dependence and impotence led easily to apathy and indifference to village cooperation. The importance of patronage in its turn was one reason for the immense store set on education, for through it a son might escape to the town and to a worthier employment in the world of clerks. With the support of a patron he might even rise to a position of influence where he could himself protect his kinsmen. But this education was, also, a channel through which the life of the national state and particularly of the capital city was unduly idealized.

By the end of the nineteenth century there were few villages without some migrants in the towns and cities of Greece or overseas. The latter after saving money often returned to spend their declining years in the village, the former would return at times of festival, the pride of their kin, the envy of others. The wonders and variety of their urban life were rehearsed to the delight or irritation of the villagers, but whatever their reaction they became aware in detail of the amenities which were lacking in their lives and the depreciation of village culture in the opinion of the great world for which their own activities and judgements were almost irrelevant. To be unconsidered was within the framework of their own values the worst humiliation.

Between the wars the late growth of light industry and the services which supported them created enough employment to increase the rate of internal migration. Nevertheless it was not sufficient seriously to undermine the demographic basis of country life. And although the villages were increasingly exposed to the influence of city practices and attitudes through newspapers and personal contact, it must be remembered that the majority of villages were approached only by mule-tracks. The two worlds of city and village were physically held apart. The village men would occasionally visit the local provincial capital on some pressing business but few of them had seen Athens unless on military service. Few manufactured goods were within the means of subsistence peasants. In many districts women still dressed in traditional clothes and if their men now wore 'European' jackets and trousers these were roughly cut from homespun cloth. For his part the Athenian, unless he had relatives or property in a village, would seldom travel into the barbarous hinterland beyond the suburbs of his city.

The resistance struggle in the mountains during the Second World war and the civil war which followed it abruptly altered the quality of relations between town and country. Many villagers were driven by the fear of reprisals to find refuge in the towns and during the civil war the authorities forcibly evacuated entire districts in northern Greece in their effort to isolate insurgent forces. From this compulsory initiation into urban life many did not return to the village and not a few of those who did lamented their decision. The effects of the subsequent American commitment to support the security and economy of Greece followed. The road network was extended into remote regions. In the decade between 1950 and 1960 urban population and employment increased. There was industrial expansion and a massive importation of domestic consumer goods which were bought by the growing middle class that had benefited by the expansion of the economy based upon foreign credit and aid. Newspaper advertisement reflected the products of European industrial production and city culture from cars and refrigerators, radios and tape-recorders, to French model dresses and cosmetics. Through the community radio which most villages had been given to receive news and anti-communist commentaries, through newspapers with many syndicated articles from abroad, and cheap magazines, the country people were instructed in the material strength of western culture, and its ability to move from one extraordinary achievement to another. In comparison the scale of their own efforts seemed insignificant. Despite the immediacy of village affairs men's imaginative aspirations were elsewhere and especially in mountainous districts ambition and success became equated with migration.

In the past the possibility of moving to a town or city in Greece often depended on education or the ability of a patron to find his client employment. But during the most recent period the demand for foreign workers removed this limitation and at the same time the increase in farmers' production and incomes due to government price support and the use of improved seed and more effective cultivation, made it possible for peasants to afford a few of the amenities and much of the bric-à-brac of urban living. Development loans brought electricity to many villages and even piped water to others. Both the ability to leave and familiarity with the culture which attracted them were increased.

Thus in many respects, physically, commercially, and in style of living, the villages have been drawn into closer and more complex relations with provincial towns and the capital city than was previously the case. The effects on village culture have been profound and destructive. This is particularly obvious in material culture where the villager without the sophisticated defence that a sense of cultural relativity or comparative aesthetics might give him, is convinced that almost any object of urban or European origin (the two terms being almost synonymous) must be superior to anything that is the product of local and traditional craftsmanship. Homespun shirts and suits for men have been replaced by machine-made shirts and suits, and younger women, even among semi-nomadic shepherd groups, now wear cheap cotton dresses and knitted cardigans instead of the traditional costume of embroidered richness or the plain homespun dresses which represent the intermediary stage in this new sensitivity to fashion. Inside village homes other advances have been made. The richly embroidered blankets, covers, and cushions give way before manufactured coverlets with printed patterns of remarkable vulgarity. Designs on glasses, tin trays, and coffee cups, mechanically patterned icons in a debased italianate style, are of a similar quality. Wooden barrels and water bottles, or earthenware jars, are replaced by plastic or tin containers. Houses of local stone and traditional style are less favoured than brick and concrete flat-roofed constructions of depressing symmetry. Neon strip lighting proves that a man has a progressive spirit. Even in finishing the cloth which they still weave they make inexpert and garish use of aniline dyes and lose the subtler tones of the vegetable colouring. Imperfectly understanding material fragments of a complex culture and technology they have no standards of judgement. The connection between the community's traditional use of the natural environment and its inherited forms of life and art, is severed; and impetus is given to new found preferences by the competitive concern for reputation which remains always a common motif in Greek society.

In the traditional community however reputation depended on the recognition of honour in terms of certain sex-linked virtues, strength in numbers of close kinsmen, wealth in stock and land to support them, a well-ordered household in a style of life which was precisely prescribed and, except for the poorest families, was common to all. In a modern village this scale must be inverted. Prestige depends on the display of a style of living which villagers believe reflects an urban sophistication, that is measured by innovation not similarity, on the management of resources which produces the money income to buy the furnishings for this style, on a small family whose dowries and education, the achievement of a provident father, are costly and prestigious. Virtue is not irrelevant but it is no longer the leading factor.

In these changes the vast rural exodus of recent years, whether abroad or to towns and cities in Greece, is an important element. In villages where many people have left, those who must remain, or those who do not have the courage to follow, feel abandoned and defeated. The personal channels of communication by letters and visits to and from the migrants only impress on them their separation from a full life. Since children will leave the village whenever the opportunity is presented there is little incentive to consider the long-term improvement or fertility of the farm, let alone the condition of community pastures. Competitive attitudes, also, require present profit for an immediate display. Thus exploitation of natural resources is often ruthless whether through improper rotations, over-grazing, or the illegal cutting of young trees. By remaining in the village they have failed; and this sense invades morale in a subtle way, for not only do life and work in the village seem a pointless drudgery but the value of the community itself is diminished and men and women are less constrained by the sovereignty of public opinion over their moral conduct. Now the only individual and collective defence of self-esteem which remains is to incorporate into village life as many aspects of what is believed to be the Athenian style of living as income and propriety will allow.

In matters of morality the situation is less simple. Villagers will formally condemn the godlessness, heartlessness, and the permissive sexual morality of those who live in cities. In the uncomplicated attitudes of honour and reverence to God they still do not give precedence to others, although they sense that these qualities, which have been the unquestioned values of their own society, are not essential, or even relevant, in the other technological world whose efficacy and power are crushing the culture of their own world. They accept and compete for the productions of the other culture while they attempt to reject the accompanying patterns of behaviour where these conflict uncomfortably with the values which, they claim, still govern them. But in practice the process is one of successive compromise. Traditional dress for women disguised sexuality: by comparison the fashions in dress, hair styles, and cosmetics now favoured by unmarried girls in many villages provoke sexual attention. And if the fashions are approved it is more difficult to be entirely censorious about what may be considered to be their consequences. Judgements are now less harsh and less certain about the condition of a pregnant girl provided the marriage eventually takes place.

In considering these processes of change we have to remember that it is only by a considerable, and to some extent forced, effort of analysis that in a traditional subsistence village we are able to separate economic, kinship, political, and religious institutions. In sowing a field, celebrating a marriage, or baptizing a child, reason, emotion, and ritual were inextricably joined. A peasant sowed his field by unquestioned methods and customary rituals, a unified sequence of pragmatic and symbolic actions in a relation between human and cosmic forces involving a man, his family, the fertility of the earth, and the beneficence of God. The fruit of this work supported in a direct and evident sense the family which, with the Church, were the institutions especially blessed and protected by God. The code of honour by which different families regulated their relations depended considerably upon the view that might was right, and on bravado and deceit, yet it was not a materialistic value as we generally understand it.

The present developments in village life have a different base. In a confused and inexplicit manner even less educated peasants now understand that the return on a crop depends on a complex of factors whose effects have been isolated by the use of merely human powers of observation and reason: among others the degree of soil exhaustion, the strain of seed, weather, and weed control. He is convinced of the truth of this by the fact that the yields of his crops are now markedly greater. After retaining what is necessary for the needs of his family the considerable surplus of grain is sold; commercial crops such as cotton are also marketed. The significance of the harvest has therefore shifted from subsistence to monetary profit. The money income is provided essentially by seed, machines, and methods introduced from outside the village. It is spent competitively on a style of living which emulates an urban ideal; and on the dowries of daughters and the education of sons whose purpose, if resources are sufficient, is their establishment in the town or city. Such values are materialistic and success depends on a rational manipulation of resources and relationships. A man probably prospers more if he feuds less; and restrains the more sensitive promptings of his *philotimo*. He may still observe the rituals which protect his crops. But these actions are fragments from a pattern whose unity is broken; and they have no necessary place in the new order of things. A man may not have lost his sense of honour or his reverence for God but he learns that the contexts where these attitudes are appropriate no longer embrace the whole of life or even that part of it which most concerns him. The integral quality of village life is gone. And in a sense a man's success in the modern village depends on his spirit and perceptions having already passed beyond it.

In giving this brief and generalized statement about a complex process we have used the simple model of opposed types of village, traditional and modern. In fact the great majority of communities fall between these extremes, including features of both types in an uncertain attempt to find an accommodation. Logically this does not exist. But men are adept at living by conflicting values which they quickly learn to manipulate for their own practical or expressive purposes. Criticism can be turned either way at choice: against the tractor-owner lacking in neighbourly feeling: against the miserly traditionalist who saves on his fertilizers: against a girl who flirts, for lacking self-regard: against a man who draws a knife in a quarrel, for having too much.

In illness both old and new remedies are often used simultaneously, an injection of an antibiotic drug with a family's own syringe and a wise woman's exorcism of the Evil Eye. For some illness is caused by 'microbes' and other illness by people's envy. However acute this recognition of the psychosomatic origin of some disease may ultimately prove to be, it reflects unwillingness to trust entirely in either science or traditional belief in matters which reach a deep level of unconscious anxiety. Illness produces other examples of conflict. Certain diseases, such as tuberculosis, are too shameful to disclose and may be reported only when the symptoms are obvious and beyond cure. And among village women the doctor is favoured who makes his diagnoses and prescribes the treatment at a single consultation and without requiring his patient to remove any clothing. For this saves both money and womanly modesty.

Some observers are impressed by the adaptability of Greek peasants to rapid social change. There is some truth in this judgement. For once an innovation is taken up by a leading personality in the community its adoption by his competitors is very probable. This tendency may often assist the introduction of improved methods of cultivation and strains of seed. If the immediate profitability of a new technique is not in doubt its acceptance meets with remarkably little resistance. It is also said that the artless combination of new styles and conventions of behaviour with surviving traditional practices and beliefs, or their modifications, indicates the flexibility of village culture. Of this we are less sure, for the texture of present village culture is a patchwork in which not all the pieces are matching. It is composed of fragments from two patterns of life which are quite different both in quality and scale. Despite individual adapt-ability this opposition disturbs the villager's understanding of his place in the world. Change is the more bewildering and dis-appointing when its possibilities are naïvely believed to be infinite elsewhere, yet what is realized locally is so clearly limited; and when each marginal increase in wealth is discounted at once by only one item in the endless inventory of material needs which commitment to values of the urban world implies. The comfort of certainty is lost and there are few standards which any longer limit expectations.

Chapter 11

The City and the State

I

The City

IN 1920 the municipality of Athens was a compact city of 293,000 people and Piraeus, its port to the south-west, a town with 133,000 inhabitants. Between 1920 and 1928 the settlement of refugees from Asia Minor, and to a lesser degree the arrival of other migrants from within Greece, created a ring of suburban communities to the west, north, and east of the city, and between it and Piraeus. This area of settlement which in 1920 was occupied by only 5·9 per cent of the population of what is now the Greater Athens area, by 1928 held 28·4 per cent of the population. Between 1928 and the present day the continued growth of the city has filled in the intervals between the original refugee settlements and the city, has physically joined Piraeus to Athens, and has extended the whole urban complex in most directions along lines of unplanned ribbon development to cover the plain as far as the lower slopes of the mountains Hymettus, Penteli, Parnes, and Aegaleus on the east, north-west, and west of the city. The physical impression of these changes on the periphery is generally unpleasant; square, flat-roofed houses, cubes of brick and concrete with one or two rooms only, 'maisons de la nuit' as Kayser[1] aptly names them. Very often they stand desolate in a bare plot of red brown earth, unfinished for lack of funds but occupied nevertheless. In contrast to this rudimentary modernism in the poorer suburbs is the sophisticated reconstruction of the heart of the city, where a decade of building investment has removed the provincial neo-classical appearance of the wartime city and replaced it with a conventional but affluent façade of modern blocks of offices, hotels, and luxury flats. The area is marked and dominated by the hills of Lykavettos and the Acropolis and the broad avenues of Venizelos and Stadiou streets which link Constitution Square to Omonia Square. Within its relatively narrow limits are the offices where political and commercial policies and decisions are made, and where popular demonstrations were previously attempted. It is also the congested terminus for the public

[1] See p. 410.

transport system; and the centre of attention and recreation for a great part of the population of 1,852,709 which now inhabits the Greater Athens area.

It follows from the rapidity of population growth in Athens that the majority of its citizens were not born in the city. A single indication of the magnitude of the population movement is that between 1951 and 1961 the net increase in population due to immigration was 330,861. Not all the provinces contributed equally to this body of new citizens. The Peloponnese, central Greece and Euboea, and the Aegean islands remained during this period, as they had in past generations, the important areas of the exodus to Athens. They account for 62·4 per cent of the migrants to the city during these years; and about two-thirds of this number came from villages or small towns with less than 10,000 inhabitants.

Greece is dominated, even paralysed, by the influence and attraction of its capital city, which is at once political, commercial, and demographic. It holds one-fifth of the country's total population and more than half its urban population. Apart from the inevitable consequences of the city's position as the seat of government, and until recently of parliament, the centralized organization of the civil service requires that administrative decisions on relatively unimportant questions are made in Athens, and to deal with this business 33·5 per cent of the country's civil servants work in the capital. Banking, shipping, and insurance institutions have their administrative headquarters in the city. Further, 59·3 per cent of industrial firms employing more than 100 workpeople are established there, and more than half the industrial workers of the country live in the city. In the professions this crushing superiority is equally evident; 85 per cent of the country's medical specialists work in Athens, which has more than half the hospital beds in Greece; and 70 per cent of the students in higher education work there. The predominance of Athens over the rest of Greece is such that with the exception of Salonika, which in the northern provinces duplicates in many respects the role and characteristics of Athens, the cultural and industrial life of other provincial towns in Greece is relatively stagnant and derivative.

Yet a consideration of the economic and occupational structure of the capital reveals that although half of the country's industry is in the city and 30 per cent of its actively employed inhabitants work in manufacturing industry, Athens is not an industrial complex. Many workers included in this category are in fact concerned with the repair or assembly of goods rather than their production. And the products of Athenian industry are generally those of light consumer goods industry; of the ninety-five larger industrial plants,

twelve are concerned with food and tobacco, thirty-three with textiles and clothing, twenty-six with light metal industry, and eight
with chemical products. The economic interests of the city are better
represented by the proportion of 57 per cent of the working population employed in commerce, transport, and other service industries.
If we add that 10 per cent of the men in the active population work
in the building industry which in recent years has found its principal
custom in the erection of residential flats, and on the other hand
that 66 per cent of the value of wholesale commerce for the country
in 1961 was attributed to Athenian businesses, it may be judged to
what extent the economic functions of the city are those of distribution and consumption rather than production. These interests
are encouraged, too, by the fact that the ports of the Athens region
at Piraeus, Megara, and Eleusis handle three-quarters of the
country's imports, a circumstance which is itself in part determined
by the concentration of consumers in the capital. The existence of
this market, the higher average annual *per capita* income in Athens
(in 1961, 13,422 drachmas against 9,932 drachmas for the whole
country), and the greater domestic expenditure which accompanies
it, are factors which attract the concentration of industry in Athens
and affect the character of its production.

It is difficult and perhaps profitless to generalize about the outward quality of Athenian city life. It is, of course, public, crowded,
noisy, and uninhibited as it might be in many other Mediterranean
cities. There is no long tradition of metropolitan life in Greece.
Athens was little more than a large village when the Greek state
was established; and until 1870 the population of the city was less
than 50,000. Although its growth during the present century has
been extraordinarily rapid and the majority of its present population
are migrants, Athenian society has not suffered the profound
modifications which industrialization of some scale normally
effects. Many manufacturing firms are of a very modest size and
in commerce the number of proprietors who work in their own
businesses is greater in aggregate than the number of salaried
employees. Personal obligations, commitments, and relationships
continue to be more significant than civic duty or the constraints
of any corporate membership. And while it is true, as we have said,
that the values of urban life have undermined the traditional values
of the countryside, it is true also that some values and institutions of
Athenian life have a certain descent from rural or provincial origins.

The priority of obligations to the immediate family, the relative
quality of moral behaviour towards others, and the intense distrust
which is its consequence, are no less marked in the city. Recognition
of a man's social personality remains perhaps the source of deepest

anxiety. In the city the threat of anonymity must be combated by as wide a circle of acquaintanceship as can credibly be claimed and by frequent appearance in public. Coffee-shops, bars, *tavernas*, restaurants, hotels, cinemas, theatres, and beaches provide the obvious opportunities in some variety. Particularly among middle-class families there is much visiting between the homes of friends and relatives in the early evening. The expedition with a large company (*parea*) of friends to a *taverna* or restaurant is favoured both for the convivial enjoyment it naturally offers and for the demonstration to oneself and to others that one is recognized and respected. Social life is intense. And the place a family is able to claim in it considerably depends on the order and style of living reflected in the home itself. The competitive pressure to excel in the sophistication of modern design, furnishing, and domestic appliances has greatly increased since 1953 when the restrictions on the importation of foreign consumer goods were relaxed. These forms of consumption and display are of a financially more serious kind than the traditional obligations of simple hospitality. Many who buy such goods with the aid of instalments cannot rationally afford to do so, and many others who cannot, or more sensibly do not, find the deposit necessary to buy them feel bitter and deprived. Given the connection between status and acquisition the incomes of most families are insufficient.

In these circumstances a family head has the duty to increase his income by almost any means that are not plainly criminal or dishonourable. The social position of his family which is his sacred trust requires it. Commercial and personal exploitation, therefore, is often ruthless and since it is generally suffered by a person outside the social circle of the exploiter, the latter is restrained only by his conscience to which his actions are conveniently justified by a reference to his familial duties. These attitudes have widespread effects in economic life, for instance in the treatment of employees, and, less rationally, in the general refusal of the owners of unrented flats to reduce their rents. Socially they merely reinforce the general distrust of men towards one another which is in part a legacy of the opposition and exclusiveness of families in village communities. The difference is that opposition and competition in small traditional communities are contained within a consensus of values sanctioned by public opinion, and are limited by a prudent avoidance of extreme behaviour.

In the city there is little to check an individualism the interests of which are wealth, status, and consumption. The family itself is not immune to its effects. Among working-class families wives and even daughters frequently go to work. A young boy may be placed as an apprentice in a workshop or as an errand boy in a grocer's business, and live away from home. There is a certain dispersion of family life, and although fathers attempt to be authoritarian in the traditional manner their control over adolescent children is often ineffective. Dowry remains an important consideration, but a girl's secure employment may be regarded as its equivalent in many instances. Young men prefer to find their own brides from among the girls they know and arranged marriages are less frequent than in the countryside. Among the middle bourgeoisie of clerks, shop-keepers, and businessmen, formal solidarity in the family is more evident. The strain which this imposes in the financial struggle to maintain a certain style of life is considerable. Yet the husband resists the idea of his wife working since this may be attributed to his personal inadequacy as a provider. And although daughters may be allowed to work in respectable institutions such as banks, some attempt is made to control the company they keep and the marriages they contract. Since a socially satisfactory match will probably involve dowry and some sacrifice in saving from income, families in this class may be more successful in these attempts. Because it is difficult to equate means with expectations, life in this stratum of society is often restricted. Mothers, in particular, cultivate unrealistic ambitions for their sons whose professional success they believe will compensate for the father's relatively modest position and income. But the children of middle-class families, like other Greek children, are indulged and praised in their early years. Unlike the experience of peasant children this unqualified admira-tion of their ability is prolonged into adolescence with the result that in many cases concentration and the will to work are enervated and a false valuation of their own qualities is accepted. Objective failure in examinations may be circumvented if a family has an influential patron, but in any case it will be attributed to the corruption and vindictiveness of others. But the essentially admirable quality of the young man is his masculinity and while his sister is expected by her parents to remain a virgin before her marriage the son is tacitly encouraged and applauded in his pursuit of erotic conquest. The contradiction in these aims is reflected in a deep anxiety about sexual impotence, and in the speciality of some gynaecologists in physically reconstructing the virginity of those who ought not to have lost it. Among the more affluent upper-class families two differences may be remarked. Husbands are less authoritarian; wives have more leisure and education, and they demand to share decisions which do not belong to the traditionally feminine sphere of competence. Secondly, since it is difficult in the prevailing climate of competitive consumption for parents to deny their children anything they can reasonably afford, richer families indulge their sons and daughters with clothes and cars and whatever else is necessary for success in fashionable *Kolonaki* society. This success is a projection of the prosperity and status of their parents who could deny them these things only at the risk of suggesting poverty or an eccentric puritanism. An inevitable consequence is that they often have less control over the movements of their children than parents in middle-class families with more modest incomes.

Thus although, in the absence of any corporate membership or loyalties of equivalent importance, the family in the city as in the countryside is the only social group which offers some form of emotional and material security, the conditions of urban life, employment, and competitive display, affect the solidarity of the family particularly in the ability of the parental generation to guide and sanction the behaviour of adult and adolescent sons and daughters. Not only do individuals distrust one another if they are not bound by the obligations of a personal relationship, but the values which in traditional rural and even urban communities checked the forms of economic and sexual exploitation no longer apply, partly because in modern Athens circles of public opinion are imprecise and their judgements confused, and more particularly because the family is an ineffective arbiter of morals in situations where its head is no longer in full control of all its members and where he himself may prefer the prestige of display to the reputation for honour. Meanwhile the younger age groups which scarcely know of the more traditional world from which their parents have moved away, are exposed through the press, intensive advertising, and the cinema (which is their particular addiction) to an unreal and deracinated version of western materialism in which the delights of consumption predominate over the problems of production. The limited incomes of the majority of the unmarried population, their relative freedom from parental control and family responsibilities, make them natural recruits for political movements and protest. It is not without significance that more than half the male migrants arriving in Athens are unmarried and that the average age of marriage for Athenian men is unlikely to be less than 28·2 years, which is the median for the whole country. The years before marriage are the time of altruistic friendship and political commitments. But just as these personal friendships have little content beyond their intense sentiments so the expression of political ideals tends to be either utopian and ineffective or violent and irresponsible as in the activities of organized bands of bravos recruited by political parties. The responsibilities of marriage and family almost immediately qualify these relationships, converting the free identification

z

of an individual without responsibility into the careful assessment of family interests.

In comments on Athenian family life we referred to social classes. In terms of occupation and wealth it is possible to describe these in extremely general terms while recognizing that the lines between them are indeterminate. The upper class includes shipowners, bankers, industrialists, and merchants of riches and influence. Descendants of the landed or Phanariot families of the nineteenth century, where these have not lost their wealth, add an illusion of continuity to the class. But essentially wealth or influence, widely interpreted, are the criteria of acceptance. The class includes, therefore, leading politicians, although they may not be personally rich, some senior officers in the forces and leaders of the professions, lawyers, doctors, and certain academics and artists. It numbers perhaps a thousand families. But although it includes many cultured persons education is not a necessary qualification. Indeed, there is admiration for the self-made industrialist or politician. Nevertheless the educated or second generation members of this class acquire a recognizably cosmopolitan culture, an indication of which is often fluency in English and French learned from their governesses. And what marks of cultural distinctiveness may separate the upper class from the rest of Greek society can be attributed almost entirely to the styles and education of western European culture. The middle class consists of professional people, entrepreneurs of different kinds, officials, and executives of a certain seniority. A lower-middle class is formed by clerks, junior civil servants, small merchants and shopkeepers, craftsmen and skilled workers. These classes represent the majority of the urban population. Between the middle and the lower-middle class the boundary is particularly uncertain and within each of these two categories there is anxiety and doubt about relative statuses. Finally there is a residual lower class of unskilled labourers, factory workers, drivers, domestic servants, and similar occupations.

In the description of village institutions we stressed the importance of patronage. An important favour which patrons regularly arrange is to find employment in Athens or the provincial town for the son of a client. Migrants usually maintain their ties with their village and, if they are successful, they act in their turn as the patron and protector of other kinsmen and fellow villagers wishing to migrate. Patronage is not simply a matter of calculated advantage. It flatters a man to have others dependent on him, draws attention to his influence and status, and in an urban setting protects him from anonymity. Its practical function for the client is also no less significant in city life than in the countryside, and for the same reasons of distrust, relative morality, and the unwillingness of one man to concede anything to another unless there is a personal motive. The working of this market in favours depends on the numerous exchanges of services between patrons within their own circles of personal and professional friendships. The negotiation of such matters, it must be added, consumes a great amount of time and energy. These affairs sometimes have their own curious rituals. A scholarship candidate before an interview board may deftly present the chairman with the visiting cards of his professors and supporters, indicators of the interests which may be offended if he is not selected. Educational opportunities, and the improved employment which may follow them, are, of course, one important route to social mobility. But more generally the dependence relationships of patronage not only cross the limits of social classes but are themselves the means by which determined individuals rise in occupation, income, and social status. Forty per cent of the fathers of the more important industrialists of the present day were men of humble occupations, craftsmen, peasants, small shopkeepers – an indication of the considerable mobility in Greek society which accompanies the imprecise lines of social stratification.

Despite differences of income, physical amenities, and conventional morality between the cities and the countryside there is no effective opposition between these two segments of the nation in political terms. The dominance and attraction of Athens, and in the north Salonika, are too great. The demand for certain kinds of unskilled and semi-skilled labour, for instance in the building trade, or the relatively easy access to secondary education, makes it possible for the more dissatisfied or determined to migrate to the city (if they do not go abroad). There the problems of assimilation are relatively slight, partly because of the essentially non-industrial quality of social life in the city, partly because patrons and kinsmen play some part in arranging employment. It is interesting that in 1961 the rate of unemployment among recently arrived migrants (7·2 per cent) was lower than the rate for the general working population of Athens (7·7 per cent). But as the efficiency of the migratory process progressively weakens the life of the countryside, the increment in population to the city does not alter its unbalanced occupational structure or the inadequacy of its industrial production.

II

Industry

We have already remarked on the degree of fragmentation in village life and economy and in the social life of urban Athens. The same phenomenon is also present to a remarkable degree in the structure of Greek industry. The results of the government Industrial Survey of 1959 reveal this very clearly. Establishments employing up to ten people represented 94·5 per cent of the manufacturing businesses in the country, produced 33 per cent of the output (value added), and accounted for 55 per cent of the employment in these firms. On the other hand firms with more than fifty employees had 0·8 per cent of the establishments, 45 per cent of the output, and 27 per cent of the employment. The building of certain large industrial plants since this date would modify these figures today, but not radically. Therefore not only is there fragmentation but also a considerable concentration of production in relatively few firms.

Naturally, technical and commercial requirements affect the size of plants. These tend to be larger, for instance, in petroleum products, basic metal industries, and tobacco manufactures. But it is significant that in food and beverages, clothing, chemicals and allied trades, textiles, light engineering and electrical goods, which together account for considerably more than half the gross domestic product of manufacturing, there is an excessive number of small producing units. In textiles, for example, the number of firms increased between 1951 and 1958 from 2,291 to 3,530. Most of these newcomers were small in scale. In the cotton industry only twenty-six out of sixty-six spinning mills had more than 5,000 spindles, a number considered to be the minimum for profitable operation; in the woollen industry 5,000 spindles are again judged to be the effective minimum, yet 38 per cent of productive capacity belonged to firms which possessed on average only 1,736 spindles. These circumstances are general in Greek manufacturing rather than peculiar to these industries. Although it is possible that small-scale operation in industry has certain social advantages, the economic consequences are clear. There is limited specialization in production and a lack of standardization. Small firms often produce for a limited and known clientele, making goods to order and particular specifications rather than producing for a market. But a further disadvantage of small size is the restricted use of mechanical power and the infrequent replacement of outdated machinery.

Historically Greek manufacturing industry largely developed out of small artisan businesses. Indeed the very large number of establishments with less than ten employees are often still little more than craftsmen's workshops. This is reflected in the startling statistic that less than one-third of the country's manufacturing establishments makes any use of mechanical power. It is true that in recent years small firms have increased their productive efficiency by using electrical power which is now more widely available to industry.

But in general Greek industry uses relatively large amounts of labour which is abundant in relation to capital equipment, which is scarce.

Unfortunately both plant and techniques are antique. Naturally there exist cases of efficiency in some industries. Modern equipment, for example, is characteristic of the cement and tobacco industries. But in many industries such as textiles, shoes, chemical products, wood and cork, electrical equipment, the generalization is justified particularly for firms of modest size. The consequences are those which would be expected: the products are expensive and difficult to export, and individuals or institutions rarely invest capital funds in firms with dilapidated equipment.

Small firms emerging from artisan workshops are family businesses. Where they have grown beyond the scale of five to ten employees however they remain bound by family limits. The business has borne the family up to a status which it supports and it becomes more than a specifically economic enterprise; rather it is a way of life which provides a modest affluence and dependants, both of which are a source of some prestige. The business is a focus for family life and solidarity. It gives its members secure employment, although often at depressed wages. And if its scale of operation is restricted it may also cut its costs by avoiding contributions to welfare funds and unemployment insurance for its employees. The importance of family participation may be judged by the fact that in 1958 entrepreneurs and assisting family members represented 32 per cent of the labour force in Greek manufacturing. Thus there are important social and practical reasons why small family businesses do not wish to increase their size, or merge with other firms, if this endangers the family's continued control of the concern. This suggests that family ownership will also predominate in medium and large-scale companies. Besides the many cases where this is known to be so, figures on the numbers of shareholders in 1,369 larger industrial concerns at least reveal how restricted the circle of shareholders is in the majority of these firms. Only 156 have more than twenty-five shareholders, and exactly 1,000 have less than ten.

The modest rate of industrial expansion in Greece, despite the continuous concern of successive governments, and the failure of individual firms to improve their techniques or increase the scale of their production, are not the result of inadequate savings by the community generally. Since 1954 savings have steadily increased and in 1962 represented the impressive proportion of 21·1 per cent of the gross domestic product. Personal savings are an important element in this amount and it is a phenomenon of some interest that while the upper income groups indulge increasingly in conspicuous consumption it is the lower and middle income groups which principally contribute to the flow of savings. The motives for this saving are naturally various but it is largely attributable to saving for dowry and, among those who have migrated to the city, the need to build a home, or the ambition to establish an independent family business. This is confirmed when we discover that in 1961 40·3 per cent of private gross fixed investment was in private housing and as little as 12·7 per cent in manufacturing. Yet private savings have so far exceeded private investment. And although deposits in the commercial banks have grown, partly from current savings and partly from the dishoarding of gold, manufacturing industry appears to have benefited remarkably little from this availability of funds. The suspicion grows that not only peculiarities in the structure of Greek firms, but also others in the structure of the capital market itself, may be responsible for this situation. Family ownership or management of businesses is a serious obstacle to expansion through equity financing. The family are unwilling to surrender control but outsiders will not entrust their money to those to whom they are not personally bound. It would be hard to convince a Greek that a company's dividend policy is not formed to suit the personal tax requirements of controlling shareholders. And it is true that an entrepreneur may pay himself a large salary and expenses while retaining the remainder of the profits for reinvestment. The institutional forms of Greek businesses are another source of misgiving for the investor. Partnerships are favoured because they are simple to establish and there is a flexibility in their management which is particularly suitable for a family business. But it is difficult for an outsider to discover the exact terms of the agreement. Since it is only necessary for one member of the partnership to be fully liable, and it may be arranged that this member possesses no material wealth, the fear of fraud is not unreasonable. Although it may be less justified, distrust of firms organized as companies is also general. Limited liability companies may be formed by two or more persons with joint capital of 200,000 drs. This type of concern for which legislation was passed in 1955 would be more valuable if the amount of initial capital required were greater. About a thousand of the larger businesses in Greece are *Sociétés Anonymes*, a form of corporate enterprise based on the French Code of Commerce. Its disadvantages are principally in the voting system for corporate directors which tends to perpetuate the existing oligarchy, and in the lack of full and reliable reports on the company's operations. In these circumstances minority shareholders feel particularly vulnerable since the market in equities at the Athens Stock Exchange is narrow (principally as a result of the distrust we have described), and they fear that they may not be able to remove their stake in a company without a considerable capital loss.

In the absence of any considerable equity financing, firms must rely for their capital requirements on loans from the commercial banks, or on the reinvestment of their own profits. But the banks like other individuals and institutions in Greece are untrusting and in view of the record of poor profitability and the high death rate of small businesses it is in practice only the larger corporations which can be confident of regular access to the banks for long- or medium-term funds. Even then, the loans must be secured against production, property, or equipment. The concentration of available credit in the hands of the three largest commercial banks which control 97·8 per cent of the total commercial banking assets of the country gives these institutions a very real power. And since the banks do not restrict their business to self-liquidating loans but involve themselves also in long-term industrial development they inevitably acquire permanent interests in particular firms. In effect a narrow alliance of bankers and leading industrialists is formed whose interests it is not easy for the government, let alone small businesses, to resist. It is significant, for instance, that the Economic Development Financing Organization (E.D.F.O.), established in 1954 to provide loan capital for industry and agriculture, favoured large companies, almost exclusively, in its grants of industrial loans. The effect of the banks' policies is that larger companies use a disproportionate amount of bank credit and operate their businesses very largely on borrowed capital, which for a selected list of companies in 1961 reached a level of 70·2 per cent. Smaller businesses, on the other hand, must manage with short-term bank loans, which are costly and whose renewal is uncertain, and sometimes with self-financing from retained profits; but this is a laboured progress and may often be simply inadequate, or too expensive, to bridge the change in technical methods of production that accompany a change in scale.

Factors other than the availability of capital are not lacking to discourage a firm from expansion or improvement. Despite the excess liquidity in the economy borrowed capital is expensive. The effective rate of interest on bank loans may be greater than 10 per cent, and in general the smaller the firm the greater the cost. Profitability is a further constraint. In Greek industry firms with less than 10 million drs. of capital seldom earn a respectable rate of profit and therefore expansion which does not aim to pass beyond this limit is unlikely to be as attractive as an equivalent investment in commerce or building construction. There is also the more general problem of the size of the domestic market. The demand for goods manufactured in Greece is limited by low average incomes in a small population, and by the preference of the upper income group for imported goods.

Factors which limit the possibility of growth for smaller firms also create conditions in which monopoly or at least oligopoly may develop. There are governmental policies and legislation, also, which tend in the same direction. Greek industry was established behind high protective tariffs and although these must become less effective through the association with the Common Market the industrial structure, which they produced, remains. Until the present time international competition has hardly touched a wide area of Greek industry. The result has been inefficiency and high costs. Equally damaging to any competitive movement in industry have been regulations, originally introduced in 1935, which controlled the establishment of new firms or the expansion of existing ones in fields which the government might judge to be 'saturated'. Since this system was used by existing firms to prevent the issue of 'expediency licences' to new rivals in the same field, accusations of corruption were frequent and predictable. In 1962 new legislation was passed which altered the criteria for the issue of a licence to include tests of international competitiveness, national economic interest, and the size of the undertaking. But in practice the negotiation of any particular case left the Minister with a discretion wide enough to embrace arrangements which his clients and friends might request, for instance in avoiding a stipulation of the law that new firms should not be established in the metropolitan province of Attica. Taken together, tariffs and licensing controls have unquestionably made industry less competitive and less efficient.

Historically competition in a narrow market with a low level of demand resulted in the growth of monopolies in certain industries. The best known is the Fix brewery which destroyed its rivals before the First World war and was alone in the field until 1961 when a quarrel between the Fix brothers led to the establishment of a second brewery. In 1962 a foreign firm, Amstelbrouwerei, was granted permission to build a third brewery. The experience of the fertilizer industry, where a monopoly resolved into limited competition, has been similar. These developments hardly presage a new competitive tension in industry, they are due rather to rapid growth in the domestic market and personal incomes and, in the case of fertilizers, to more technical and informed attitudes among farmers. Shipbuilding however is dominated by a single firm, that of Niarchos, a monopoly which has been defended by his candid threat to go to another country if the government issues a licence to a competitor.

Other industries such as the chemical, metallurgical, paper, and cement are controlled exclusively by a few large firms, which either divide the market by tacit understanding, or, as in the paper industry, tend to specialize in making different qualities of the same product. There are, too, among smaller businesses many local monopolies, for instance in milling and olive pressing.

It is however the peculiar coexistence in the same industry of a few large firms and many small ones which particularly characterizes Greek industry. Out of 3,119 textile firms, 2,145 employed one to four persons, 895 employed five to ninety-nine, seventy-seven employed 100–500, one employed 1,500, and the Piraiki–Patraiki employed 3,500. Protected by tariffs from foreign competition, the larger firms allow their small competitors to remain in business and set their own prices to those of the marginal producer. Driving out the small family producer is, in any event, a difficult enterprise since he works to live rather than to make commercially respectable profits. In addition small firms are numerous and influential enough through the aggregate pressure of their individual political patrons to win tax concessions, and other kinds of assistance from the government which help them to survive. Small firms will also protect themselves from open competition by manufacturing for individual requirements and by enmeshing themselves and their patrons in a network of social and political obligations which they hope will offset any purely economic advantage the latter might gain by dealing with larger and more modern businesses.

Not surprisingly the organization of labour in Greece shows evidence of the same incapacitating fragmentation as the structure of industry. The trade union movement is represented in its relations with the government by the General Confederation of the Workers of Greece (G.S.E.E.). This includes a plenitude of unions among which a few are relatively large; but the great majority are very small – indeed, often restricted to a particular locality. It may even occur that in the same town a single trade is represented by two antagonistic bodies. And among the larger firms in an industry there is a tendency for separate unions, or independent branches of unions, to form within each company.

In these circumstances the pressure of organized labour to improve wage rates has been uneven in its incidence and its success. In trades where labour was in demand and organization militant, for instance among building workers, there have been important gains. But generally in industry such conditions do not exist. Among the smaller firms in manufacturing industries, especially, employers may succeed in compelling workmen to accept a wage lower than the amount stipulated in a negotiated agreement. Moreover, in many cases where workers have been well organized, as in public utilities or services where the withdrawal of labour was a weapon with some force, strikes were handicapped by the article of the Greek constitution which denies the right to strike to civil servants and those employed in other corporations and undertakings of the state, and imposes the penalties of dismissal or imprisonment. In practice, it is true, this did not always prevent state servants from striking; school teachers, postmen, and the employees of the Electricity Corporation, for example, have done so. In these instances the government has had resort to a law enacted by Metaxas in 1939 which enables it to declare a civil mobilization of the workers in the affected industry. This procedure has also been directed against employees of undertakings which at law have the status of a private company but whose operation affects essential public services, for instance in public transport and telegraphic services. Also by legislation passed in 1955 the Minister of Labour may intervene in a dispute to refer it to an arbitration court consisting of an equal number of representatives from the two parties. While the claim is under consideration strikers must return to work and if an agreement results its recommendations are legally binding. By such powers, by the intimidatory presence of the police and the army, and by judicious concessions on wages, the government has had no difficulty in recent years in containing trade union activity despite the undoubted discontent.

Greek governments have been careful to prevent the political consolidation of the movement. In the period of the civil war the communist elements in the leadership of the General Confederation were forcibly removed and since then the Confederation itself has been under security surveillance. The voting rules within the Confederation favoured the manipulation of small unions. Since no union could claim in relation to the size of its membership more than seven votes or less than one, a large and politically active union was easily outvoted by a number of smaller unions whose aggregate membership was no greater than that of the larger union. In 1965 during Papandhreou's premiership an attempt to introduce legislation which would have related, proportionately, voting powers to membership was blocked by those who feared a resurgence of extreme left influence, and a compromise bill was passed which limited the voting power of any union to not more than one-tenth of the total votes. It was also arranged that dissident unions with supposed extreme left policies which had been expelled from, or by preference had remained outside, the Confederation should have direct access to the Ministry of Labour.

After Papandhreou's resignation the Confederation under its

general secretary Papageorgiou, a Centre Union nominee, attempted to retaliate by the organization of a general strike. Significantly, despite the popular agitation at the time, it failed. And for technical misdemeanours against the constitution of the Confederation Papageorgiou was soon replaced by the reliably conservative Makris who had previously held office when E.R.E. was in power. Under his leadership the Confederation was among the first national organizations to telegraph its congratulations to the Colonels after the *coup* of 21 April. Inevitably, '115', as the group of dissident left-wing unions is generally known, and the unions which followed Papageorgiou out of the Confederation after his dismissal, were subsequently banned by the military government.

Generally the organization of labour is still weak and fragmented. Quite apart from the political difficulties it faces in its relations with the government, and the fragmentation of its own organization, the modest role, until recently, of industry in the Greek economy is a fundamental condition which not only limits the effectiveness of organized labour but also affects the character of the country's political parties. We return to this problem in the final section of this chapter.

III

The Civil Service and Education

The effectiveness of economic planning since the civil war and the manner of its impact on the practical interests and personal sensibilities of private citizens, has depended very largely on the quality of the civil service.

In view of what has already been said about the structure of the family in the countryside and in the city, and about the functional significance of patronage in a society where familial obligations have a moral priority, it is scarcely surprising that relations between the public and the civil service are distant and unsatisfactory. Neither in terms of his own status, nor the dignity of his service, does a civil servant believe he is bound to serve or assist his fellow citizens. It is, naturally, another matter if they are personal friends, or clients of political figures and other personalities with influence who may affect a man's professional or social position. Otherwise the civil servant's duty, as he is instructed to see it, is the administration of the laws which fall within the competence of his Ministry's activities, in an adamantly legalistic spirit. This enables the service to resist the importunities of unimportant people which cost the state scarce resources and give its servants unnecessary work. Since it denies junior officials any exercise of their own initiative it also safeguards them from the criticism of superiors and supports the centralized structure of the service. The ill effects of these attitudes are plain. Since every imagined contingency must be provided for, the work of the legislator, and subsequently the administrator, is made absurdly burdensome and complex. The more serious disadvantage is that the original aims of the legislation are distorted or lost to sight. Civil servants are not accustomed to ask themselves what were the original intentions of the legislator and to adapt their administrative acts to that interpretation. The law offers a convenient means of defence or excuse, but it seldom expresses a pattern of behaviour that is believed in. At the same time the legalistic attitude itself encourages the search for loopholes in the law and is intimately connected with the need for the support of patrons.

The defects in the structure of the civil service and in its practical procedures are consistent with these attitudes. The administration of the country is excessively centralized, partly because this was inherent in the French model from which the organization was copied, partly because the coherence and security of good government in a geographically and socially fragmented society appeared to demand it. The concentration in Athens of the senior officials who alone are able to make decisions, adds a geographical dimension to the sense of division between those who administer and those who are administered, which we have already remarked. It also creates, within the service itself, a sense of distance between the outside men in the provinces, who are nearer to many of the problems which must be dealt with but further from the place of decision, and those in the Ministries in Athens who are in exactly the reverse position. Senior officials do not want to delegate authority. As long as juniors must refer questions to them, even if this is only the formality of a countersignature in a matter of routine, the senior official's authority is unquestioned and his presence, for the proper functioning of his department, is seen to be indispensable This attitude is no doubt present to some extent in all administrative hierarchies; but it is peculiarly apparent in Greece where the social recognition conceded to a man partly depends on the number and quality of persons seen to be dependent on him. In the civil service the consequence is that junior officials find safety in the letter of the law, inertia, or reference to a higher authority. Indeed those who show too much initiative may be classed as 'rebels' and this judgement entered in the yearly report submitted on each official by the head of department could handicap his career.

The centralization of the civil service is not however that of a unified body. The administration of the country is divided between nineteen Ministries. Although the coordination of their work is the particular care of a separate Ministry, this is only partially achieved and at the cost of much effort, since jurisdictions overlap and responsibilities are confused. The Ministries have been described not inappropriately as 'separate fiefdoms' operating in relative isolation from each other, which is often accentuated by the political pressures and competitive manoeuvres of Ministers, and by the convention that the posting of an official from one Ministry to another is an extremely rare occurrence. Such exclusiveness leads too often to the wasteful duplication of work by different Ministries and is a depressing but not unexpected reiteration of the theme of fragmentation to which we have frequently drawn attention. It must be added that the same fragmentation of effort is to be observed within Ministries between Directorates-General, and within these between the Directorates. These relations are inevitably repeated in the fifty-two provincial divisions of the country into Nomes. At that level many of the Ministries have their local representatives or agencies whose cooperation is guided by the Nomarch who is the local representative of the central government. Since any problem may be referred to a number of Ministries in Athens his task is formidable. Generally at all levels in public administration parochial interests and reciprocal mistrust between Ministries are evident. Confusion is increased by the setting up of various agencies to deal with temporary needs or problems, without proper delimitation of their tasks or consideration of the destructive effects they produce in the Ministries with whose work they overlap. And responsibility is diffused by the proliferation of consultative bodies convened by the government without clearly stated terms of reference, whose main purpose is often to delay decisions on controversial questions, and incidentally to provide those invited with an additional income.

In the practical dispatch of business the scene is equally discouraging. The procedures of most Ministries are slow, complicated, and inefficient. The pressure of political patronage to assist people into the service, and afterwards to protect their careers, has in the past created a proliferation of unneeded posts which various attempts at rationalization have only partly remedied. The meaningless passage of an individual or an application through a circuit of officials who copy the same information into different ledgers is typical of methods which affront the intelligence of a public increasingly used to the relatively modern techniques and more cooperative attitudes which they meet in banks and other business institutions.

The efficiency of the civil service is not increased by the morale of its members, methods of entry into the service, and the quality of recruits. The service is divided into three categories of official. Category 'A' includes those with university or equivalent qualifications, category 'B' those who have completed secondary school courses, category 'C' the remaining staff, porters and messengers, who have no formal qualifications. It is surprising to discover that of the total of almost 37,000 civil servants 42 per cent are in category 'A'. Since in England and France only 4 to 5 per cent of the civil service are in the equivalent class it might be supposed that the Greek civil service was particularly rich in human resources. Unhappily this does not follow. Not all degrees and diplomas have comparable merits. The better graduates from the universities of Athens and Salonika seldom enter the service, for salaries are unattractive and the civil servant enjoys little prestige in the city. On the other hand no fewer than 60 per cent of the candidates for the civil service examinations come from the Pantios School of Administrative Studies, whose standards, to put it charitably, are hardly elevated. This school draws its students very largely from the secondary schools of provincial towns where standards of secondary education are variable but where a career in the public service has considerable prestige and is often the ambition of an artisan or farmer for his son.

Within the service competition for entry varies greatly since each Ministry holds its own examinations. As some Ministries are more favoured than others the distribution of scarce talent is extremely uneven. Once in the service a category 'A' official is promoted automatically from grade 9 to grade 6, but at this point the pressure for promotion to the higher ranks becomes intense and it is generally believed that further advance depends upon political relationships and affiliations both inside and outside the service.

The frustrations of this situation dull the conscience and the appetite for honest work. Earnings have a similar effect. The basic salary rates are inadequate and many lower-grade officials have an additional job in the afternoon after their office has closed, although, strictly, pluralism of employment is not permitted. More senior men are given appointments to various consultative bodies and commissions for which they receive an honorarium. There are also indemnities and bonuses. The result is that the concentration and interest of officials is distracted from their essential duties; and that men who do the same work are paid different effective salaries, the level of which depends on their relations with superiors. Morale is also lowered by the fact that although appointment to categories 'A' and 'B' is in principle restricted to those who have been successful at examination, and who also hold the required degree or diploma, in fact many temporary civil servants originally recruited by contract are later 'established'. Moreover, any person appointed to categories 'C' or 'B' can subsequently advance to a higher category by passing the degree or diploma that is the qualification for that category. He is not required to submit himself for examination. These are particularly the routes into the civil service that can be arranged through political influence and patronage. But undoubtedly the insecurity of the unpredictable connections between professional advancement and political events makes a career in the civil service unattractive to most men of talent; and therefore condemns it to mediocrity.

There is some supervision of civil service affairs from outside the organization. The Council of State established in 1929 examines the legality of administrative acts and therefore protects public servants from demotion or unjust dismissal. The Higher Council for the Civil Service was created in 1951 to act in a consultative capacity on all matters concerning the civil service. And it is charged with the duty of selecting candidates for categories 'A' and 'B'. Almost all considerations of reform in the past, particularly Venizelos' legislation in 1911, and the reforms of 1951, have been concerned with establishing the political neutrality of civil servants, and consequently their security of tenure and the continuity of public administration whatever party is in power. But in practice these aims, even when protected by law, have been defeated by justifications of public safety as is now the case. Earlier, Papagos purged the service in 1953, Papandhreou by retiring officials of more than thirty-five years' service ingeniously did the same without appearing to do so. And on other occasions the rules concerning selection by examination have been temporarily set aside. But reforms in the structure of the service itself, or in training and methods, have generally been resisted or evaded. It is hard to penetrate the thickets of a sacred and traditional routine. Officials who in recent years on the initiative of a few determined reformers in the Ministry of Coordination have been sent for training to Britain, Holland, and France return to find that the techniques they have learned are impractical in departments where their seniors cannot publicly admit that they have anything to learn.

The deficiencies of the bureaucracy inevitably affect the economy. In setting up a new industry, building an extension to a plant, or forming a company, the citizen is faced with unimaginable difficulties, despite the concessions and exhortations of successive governments to industrialists to undertake exactly these developments. The relatively unenterprising quality of Greek entrepreneurship in industry as opposed to commerce has been attributed to management by owners, an unsatisfactory capital market, inappropriate education, and the lack of technical training. But it is also due in no small measure to the extraordinary waste of time and ingenuity on the endless struggle of personal manoeuvre to obtain licences, permits, tax allowances, and generally to ensure that the entrepreneur has friendly and profitable relations with persons who politically or administratively might damage the business, whether out of malice, common interest with a rival, or bureaucratic legalism. Indeed, the manufacturer must lavish the greater part of his time on protecting his business from the external environment at the expense of the proper organization of the process of production in his factory.

*   *   *

It is generally recognized today that there is a relation between productivity and educational standards. There is little doubt, for instance, that the failings of the Greek system of education handicap industry by the scarcity of technically trained graduates, and that they affect the quality of the civil service by providing it with too many candidates indifferently and dogmatically educated in the faculties of law and political science. To explain these deficiencies we must refer to the regulations which existed before Papandhreou's reforms of 1964, which in any event have now been mainly reversed.

Since 1929 six years of primary education from the age of six have been compulsory for Greek children. In practice few children avoid this schooling today and although some illegally drop out in the later years the quite considerable proportion of 87 per cent complete the six years course. The weaknesses of primary schools reflect most of the problems which also exist at secondary and university level: lack of teachers, lack of space and books, the poor quality of existing text books, outdated curricula and teaching methods, and a serious imbalance of resources and opportunity between the cities and the more remote areas of the countryside. In 1961 the average teacher: pupil ratio in primary schools was 1:40. This figure which in itself is unsatisfactory disguises two more serious conditions; that in many village schools one teacher must instruct the six primary grades in a single classroom (indeed of the 9,300 primary schools, 4,300 have only one teacher); and that in primary schools in the cities, although each grade may have its own teacher, the class may include as many as seventy children and in some instances more. In these difficult conditions teaching is unimaginative, and learning is by rote. Apart from a generally indifferent standard in reading, writing, and arithmetic, the most considerable achievement of these first years at school is the assimilation of heroic myths which stand for the historical experience of the infallible Greek people during the classical, Byzantine, and modern periods. This includes some exposition of the position and dogma of the Orthodox Church interpreted as an aspect of Greek nationality.

Until 1964 entry into a secondary school (gymnasium) was by examination. In 1961, 46 per cent of the students leaving primary schools were accepted at gymnasia. In that year there were 544 state gymnasia with 233,490 pupils. The teacher: pupil ratio at 1 :38 was little different from the situation in the primary schools and there were the same extreme examples of congestion in urban gymnasia, some of which operated a two-shift system. Since outside the cities these schools are normally established in small towns, the country child in 1961 paid not only for books and fees but also for food and lodging. The quality of teaching and hence the value of the graduation diploma varies greatly but generally the standard is dangerously low. Again the country child may suffer disproportionately. Private secondary education, which is encouraged by the government because it relieves the state of the investment burden of building more gymnasia, is concentrated almost exclusively in the cities and in 1961 accounted for 44,306 students in 285 schools with a teacher: pupil ratio of 1:11. Although these schools, too, vary widely in quality, they attract by the offer of higher salaries many of the more gifted teachers who prefer to live in Athens or Salonika. The effect on the quality and number of gymnasium teachers in the provinces, where a large percentage of the children come from villages, is inevitably adverse.

In quality the most general fault in secondary teaching, as also at the university level, is the confusion of the teacher's personality, and what he considers to be due to it, with the process of learning itself. The student is given little encouragement to exercise his intellect apart from memory, and his role is simply to accept his instructor's authority and passively admire his performance.

The content of secondary education as it existed before 1964 was overwhelmingly 'classical'. There were some secondary schools with syllabuses directed to commercial or technical subjects, but in each of these categories the number of students was only about 3 per cent of those attending classical gymnasia. In the latter the emphasis on the teaching of classical languages and the cultural heritage of Hellenism is evident in the distribution of 6,351 hours of instruction in the six-year course: 1,479 were given to ancient Greek, 1,044 to history and modern Greek, 638 to mathematics, and 551 to natural sciences. The disproportionate attention lavished on classical

AA

subjects was certainly inconsistent with national policies of economic and technical development, but fundamentally what was, and still is, alarming, is the low standard of attainment even in these favoured subjects.

In 1961 about two-fifths of the students who originally enrolled in the first year eventually graduated from their course of six years study. Since the graduation diplomas from gymnasia are not greatly respected by employers the common ambition is to go to university or to a recognized college of higher education. In 1961 entrants to universities and equivalent institutions were 43 per cent of the number of students graduating from gymnasia in that year. Although competition for the limited number of places, particularly at the two universities, was intense, the quality of the education which students so anxiously sought was indifferent. While professors have some cause for complaint that they have few lecturers or tutors to assist them, they are too often complacent, delivering lectures whose content would be considered inadequate by the standards of western scholarship, and paying more attention to additional obligations which they commonly have on consultative bodies outside the university than to the problems of students. Seminars, or tutorials, are rare where they exist at all; and, as in the gymnasia, the student has few opportunities to write or express an opinion until the ordeal of examination, when conformity and influence rather than originality serve him better. There are exceptions to this state of affairs but this is the general condition. Of the 24,000 students in higher education in 1961, 14,500 were at the two universities of Athens and Salonika, the remainder at other schools which have an accepted university status. It is in certain of these schools which specialize in commercial, political, and administrative studies that standards are particularly questionable. Students study a range of subjects such as law, public administration, pure economics, and accounting at a level of some abstraction, or in relation to developed economies, so that knowledge is both superficial and effectively divorced from any Greek reality while it flatters naïve students with the illusion of acquired omniscience.

Higher education is still dominated by the law faculties; both the legalistic approach of the government administration and the character of political patronage encourage this kind of training. Of the 129,000 graduates of higher education 23,600 have law degrees, 11,300 graduated from the medical faculties, 10,400 from the humanities, and only 8,800 from the natural sciences. In 1961 three-quarters of the students enrolled at the universities of Athens and Salonika were in the faculties of law, philosophy, and the humanities. Facilities for the study of engineering science are notably lacking. But it is no longer the case that this reflects a snobbish contempt for technical subjects. On the contrary these are increasingly fashionable and it is significant that 59 per cent of the 8,000 Greek students in foreign universities study scientific or technical subjects. Probably only the lack of laboratories limits the number of science and engineering graduates.

In the past the legal requirements of the education system have not been met. The 1961 census revealed that there were 1,222,000 illiterates over the age of ten, nearly a million of whom were women. Many factors account for this disturbing number; they include war, the arrival of refugees, lack of teachers in mountainous districts, and simply non-attendance. Nevertheless there is generally among Greeks an ambition for education. This is, perhaps, less the result of a traditional respect for learning as such than the belief that it provides the key to increased wealth and status. A peasant saves with difficulty to support a son during six years at gymnasium in the hope that he will later study law at university. He sees in his son the future protector of the family, established in some stronghold of the other world. From the earliest years of the Greek state in 1834 when four years of primary schooling were made free and compulsory until the legislation of the Papandhreou government in which education at all levels was at the state's expense, the principle has been established that access to education is a right as well as an obligation of citizenship. In the particular conditions of Greek parliamentary democracy these educational rights supported by the arrangements and manipulations of political patrons partly explain the considerable social mobility in Greek society. It is a remarkable fact that forty per cent of the students enrolled at the universities of Athens and Salonika come from the families of farmers or labourers.

Unfortunately in education, as in many other aspects of Greek life, the gap is wide between what is attempted and what the means available could reasonably be expected to achieve. Eighteen per cent of the population aged eighteen in Greece have completed the full course of secondary education in comparison with 11 per cent in France and Sweden, and 6 per cent in Great Britain. Similarly as a proportion of the relevant age group, university graduates represent 3·6 per cent in Greece, in comparison with 3·4 per cent in France and Great Britain, and 2·7 per cent in West Germany. Allowing for the difficulties of international comparison these figures, at first sight, are impressive. Yet, although between 1955 and 1961 total expenditure on education in Greece increased by 76 per cent, it had actually fallen as a percentage of the national budget, and in the latter year represented only 2·1 per cent of the gross

AA*

national product in comparison with 4·1 per cent in Sweden, 3·7 per cent in Great Britain, 3·5 per cent in France, 2·8 per cent in West Germany, countries which Greece has apparently surpassed, at least in numbers, in her ambition to educate her population. The disparity between means and ambitions underlies the very un-satisfactory quality of Greek education, which in its turn explains how relatively small a return the country enjoys from a civil service which has ten times as many university graduates as the civil services of France and Great Britain; and from a system of primary education in which four-fifths of the teachers have had higher education.

Although in themselves many of the details of the educational reform of the Papandhreou government, which became law in 1964, were admirable, their effect was to make education yet more extensive and more accessible. Given the connections between education, movement to the city, and social mobility, this was politically a sensible and attractive programme. But it inevitably made the problem of improving the quality of education even more intractable. Under the new regulations fees for education at every level, including university, were abolished. Compulsory education was extended from six to nine years to include the first three years of secondary education. Instead of the university entrance examina-tion there was now a standardized graduation examination at the end of the six years of secondary education which demanded a more rigorous and uniform standard than the old diploma examination which each gymnasium administered for itself. This new leaving certificate was centrally examined and success entitled an individual, in principle, to a place at a university or equivalent institution. There can be no quarrel with the changes in curricula which radically altered the distribution of time between subjects and place a proper emphasis on modern and technical subjects. The use of the demotic form of modern Greek in secondary education was also adopted. However, as soon as Papandhreou fell from power the revision of his educational programme began with the reintroduction by Stephanopoulos of the *katharevousa* language as the principal med-ium for teaching in secondary schools. For whatever may be the intellectual arguments in the language question, *katharevousa*, the language of government that is learned at gymnasium, symbolically and practically divides those who generally administer from those who are generally administered. The Colonels' regime has further dismantled the new structure by reducing compulsory education to six years of primary education as before, and by abolishing the new secondary school graduation exam. The first step in this reversed policy was no doubt partly a question of economy but it probably contained some notion of social control, while the second makes it easier once more for universities to choose their entrants by whatever criteria seem currently suitable. For the rest, the establishment of a new modern university, the development of schools for technical training, credits for school building, measures to train teachers in modern educational techniques, inevitably depend on a continuous flow of public funds into educational investment and their practical effects must lie some distance in the future; if, indeed, the present military regime allows these plans to mature.

It is not, of course, easy to reform a system of education which is itself the product of the society which it instructs. Even external reforms in curricula depend on a difficult redistribution of staff which can be imagined from the fact that in 1961 there were more teachers of theology in the gymnasia than of the natural sciences. But the quality of teaching is a more subtle problem. Education concerns a personal relationship between teacher and pupil, the pattern of which is a reflection of attitudes and values more generally current. One cannot credibly hope that this relationship in Greece will now develop in the direction of reasonable debate in which the teacher's intention is to present knowledge in a manner which stimulates the student to make considered suggestions of his own, and above all to appreciate that both in matters of historical interpretation and scientific hypothesis there may be no absolute truth. One must expect that unilateral instruction based on authority and emotion will continue to impress on young Greek boys and girls habits of thought which subsequently in adult life make it very difficult for them to retreat openly from any intellectual position even when they have ceased to believe in it. Such attitudes have practical effects. Even in businesses of some size it is difficult for the manager to discuss with his staff a rational internal organization and a practical delegation of authority. Instead coordination and decision making, essentially without objective discussion, are concentrated upon a single man whose absence or indisposition prevents all but simply routine operations. Similarly in the many consultative bodies and *ad hoc* committees established in the orbit of government proceedings typically consist of lengthy and categorical statements of position, rhetorically presented. There is little time or willingness for cooperative consideration of the problems which the body was supposedly constituted to discuss.

It is probably true, without calculating what might have been the effects of the attempted extension of educational rights, that with limited resources and her particular social and economic structure Greece has produced too many graduates of classical gymnasia, and too many university graduates in the humanities and social sciences. With rising incomes in the past fifteen years the number of children setting out on this type of academic course has increased spectacularly. If they do not go to university after the gymnasium the difficulty is not only that their learning equips them for no particular calling but that social and practical reasons do not make it easy for the children of peasants or craftsmen to return to the farms and workshops which their families own. The already fragmented farm, or the small workshop, may be assigned to another brother and in any event such a retreat would be a mark of failure. If they complete a university course their suitability for most occupations is hardly improved, but in practice the range of possible employment open to them in banks, business, the public service, or teaching is wider. Yet except for the minority whose connections or, more rarely, outstanding merit place them immediately in a satisfying post, the work to which most graduates must resign themselves fits ill with their dreams and pretensions. With so many graduates competing for work underemployment is common and promotion is blocked. Intrigue is the common pursuit for men whose talent and energy is not properly used. The consequence has been the creation of a disaffected intellectual proletariat with faith in very little except their own abused worth.

IV

The Political Structure

In this brief account of political structure in Greece we speak for convenience in the present tense of the situation as it existed before the *coup d'état* of 21 April 1967. The form of government is a constitutional monarchy whose powers, deriving wholly from the nation, are set out in the one hundred and fourteen articles of the constitution, in its revised form of 1952. The legislative function is discharged by King and parliament, but the right to propose legislation can only be exercised by the King through his Ministers. The legislative body consists of a single chamber whose members are elected for four years by secret universal ballot; although for women the right to vote was conceded only as recently as 1952. However, while the principles governing election to parliament and the functions of the Assembly are included in the constitution, the electoral system itself may be subject to the legislation of the majority in the outgoing chamber. The cynical legalistic ingenuity of political leaders who through the command of a majority, or as a result of an electoral bargain between parties, construct an electoral system, sometimes of considerable complexity, to suit their parties' interests, indicates again how little the notion of respecting the popular will is yet a matter of conscience in Greek politics. In practice the distance between such manipulations and a physical *coup d'état* is not so great.

The King, acting through his responsible Ministers, is the head of the executive and the Commander-in-Chief of the armed forces. On the advice of his Ministers he declares war and concludes peace. Commercial treaties however are not valid without the consent of parliament. The King appoints and dismisses his Ministers; but the Prime Minister must advise him on the appointment of his colleagues. The King convenes, prorogues, and dismisses parliament, but this power is subject to certain well-defined limitations. In general the King may only exercise his powers through his Ministers. His assent is necessary for bills passed by parliament but no act of the King is valid unless it is also signed by the appropriate Minister. The latter assumes the responsibility. The person of the King is inviolable and free of responsibility. Such at least are the indications of the constitution.

The government is composed of Ministers and under-secretaries. It is directed by the Council of Ministers presided over by the Prime Minister. The legalistic spirit of Greek administrative arrangements has not spared this cabinet. Its functions and procedures are determined by law. Decisions of the Council are taken by majority vote and a quorum of more than half its members must be present. The greater volume and complexity of business in recent years has resulted in the establishment of smaller ministerial committees which attend to particular problems of coordination, but here again the powers and jurisdictions of these bodies are defined by law.

Despite this legal framework the practice of government in many instances is different. The legal formalities of majority decisions in the Council of Ministers were little respected by Karamanlis or Papandhreou. And while the constitution of 1952 is clearly based on the principle that the monarch reigns but does not govern, yet if it is interpreted strictly by the letter of its articles the extent of the King's authority in certain situations remains equivocal.

Constitutionally the King is the highest agent of the state, and in this office certain powers have been entrusted to him. His distinctive function is that of a moderator or regulator of the constitution and in this role he ought to ensure that the policies of the elected parliament remain in reasonable harmony with the will of the people. The right to dissolve parliament and hold elections is, appropriately, his constitutional weapon in such a situation.

After elections have been held, or after the resignation of the Prime Minister at any other time, the King is also empowered by the constitution to appoint a successor who, not later than fifteen days after the formation of his government, must appear before the Assembly and ask for a vote of confidence. If the government is unsuccessful it must resign.

If a Greek King could appear to be impartial and if it were possible to discover objectively, and to the satisfaction of the majority, when the will of the people was being seriously frustrated by parliament, such arrangements might achieve their purpose. In practice, unfortunately, the exercise of these powers in any particular instance is almost certainly displeasing to one or other of the political factions; and their judgements of the King's motives vary accordingly. Moreover, by his right to appoint a Prime Minister the King may sometimes create or destroy a political career. It might be thought the requirement that a government must enjoy the confidence of the Assembly would be a sufficient safeguard against the imposition of a Prime Minister, if not unwanted, at least not chosen by the majority party. Yet if the King chooses his candidate with careful reference to personal followings and animosities, the absence of corporate solidarity and organization in the parties of the Centre and the Right makes such an outcome possible. The premiership of Karamanlis is one example.

Other powers of the Greek King add to the possible ambiguities of his constitutional position. If it is true that on the advice of his responsible Prime Minister he appoints Ministers, gives his assent to bills passed in parliament, and may dissolve parliament, there is no explicit indication that he must do any of these things. In 1965 King Constantine declined to appoint Papandhreou as Minister of Defence or to dissolve parliament. The King was not acting unconstitutionally in finding another Prime Minister who eventually formed a government and successfully faced the ordeal of a confidence vote in the existing chamber. On the other hand his opponents argue with some justice that since apparently a majority of the people wished to resolve the crisis by a general election and since his Prime Minister had made the same request, it was his constitutional duty to accept this advice. There is, also, the moral question of whether it was right to promote an alternative government whose success depended on undermining the stability of the Centre Union Party by the distribution of ministerial posts to those who deserted it.

The political differences of July 1965 showed how the flexibility or perhaps imprecision in the drafting of the constitution where it describes the duties and powers of the King, was inevitably exploited by the parties to the dispute. As in the matter of electoral systems the constitution enjoys no particular or patriotic respect except when it is infringed by political opponents. It is a code of rules to be manipulated in the interests of a party, or if they will not serve it, to be altered by political manoeuvre in the case of moderate parties, by force in the case of militant groups of the extreme Left and Right. Certainly Greek Kings have often believed that when the safety of the established social order is threatened, its defence may justify action not foreseen, or permitted, in the constitution.

That there has been legitimate concern for the country's safety (variously interpreted from different positions) on too many occasions, is partly to be attributed to peculiarities in the internal structure of Greek political parties. It is true that between 1952 and 1965 there was an apparent stability in political life which encouraged some observers to believe that economic growth, however unbalanced, and the rural migration which accompanied it, were leading to the development of modern political parties radically different from the traditional groupings of notabilities supported by local dependants. In 1946 there were six parties in parliament; in 1950 fourteen. By 1964 this number had been reduced to four. After 1952, moreover, there were no instances of government by loose coalitions, and some proof of party discipline of a kind previously unknown in Greek parliamentary experience. However, some of the factors which may account for these changes are external and perhaps temporary.

The exhausted resources of the country after the civil war forced successive Greek governments into extreme dependence on the Americans. The reward for political stability and disciplined parliamentary behaviour was the confidence of allies and funds to rebuild the country's roads, to give it adequate electric power, irrigation, and the other facilities necessary for the economy's repair. In effect this placed in the hands of the Prime Minister resources of patronage of such importance, in the form of contracts and local employment which offered a living for constituents and profits for political intermediaries and contractors at different levels, that few deputies could afford to show much independence of spirit. Karamanlis' period of power between 1956 and 1963 was marked by some display of rebellion in 1958 when fifteen deputies left the party over the issue of the electoral law which introduced the weighted form of proportional representation. An incidental but illustrative complaint of Papaligouras, one of the two Ministers among the dissidents, was that Karamanlis had almost ceased to use the Council of Ministers for either holding discussions or taking decisions. Yet after the election which was forced on the government by these resignations Karamanlis' National Radical Union (E.R.E.) Party was returned to power and before the next election in 1961 most of the rebels had rejoined.

The process we have described reinforces itself. In Greece a party continuously in power over a period of years begins to dominate and use the machinery of the state as by right. The electoral advantages which result from this illegal convention as well as others which the weighted electoral system gives to the larger parties have been arguments to dissuade dissatisfied deputies from forming small independent parties whose electoral experience would very probably be unprofitable. The same arguments in 1961 enabled Papandhreou to join in a Centre Union Party the many political groups and interests inhabiting the territory between E.D.A., the communist-affected left-wing party, and the traditional conservatism of E.R.E. Only a few of these were represented in parliament but in aggregate they had greater electoral strength than the Liberal Party whose defeat as a single party at the 1958 election had been disastrous. By 1961 centre parties had not shared in government for nine years, during a period when both the means to support programmes of development and reform, and the resources of government patronage, had visibly increased. Under the spur of desperation the achievement was considerable but the balance precarious. In June and July 1961 the foundation of the alliance was strengthened by unofficial conversations which a senior State Department official held with different centre personalities. There was a hint, perhaps, that if its unity was proved and its liberalism remained conservative it might in certain circumstances be acceptable to the Americans as an alternative government.

An examination of the structure of the E.R.E. Party which for seven years held power under Karamanlis' leadership at once reveals that this is not a modern mass party with a corporate identity apart from the personalities of its leaders; or a formal organization permanently linking the parliamentary group with constituency organizations whose existence has little to do with the personal influence of their parliamentary candidates. It is true that E.R.E. has published a charter which provides for a General Assembly, a secretariat, a General Council, an Executive Committee, and other specialist committees for research, finance, and discipline. Political centres were to be set up in each constituency with sections in villages and the wards of towns and cities. The General Assembly which by the statutes must be convened every two years includes the members of councils and committees, the members of parliament, other candidates at the preceding election, representatives of the local organizations. By its own constitution the Assembly appears as a rally of political personalities and local notabilities rather than the representative assembly of a party which at times embraces half the nation.

In reality the structure we have described does not exist. In the first eight years of the party's existence the Assembly never met. Apart from some sketchy attempts at organization in the cities the party is represented in the constituencies through the persons of its deputies and candidates, their friends and clients. Of the party's superstructure only three elements are important, the leader, the parliamentary group, and the secretariat. We have already remarked on the dominance of Karamanlis over his deputies. What characterized the secretariat was the degree to which it was absorbed into the Prime Minister's office, a department of state. Indeed since the party was in power from its earliest days, it had until 1963 no separate existence apart from the government. Although in Greece this confusion is traditional and convenient for party interests, the scale of Karamanlis' employment of state machinery was extreme. Not only did the civil servants in his department deal with the problems and solicitations of the party's more important clients; the official information services never failed in their eulogies of the leader and his achievements to make the equation between the government and the party very explicit; and in the pre-election periods the state services, not excluding the police and army, created an atmosphere both of inducement and apprehension directed particularly at voters in the countryside where it is difficult to conceal a political allegiance.

The situation of the Centre Union Party differs little from that of E.R.E. There is provision for the same ambitious political organization which has never been established. And a Congress which does not meet. If it is true that Papandhreou never dominated his members of parliament with the same contemptuous ease of Karamanlis, his control over the party until his resignation in 1965 was the more remarkable since it included some men who in certain circumstances might have joined E.D.A. and others who were soon to establish a tacit coalition with E.R.E. As in the case of E.R.E. this acceptance of discipline had little to do with any inherent qualities of the party's organization. If anything this was less coherent than arrangements in E.R.E., certainly while the party was in opposition. The secretariat was embryonic and affairs were largely conducted from the personal political offices of the leading personalities of the different groups which had formed the union. In the cities there was initially some attempt to establish local branches of the party. The account given to one of the authors by a senior woman delegate of the first meeting of an Athenian constituency organization after the electoral victory in February 1964 is instructive. After mutual congratulation the chairman explained that the meeting was, of course, a formality since with the new government successfully established their purpose was achieved and in the future party problems and programmes could be discussed directly with the appropriate Minister. In justice to Papandhreou it should be said that during his premiership Ministers were forbidden to conduct political business from their ministerial offices. But even if his edict was respected, it may be doubted if the simply physical separation of these activities has in fact altered their practical confusion.

In saying that the framework of party organization is based upon networks of friendship and patronage we are not claiming that political behaviour is reducible to these kinds of personal relationship. Even in the countryside the personal obligations and relationships which at various removes link a deputy, or a candidate, to the voters are not, of course, unaffected by the scale and power of the national party he represents. A man is adopted as a candidate on a party list because he is influential and possesses an existing social or professional clientele. Equally the fact that he has been chosen by a party who may form the government adds considerably to his influence, particularly if the government's potential patronage is considerable. Today it is only rarely the case that a member of parliament who resigns from a national party to become an independent, or to join another party, is able to carry with him the majority of his electoral supporters. Influential persons in villages and towns with clients of their own may judge it to be more prudent to join their forces to the party's new candidate. But this decision is not a matter of principle, or of customary loyalty to a party, or mainly even of interest, if this is judged by the general advantages likely to result from a party programme, although these considerations are not entirely absent. It is a question of the protection of interests which clients feel may be threatened under any system of administration, and possibly of winning particular privileges if the patron's influence is effective. Indeed if his efficiency is not proved, some at least of his dependants will fall away. A characteristic of patronage networks in Greece is the attempt to keep open a number of lines of relationship with influential persons. From time to time the failure of a patron or the ingratitude of a client leads to a new arrangement of alliances.

In the cities, too, despite the scale of society and the division of interest between a man's residence and his place of work, the frequent coincidence between political affiliation and the receipt or hope of patronage, organized, for instance, through the clienteles of lawyers, doctors, and shopkeepers who offer more liberal credit to political sympathizers, indicates the persistence of political attitudes of rural origin. But in the city, inevitably, patronage does not account, even approximately, for political behaviour. The problems and apprehensions of the urban population are too complex and demanding for solution or reassurance by the traditional manipulations. Various factors such as an inherited party affiliation, the attraction of electoral promises, or access to patronage may determine many individual allegiances. But the fluctuations in the voting strength, for instance, of E.R.E. in different elections since its foundation, the sudden access of strength to E.D.A. in 1958, or to the Centre Union Party between the elections of November 1963 and February 1964, suggest that a considerable body of voters habitually change the party of their choice. It is typical of comment on these changes that individuals first refer either to the personal morality of leaders of the party they are deserting or to present frustrations in their own affairs. Objections are often negative and particular and have little to do with the merits of policies. Behind these complaints there is the general discontent which is created by the visible and extravagant consumption of the upper class, which others are encouraged to emulate but cannot afford. Thus in a gesture of alienation, in protest rather than conviction, they change their party. One aspect of this act is a reassertion of the independence of personality in a situation where either one has no effective political connections or even these cannot solve the problem. To protest may be added calculation. In a society dominated by notions of patronage and favours it is crucial to be on the winning side if only in the negative sense that it may save a man from undue administrative harassment. And, especially in villages, voters who change their allegiance to the party which it is presumed will win, make sure that their new convictions are generally known.

Therefore such organization as E.R.E. or the Centre Union Party can claim, either in the city or the countryside, is imposed from above. Its basis among the electorate is not that of a corporate local membership of party workers, and of committees elected by them which have an existence independent of the member of parliament. It is simply a personal circle and the dependants and allies of those who belong to it. It follows that if a considerable fraction of the parliamentary group deserts there are no constituency organizations which can immediately expel the rebels and replace them with other men. The party divides. After Papandhreou's resignation in July 1965 this happened to the Centre Union.

BB

Certain conditions made it possible for the union of centre parties between 1958 and 1963 to persist in its struggle for office, to win its electoral victory, and to form a government. For a time, with guarded reservations, it was acceptable to the army, the King, and the Americans, in that order of increasing enthusiasm. Initially like the preceding governments it had important resources of patronage. Changes in the same factors which brought it to power, destroyed it. It lost the political confidence of the army and the King; and it met economic difficulties. There followed the spectacle of a government of Centre Union rebels supported but not joined by E.R.E., which had no difficulty in recruiting new members from the remainder of the Centre Union by the offer of ministerial portfolios and under-secretaryships. After the initial breach of unity, and once the source of patronage was located elsewhere, the tendency to fragmentation could not be resisted.

Until it was dissolved by the present regime E.D.A. was the party which represented the left opinion of those who sympathized with the banned Communist Party or whose reformist socialism was too radical for the Centre Union. Alone of Greek political parties it possessed a formal organization which was an integral part of its political life. Sections, or cells, recruited on the basis of neighbourhood, factory, or professional association, are grouped into sections which in turn form a provincial association. At each level affairs are ordered by an elected committee. The party Congress is the supreme authority. Its members, representing the provincial and urban organization of the party, decide on policy and elect a steering committee, the president of which is also the president of the party. The latter also presides over the executive committee whose members are drawn from the steering committee. At all levels there is freedom of discussion, but once a decision has been taken disciplined acceptance is obligatory. In this formal structure all the organs of party authority must answer to the Congress which is itself representative of the entire party. Although in organizations of this kind the origin and manipulation of effective power lie elsewhere than in the institutional forms, nevertheless its members have a sense of corporate participation which is absent in other parties. The agent of E.R.E. in a village, for example, supports the party and draws benefits from it but his commitment is contingent, external, and easily reversible.

One reason for these differences is that while the 'bourgeois' parties, E.R.E. and Centre Union, accept the country's existing social and political institutions, subject to the reforms presented in their programmes, and therefore in their own organization tend merely to reflect the kind of institutional arrangements which characterize Greek society, for example the difficulty of building any corporate loyalty which conflicts with the obligations of family and the alliances of patronage, E.D.A. on the other hand does not accept the existing social framework but wishes, sooner or later, to change it. These aims are indicated in the popular democratic and hierarchical institutions of the party which do not find their models in Greek society.

Since industry is weak and firms are generally very small, industrial trade unions are not strongly organized. Nor has there been any considerable agrarian movement in a countryside where peasants own their farms. There has thus never been any basis for the growth of an organized labour party in Greece with its electoral strength drawn from particular social and occupational classes. The Centre Union Party despite its reformist programme is essentially conservative. It may advocate a planned economy but there is no suggestion of interference with private ownership and profit. Its notions of social justice are those of liberalism: educational opportunity and equitable taxation. In principle, E.R.E., too, accepts the same policies, but with less enthusiasm for planning, and with the reservation that any measure of social welfare must not conflict with the requirements of monetary stability. Although in the absence of detailed studies one may hazard the guess that in recent years more owners of shops and businesses cast their vote for E.R.E. and more salaried employees for the Centre Union, the more important generalization is that both these parties draw their votes from all strata of society, from peasants to industrialists; in this, again, they merely follow the structure of Greek society in which individuals are linked to kinsmen and dependants across ill-defined lines of social class.

In the case of E.D.A. the majority of the party's supporters are among industrial workers, labourers, and the lower paid employees in service industries, particularly among the families of Asia Minor refugees. Yet the party also has numerous adherents among the frustrated, half-educated, intellectual proletariat which the democratic, but inefficient, education system of the state so prodigally produces. Until the present time, the barrier to any decisive extension of the influence of the Left in Greece has been the inherently conservative interests of the family. The extent of these interests is, indeed, extraordinary. Half the population are dependent on agriculture which is almost exclusively in the hands of peasants who own their farms, 32 per cent of those working in manufacturing industry are the owners of firms or members of their families, in commerce the owners of shops and businesses actually outnumber their employees. The economy of the country is fragmented into an infinite number of petty enterprises, the great majority of which exist to support a family. Men with such interests inevitably believe that any extension of the state's administration over their affairs, particularly in the form of radical legislation which might lead to such measures as compulsory land consolidation or the socialization of industry, would destroy their independence. Although their present situation may not be flourishing they prefer to put their trust in personal arrangements and relationships which the traditional 'bourgeois' parties encourage. They are conscious of the general scarcity of resources, of the particular difficulties of their farm or their firm, of the needs of their families, and of their deep distrust of administrators and competitors. And at all levels of the political parties through which they attempt to protect themselves, the same fragmentation of concern is manifest. A politician, even the leader of a party, must honour his obligations to friends and clients who have supported him, as he also owes it to his own *philotimo* and self-regard not to accept any modification of his status in relation to colleagues, even for the good of the party. All this is in plain contrast to political attitudes in industrial nations where group interests, whether those of owners and management, or of industrial labour, accept the cause of their common situation and express their policies through corporate political parties.

In Greece only two institutions, the King and the army, can make a formal claim to represent national solidarity. We have already traced in a previous chapter the development of the 'schism' in the nation first expressed in the opposition of King Constantine and Venizelos in the years 1915–17. Since the events of the First World war and the subsequent catastrophe in Asia Minor there have been only two occasions when the people have rallied spontaneously about their King; the Italian invasion in 1940 was the first, the civil war of 1947–49, if we except those willingly or unwillingly recruited into the ranks of the Democratic Army, was the second. During the latter period King Paul and Queen Frederika travelled courageously and indefatigably about their realm in a manner which impressed their people. Politically, opposition to the Left reconciled sincerely republican politicians such as Kanellopoulos and Kassimatis both to the Crown and to alliance with men of a genuinely right-wing populist lineage, colleagues or relations of the six martyrs shot in 1922. Even Papandhreou for a short time served as a deputy of Papagos' Greek Rally Party.

The situation did not endure. The elevation of Karamanlis to power by the choice of the King, his too successful use of the apparatus of the state to retain that power, soon led the less inhibited members of the opposition, particularly after the elections of 1961, to speak of the Karamanlis government as a monarcho-fascist dictatorship. Since that time the identification of the King with the Right has been generally accepted. Various aspects of the monarchy had already been the subject of critical comment. The autonomous regime of the Queen's Fund, a charitable institution fed with special tax receipts but not accountable to parliament, was declared to be the organization of a royal clientele with clear political overtones which was recruited in two ways, from those employed by the Fund, and those benefiting from it. The public image of the Queen suffered. She was characterized as authoritative, arrogant, and interfering. Her dynastic ambition was held responsible for the payment by the nation of a dowry of $300,000 for her daughter, Princess Sophia, on her marriage to Prince Juan Carlos, son of the claimant to the Spanish throne. Furthermore there was a circle of personalities about the Court, apart from the official military and civilian members of the Royal Household, on whom the King relied for advice and information, men such as Niarchos, Paraskevopoulos the banker, Pipinelis the former diplomat. Both the material benefits which these royal clients were assumed to enjoy from their relationship with the King and the privilege of offering him their advice, offended the political world of the Centre Union who partly attributed the King's policy to their manoeuvres. In such an atmosphere it was idle to refer to the provision of the constitution which states that the King's person is free of responsibility; on the contrary for the Left, and for a majority of the Centre Union, the King was at least the accomplice and often the instigator of every unfair practice used against their parties. There was a brief period after Constantine came to the throne and Papandhreou became Prime Minister, when some imagined they saw the flowering of a piquant relationship between a King too young to have political ambitions beyond constitutional propriety and a Prime Minister too sagacious to be distracted by the republican convictions of his earlier career. The controversy which ended the prospect of this happy *entente* concerned their relations with the army.

The army is the one effective corporate organization with a wide membership in the Greek state. Since its ranks are filled by conscripts who serve for two years it can also claim in a certain sense to be representative of the nation whose traditional patriotism it naturally expresses. From 1915, with increasing ill effects, the political allegiance of the officer corps was divided between Venizelos and the King. But after the electoral victory of the Populist Party in 1933 and the return from exile of King George II in 1935, this division was suppressed by purging the force of its republican elements, and since that time, if we except some of the units stationed in the Middle East during the Second World war, the Greek army has been overwhelmingly conservative and, until recently, monarchist in its loyalties.

Its experience during the civil war of 1947–49, and training and equipment with American arms and advice, have made it an efficient force whose duties have clearly had two aspects: within the command structure of N.A.T.O. to guard the extended northern frontiers with the three communist neighbours, and to provide an assurance of internal security. Not the least important of the means for achieving the second of these purposes is the political indoctrination of recruits. Similarly the screening of candidates for commissions has explicitly aimed at rejecting men with left or even liberal opinions. Some no doubt have misled their interrogators and others have changed their views, sometimes with an eye to promotion after the possibility of a Centre Union government first appeared. But in general the opposition to communism is an accepted obsession; and opinion which is not impeccably conservative is suspect. Many senior officers learned their profession in the civil war and they would not have reached their present positions unless their anti-communist sentiments were beyond question. Not only do they sincerely believe that the army's task is to support the established order, as they interpret this, but clearly their own careers depend on it.

Thus the arrival in power of Papandhreou was regarded as a development which threatened national security, opening the road to closer relations with eastern European countries and suggesting a dangerous concern with individual liberties. The attempt by Papandhreou to make changes in the military hierarchy and to remove the Minister of Defence, Garoufalias, a man in the King's confidence; and the discovery of a conspiratorial group of officers known as 'Aspida', with leftist sympathies and a supposed plan for a *coup d'état*, with which Papandhreou's son Andreas, the deputy Minister of Coordination, was said to be connected, were events which merely confirmed what the army believed it already knew.

These happenings estranged the King from Papandhreou. For although the constitutional practice is that the King should accept the list of Ministers and military commanders chosen by his Prime Minister, nevertheless until the *coup* it was the King who formally made these appointments. With the justification that the army and the nation were in danger, and at the cost of perhaps precipitating a constitutional crisis, the King could decline to take his Prime Minister's advice. Such were the circumstances in which King Constantine refused to allow Papandhreou to become his own Defence Minister. The fact that it was known that the King was prepared not to agree to appointments which either offended the conventions of seniority or might alter the political orientation of the army, gave the officer corps an assurance against interference in its affairs, just as the loyalty of the army allowed the King to face with some equanimity anti-dynastic propaganda. If we accept that the King was not a party to the *coup* of 21 April and that his visible annoyance was sincere, the speedy *rapprochement* with the military leaders appears to be an example of this inevitable interdependence, which after the change of regime was quite as marked as before, in the somewhat different sense that the relatively junior officers who carried through the *coup* required at least the King's recognition of their government to pacify the generals whose services they still needed but whose position in the military hierarchy they had, in effect, usurped; while the King, compromised in the view of his opponents by his supposed complicity in the *coup*, depended generally on the army for the existence of his throne.

However, as the months of dictatorial rule lengthened the situation changed. With the ruthless retirement of men whose loyalty was even marginally in question ambitious officers learned to identify employment and quick promotion with an attachment to the regime rather than to the King, from whom in any case they were effectively isolated. Despite the oath which every officer takes to his sovereign, and the attempts from time to time to remind him of the religious element in the relationship between the army and the King (once explicitly expressed in an address to officers by King Paul when he said that he and they were united by God), there was already before the *coup* less mystique of monarchy among junior officers than among their elders. For the younger officers the bond between King and army was essentially one of common, and particularly anti-communist, interest. It must be remarked, too, that the majority of officers are recruited from a lower-middle class, sons of tradesmen, shopkeepers, and minor civil servants. Many come from the provinces. Among the younger officers from this background, with social and professional pretensions and generally limited means, there is a mixture of envy and contempt for the prosperity of politicians, businessmen, and the upper bourgeoisie, which is partly expressed in the social discipline and puritanism which officers often advocate for society; and in their own obsessed pursuit of the less tangible honours of military rank and power in which their loyalties to patrons inside or outside the army are remarkably flexible and opportunist, although not in many cases to the extent of abandoning an anti-communist position. These were the attitudes which the King's *coup* encountered in December 1967. There were senior officers who from accustomed loyalty to the throne and resentment against a junta of subordinate officers which now dominated them, were prepared to stand with the King; yet their junior commanders were not prepared to share the risk and refused to join them. From the evidence that they remained in command of combatant units it is now clear that they had already come to terms with the regime.

Although it is true that the army supported the Rally Party of Papagos and its successor, E.R.E., under Karamanlis, both by the great majority of its own votes and its threatening presence, it would be too simple to regard its recent action as indicating merely a preference for the politics of the Right. Army officers accustomed to the ponderous efficiency which military needs and training require, despise the anarchic apparatus of civilian political control as it functions in Greece. The antipathy is mutual. The politician characterizes the soldier as *stenokephalos*, narrow-headed or stupid, the soldier criticizes politicians and their intermediaries as immoral and self-seeking, concerned only with the buying and selling of favours. The soldiers sincerely believe that a government of the kind which is now in power can reform the morals of the nation. Unhappily, these are not matters for which authoritarian government, or even wise legislation, provides a cure. The aspects of political life which offend the army are, as we have attempted to show, an expression of certain particularities of social values and the institutional structure of the country. It is Greece's misfortune that she has achieved an efficient national army before she found political parties with organizations and memberships which could restrict it to its proper place and function in a parliamentary regime.

Bibliography

The select bibliography which follows is generally confined to works in western languages. In three instances books in Greek are noted which deal with subjects not adequately treated in works by western authors. The bibliography also serves, imperfectly, as an acknowledgement of the work of other scholars on which this book is mainly based. In addition to the works listed we have consulted newspaper files, mainly the *Kathimerini*, *Vima*, *The Times*, *The Guardian* and *The Economist*. We also wish to acknowledge the use we have made of papers or unpublished material provided by Mrs Tina Gioka on urbanization, Mrs Constantina Safilios-Rothschild on Greek family structure, Miss Julie du Boulay on village society in Euboea, and Mr Dimitrios Argyriades on the Greek Civil Service.

General Histories of Greece, Turkey, and the Balkans
Anderson, M. S., *The Eastern Question* (London, 1966).
Driault, E., and Lhéritier, M., *Histoire diplomatique de la Grèce de 1821 à nos jours*, 5 vols. (Paris, 1925).
Finlay, George, *History of Greece*, 7 vols. (Oxford, 1877).
Forster, E. S., *A Short History of Modern Greece, 1821–1956* (London and New York, 1957).
Heurtley, W. A., Darby, H. C., Crawley, C. W., Woodhouse, C. M., *A Short History of Greece from Early Times to 1964* (Cambridge, 1966).
Lewis, Bernard, *The Emergence of Modern Turkey* (London, 1961).
Lewis, G. L., *Turkey* (3rd ed. London and New York, 1965).
Mavrogordato, J., *Modern Greece, 1800–1931* (London, 1931).
Miller, W., *The Ottoman Empire and Its Successors, 1901–1927* (Cambridge, 1936).
Stavrianos, L. S., *The Balkans since 1453* (New York, 1958).
Svoronos, N. G., *Histoire de la Grèce moderne* (Paris, 1953).
Woodhouse, C. M., *The Story of Modern Greece** (London, 1968; also issued as *A Short History of Modern Greece*, New York, 1968).

Chapter 1. The Idea of the Greek Nation
Chaconas, S. G., *Adamantios Korais, A Study in Greek Nationalism* (New York, 1942).

Hadjiantoniou, G. A., *Protestant Patriarch: The Life of Cyril Lucaris (1572–1638)* (London, 1961).

Jenkins, R. H. J., *Byzantium and Byzantinism* (Cincinnati, 1963).

Makriyannis, *Memoirs*, translated and edited by H. A. Lidderdale (London, 1966).

Masai, F., *Pléthon et le Platonisme de Mistra* (Paris, 1956).

Sherrard, Philip, *The Greek East and the Latin West* (London, 1959).

Spencer, Terence, *Fair Greece Sad Relic* (London, 1954).

Tsourkas, C., *La Vie et l'oeuvre de Théophile Corydalée (1563–1646)* (Bucharest, 1948).

Chapter 2. The Approach to Independence, and Chapter 3. The War of Independence

Botzaris, N., *Visions Balkaniques dans la Préparation de la Révolution Grecque, 1784–1821* (Geneva and Paris, 1962).

Crawley, C. W., *The Question of Greek Independence* (Cambridge, 1930).

Dakin, Douglas, (1) *British and American Philhellenes* (Salonika, 1955); (2) *British Intelligence of Events in Greece 1824–1827* (Athens, 1959).

Dascalakis, A., *Rhigas Velestinlis* (Paris, 1937).

Dontas, D. N., *The Last Phase of the War of Independence in Western Greece, 1827–1829** (Salonika, 1966).

Gibb, H. A. R., and Bowen, H., *Islamic Society and the West*, Vol. 1, Parts I and II (London and New York, 1950 and 1957).

Hasluck, F. W., *Christianity and Islam under the Sultans* (Oxford, 1929).

Papadopoullos, T. H., *Studies and Documents relating to the History of the Greek Church and People under Turkish Domination* (Brussels, 1953).

Sakellariou, M. B., *The Peloponnese during the Second Turkish Occupation, 1715–1821* (Athens, 1939). In Greek.

Svoronos, N. G., *Le Commerce de Salonique au XVIIIe siècle* (Paris, 1952).

Temperley, H., *The Foreign Policy of Canning, 1822–1827* (London, 1925).

Woodhouse, C. M., (1) *The Greek War of Independence* (London, 1952); (2) *The Battle of Navarino* (London, 1965).

Chapter 4. The New State and the Great Idea

Alastos, D., *Venizelos* (London, 1942).

Dakin, Douglas, *The Greek Struggle in Macedonia, 1897–1913* (Salonika, 1966).

Dontas, D. N., *Greece and the Great Powers, 1863–1875** (Salonika, 1966).

Helmreich, E. C., *The Diplomacy of the Balkan Wars, 1912–13* (Cambridge Mass., 1938).

Jenkins, Romilly, *The Dilessi Murders, 1870* (London, 1961).

Kaltchas, N., *Introduction to the Constitutional History of Modern Greece* (New York, 1940).

Korisis, Hariton, *Die Politischen Parteien Griechenlands* (Hersbruck, Nürnberg, 1966).

Langer, W. L., *The Diplomacy of Imperialism 1890–1902* (New York, 1935).

Levandis, J. A., *The Greek Foreign Debt and the Great Powers, 1821–1898* (New York, 1944).

Llewellyn Smith, Michael, *The Great Island. A Study of Crete* (London, 1965).

Miller, William, *Travels and Politics in the Near East* (London, 1898).

Pallis, A. A., *Greece's Anatolian Venture, and After* (London, 1937).

Palmer, Alan, *The Gardeners of Salonika, The Macedonian Campaign 1915–1918* (London and New York, 1965).

Pournaras, D., *Charilaos Tricoupis*, 2 Vols. (Athens, 1950). In Greek.

Prevelakis, E., *British Policy towards the Change of Dynasty in Greece* (Athens, 1953).

Chapter 5. Catastrophe and Reaction

Barker, Elizabeth, *Macedonia* (London, 1950).

Daphnis, G., *Greece between the Two Wars* (Athens, 1955). In Greek.

Greek Ministry of Foreign Affairs. *The Greek White Book.* Documents relating to Italy's Aggression against Greece (London, 1942).

Kousoulas, D. George, *Revolution and Defeat. The Story of the Greek Communist Party* (London and New York, 1965).

Leeper, Sir Reginald, *When Greek Meets Greek* (London, 1950).

Myers, E. C. W., *Greek Entanglement* (London, 1955).

O'Ballance, Edgar, *The Greek Civil War, 1944–1949* (London, 1966).

Papagos, Alexander, *The Battle of Greece, 1940–41* (Athens, 1949).

Pentzopoulos, D., *The Balkan Exchange of Minorities and Its Impact on Greece* (Paris and The Hague, 1962).

Toynbee, A. J., *The Western Question in Greece and Turkey* (2nd edn., London, 1923).

Woodhouse, C. M., *Apple of Discord* (London, 1948).

Chapter 6. The Orthodox Church in Greece

Cabasilas, Nicholas, *A Commentary on the Divine Liturgy*, translated by J. M. Hussey and P. A. McNulty (London, 1960).

Hammond, P., *The Waters of Marah* (London and New York, 1956).

Lossky, V., *The Mystical Theology of the Eastern Church* (London, 1957).

Ouspensky, L., and Lossky, V., *The Meaning of Icons* (Olten, 1952).

Sherrard, Philip, *Athos, The Mountain of Silence* (London, 1960).

Ware, Timothy, (1) *The Orthodox Church* (Harmondsworth, 1963); (2) *Eustratios Argenti* (Oxford, 1964).

Chapter 7. Modern Greek Literature
The Poems of C. P. Cavafy, translated by John Mavrogordato (London, 1951).
Jenkins, R. H. J., *Dionysius Solomos* (Cambridge, 1940).
Keeley, Edmund, and Sherrard, Philip, *Six Poets of Modern Greece* (London, 1960).
Keeley, Edmund, and Sherrard, Philip, *George Seferis, Collected Poems, 1924–1955* (Princeton, 1967).
Sherrard, Philip, *The Marble Threshing Floor: Studies in Modern Greek Poetry* (London, 1956).
Trypanis, C., *Medieval and Modern Greek Poetry* (Oxford, 1951).

Chapter 8. Political Events Since the Civil War
Couloumbis, Theodore A., *Greek Political Reaction to American and N.A.T.O. Influences* (New Haven, 1966).
Meynaud, Jean, *Les Forces Politiques En Grèce* (Lausanne, 1965).
Stephens, Robert, *Cyprus: A Place of Arms* (London and New York, 1966).
Sweet-Escott, Bickham, *Greece. A Political and Economic Survey 1939–1953* (London, 1954).
Xydis, Stephen G., *Greece and the Great Powers, 1944–1947* (Salonika, 1963).

Chapter 9. Economic Dilemmas
Break, George F., and Turvey, Ralph, *Studies in Greek Taxation* (Athens, 1964).
Economist Intelligence Unit, *Greece*. Quarterly Economic Reviews.
Ellis, Howard S., *Industrial Capital in Greek Development* (Athens, 1964).
Meynaud, Jean, op. cit.
O.E.C.D., *Annual Economic Surveys of Greece* (Paris).
Ward, Benjamin, *Greek Regional Development* (Athens, 1963).
Zolotas, Xenophon, *Monetary Equilibrium and Economic Development* (Princeton, 1965).

Chapter 10. The Greek Countryside
Blum, Richard and Eva, *Health and Healing in Rural Greece* (Stanford, 1965).
Burgel, Guy, *Pobia, Étude Géographique d'un Village Crétois* (Athens, 1965).
Campbell, J. K., *Honour, Family and Patronage* (Oxford, 1964).

Friedl, Ernestine, *Vasilika, A Village in Modern Greece* (New York, 1962).

Kayser, Bernard, *Géographie Humaine de la Grèce* (Paris, 1964).

Kayser, Bernard, and Thompson, Kenneth, *Social and Economic Atlas of Greece* (Athens, 1964).

Lambiri, Ioanna, *Social Change in a Greek Country Town* (Athens, 1965).

McCorkle, Chester O., *Fruit and Vegetable Marketing in the Economic Development of Greece* (Athens, 1962).

O.E.C.D., *Problems of Agriculture Co-operation* (Paris, 1964).

Papelassis, Adam A., and Yotopoulos, P. A., *Surplus Labor in Greek Agriculture, 1953–1960* (Athens, 1962).

Sanders, Irwin T., *Rainbow in the Rock* (Cambridge, Mass., 1962).

Thompson, Kenneth, *Farm Fragmentation in Greece* (Athens, 1963).

Chapter 11. The City and the State

Alexander, Alec P., *Greek Industrialists* (Athens, 1964).

Coutsomaris, George, *The Morphology of Greek Industry* (Athens, 1963).

Kayser, Bernard, op. cit.

Kayser, Bernard, and Thompson, Kenneth, op. cit.

Meynaud, Jean, op. cit.

O.E.C.D., Country Reports: *Greece* (Paris, 1965).

O.E.C.D., *Reorganization of Public Administration in Greece* (Paris, 1964).

* Books not available to the authors during the preparation of their manuscript.

Index

Index

Abdul Hamid, 109
Aberdeen, G. H. Gordon, earl of, 90
Abraham's Sacrifice, 221
Acarnania, 78, 79, 94, 326
Ackerman, Convention of, 74
Adalia, 123, 125
Adrianople, 104, 114
Adrianople, Peace of, 72, 77
Aegean Islands, 27, 66, 67, 115, 164, 322
Aetolia, 79, 322, 326
Aghia Lavra, 65
Agrarians, 112, 151, 265
Agriculture, *see* Farming
Akrotiri, 262
Alaric, 21
Albania, 115, 168, 171, 172
Alexander the Great, 21, 28
Alexander I, Tsar, 59, 63, 71, 72, 90
Alexander, King, 122, 124
Alexandretta, 128
Ali Pasha, 58, 61-2, 66, 86
Amalia, Queen, 91, 94
Ambatielos, Antony, 265
American Aid, 250, 251, 253, 260, 263, 266, 295, 298, 300, 304, 312-14, 318, 393
American Red Cross, 138
Amstelbrouwerei, 376
Amurath III, 31
Anamnesis, 202
Anastasis, 206

Anatolia, 54, 123
Andrismos, 44, 45, 216
Androutsos, Odysseus, 217
Ankara, 126
  convention, 142
  pact, 253
Apostoliki Diakonia, 209
Argyrokastron, 171
Aristotle, 29, 35, 37, 39
Armatoles, 57, 83, 86, 88
Arta, 66
'Aspida' group, 274, 278, 279, 281, 284, 402
Aspropotamos, 78
Assemblies, National, 67-8, 69, 76, 86, 95, 96, 111, 112, 130, 133, 134, 196, 250, 390, 394-5
Ataturk, *see* Mustapha Kemal
Athanasiades-Novas, George, 276
Athens, 33-5, 67, 75, 92, 93, 94, 98, 110, 121, 122, 172, 177, 180, 181, 283, 351, 364-71
  class structure, 370-71
  population, 364-5, 366
  social life, 367, 369
Athens, philosophical school, 20, 37
Athens, Treaty of, 263, 318
Athos, 39, 192, 205
Austria, 72, 109
Averro-Aristotelian schools, 29, 37, 38

Averof, Evangelos, 292

Baarlam, 26
Baghdad Pact, 256, 259, 262
Balkan Entente, 167, 168
Balkan League, 114
Ballads, 214, 215, 216, 219, 229
Banking, 98, 101, 272, 277, 278,
    304, 305–6, 311, 374, 375
    Agricultural Bank, 145, 331,
        351, 353, 355
    savings, 374
Barsanuphius and John, 211
Beret, 190, 191
Berlin, Congress of, 104
Bessarion, Caloyer, 34
Bologna, 29, 37
Bosnia, 103, 109
Breweries, 376
Brigands, *see Klephts*
Brussa, 124
Bucharest, Peace, 115
    Treaty, 71, 167
Bulgaria, 102, 103, 104, 107,
    109, 114, 115, 117, 118,
    119, 167–8, 273
Byron, George Gordon, Lord,
    26, 32, 37, 73, 224–5
Byzantine Empire, 19, 20, 21,
    24, 25
Byzantine studies, 210

Cabasilas, Nicholas, 195
Canning, George, 73, 74, 75, 76
Canning, Stratford, 75
Capodistrias, Agostino, 79
Capodistrias, John, 59, 76, 78,
    79, 83, 84, 356
Capuchins, 33
Censorship, 160, 164, 292
Centre Union Party, 264, 265,
    267, 268, 272, 273, 274,
    275, 276, 278, 280, 281,
    282, 394, 395, 397, 399

Cervi, 90
Chania, 110
Charles X, 74
Chatzikyriakos, Adm.
    Constantine, 130, 132, 152
Chiftliks, 55, 97
Child-tribute, 32
Chios, 31, 39
    massacre of, 73
Chrysostomos, Archbp., 212
Church, *see* Orthodox
    Christianity
Church, Sir Richard, 75
Churchill, Sir Winston, 181
Cilicia, 125, 127
Civil Service, 289–90, 349, 350,
    379–84
    in Athens, 365, 380
    Higher Council for, 383
    Ministries, 381
    procedure, 381–2
    salaries, 382–3
    school of Administrative
        Studies, 382
Civil War, 180-82, 183–5
Climate, 323
Cochrane, Thomas (earl of
    Dundonald), 76
Codrington, Sir Edward, 75
'Colonels', *see* Junta
Commercial colonies, 40, 50, 51
Common Market, 263, 264, 266,
    267, 294, 301, 315, 318,
    319, 320
Communications, 91, 97, 101,
    108, 357–8
Communist Party, 142, 143,
    146, 158, 159, 160, 164,
    174, 175, 177, 182, 248,
    297, 398
Constantine the Great, 20
Constantine I, King, 110, 113,
    117, 118, 119, 120, 122,
    125, 127, 161

Constantine II, King, 272, 275, 276, 277, 279, 281, 284, 285, 286, 288–9, 291, 296, 392, 401, 402–3
Constantinople, 19, 24, 25, 30, 33, 34, 37, 93, 122
see also Istanbul
Constitution, 136, 296–7, 391
Corfu, 121, 166
Corinth, Isthmus, 21, 23, 31, 67
Corydaleus, Theophyllos, 39, 192
Costume, 359, 360–61
Cotton, 299, 310, 326, 332
Councillors, 83, 344–5
Courts-martial, 291
Crete, 31, 78, 102, 103, 104, 105, 107, 109, 110, 115, 155, 164, 172, 221, 322
Crimean War, 89, 91–3
Crusades, 33
Currant trade, 31, 73, 97, 105, 301, 310, 325
Curzon, George N., Marquis, 127, 128
Cyclades, 77
Cyprus, 128, 254–9, 261–3, 268–70, 280, 287, 288

Damaskinos, Archbp., 181
Dardanelles, 117
Deligiannis, Theodore, 100, 101, 104, 105, 106
Deligeorgis, Epaminondas, 94
Demarchs, 87
Demertzis, Constantine, 157, 158
Demes, 84, 85
Democratic Front, 249
Democratic Union, 258
Denktash, Rauf, 287
Deputies, 99, 100, 102, 116
Devaluation, 252, 300
Dhekelia, 262

Diaspora, 28, 59
Dighenis, *see* Grivas
Digenis Acritas, 215, 216
Disraeli, Benjamin (earl of Beaconsfield), 104
Dobruja, 115
Dodecanese, 123, 128, 166
Dormition of the Mother of God, 206, 207
Dovas, Constantine, 265
Dragatsani, Battle of, 63
Dragoman, 53
Dragoumis, Ion, 108, 117
Drama, 118, 326
Dramali, Ali, Pasha of, 67, 68, 69
Drope, 44, 45
Drosinis, George, 240
Dulles, John F., 257

E.A.M., 174, 175, 176, 177–83 *passim*
Economics, 300–21
E.D.A., 250, 251, 260, 264, 265, 267, 268, 273, 298, 394, 398, 399
Eden, Anthony, 181, 259
E.D.E.S., 176–81 *passim*
Education, 29, 42, 53, 146–7, 271, 292–3, 305, 384–90
  expenditure, 387–8
  free, 388
  graduates, 389–90
  illiterates, 387
  law faculties, 386
  primary schools, 146, 384
  reduction of compulsory, 388–9
  secondary schools, 146, 385–6, 387
  universities, 146, 386
E.E.C., 263, 295, 311
E.F.T.A., 263
E.K.K.A., 176

E.L.A.S., 174, 175, 176, 177–82
 passim
Elections, 99–100, 135, 136–7,
 151, 155–6, 157, 248, 250,
 260, 264–5, 267, 268, 273,
 280–82, 295
 false inscriptions, 265
 proportional representation,
 135, 247, 249, 260
 return to majority system,
 137, 154, 247, 251
Elytis, Odysseus, 214, 228, 236
Emigration, *see* Migration;
 U.S.A.
Enosis, 254, 260, 268, 270, 280,
 287, 313
E.O.K.A., 256, 261
Eparchies, 84
E.P.E.K., 249, 250
Epidaurus, 67
 constitution of, 73
Epirus, 39, 54, 63, 66, 91, 103,
 104, 109, 115, 123
E.R.E., 258, 260, 261, 263, 264,
 265, 267, 268, 271, 273,
 276, 278, 281, 282, 298,
 394, 399
Erophile, 221
Erotocritos, 215, 221
Esso-Papas, 302, 310, 316
Ethnos, 20, 108, 173, 349
Evil Eye, 340–41, 362
Exarchate, 103, 105–6
Exports, 303, 309, 310–11, 318,
 319, 326

Family, 44–7, 117, 124, 334–42
 in Athens, 368–70, 399
 dowry, 337–8, 368
 marriage, 336–9
Farming, 139–40, 162, 278, 293,
 299, 301, 310, 323–33, 352–3
 animal husbandry, 326–7
 cooperatives, 353–5

irrigation, 331
 mechanisation, 327, 328, 330
 productivity, 331
Ferdinand, King of Bulgaria,
 119
Finlay, George, 90
Fix brewery, 376
Foot, Sir Hugh, 261
Forests, 327
Fort Rupel, 121
Foscolo, Ugo, 220, 224
Frederika, Queen, 265, 400, 401
Free beseiged, 222–4, 231
Free Opinion Party, 135, 137
Fruit, 301, 310, 319, 325

Gargalides, Gen. Panayiotis,
 130
Garoufalias, Petros, 275, 402
Gaza, Theodore, 34
General Confederation of the
 Workers of Greece
 (G.S.E.E.), 377–9
Gennimatas, Gen. John, 280
Genoan Republic, 31, 33
George I, King, 95, 96, 103,
 111, 117
George II, King, 107, 127, 160,
 161, 172, 178
 dethroned, 131
 dissolves Parliament, 160
 exiled, 172
 restored, 157, 183
George of Trebizond, 24, 34
Germanos, Bishop, 59, 65
Gerontikon, 211
Gibbon, Edward, 31
Gold standard, 150
Gonatas, Stylianos, 127, 128,
 147
Gorgopotamos, 177
Gounaris, Dimitrios, 116, 119,
 126, 127
Grazzi, Emmanuele, 170

'Great Idea', 83–126 *passim*, 129
Greco, El, 221
Greco–Turkish War, 97, 106–7
Greek language, 28, 41, 60
  demotic, 146, 242
  Katharevousa, 237, 242, 292, 388
  liturgical, 41
Greek literature, 30, 214–44
  fiction, 237–44
  poetry, 214–37
Greek Rally party, 247, 250, 251, 257
Gregory Palamas, St, 195
Gregory V, 52, 72, 193
Grey, Sir Edward, 117
Grivas, George, 254, 255, 264, 270, 280, 287
Grivas, Theodore, 94
Gross national product, 307, 312, 319
Guilford, Frederick North, earl of, 225
Guillet de St Georges, Georges, 33
Guizot, François, 89

Hadjianestis, Gen. George, 122
Halepa Pact, 104
Harding, Sir John, 258, 261
Helladics, 21
Helle, sinking of, 170
Hellenes and Hellenism, 19, 20, 21, 22, 23, 24, 27, 28, 35, 36, 39, 53, 73, 103, 126, 192, 207, 230, 385
  see also 'Great Idea'
Herules, 21
Herzegovina, 103, 109
Hesychasm, 20, 195
Hetairists, 58–64, 66
Hitler, Adolf, 158, 170, 171
Holy Alliance, 71, 72
Homer, 28, 215

Hopkinson, Henry (Lord Colyton), 255
Humanism and humanists, 27, 29, 30
Hypsilantis, Alexander, 59, 60, 62, 63, 72

Ibrahim Pasha, 67, 70–71, 74, 75
Iconostasis, 200–1
Icons, 201, 209
'Idionym' Law, 159
Imbros, 123, 128
Imports, 301, 303, 308, 311, 366
I.M.R.O., 106
Independence, War of, 35, 38, 43, 65–80, 86, 91, 217, 238–9
Industry, 98, 141, 293, 299, 300, 302, 316, 371–9
  in Athens, 365
  expansion, 373–4
  small units, 372–3
  Sociétés Anonymes, 374
  structure, 372–5
International Financial Commission, 108, 109
Investment, foreign, 294, 302, 310, 315, 316–18, 320
Ioannides, 180
Ionian Islands, 31, 96, 322
Irredentism, 90, 96
Irregulars, *see Armatoles*
Ismet Inonu, 128
Istanbul, 256
Italo–Turkish War, 114
Italy, 123, 166, 170
Izmit Peninsula, 124

Jannina, 66, 114
Jassy, Treaty of, 50, 71
Jesuits, 33
Johnson, Lyndon B., 288, 295

Juan Carlos, Prince, 401
Julian the Apostate, 20
Junta, 283–98 *passim*, 324,
    388–9
Justinian, Emperor, 20

Kallergis, Gen. Dimitrios, 86
Kalligas, Pavlos, 240
Kalvos, Andreas, 220, 224–8,
    229
Kanaris, Constantine, 95
Kanellopoulos, Panayiotis, 248,
    250, 268, 281, 282, 286–7
Kaphantaris, George, 132, 136,
    148, 149, 158
Karageorge (George Czerny),
    60
Karaiskakis, George, 71
Karamanlis, Constantine, 252,
    257, 258, 259, 260, 262,
    264, 265, 268, 288, 305,
    313, 317–19, 393–5,
    400–1
Karapanayiotis, Byron, 147,
    149
Karkavitsas, Andreas, 240, 241
Katharevousa, see Greek
    language
Kathimerini, 147, 286, 292
Kavafy, Konstantinos, 228,
    229, 234
Kavalla, 105, 115, 118, 141,
    326
Kazantzakis, Nikos, 228, 244
Kennedy, John F., 267
Khrushchev, Nikita, 267
Khurshid Pasha, 66
Kiutahi (Reshid Pasha), 70
K.K.E., *see* Communist Party
Klephts, 45, 57, 83, 88, 92, 107,
    108, 154, 216, 217
Kodjabashis, see Notables
Koimisis, see Dormition
Koinotis, 344

Kokkina, 269
Kolettis, John, 79, 86, 87, 88,
    89, 90
Kollias, Constantine, 285, 288
Kollyvades group, 211, 241
Kolokotronis, Theodore, 59, 67,
    68, 69, 70, 71, 79, 92, 217
Kolonaki society, 369
Komitadji, irregulars, 106, 107
Kondouriotis, George, 70
Kondylakis, Yannis, 240
Kondylis, George, 130, 132,
    133, 135, 148, 149, 152,
    153–4, 155, 156, 157, 158
Kontoglou, Photis, 209
Korais, Adamantios, 40–42, 207,
    208
Koritsa, 171
Kornaros, Vizentzos, 215, 221
Koryzis, Alexander, 172
Kotsonis, Jerome, Archbp., 212
Koumoundouros, Alexander,
    102, 103
Koundouriotis, Adm. Paul, 148
Koutsovlachs, 86, 97, 322
Kratos, 108, 349
Kutchuk, Fadil, 262, 269
Kutchuk Kainardji, Treaty of,
    50, 71

Ladas, Christos, 249
Lambrakis, Gregory, 266, 279
Lamia, 66
Larissa, 66, 288
Lausanne, Treaty of, 127, 128,
    129, 134, 254
Lausiac History, 211
Law of Vilayets, 102
League of Nations, 138, 139
Lebanon Charter, 179
Lennox-Boyd, Alan (viscount
    Boyd), 259
Leonardopoulos, Gen. George,
    130

Leopold of Saxe-Coburg, Prince, 78
Leros, 284
Levant Company, 31
Liberal Party, 115, 116, 119, 120, 124, 125, 131, 147, 151, 247, 249, 260, 394
Limassol, 269
Little Entente, 168
Lloyd George, David, 125
London, Treaty of (1829), 74 (1913), 114–15 (1915), 123
Londos, Andreas, 70

Macarius, St, 195, 211
Macedonia, 39, 54, 91, 103, 104, 105, 106, 107, 109, 114, 115, 119, 129, 135, 142, 143, 172, 322, 326, 327, 328
Macmillan, Harold, 256, 261
Mahmoud II, 62
Mahomet II, 189, 190
Makarezos, Nicholas, 285, 289, 293, 294
Makarios, Archbp., 254, 255, 259, 261, 262, 263, 269, 270, 280, 287
Makris, Photios, 379
Makriyannis, John, 48, 49, 92, 217, 239
Malmsey wine, 31
Manettas, Gen. Theodore, 153
Maniadakis, Constantine, 164, 174
Maniotes, 79
Manuel III, Emperor, 23
Maris, George, 144
Markezinis, Spyros, 249, 250, 252, 253, 258, 265, 267, 280, 298, 300
Markos, see Vafiades
Marmora, Sea of, 124

Matthopoulos, Eusebius, 209
Mavrocordatos, Alexander(1), 53
Mavrocordatos, Alexander (2), 66, 68, 70, 73, 87, 89, 90, 91
Mavromichalis, Constantine, 79
Mavromichalis, George, 79
Mavromichalis, Kyriakoulis, 110
Mavromichalis, Petrobey, 59, 65, 69, 217
Mavromichalis, Stylianos, 267
Mayors, 345–6
Menderes, Adnan, 262
Merchants, 50, 92, 93, 351, 352
Mesolonghi, 66, 67, 70, 73, 222
Metaxas, Andreas, 89
Metaxas, John, 118, 129, 131, 152, 155–6, 157, 158, 159, 160, 161–2, 170, 173, 247
dictatorship of, 161–6, 344n.
foreign policy of, 168–9
strategy of, 170–71
Metsovo, 171
Metternich, Clemens, Prince, 71, 72, 78
Miaoulis, Andreas Vokos, 70
Michalocopoulos, Andreas, 132, 133, 164
Middle class, 98, 368–70
Migration, 97–8, 260, 272, 301, 310, 328, 357–8, 360, 365, 371
Military League, 110, 111, 113, 129–30, 131, 132, 151
Millet, 32, 52, 53, 189
Minorities, 143
compulsory exchange, 128–9, 166
Mistra, 30
Mitsotakis, Constantine, 274
Moldavia, 62
Monasteries and Monasticism, 194, 205, 208, 210, 211–12
female, 211–12
Montenegro, 102, 103, 114

Moral regulation, 291
Morea, 33
Morosini, Francesco, 33
Mussolini, Benito, 166, 168, 170
Mustapha Kemal, 123, 124
Myers, E. C. W., 181n.
Mykonos, 56
Myrivilis, Stratis, 244

Napoleon III, 94
Nasser, Gamal Abdel, 270
National Assembly, see Assemblies
National and Social Liberation, see E.K.K.A.
National Liberation Front, see E.A.M.
National Loan, 135
National Opinion Party, see Populist Party
National Organization of Cypriote Fighters, see E.O.K.A.
National Popular Liberation Army, see E.L.A.S.
National Progressive Union, see E.P.E.K.
National Radical Union, see E.R.E.
National Republican Greek League, see E.D.E.S.
National Schism, 120
National Society, 106
N.A.T.O., 250, 253, 255, 257, 258, 259, 263, 273, 274, 283, 287, 293, 295, 402
Nauplion, 69, 70, 94, 196, 212
Navarino, Battle of, 75
Negris, Theodore, 68
Nektarios Kephalas, St, 211
Neuilly, Treaty of, 143, 167
Newspapers, 93

Niarchos, Stavros, 376, 401
Nicaea, Council of, 201
Nicodemus the Hagiorite, St, 195
Nicosia, 269
Nikousios, Panayiotis, 53
Nomarchies, 84, 345, 381
Notables, 65, 84
Nuri Said, 262

Obrenovitch, Milosh, 61, 63
Ochtoechos, cycle of, 206
Old Calendarists, 212
Olga, Queen, 198
Olives, 324–5
Organic Statute, 103
Orthodox Christianity and Church, 24, 25, 32, 33, 34, 36, 37, 38, 42, 51, 52, 71, 127, 144, 189–213, 230, 234, 241, 291, 385
chief hierarch, 197
liturgical poetry, 214
liturgy, 195–6, 198–9, 202–5
spiritual writings, 195, 211
Synod, 197–8
Typikon, 206–7
Otho, King, 79, 83–95 passim.
Othonaios, Gen. Alexander, 130, 147, 153, 155
Ottoman Empire, 19, 36, 71, 102, 109
see also Turkey

Pacifico, Don, 90
Padua, 29, 37, 38, 39, 220
Palamas, Kostis, 228, 229, 231, 232, 234, 237
Pallikari, 219
Pallis, A. A., 198
Palmerston, H. J. Temple, viscount, 79, 90
Pangalos, Theodore, 128, 130, 134–5

Papadiamantis, Alexandros, 211, 240, 241, 242
Papadopoulos, George, 283, 285, 289, 291, 293, 295, 296, 297
Papageorgiou, 379
Papagos, Alexander, 156, 157, 158, 163, 172, 184, 247, 249, 250, 251, 253, 255, 305, 383
Papaligouras, Panayiotis, 393
Papanastasiou, Alexander, 131, 132, 133, 136, 148, 149, 151
Papandhreou, Andreas, 271, 273-4, 281, 284, 402
Papandhreou, George, 179, 180, 248, 249, 251, 258, 264, 266, 267, 269-83 passim, 378, 383, 387, 388, 392, 394, 395, 401, 402
  education policy, 398
  economic policy, 305, 307-9, 311, 317
Papaphlessas, Dikaios, 63, 65
Papapolitis, Savas, 272
Paraskevopoulos, John, 281, 401
Parthenon, 26
Parties, Political, see individual names
Patmos, 39
Patriarchate, Academy, 39, 192
Patriarch of Constantinople, 20, 32, 51, 52-3, 73, 103, 189, 190, 191, 192, 193, 196
Patridha, 47
Patronage, 116, 349-51, 357, 370-71, 393, 396-7
Pattakos, Stylianos, 283, 285, 289, 295
Paul, King, 124, 184, 248, 257, 265, 266, 272, 400
Péchiney, 302, 310, 316
Peloponnese, 22, 23, 50, 56-7, 60, 61, 64, 65, 67, 68, 74, 75, 77, 91, 323
Peridis, Lt. Gen. George, 288
Peta, 67, 73
Petrarch (Francesco Petrarca), 26, 29
Peurifoy, John E., 251
Phalanx, 87
Phalerum, Battle of, 76
Phanariots, 40, 53-4, 60, 62, 70, 92, 190, 193
Pheraios, Rhigas, 60
Philanthropia, 202
Philhellenism, see Hellenes
Philiki Hetairia, see Hetairists
Philokalia, 195, 211
Philotimo, 44, 340, 341, 342, 346, 359-60, 361, 400
Pipinelis, Panayiotis, 267, 287, 401
Piracy, 73, 74
Piraeus, 91
Pirelli, 316
Plastiras, Nicholas, 127, 128, 129, 130, 131, 147, 152, 153, 155, 249, 250, 251
Plato and Platonism, 22, 23, 35
Pletho, George Gemistos, 23-5, 34, 35, 40
Plutarch, 27
Poetry, 214-37
  metre, 215, 220
Political prisoners, 283, 284
Political structure, 390-404
  Army, 401-4
  King, 391-3, 400
  Ministers, Council of, 391
  parties, 393
  party congress, 398
  see also Assemblies, Elections, names of political parties
Politis, K., 243
Politis, Nikolas, 240
Popov, Col., 180
Population, 93, 98, 322-3

Populist Party, 116, 130, 135, 136, 137, 148, 149, 150, 151, 152, 154, 155, 156, 183, 247, 249, 250, 251
Prevelakis, Pandelis, 244
Priests, 347
Progressive Party, 264, 267, 276, 280
Psaros, Col. Dimitrios, 176
Psellus, Michael, 22–3
Psycharis, Yannis, 107, 242–3
Public Works, 145, 162, 311, 320

Queen's Fund, 401
Quinine scandal, 149

Rallis, Dimitrios, 110
Rallis, John, 176
Refugees, 129, 138–40, 141
    settlement commission, 138–9, 141
    urban, 140
Regional Cooperative Unions, 353–5
Renaissance, 26, 27, 29
Republic, 133 et seq.
    constitution, 136
Republican Union, 131, 132, 135, 136
Ricaut, Sir Paul, 194
Romania, 115, 118, 167
Romanos the Melodist, 214
Rommel, Erwin, 177
Roumeliots, 70, 79
Rousfetia, 163
Rousseau, Jean Jacques, 36
Roussos, George, 132
Russia, 59, 62, 71, 77
Russo–Turkish war, 91, 103

St Petersburg Protocol, 74, 76
Saints, 205–6, 216
Salonika, 50, 51, 93, 104, 109, 114, 115, 120, 121, 141, 159–60, 172, 177, 266, 326, 351, 365
    free zone, 166
Samos, 78
Sandys, George, 31
Sanjak of Novi Bazar, 114
San Stefano, Treaty of, 103
Sapienza, 90
Saraphis, Gen. Stephanos, 176
Scholarchs, 39
Scholarios, George, 20, 189
Schoolmasters, 346
Scobie, Lt. Gen. Sir Ronald, 180
Scutari, 114
Seferis, George (Seferiades), 215, 228, 229, 230, 231, 232, 235
Serbia, 60, 61, 74, 102, 103, 114, 115, 117, 119, 135
Sèvres, Treaty of, 123, 125
Shelley, Percy Bysshe, 73
Shipping, 51, 98, 301, 306
Siantos, George, 180
Sikelianos, Angelos, 228, 229, 230, 231, 234, 236
Simony, 191
Simovitch, Gen. Dushan, 172
Sinope, 34, 37
Sivri Hissar, 126
Skoulas, Nicholas, 144
Smallholdings, 43, 92, 112, 145, 329–30
Smyrna, 50, 51, 93, 118, 123, 126
Societas christiana, 29
Societas humana, 29
Sociological society, 109
Solomos, Dionysios, 220, 221–4, 231, 236, 242
Sophia, Princess, 401
Sophoulis, Themistocles, 132, 133, 158, 160, 184, 248, 249

Sossidis, 280
Sotir, 213
Soutsos, Alexander, 237
Soutzos, Michael, 62
Soviet Military Mission, 180
Spahis, 54–5
Spandidakis, Gregory, 286
Stalin, Joseph, 180
Standard Oil (N.J.), 316
Stephanopoulos, Stephanos,
    250, 257, 258, 274, 276,
    277, 302, 309
Strikes, 160, 162, 278
    General Strike, 161
Svolos, Prof. Alexander, 178
Symeon, St, 215

Tapu, 55
Tariffs, 145, 302, 318–19, 376
Taxes, 47, 54–5, 85, 101, 271,
    306, 307
    Income Tax, 277
Tenedos, 123, 128
Textiles, 140, 377
Theodorakis, Michael, 292
Theotokas, George, 144, 243–4
Theotokis, George, 126
Theotokis, John, 158, 160
Theotokis, Konstantine, 240,
    241
Thessaly, 91, 103, 104, 107,
    108, 322, 327, 328
Thrace, 54, 104, 115, 123, 124,
    128, 135, 172, 322, 326,
    328
Time, 44, 46, 58
Tithes, 54, 97
Tito (Josip Broz), 182, 184
Tobacco, 140, 141, 142, 169,
    273, 299, 301, 310, 322,
    326
'Torch', 298
Tourism, 301
Trade Unions, 109, 377–9, 399

Tricoupis, Charilaos, 95, 100,
    104, 105
Tripolitza, Massacre of, 65
Truman doctrine, 248
Tsaldaris, Panayiotis 137,
    138, 148, 150, 151, 152,
    153, 154, 155, 156, 157
Tsaldaris, Constantine, 248
Tsirimokos, Elias, 264, 272, 276
Tsolakoglou, Gen. George, 172,
    173
Tsoudheros, Emmanuel, 172,
    178–9
Turkey, 77, 106–7, 167, 253,
    287
Turks, 21, 22, 33, 51, 66
    Young Turks, 109, 110
Typikon, see Orthodox
    Christianity

United Democratic Left, *see*
    E.D.A.
United Nations, 255, 269, 288
U.S.A., migration to, 97
U.S.S.R., 167, 169, 171, 175,
    182, 183–4, 273, 318

Vafiades, Markos, 183, 184
Vance, Cyrus, 288
Vardinoyannis, Paul, 281
Varkiza, agreement, 181, 249
Varvatos, 44
Vekyls, 56, 57
Velouchiotis, Aris, 175
Venetian Republic, 31, 33, 38,
    39, 220
Venizelos, Eleutherios, 110–13
    passim, 115–25 *passim*,
    131–2, 136–8 *passim*, 144,
    147–58 *passim*, 383
Venizelos, Sophocles, 248, 249,
    250, 258, 264, 272
Venezis, Ilias, 244
Vikelos, Dimitrios, 240

Vilayets, 56, 102
Village communities, 43–4, 46–9, 52, 55, 85, 108, 239–40, 241, 322–3, 333–4, 342–8, 355–63
Viziers, 56
Vlachou, Helen, 286, 292
Vladimirescu, Tudor, 62, 63
Voulgaris, Dimitrios, 95

Wages and salaries, 308
Wallachia, 62, 63
Wavell, Archibald, earl, 171, 172
Wellington, Arthur Wellesley, duke of, 76, 77, 78
Wheat, 323–4, 332, 354
Wheler, Sir George, 191
Woodhouse, C. M., 69, 181n.
World War I, 117
World War II, 169–81
   Invasion of Greece, 172

'X', 254
Xanthos, Emmanuel, 59
Xenopoulos, Gregorios, 243

Yioura, 283, 284
Young Turks, *see* Turks
Youth Movement (E.O.N.), 165
Yugoslavia, 135, 166, 167, 168, 172, 253

Zachariades, Nikos, 182, 184
Zaimis, Alexander, 69, 70, 135, 136, 148
Zante, 220
Zavitsianos, Constantine, 148, 149
Zervas, Napoleon, 176, 178, 249
Zoë Brotherhood, 209–10, 212, 213
Zoitakis, Georgios, 284, 289
Zola, Emile, 239

*Printed in Great Britain
by C. Tinling & Company Limited
Liverpool · London · Prescot*